Cybersecurity Sustainability

Future Directions

Roland Berry

ISBN: 978-1-77961-308-0
Imprint: Telephasic Workshop

Contents

Introduction

Overview of Cybersecurity Sustainability

Definition of Cybersecurity Sustainability

In this section, we will explore the concept of cybersecurity sustainability and provide a comprehensive definition for it.

Understanding Sustainability

Before delving into the specifics of cybersecurity sustainability, let us first understand the concept of sustainability in a broader context. Sustainability refers to the ability to maintain and support a certain level of functionality and continuity over an extended period. It encompasses various dimensions, including environmental, economic, and social factors. In the context of cybersecurity, sustainability extends to the ability to ensure the ongoing protection of critical information, systems, and networks against evolving cyber threats and challenges.

Cybersecurity Sustainability

Cybersecurity sustainability encompasses the set of practices and measures aimed at maintaining the long-term effectiveness and resilience of cybersecurity systems and processes. It involves the proactive management of risks and the implementation of strategies to ensure the availability, integrity, and confidentiality of information and systems. Cybersecurity sustainability is not limited to a single organization or system; rather, it emphasizes the collective responsibility of stakeholders, including individuals, organizations, and governments, to work together towards maintaining a secure and robust cyber environment.

Core Principles of Cybersecurity Sustainability

To better understand cybersecurity sustainability, let's explore its core principles:

1. **Risk Management:** Cybersecurity sustainability requires the adoption of a risk-based approach to identify, assess, and mitigate potential threats and vulnerabilities. This involves conducting regular risk assessments, implementing appropriate controls, and continuously monitoring and updating security measures to adapt to emerging threats.

2. **Resilience and Continuity:** Cybersecurity sustainability focuses on building resilience in the face of cyber incidents and maintaining the continuity of operations. This involves implementing robust incident response plans, incorporating effective backup and recovery strategies, and conducting regular drills and simulations to test the effectiveness of these measures.

3. **Collaboration and Cooperation:** Cybersecurity sustainability cannot be achieved in isolation. It requires cooperation and collaboration among various stakeholders, including government agencies, industry organizations, academia, and users. Information sharing, joint research efforts, and coordinated response mechanisms are essential for effectively addressing cyber threats.

4. **Adaptability and Innovation:** The field of cybersecurity is constantly evolving, with new threats and technologies emerging regularly. Cybersecurity sustainability necessitates a culture of adaptability and innovation to stay ahead of cyber attackers. This involves staying abreast of the latest security trends, investing in research and development, and continuously updating security practices and technologies.

5. **Privacy and Ethical Considerations:** Cybersecurity sustainability must also take into account privacy and ethical considerations. It involves protecting individuals' privacy rights while implementing robust security measures. Respecting ethical guidelines and adhering to legal and regulatory frameworks is paramount in ensuring the sustainability of cybersecurity practices.

Benefits of Cybersecurity Sustainability

Implementing cybersecurity sustainability practices offers numerous benefits, including:

- **Enhanced Security:** By adopting sustainable cybersecurity practices, organizations can effectively mitigate risks and reduce the likelihood of successful cyberattacks. This leads to improved overall security posture and increased protection against threats.

- **Business Continuity:** Cybersecurity sustainability ensures the continuity of business operations, even in the face of cyber incidents. By implementing robust incident response plans and disaster recovery strategies, organizations can minimize downtime and quickly resume operations.

- **Trust and Reputation:** Sustainable cybersecurity practices help build trust with customers, partners, and stakeholders. Organizations that prioritize cybersecurity sustainability demonstrate their commitment to safeguarding sensitive information, which enhances their reputation and competitiveness.

- **Compliance and Legal Requirements:** Many industries have legal and regulatory requirements related to cybersecurity. By adopting sustainable cybersecurity practices, organizations can ensure compliance with these requirements, avoiding costly penalties and legal complications.

- **Innovation and Competitive Advantage:** Organizations that prioritize cybersecurity sustainability can leverage it as a competitive advantage. By staying ahead of emerging threats and investing in innovative security solutions, they can differentiate themselves in the market and attract customers who value a secure and resilient environment.

The Role of Cybersecurity Professionals

Cybersecurity professionals play a crucial role in ensuring the sustainability of cybersecurity practices. They are responsible for:

- Conducting risk assessments and implementing appropriate controls to manage cyber threats.

- Monitoring and analyzing the evolving threat landscape to identify emerging risks and vulnerabilities.

- Developing and implementing incident response plans to mitigate the impact of cyber incidents.

- Educating users and stakeholders about cybersecurity best practices and promoting a culture of security awareness.

- Collaborating with stakeholders to share information and coordinate efforts in response to cyber threats.
- Keeping abreast of emerging technologies and trends in cybersecurity to continuously enhance security measures.

Conclusion

In conclusion, cybersecurity sustainability is the key to maintaining the long-term effectiveness and resilience of cybersecurity systems. It involves a proactive and risk-based approach to identify, manage, and mitigate cyber threats in collaboration with various stakeholders. By adopting sustainable cybersecurity practices, organizations can enhance security, ensure business continuity, build trust, and gain a competitive advantage in today's digital landscape. Cybersecurity professionals play a pivotal role in achieving cybersecurity sustainability through their expertise and contributions.

Importance of Cybersecurity Sustainability

Cybersecurity sustainability is a critical aspect of protecting our digital systems and infrastructure from cyber threats. In today's interconnected world, where almost every aspect of our lives relies on technology, ensuring the long-term viability and effectiveness of cybersecurity measures is of utmost importance.

The importance of cybersecurity sustainability can be understood from multiple perspectives, including economic, social, and national security considerations.

Economic Importance

In a highly digitized and interconnected economy, the reliance on technology and digital systems poses significant risks to businesses and organizations. Cyber attacks can disrupt operations, lead to financial losses, damage brand reputation, and result in the loss of customers' trust. The consequences of a successful cyber attack can be devastating, both in terms of immediate financial impact and long-term sustainability.

By investing in cybersecurity sustainability, organizations can mitigate the risks associated with cyber threats and ensure the continuity of their operations. This includes implementing robust security measures, regularly updating and patching systems, and establishing incident response plans. By protecting their digital assets and sensitive information, businesses can safeguard their intellectual property, maintain customer trust, and ultimately secure their long-term viability and competitiveness in the market.

Social Importance

Cybersecurity sustainability is not just about protecting businesses; it is also about safeguarding individuals in their online activities. With the increasing reliance on digital technologies for communication, entertainment, and personal financial transactions, individuals are more vulnerable than ever to cyber attacks. Personal data breaches can result in identity theft, financial fraud, and other forms of cybercrime that can have long-lasting effects on individuals' lives.

Cybersecurity sustainability ensures the protection of personal information, preserving privacy and ensuring the safe use of digital services and platforms. By promoting a secure online environment, cybersecurity sustainability fosters trust among individuals, encouraging greater engagement in digital activities and the sharing of information. This, in turn, drives innovation, economic growth, and social development.

National Security Importance

Cybersecurity sustainability is a matter of national security. In today's digital age, nations are increasingly reliant on interconnected information systems and digital infrastructure. Critical sectors such as energy, transportation, healthcare, and finance are all heavily dependent on technology. A successful cyber attack on any of these sectors could have severe consequences for national security, public safety, and the economy.

By investing in cybersecurity sustainability, governments can protect not only their own digital infrastructure but also the interconnected global ecosystem. Strong cybersecurity measures, collaboration between nations, and international standards and frameworks are necessary to prevent cyber attacks and ensure the stability and resilience of the global digital infrastructure.

Conclusion

The importance of cybersecurity sustainability cannot be overstated. It is crucial for businesses, individuals, and nations to recognize the risks posed by cyber threats and take proactive measures to protect their digital systems and infrastructure. By doing so, we can ensure the long-term viability, security, and stability of our digital world. Investing in robust cybersecurity measures, promoting a secure online environment, and fostering international cooperation are key components in achieving cybersecurity sustainability.

Scope of the Book

The scope of this book, "Cybersecurity Sustainability: Future Directions," is to provide a comprehensive overview of the field of cybersecurity and its sustainable practices. It aims to equip readers with the knowledge and understanding of the evolving threat landscape, emerging technologies, governance and risk management, architectural design, threat intelligence, legal aspects, workforce development, and future challenges and opportunities in cybersecurity sustainability.

1. The evolving threat landscape: This section explores the historical context of cybersecurity and the major milestones that have shaped its development. It delves into the emergence of computer security, the birth of cybersecurity as a specialized field, and the evolution of cybersecurity threats over time. It highlights the impact of technological advancements and trends in cyber attacks that have shaped the current state of cybersecurity.

2. Governance and risk management: This section focuses on the principles of cybersecurity governance and the role of key stakeholders. It discusses the responsibility of the board of directors, the integration of cybersecurity governance with enterprise risk management, and the development of risk assessment and management frameworks. It also addresses incident response and business continuity planning as key elements of cybersecurity risk management.

3. Architectural design: This section explores the fundamentals of cybersecurity architecture and design principles. It discusses the components of a cybersecurity architecture, various security frameworks and models, and the concept of defense in depth and layered security approaches. It also covers network security architecture, application security architecture, and cloud security architecture, providing insights into secure design principles and best practices.

4. Threat intelligence and analytics: This section provides an introduction to cyber threat intelligence and its role in cybersecurity. It discusses various sources of threat intelligence, the importance of collaboration and sharing, and the analysis and reporting of threat intelligence. It also delves into the application of data analytics techniques, such as machine learning and predictive analytics, in cybersecurity to detect and respond to threats effectively.

5. Privacy and legal aspects: This section explores the right to privacy in the digital age and the relevant laws and regulations. It discusses privacy by design principles, data protection, and privacy impact assessments. Additionally, it covers

cybersecurity-related legal compliance, including incident notification and reporting, digital forensics, and cybersecurity liability and insurance. International cooperation in cybersecurity and public-private partnerships are also addressed.

6. Workforce development: This section focuses on building a skilled cybersecurity workforce. It discusses the demand for cybersecurity professionals, various job roles and functions, and the required skills and competencies. It also covers cybersecurity education and training programs, certification and accreditation, and continuous professional development to meet the evolving demands of the industry.

7. Future challenges and opportunities: This section explores the intersection of cybersecurity with emerging technologies, geopolitical factors, social implications, environmental sustainability, and ethical considerations. It discusses the impact of technologies such as artificial intelligence, the Internet of Things, quantum computing, and blockchain on cybersecurity. It also addresses the geopolitical aspects of cybersecurity, ethical considerations in decision-making, and the importance of corporate social responsibility.

The book provides a comprehensive treatment of these topics, offering theoretical foundations, practical insights, real-world examples, and thought-provoking exercises to enhance the understanding and application of cybersecurity sustainability. Through its holistic approach, it aims to equip readers with the knowledge and skills to navigate the constantly evolving cybersecurity landscape and contribute to the development of sustainable cybersecurity practices.

Organization of the Book

The book "Cybersecurity Sustainability: Future Directions" is organized into seven main sections, each focusing on a different aspect of cybersecurity sustainability. This section aims to provide an overview of how the book is structured and the topics covered in each section.

Section 1: Introduction

The first section of the book serves as an introduction to cybersecurity sustainability. It begins with an overview of the concept, defining cybersecurity sustainability and discussing its importance. The section then delves into the scope of the book, explaining the areas it will cover and the specific challenges associated with cybersecurity sustainability. The role of stakeholders and ethical considerations in cybersecurity sustainability are also discussed. Lastly, the section outlines the research methodology and approach used throughout the book.

Section 2: The Evolution of Cybersecurity

The second section focuses on tracing the evolution of cybersecurity. It starts by exploring the early developments in computer security and the birth of cybersecurity as a field. Key milestones in the history of cybersecurity are highlighted, along with an examination of the evolving nature of cybersecurity threats. The section also discusses the impact of technological advancements on cybersecurity and provides insights into the current state of cybersecurity, including an analysis of the existing landscape, trends in cyber attacks, cybersecurity policies and regulations, and the role of governments in cybersecurity. The section concludes by exploring future directions in cybersecurity, with a particular emphasis on emerging technologies and their implications for cybersecurity.

Section 3: Cybersecurity Governance and Risk Management

Section 3 delves into the principles of cybersecurity governance and risk management. It begins by discussing the responsibilities of the board of directors in cybersecurity governance and the establishment of a cybersecurity governance framework. The section then explores the role of the Chief Information Officer (CIO) and Chief Information Security Officer (CISO) in cybersecurity governance. It also highlights the integration of cybersecurity governance with enterprise risk management, as well as frameworks for assessing and prioritizing cybersecurity risks. The section concludes with a focus on incident response and business continuity planning, emphasizing the importance of continuous improvement in cybersecurity risk management and the assurance and compliance of cybersecurity measures.

Section 4: Cybersecurity Architecture and Design

Section 4 introduces the fundamentals of cybersecurity architecture and design. It begins by discussing the components of a cybersecurity architecture and the various security frameworks and models that can be employed. The section then explores security architecture design principles, such as defense in depth and layered security approaches, as well as the importance of adhering to security standards and best practices. The section further delves into network security architecture, including secure network design principles, perimeter security controls, intrusion detection and prevention systems, virtual private networks (VPNs), and wireless network security. It also covers application security architecture, cloud security architecture, and web application security.

Section 5: Cyber Threat Intelligence and Analytics

Section 5 focuses on the importance of cyber threat intelligence and analytics in cybersecurity. It begins by providing an introduction to cyber threat intelligence, highlighting the various sources of threat intelligence and its role in cybersecurity. The section then explores the intersection of data analytics and cybersecurity, including the use of big data and machine learning techniques for threat detection and anomaly detection. It also delves into security information and event management (SIEM) systems and the application of predictive analytics in cybersecurity. The section concludes with an overview of cybersecurity incident response, covering incident identification, classification, and escalation, as well as incident investigation, evidence collection, and post-incident analysis.

Section 6: Privacy and Legal Aspects of Cybersecurity

Section 6 addresses the privacy and legal aspects of cybersecurity. It begins by examining the right to privacy in the digital age, focusing on relevant privacy laws and regulations. The section then delves into privacy by design principles, data protection and privacy impact assessments, privacy policies, and consent management. The legal framework for cybersecurity is also explored, along with topics such as cybersecurity incident notification and reporting, electronic evidence and cybercrime investigations, digital forensics, cybersecurity liability, and insurance. The section further explores international cooperation in cybersecurity, particularly in the context of cross-border data protection and privacy, international cybersecurity agreements and treaties, and public-private partnerships.

Section 7: Cybersecurity Education and Workforce Development

The final section of the book addresses cybersecurity education and workforce development. It begins by discussing the demand for cybersecurity professionals and the various roles and job functions within the field. The section then focuses on cybersecurity education and training, covering cybersecurity curricula and programs, certification and accreditation, professional development, continuous learning, and cybersecurity awareness and training for end users. The section also highlights the importance of cybersecurity research and innovation, exploring emerging trends in cybersecurity research, research funding and collaboration, open-source security solutions, startups and entrepreneurship in cybersecurity, and ethical considerations in cybersecurity research.

By organizing the book into these seven sections, "Cybersecurity Sustainability: Future Directions" provides a comprehensive and structured approach to understanding and addressing the challenges and opportunities in the field of cybersecurity sustainability. Each section builds upon the previous ones, providing readers with a well-rounded understanding of the various aspects of cybersecurity sustainability and equipping them with the knowledge and skills needed to navigate the rapidly evolving landscape of cybersecurity.

Challenges in Cybersecurity Sustainability

As the field of cybersecurity continues to evolve and adapt to new technologies and threats, it faces numerous challenges in achieving sustainability. These challenges arise from various factors, including the constantly changing threat landscape, the rapid development of new technologies, and the interconnected nature of modern systems. In this section, we will discuss some of the key challenges that cybersecurity professionals and organizations face in ensuring the long-term sustainability of their cybersecurity practices.

1. Rapidly Evolving Threat Landscape

One of the biggest challenges in cybersecurity sustainability is the continuously evolving nature of cyber threats. Cyber attackers are constantly finding new ways to exploit vulnerabilities in systems and networks, making it difficult for cybersecurity professionals to keep up. New attack vectors, such as social engineering techniques and zero-day vulnerabilities, pose significant challenges in detecting and mitigating cyber threats.

To address this challenge, organizations need to adopt a proactive approach to cybersecurity, rather than relying solely on reactive defense mechanisms. This includes implementing robust threat intelligence programs, staying updated on the latest threat trends, and conducting regular risk assessments. By continuously monitoring the threat landscape and adapting their defenses accordingly, organizations can enhance their cybersecurity sustainability.

2. Lack of Skilled Workforce

Another significant challenge in cybersecurity sustainability is the shortage of skilled cybersecurity professionals. The demand for cybersecurity experts far exceeds the current supply, leading to a significant skills gap. This shortage is exacerbated by the rapidly evolving nature of the field, as traditional educational programs struggle to keep up with the latest developments.

To address this challenge, organizations and educational institutions need to invest in cybersecurity education and workforce development programs. This includes offering specialized training and certification programs, fostering partnerships between academia and industry, and promoting the field of cybersecurity as an attractive career option. By closing the skills gap and nurturing a skilled cybersecurity workforce, organizations can enhance their long-term cybersecurity sustainability.

3. Constant Technological Advancements

The rapid pace of technological advancements presents both opportunities and challenges for cybersecurity sustainability. On one hand, new technologies such as artificial intelligence, cloud computing, and the Internet of Things offer innovative solutions for enhancing cybersecurity. On the other hand, these technologies introduce new vulnerabilities and attack surfaces that can be exploited by cyber attackers.

To address this challenge, organizations need to adopt a proactive approach to cybersecurity architecture and design. This includes implementing robust security controls during the development and deployment of new technologies, conducting regular security assessments, and establishing comprehensive security frameworks. By integrating cybersecurity into the design and development of new technologies, organizations can enhance their overall cybersecurity sustainability.

4. Complexity of Interconnected Systems

Today's interconnected systems, such as smart grids, industrial control systems, and critical infrastructure, present unique challenges in terms of cybersecurity sustainability. These systems often rely on various interconnected components and devices, making them more vulnerable to cyber attacks. Furthermore, the compromise of one system can have cascading effects on other interconnected systems, resulting in significant disruptions.

To address this challenge, organizations need to adopt a holistic approach to cybersecurity, focusing not only on individual systems but also on the broader ecosystem. This includes implementing robust network segmentation, conducting regular vulnerability assessments, and establishing clear incident response and recovery plans. By taking a holistic approach to securing interconnected systems, organizations can enhance their cybersecurity sustainability.

5. Compliance with Regulations and Standards

Compliance with cybersecurity regulations and standards is a critical aspect of cybersecurity sustainability. However, the complexity and constantly changing nature of these regulations pose significant challenges for organizations. Compliance requirements often vary across different jurisdictions and industries, making it difficult to navigate the regulatory landscape.

To address this challenge, organizations need to establish a robust cybersecurity governance framework that includes regular compliance assessments. This includes staying updated on the latest regulatory developments, conducting gap assessments, and implementing appropriate controls to meet regulatory requirements. By ensuring compliance with regulations and standards, organizations can enhance their cybersecurity sustainability and mitigate legal and reputational risks.

6. Balancing Security and Usability

A common challenge in cybersecurity sustainability is finding the right balance between security and usability. While stringent security measures can enhance protection, they can also create usability challenges for end-users. Complex authentication mechanisms, frequent password changes, and strict access controls can hinder productivity and create user frustration.

To address this challenge, organizations need to adopt user-centric approaches to cybersecurity. This includes leveraging technologies such as multi-factor authentication, single sign-on, and user-friendly encryption. Organizations should also invest in user awareness and training programs to educate users about cybersecurity best practices. By finding the right balance between security and usability, organizations can enhance their cybersecurity sustainability while maintaining user satisfaction.

Conclusion

Cybersecurity sustainability faces various challenges in the ever-evolving landscape of cyber threats, technological advancements, and compliance requirements. Organizations need to address these challenges by adopting proactive cybersecurity approaches, investing in cybersecurity education and workforce development, integrating security into technological advancements, taking a holistic approach to securing interconnected systems, ensuring compliance with regulations, and balancing security with usability. By addressing these challenges, organizations can enhance their long-term cybersecurity sustainability and protect their critical assets from emerging threats.

The Role of Stakeholders in Cybersecurity Sustainability

In the realm of cybersecurity sustainability, stakeholders play a vital role in ensuring the long-term effectiveness and resilience of cybersecurity measures. Stakeholders refer to any individuals or groups that have an interest or involvement in cybersecurity, including organizations, government bodies, individuals, and the general public.

Importance of Stakeholders

Stakeholders have a significant impact on cybersecurity sustainability in various ways. They contribute to the development and implementation of cybersecurity policies, strategies, and practices. They also play a crucial role in raising awareness, promoting best practices, and fostering collaboration among different sectors. The involvement of stakeholders is crucial because:

1. **Diverse perspectives and expertise:** Stakeholders bring a wide range of expertise and knowledge to the table, enabling a more comprehensive understanding of the cybersecurity landscape. This diversity of perspectives helps in identifying potential vulnerabilities, threats, and countermeasures.

2. **Collaboration and information sharing:** Cybersecurity threats are not restricted to any single organization or sector. Stakeholders facilitate collaboration and information sharing, allowing for a more coordinated response to emerging threats. By working together, stakeholders can exchange knowledge, share best practices, and benefit from collective intelligence.

3. **Policy formulation and regulation:** Stakeholders are instrumental in the development and implementation of cybersecurity policies and regulations. Their active participation ensures that policies and regulations are practical, effective, and aligned with the needs and realities of various sectors. Stakeholders provide valuable input during the policy-making process, ensuring that diverse interests are represented.

4. **Risk management and mitigation:** Stakeholders help in identifying, assessing, and mitigating cybersecurity risks. By actively engaging in risk management processes, stakeholders contribute to the development of

robust risk assessment frameworks and the implementation of effective risk mitigation strategies.

5. **Education and awareness:** Stakeholders play a critical role in raising awareness about cybersecurity threats, best practices, and the importance of sustainability. They can engage in educational initiatives, awareness campaigns, and training programs to ensure that individuals and organizations have the necessary knowledge and skills to protect themselves against cyber threats.

6. **Advocacy and accountability:** Stakeholders hold a level of responsibility and accountability in cybersecurity sustainability. They advocate for improved cybersecurity practices, policies, and regulations, and promote a culture of cybersecurity within their respective domains. Stakeholders can contribute by highlighting emerging threats, advocating for stronger cybersecurity measures, and holding organizations and governments accountable for their cybersecurity efforts.

Types of Stakeholders

Stakeholders in cybersecurity sustainability can be broadly categorized into the following groups:

1. **Government and regulatory bodies:** Governments play a pivotal role in setting cybersecurity policies, regulations, and standards. They also enforce compliance and may provide resources and funding to support cybersecurity initiatives. Regulatory bodies oversee specific sectors, such as finance or healthcare, and ensure that organizations within those sectors adhere to cybersecurity requirements.

2. **Industry and private sector:** The private sector, including businesses and organizations, plays a critical role in cybersecurity sustainability. They are responsible for implementing cybersecurity measures within their own operations and supply chains. The private sector also contributes to research and development, innovation, and the creation of cybersecurity products and services.

3. **Academia and research institutions:** Academia and research institutions are essential stakeholders in cybersecurity sustainability. They provide valuable research and insights into emerging threats, technologies, and best

practices. They also play a role in educating and training future cybersecurity professionals.

4. **Non-profit organizations and advocacy groups:** Non-profit organizations and advocacy groups focus on cybersecurity awareness, education, and advocacy. They often bridge the gap between different sectors and stakeholders, promoting collaboration and information sharing. These organizations also work towards policy development, resource allocation, and public engagement.

5. **Individuals and end-users:** Individuals have a crucial role in cybersecurity sustainability. By adopting safe online practices, practicing good cyber hygiene, and being aware of potential threats, individuals contribute to their own protection and overall cybersecurity resilience. End-users also provide feedback and insights that can help in improving cybersecurity products and services.

Collaboration and Challenges

While stakeholders play a vital role in cybersecurity sustainability, collaboration among different stakeholders can be challenging due to a variety of factors. These challenges include:

1. **Differing priorities and interests:** Different stakeholders may have varying priorities and interests when it comes to cybersecurity. Finding common ground and aligning interests can be a significant challenge in developing cohesive cybersecurity strategies.

2. **Information sharing barriers:** Sharing sensitive cybersecurity information can be challenging due to concerns about confidentiality, liability, and competitive advantage. Overcoming these barriers requires building trust and establishing secure channels for information sharing.

3. **Resource constraints:** Stakeholders may face resource constraints, such as funding, skilled personnel, and technological capabilities. Limited resources can hamper their ability to contribute effectively to cybersecurity sustainability efforts.

4. **Lack of awareness and education:** Limited awareness and education about cybersecurity among stakeholders can impede collaboration and hinder the development of effective cybersecurity practices. Addressing this challenge

requires investing in education and awareness programs targeted at different stakeholder groups.

5. **Compliance and regulatory issues:** Compliance with cybersecurity regulations and standards can be complex and costly for organizations. Striking a balance between compliance and innovation is a challenge that requires ongoing dialogue between regulators and industry stakeholders.

Despite these challenges, collaboration among stakeholders is essential to address the evolving cybersecurity landscape effectively. By working together, stakeholders can overcome barriers and leverage their collective expertise, resources, and influence to build sustainable and resilient cybersecurity ecosystems.

Case Study: Multi-Stakeholder Collaboration

To illustrate the role of stakeholders in cybersecurity sustainability, let's consider a case study involving the development of a national cybersecurity strategy. In this scenario, the stakeholders involved include government representatives, industry leaders, academic experts, and non-profit organizations.

The stakeholders convene in a series of meetings and workshops to identify the country's cybersecurity challenges, assess the current state of cybersecurity, and define strategic objectives and action plans. Each stakeholder brings their unique knowledge, expertise, and perspectives to the table.

Government representatives provide insights into emerging cyber threats, regulatory requirements, and national security considerations. Industry leaders contribute their knowledge of the latest technologies, best practices, and sector-specific challenges. Academic experts offer research-based insights, innovative ideas, and educational resources. Non-profit organizations advocate for the public interest, promote cybersecurity awareness, and provide support for vulnerable groups.

Through dialogue and collaboration, the stakeholders draft a comprehensive cybersecurity strategy that addresses the identified challenges and aligns with national priorities. The strategy includes provisions for public-private partnerships, information sharing mechanisms, capacity building initiatives, and international collaboration.

After the strategy is finalized, the stakeholders continue to work together to implement and monitor its effectiveness. Regular meetings, progress reports, and evaluations ensure that the strategy remains relevant and adaptive to the evolving cybersecurity landscape.

This case study exemplifies the critical role of stakeholders in driving cybersecurity sustainability. Their collective efforts lead to the development of effective strategies, collaboration frameworks, and initiatives that contribute to the overall resilience of the cybersecurity ecosystem.

Conclusion

The role of stakeholders in cybersecurity sustainability cannot be understated. Stakeholders bring diverse perspectives, expertise, and resources to the table, fostering collaboration, innovation, and knowledge sharing. By working together, stakeholders can address challenges, mitigate risks, and build resilient cybersecurity ecosystems. It is imperative for organizations, governments, and individuals to actively engage with stakeholders and leverage their collective strength to ensure a sustainable and secure cyber future.

Exercises

1. Identify three key challenges in stakeholder collaboration in the context of cybersecurity sustainability and suggest strategies to overcome them.

2. Research and identify a case where collaboration among stakeholders led to a significant improvement in cybersecurity sustainability. Explain the roles played by different stakeholders in the case and the outcomes achieved.

3. Discuss the importance of cybersecurity education and awareness among stakeholders. Identify three strategies that can be employed to improve cybersecurity education and awareness at different stakeholder levels.

4. Analyze the role of individuals as stakeholders in cybersecurity sustainability. Provide three real-world examples of how individual actions can impact the overall cybersecurity resilience of organizations or communities.

5. Investigate the cybersecurity regulations and standards in your country or region. Identify the stakeholders involved in the development and enforcement of these regulations. Discuss how the involvement of these stakeholders contributes to cybersecurity sustainability.

Resources

- Infosec Institute. (2021). Stakeholders in Cybersecurity. Retrieved from `https://resources.infosecinstitute.com/topic/stakeholders-in-cybersecurity/`

- National Institute of Standards and Technology. (2018). NIST Cybersecurity Framework. Retrieved from `https://www.nist.gov/cyberframework`

- World Economic Forum. (2018). Advancing Cybersecurity through Public-Private Collaboration. Retrieved from `http://www3.weforum.org/docs/WEF_Advancing_Cybersecurity_through_Public-Private_Collaboration.pdf`

- World Health Organization. (2021). Cybersecurity and Health: Stakeholder Mapping. Retrieved from `https://www.who.int/global-coordination-mechanism/working-groups/cybersecurity-stakeholder-mapping.pdf`

Ethical Considerations in Cybersecurity Sustainability

In the realm of cybersecurity sustainability, ethical considerations play a vital role in ensuring the responsible use and management of technology. As the digital landscape continues to evolve, it is crucial to address the ethical challenges that arise in the context of cybersecurity. This section explores the ethical dimensions of cybersecurity sustainability and presents guidelines for navigating these complex issues.

The Importance of Ethical Considerations in Cybersecurity

Ethical considerations in cybersecurity sustainability are essential for several reasons. Firstly, they help to establish trust and maintain the integrity of the cybersecurity ecosystem. When individuals, organizations, and governments adopt ethical practices, it fosters a sense of security and confidence in the digital domain. Secondly, ethical considerations protect the rights and privacy of individuals, ensuring that their personal information is safeguarded against unauthorized access and misuse.

Moreover, ethical principles guide the behavior of cybersecurity professionals and stakeholders, ensuring responsible decision-making and accountability. By adhering to ethical standards, cybersecurity professionals can avoid conflicts of interest, protect sensitive data, and prioritize the well-being of users and society at large.

Ethical Principles in Cybersecurity Sustainability

Several ethical principles can guide cybersecurity professionals in their efforts to promote a sustainable and secure digital environment. These principles include:

- **Respect for Privacy:** Cybersecurity professionals should respect the privacy and confidentiality of individuals and organizations. They should handle personal data responsibly and ensure that privacy laws and regulations are followed.

- **Transparency and Informed Consent:** It is essential to be transparent about data collection, processing, and sharing practices. Individuals should be informed about the purpose and potential risks associated with the use of their data and provide their consent willingly.

- **Fairness and Equity:** Cybersecurity professionals should strive for fairness and equity in their practices. They should ensure that cybersecurity measures do not disproportionately impact certain individuals or communities and work towards bridging the digital divide.

- **Integrity and Honesty:** Maintaining one's integrity and honesty is crucial in cybersecurity sustainability. Professionals should avoid engaging in deceptive practices, such as hacking or unauthorized access to systems, and be truthful and accurate in their communication.

- **Responsible Use of Technology:** Cybersecurity professionals have a responsibility to ensure that the technology they develop, deploy, or manage is used for legitimate and ethical purposes. They should consider the potential societal impact of their work and take steps to mitigate harmful consequences.

Adhering to these ethical principles promotes the overall sustainability and societal well-being in the field of cybersecurity.

Ethical Challenges in Cybersecurity Sustainability

While ethical principles provide a framework for responsible behavior, cybersecurity sustainability faces several ethical challenges. These challenges include:

- **Balancing Privacy and Security:** Finding the right balance between privacy and security is a significant challenge in cybersecurity sustainability. Striking a balance between protecting sensitive data and ensuring effective cybersecurity measures is essential but can be complex.

- **Emerging Technologies:** The rapid development of emerging technologies, such as artificial intelligence, blockchain, and IoT, introduces ethical challenges. Cybersecurity professionals must navigate the ethical implications of these technologies, such as potential biases in AI algorithms or the risks associated with decentralized systems.

- **Ethical Dilemmas in Incident Response:** Incident response can pose ethical dilemmas, such as determining the appropriate level of response and disclosure, as well as protecting user privacy in the aftermath of a cybersecurity incident. Balancing the interests of affected parties while maintaining transparency can be challenging.

- **Global Differences in Ethical Standards:** Cybersecurity sustainability operates in a global context with varying ethical standards and cultural norms. Balancing these differences while maintaining a global cybersecurity framework can be a challenge.

Addressing these ethical challenges requires ongoing dialogue, collaboration, and commitment towards ethical practices among cybersecurity professionals, policymakers, and society at large.

Ethical Decision-Making Framework in Cybersecurity Sustainability

To navigate ethical challenges effectively, cybersecurity professionals can employ an ethical decision-making framework. This framework involves the following steps:

1. **Identify the Ethical Issue:** Recognize the ethical dimensions of the situation at hand and the potential implications of different courses of action.

2. **Gather Relevant Information:** Gather all information necessary to make an informed decision, including legal and regulatory requirements, stakeholder perspectives, and potential risks and benefits.

3. **Consider Ethical Principles and Values:** Evaluate the situation in light of ethical principles and values, such as privacy, fairness, and integrity. Consider how each potential course of action aligns with these principles.

4. **Explore Alternatives:** Identify alternative solutions or courses of action that address the ethical issue while achieving the desired cybersecurity outcomes.

5. **Make a Decision:** Select the course of action that best aligns with ethical principles, taking into account the potential consequences and trade-offs.

6. **Implement and Evaluate:** Act on the decision, monitoring its implementation and assessing its effectiveness. Adjust the course of action if necessary.

By following this ethical decision-making framework, cybersecurity professionals can navigate complex ethical challenges and promote cybersecurity sustainability.

Case Study: Ethical Responsibility in Data Breaches

A real-world example that highlights the ethical considerations in cybersecurity sustainability is the issue of data breaches. When a data breach occurs, organizations face ethical and legal responsibilities to address the incident effectively.

Consider the following scenario: Company X, a popular e-commerce platform, experiences a data breach resulting in the unauthorized access of customer information, including names, email addresses, and credit card details. In this case, several ethical considerations arise:

- **Transparency and Communication:** Company X has an ethical responsibility to inform affected customers about the breach promptly. Transparent communication about the extent of the breach, the potential risks involved, and the steps taken to mitigate the impact demonstrates integrity and helps affected individuals protect themselves.

- **Data Protection and Privacy:** Company X must take immediate action to address security vulnerabilities and prevent further exploitation of customer data. This includes implementing encryption measures, updating security protocols, and assessing the overall cybersecurity posture to ensure the protection of individuals' privacy.

- **Accountability and Remediation:** Company X should take responsibility for the breach by promptly rectifying the vulnerabilities and offering appropriate remedies to affected individuals. This may include providing credit monitoring services, financial compensation, or other forms of assistance to mitigate the potential harm resulting from the breach.

By addressing these ethical considerations, Company X can demonstrate its commitment to cybersecurity sustainability and regain the trust of its customers.

Conclusion

Ethical considerations are fundamentally important in the field of cybersecurity sustainability. By adopting ethical principles and decision-making frameworks, cybersecurity professionals can ensure responsible practices, protect privacy rights, and build trust in the digital world. Furthermore, addressing the ethical challenges in cybersecurity sustainability contributes to the overall well-being of society and promotes the long-term sustainability of the cybersecurity ecosystem.

Research Methodology and Approach

In this section, we will discuss the research methodology and approach employed in this book on cyber security sustainability. A sound research methodology is crucial for producing reliable and valid findings. It provides a systematic framework for conducting research and ensures that the research process is scientific, rigorous, and transparent.

Research Methodology

The research methodology used in this book is a combination of quantitative and qualitative approaches. Quantitative research involves the collection and analysis of numerical data, while qualitative research focuses on the collection and analysis of non-numerical data, such as texts, images, and videos. By employing both approaches, we aim to provide a comprehensive understanding of the complex issues surrounding cyber security sustainability.

Research Approach

The research approach used in this book is primarily exploratory and descriptive in nature. An exploratory approach is used to gain insights into new and emerging topics, while a descriptive approach is used to provide a detailed description of a phenomenon. As cyber security sustainability is a rapidly evolving field, an exploratory approach is essential to identify emerging trends and challenges. At the same time, a descriptive approach allows us to provide a comprehensive overview of the current state of cyber security sustainability.

Data Collection

The data collection process for this book involves the gathering of information from a variety of sources. Primary data is collected through interviews with industry experts, practitioners, and researchers in the field of cyber security sustainability. These interviews help us gain insights into real-world challenges and strategies for achieving cyber security sustainability. Secondary data is collected from published articles, reports, and academic literature, which provide a foundation of knowledge and support our research findings.

Data Analysis

The data collected through interviews and secondary sources is analyzed using a combination of qualitative and quantitative methods. Qualitative data analysis involves identifying patterns, themes, and categories within the data, while quantitative data analysis involves the use of statistical techniques to analyze numerical data. By integrating both approaches, we can gain a comprehensive understanding of the issues related to cyber security sustainability.

Ethical Considerations

Throughout the research process, ethical considerations are paramount. This includes obtaining informed consent from participants, ensuring the confidentiality and anonymity of data, and conducting the research in an ethical and responsible manner. These considerations are essential for maintaining the integrity and validity of the research findings.

Research Limitations

It is important to acknowledge the limitations of any research study. In this book, one limitation is the reliance on self-reported data collected through interviews, which may be subject to bias and memory recall errors. Additionally, the rapidly evolving nature of cyber security technology and practices may challenge the generalizability of the findings. However, efforts have been made to mitigate these limitations by employing a rigorous research methodology and triangulating data from multiple sources.

Example Research Question

To illustrate the research methodology and approach used in this book, let us consider an example research question:

What are the key challenges and opportunities in securing Internet of Things (IoT) devices to achieve cyber security sustainability?

To address this research question, we would conduct interviews with experts in the field of IoT security, analyze existing literature on IoT security challenges and best practices, and explore case studies of successful IoT security implementations. By employing a combination of qualitative and quantitative analysis, we would identify common themes and trends, and provide practical recommendations for achieving cyber security sustainability in the context of IoT devices.

Summary

In this section, we discussed the research methodology and approach used in this book on cyber security sustainability. We highlighted the importance of employing a sound research methodology to ensure the validity and reliability of the findings. The research methodology used a combination of qualitative and quantitative approaches, and the research approach was primarily exploratory and descriptive. The data collection process involved gathering primary data through interviews and secondary data from published sources. Data analysis employed both qualitative and quantitative methods to gain a comprehensive understanding of the subject. Ethical considerations were also emphasized throughout the research process. Finally, we provided an example research question to illustrate the application of the research methodology and approach.

The Evolution of Cybersecurity

Early Developments in Cybersecurity

Emergence of Computer Security

In the early days of computing, the concept of security was non-existent. Computers were mainly used for scientific and military purposes, and the focus was on improving technology and functionality rather than protecting the systems from malicious actors. However, as computers became more prevalent and interconnected, the need for security measures became apparent.

The birth of computer security can be traced back to the 1960s when multi-user systems started to appear. These systems allowed multiple users to access a mainframe concurrently, which introduced new security challenges. With users having access to shared resources, there was a need to ensure the confidentiality, integrity, and availability of data.

At this time, the primary concern was unauthorized access to systems and data. The first computer security threats emerged in the form of insiders who abused their privileged access to gain unauthorized information or manipulate data for personal gains. These threats led to the development of access control mechanisms, such as user authentication and authorization, to restrict access only to authorized individuals.

In response to the growing threats, the field of computer security began to take shape. Researchers and practitioners started to develop techniques and best practices to address the emerging security challenges. One of the key milestones in the field was the development of the password-based authentication system, which allowed users to authenticate their identity by providing a secret password.

As the technology advanced and computing systems became more complex, new security threats and vulnerabilities emerged. The introduction of networking technologies further increased the attack surface, enabling attackers to target systems remotely. This led to the development of network security protocols and technologies to protect data in transit.

The evolution of computer security can be attributed to various factors, including technological advancements, increasing connectivity, and the expansion of the digital landscape. As computers became more prevalent in businesses, governments, and everyday life, the need for robust security measures became critical.

In recent years, the rise of cybercrime and sophisticated hacking techniques has highlighted the importance of computer security. Organizations have recognized the need to invest in cybersecurity to protect their sensitive data and ensure the integrity of their systems. Governments have also implemented regulations and standards to promote cybersecurity practices and protect their national interests.

Today, computer security encompasses a wide range of disciplines, including network security, application security, data security, and incident response. It involves the implementation of technical controls, such as firewalls and encryption, as well as policies and procedures to mitigate risks and respond to security incidents.

However, despite the advancements in computer security, the field continues to face new challenges. The increasing complexity of technology, the emergence of new attack vectors, and the evolving nature of cyber threats require constant vigilance and innovation in the field of computer security.

In conclusion, the emergence of computer security can be traced back to the need for protecting systems and data in the early days of computing. Over the years, computer security has evolved in response to the changing technological landscape and the growing threats posed by cybercriminals. To ensure the sustainability of cybersecurity, organizations and individuals must continue to invest in the development and implementation of robust security measures.

The Birth of Cybersecurity

The birth of cybersecurity can be traced back to the early days of computer technology when the need for protecting information and systems from unauthorized access and malicious attacks became evident. This section will explore the key milestones that marked the emergence and development of cybersecurity as a distinct field. We will also discuss the challenges and advancements that shaped its evolution.

Early Developments in Cybersecurity

In the early days of computer technology, security was not a major concern. Computers were mainly used for scientific and military purposes, and the focus was on functionality rather than safeguarding data. However, as computer networks grew in size and complexity, it became evident that robust security measures were necessary to protect sensitive information.

Emergence of Computer Security The notion of computer security began to gain attention in the 1960s when the first multi-user operating systems, such as CTSS (Compatible Time-Sharing System), were developed. With multiple users sharing a single system, there was a need to ensure that each user's data and programs were protected from unauthorized access. This led to the development of access control mechanisms, such as user authentication and file permissions.

The Birth of Cybersecurity The term "cybersecurity" was not coined until much later, but the foundations of the field were laid in the 1970s with the advent of computer networks. The ARPANET (Advanced Research Projects Agency Network), developed by the U.S. Department of Defense, was the precursor to the modern internet. As ARPANET connected more and more computers, the need for secure communication and data protection became critical.

Key Milestones in Cybersecurity Throughout the 1980s and 1990s, several milestones further propelled the field of cybersecurity. One of the most significant events was the Morris worm attack in 1988, which infected thousands of computers and brought attention to the vulnerability of computer systems. This incident led to the development of early intrusion detection and prevention systems.

Another milestone was the establishment of the Computer Emergency Response Team (CERT) at Carnegie Mellon University in 1988. CERT was created to coordinate responses to network security incidents and share information about emerging threats. This marked the beginning of organized efforts to address cyber threats and collaborate on security solutions.

Evolution of Cybersecurity Threats As technology continued to advance, so did the sophistication of cyber threats. The early days of cybersecurity focused primarily on protecting against external attacks, such as viruses and worms. However, as networks and systems became more interconnected, new threats emerged, including insider threats, social engineering, and advanced persistent threats (APTs). Cybersecurity had to evolve to address these evolving threats.

Impact of Technological Advancements on Cybersecurity Advancements in technology have had a profound impact on cybersecurity. The rise of the internet, the proliferation of mobile devices, and the widespread adoption of cloud computing have all introduced new security challenges. Cybersecurity had to adapt to protect against new attack vectors and vulnerabilities introduced by these technologies.

Current State of Cybersecurity

The current state of cybersecurity is characterized by an ever-evolving threat landscape and the increasing importance of protecting critical infrastructure and sensitive data. This section will provide an overview of the current cybersecurity landscape, including trends in cyber attacks, policies and regulations, and the role of governments in cybersecurity.

Current Cybersecurity Landscape Cyber attacks have become more frequent, sophisticated, and damaging in recent years. Organizations of all sizes and sectors are being targeted, and the potential impact of cyber attacks on individuals, businesses, and even nations is significant. Cybersecurity has become a top priority for organizations worldwide, leading to increased investment in security technologies and personnel.

Trends in Cybersecurity Attacks Cybersecurity attacks are constantly evolving, driven by technological advancements and the emergence of new attack vectors. Some notable trends include the rise of ransomware attacks, which encrypt victims' data and demand a ransom for its release, and the increasing use of social engineering techniques to manipulate individuals into revealing sensitive information or performing certain actions.

Cybersecurity Policies and Regulations Governments around the world have recognized the importance of cybersecurity and have implemented various policies and regulations to protect their citizens and critical infrastructure. These policies and regulations often require organizations to implement specific security measures, conduct regular risk assessments, and report any security incidents. Compliance with these regulations is important not only for legal reasons but also for maintaining customer trust and mitigating the risk of reputational damage.

Cybersecurity Compliance and Standards Compliance with cybersecurity standards helps organizations establish a baseline of security controls and best practices. Standards such as ISO 27001, NIST Cybersecurity Framework, and PCI DSS provide guidelines for implementing effective cybersecurity strategies. Compliance with these standards not only improves an organization's security posture but also demonstrates a commitment to protecting sensitive data and maintaining a secure environment for customers and partners.

Role of Government in Cybersecurity Governments play a crucial role in cybersecurity, both in terms of protecting their own networks and infrastructure and in ensuring the overall security of the nation. Governments invest in cybersecurity research and development, establish cybersecurity agencies and organizations, and collaborate with other countries to combat cyber threats. Government cybersecurity initiatives are often aimed at addressing national security concerns, protecting critical infrastructure, and promoting economic growth.

In conclusion, the birth of cybersecurity can be traced back to the early days of computer technology when the need for protecting information and systems became evident. The concept of computer security emerged with the development of multi-user operating systems, and the birth of cybersecurity followed with the advent of computer networks. Key milestones in cybersecurity, such as the Morris worm attack and the establishment of CERT, further shaped the field. The evolution of technology has brought new challenges, and cybersecurity has had to adapt to protect against sophisticated threats. The current state of cybersecurity is characterized by an ever-evolving threat landscape, increasing regulations, and the role of governments in addressing cyber threats.

Key Milestones in Cybersecurity

Cybersecurity has evolved significantly over the years, with several key milestones shaping its development. In this section, we will explore some of these pivotal moments and their impact on the field of cybersecurity. These milestones highlight the progress made in protecting digital systems and networks from various threats and vulnerabilities.

1. The Morris Worm (1988): One of the earliest milestones in cybersecurity was the Morris Worm, created by Robert Morris in 1988. This self-replicating malware infected thousands of computers connected to the early internet, causing widespread disruption. The Morris Worm served as a wake-up call, emphasizing the need for effective cybersecurity measures to prevent and mitigate such attacks.

2. The Computer Emergency Response Team (CERT) (1988): In response to the Morris Worm incident, the Computer Emergency Response Team (CERT) was established at Carnegie Mellon University. CERT became the first formal cybersecurity incident response organization, providing guidance and assistance to individuals, organizations, and governments in dealing with cyber threats. The establishment of CERT marked a significant milestone in the development of incident response capabilities.

3. The Computer Fraud and Abuse Act (1986): The Computer Fraud and Abuse Act (CFAA) is a federal law in the United States that was enacted to combat computer-related crimes. It addressed various cyber offenses, including unauthorized access, identity theft, and computer fraud. The CFAA played a crucial role in establishing legal frameworks to prosecute cybercriminals and protect individuals and organizations from cyber threats.

4. The Trusted Computer System Evaluation Criteria (1983): The Trusted Computer System Evaluation Criteria, commonly known as the Orange Book, was published by the U.S. Department of Defense in 1983. The Orange Book introduced a set of criteria for evaluating the security capabilities of computer systems. It established a framework for categorizing and assessing system security levels, laying the foundation for future cybersecurity standards and guidelines.

5. The First Virus (1981): Elk Cloner, created by Richard Skrenta in 1981, became the first computer virus to spread in the wild. It infected Apple II computers through floppy disks and displayed humorous messages. Elk Cloner raised awareness about the potential dangers of viruses and showcased the need for antivirus software to protect against such threats.

6. The Internet Engineering Task Force (IETF) (1986): The Internet Engineering Task Force (IETF) emerged as an important organization for developing and promoting internet standards. Through its various working groups, the IETF has played a significant role in shaping the security protocols and standards that underpin the internet, such as the Transport Layer Security (TLS) protocol and the Internet Protocol Security (IPsec) framework.

7. The CISSP Certification (1994): The Certified Information Systems Security Professional (CISSP) certification was introduced in 1994 by the International Information System Security Certification Consortium $(ISC)^2$. It became one of the most recognized and sought-after certifications in the field of cybersecurity. The CISSP certification provided a standardized framework for assessing and validating the knowledge and skills of cybersecurity professionals, contributing to the professionalization of the industry.

8. The Stuxnet Worm (2010): The Stuxnet worm, discovered in 2010, targeted industrial systems, specifically those used in Iran's nuclear program. It was

a highly sophisticated cyber weapon designed to sabotage centrifuge machines. The Stuxnet worm demonstrated the potential of cyberattacks to cause physical damage and highlighted the importance of critical infrastructure protection within the field of cybersecurity.

These key milestones in cybersecurity history illustrate the evolution and progress made in combating cyber threats. They have paved the way for improved strategies, technologies, and regulations to safeguard digital systems and networks. It is crucial to understand these milestones to appreciate the challenges faced and the advancements achieved in the ongoing battle for cybersecurity.

Evolution of Cybersecurity Threats

The evolution of cybersecurity threats has been a significant concern for individuals, organizations, and governments alike. As technology has advanced, so have the tactics and techniques employed by cybercriminals to exploit vulnerabilities and gain unauthorized access to systems and data. This section explores the historical progression of cybersecurity threats, highlighting key milestones and the impact of technological advancements.

Early Forms of Cybersecurity Threats

In the early days of computing, cybersecurity threats were relatively simple and primarily focused on exploiting system vulnerabilities. Viruses and worms were among the earliest forms of cyber threats that spread through infected files and network connections. These malicious programs had the potential to cause significant damage to computer systems, leading to data loss and disruption of critical services.

Additionally, hackers at this time were motivated by the desire to demonstrate their technical skills or gain notoriety. They would infiltrate systems by exploiting weak passwords, misconfigured services, or using social engineering techniques. The primary goal was often to gain unauthorized access to sensitive information or disrupt system operations.

The Rise of Cybercrime

As computing became more prevalent and interconnected, cybercrime began to emerge as a serious threat. Criminals realized the potential economic benefits of exploiting technology for illicit activities. The advent of e-commerce and online banking introduced new vulnerabilities that attackers could exploit to steal personal and financial information. Phishing attacks, where attackers trick individuals into providing confidential information, became a popular method for identity theft and financial fraud.

Moreover, the introduction of botnets revolutionized cybercrime by enabling large-scale attacks. Botnets are networks of compromised devices that can be controlled remotely. These networks were used to launch Distributed Denial of Service (DDoS) attacks, flooding systems with an overwhelming amount of traffic to render them inaccessible. This tactic was employed by cybercriminals to extort money, disrupt services, or exact revenge on specific targets.

Technological Developments and Advanced Threats

Advancements in technology have not only transformed society but also presented new challenges in cybersecurity. As computing moved to the cloud and mobile devices became ubiquitous, cyber threats adapted accordingly. Here are some of the significant technological developments and the corresponding cybersecurity threats that emerged:

Mobile Devices and Mobile Malware

The proliferation of smartphones and tablets led to the development of mobile malware. Malicious applications disguised as legitimate ones could compromise devices, steal personal information, and perform unauthorized activities. Mobile malware often spread through app stores or via malicious links sent through text messages or emails.

IoT and Botnets

The Internet of Things (IoT) brought about a new era of interconnected devices, but it also created a vast attack surface for cybercriminals. Insecure IoT devices have been exploited to create botnets capable of launching massive DDoS attacks, such as the Mirai botnet in 2016.

Ransomware

Ransomware emerged as a major cybersecurity threat, causing significant financial losses worldwide. This type of malware encrypts a victim's data and demands a ransom to provide the decryption key. Attacks often target individuals, businesses, and even critical infrastructure, paralyzing operations until a ransom is paid.

Advanced Persistent Threats (APTs)

Advanced Persistent Threats (APTs) are highly sophisticated and targeted attacks, often attributed to nation-state actors or well-funded criminal organizations. APTs involve a prolonged and stealthy campaign of network infiltration to steal sensitive information or disrupt critical operations. Attackers utilize advanced techniques, such as zero-day exploits and social engineering, to bypass traditional security measures.

Mitigation Strategies and Future Outlook

The evolving nature of cybersecurity threats necessitates innovative approaches to mitigate their impact. Organizations and individuals must adopt a multi-layered defense strategy that includes the following measures:

Threat Intelligence

Threat intelligence involves gathering and analyzing information about potential threats and adversaries to enhance situational awareness. By proactively monitoring the threat landscape, organizations can identify emerging risks and tailor their security measures accordingly.

Endpoint Security

Endpoint security solutions provide protection against malware, unauthorized access, and data exfiltration on individual devices. This includes implementing robust anti-malware software, regularly patching systems, and enforcing strong authentication mechanisms.

Network Segmentation

Segmenting networks and implementing strict access controls helps prevent lateral movement by attackers. By dividing the network into smaller, isolated segments, organizations can limit the impact of a breach and protect sensitive data.

Employee Training and Awareness

Human error remains a significant vulnerability in cybersecurity. Training employees on best practices, such as identifying phishing emails, using strong passwords, and reporting suspicious activities, helps reduce the risk of successful attacks.

Continuous Monitoring and Incident Response

Implementing a robust incident response plan, including continuous monitoring and threat hunting, is crucial for detecting and responding to cybersecurity incidents promptly. Organizations should regularly test their incident response procedures and conduct post-incident analysis to improve future response efforts.

Looking ahead, emerging technologies such as artificial intelligence and machine learning present both opportunities and challenges in combating cybersecurity threats. While AI-powered tools can enhance threat detection and response capabilities, they can also be exploited by malicious actors. Therefore, it is crucial to maintain a proactive and adaptive approach to cybersecurity, keeping pace with the evolving threat landscape.

In conclusion, the evolution of cybersecurity threats has mirrored the advancements in technology. From early viruses to sophisticated APTs, cybercriminals have continually adapted their tactics to exploit vulnerabilities. Organizations and individuals must stay vigilant, employing a combination of technical measures, employee training, and robust incident response practices to mitigate the evolving cybersecurity risks. By understanding the historical context and staying informed about emerging threats, we can collectively work towards a more secure digital future.

Impact of Technological Advancements on Cybersecurity

The field of cybersecurity has evolved significantly over the years due to rapid technological advancements. Emerging and evolving technologies have not only presented new opportunities but also challenges in securing cyberspace. In this section, we will explore the impact of technological advancements on cybersecurity and discuss the implications for organizations and individuals.

Technological Advancements in Computing

The advancements in computing have played a crucial role in shaping the cybersecurity landscape. The exponential increase in computing power and storage capabilities has enabled organizations to process large volumes of data in real-time. However, this rapid advancement has also empowered cybercriminals with sophisticated tools and techniques.

One of the significant technological advancements that have had a profound impact on cybersecurity is cloud computing. The adoption of cloud services has allowed organizations to scale their infrastructure and store critical data off-site.

However, this shift has introduced new security challenges, such as the risk of data breaches and unauthorized access to sensitive information.

Similarly, the Internet of Things (IoT) has revolutionized the way we interact with the digital world. IoT devices, such as smart home appliances, wearables, and industrial sensors, have become pervasive in our daily lives. However, the widespread adoption of IoT has raised concerns about the security and privacy of personal and sensitive data. Vulnerabilities in IoT devices can lead to large-scale cyber-attacks, compromising not only individual privacy but also critical infrastructure.

Artificial Intelligence and Machine Learning

Artificial Intelligence (AI) and Machine Learning (ML) have emerged as powerful technologies with a wide range of applications. In the context of cybersecurity, AI and ML have the potential to augment human capabilities in threat detection, analysis, and response. AI-based tools can process vast amounts of data, identify patterns, and detect anomalies that may indicate a cyber-attack.

However, as with any technology, AI and ML also come with their own set of challenges. Adversarial ML, for example, is a technique that manipulates machine learning algorithms to generate false outputs. Cybercriminals can exploit vulnerabilities in AI systems to bypass security mechanisms and launch sophisticated attacks.

Moreover, the use of AI in cybersecurity raises ethical considerations. The decisions made by AI systems may have far-reaching consequences, such as identifying potential threats or determining access controls. It is crucial to ensure transparency, accountability, and fairness in the design and deployment of AI technologies to avoid unintended biases and discrimination.

Blockchain and Distributed Ledger Technology

Blockchain and distributed ledger technology (DLT) have gained significant attention in recent years due to their potential to improve security and privacy. Blockchain, the underlying technology behind cryptocurrencies like Bitcoin, provides a decentralized and tamper-resistant ledger of transactions.

From a cybersecurity perspective, blockchain can enhance data integrity, transparency, and authentication. The decentralized nature of blockchain makes it challenging for malicious actors to manipulate or tamper with data stored on the ledger. This technology has applications in various sectors, including supply chain management, financial services, and healthcare.

However, it is essential to recognize that blockchain and DLT are not a panacea for all cybersecurity challenges. While they offer certain security properties, they also introduce new vulnerabilities and risks. Smart contract vulnerabilities, for example, can lead to unauthorized execution of code and potential financial losses. Moreover, the immutability of blockchain can also pose challenges when it comes to data protection and privacy regulations.

Quantum Computing

Quantum computing is an emerging technology that has the potential to revolutionize various industries, including cybersecurity. Quantum computers leverage the principles of quantum physics to perform complex computations at a speed exponentially faster than classical computers.

While quantum computing holds promise for solving difficult cryptographic problems, such as factorization and discrete logarithms, it also poses a significant threat to current encryption algorithms, which rely on the computational infeasibility of certain mathematical operations.

The advent of quantum computers could render existing encryption methods obsolete, compromising the security of sensitive information. To address this challenge, researchers are exploring the development of quantum-resistant encryption algorithms that can withstand attacks from powerful quantum computers.

Striking a Balance: Opportunities and Challenges

Technological advancements have opened up new opportunities for organizations and individuals to enhance their cybersecurity capabilities. However, they also introduce new challenges that need to be addressed proactively.

Organizations must continuously adapt and evolve their cybersecurity strategies to keep up with the rapidly changing technological landscape. This includes investing in robust cybersecurity frameworks, adopting best practices, and leveraging emerging technologies to detect and mitigate cyber threats.

Individuals also play a vital role in ensuring their cybersecurity. Practicing good cyber hygiene, such as using strong and unique passwords, regularly updating software, and being cautious of phishing attacks, can go a long way in protecting personal and sensitive information.

In conclusion, technological advancements have significantly shaped the field of cybersecurity. The evolution of computing, AI and ML, blockchain, and quantum computing presents both opportunities and challenges. By understanding the impact of these technologies, organizations and individuals can stay ahead in the race against cyber threats and ensure a secure cyberspace for all.

Current State of Cybersecurity

Current Cybersecurity Landscape

The current cybersecurity landscape is constantly evolving due to advancements in technology, the proliferation of cyber threats, and the increasing dependency on digital infrastructure. In this section, we will explore the key components and trends within this ever-changing landscape.

Threat Actors

Cybersecurity threats emanate from various actors, each with their motives and capabilities. The following are some of the prominent threat actors in today's cybersecurity landscape:

1. **Cybercriminals:** These individuals or organized groups aim to profit from their malicious activities. They engage in activities such as financial fraud, ransomware attacks, and identity theft.

2. **Nation-State Actors:** Governments and state-sponsored groups conduct cyber operations for political, economic, and military advantages. They target critical infrastructure, engage in espionage and carry out disruptive attacks.

3. **Hacktivists:** These are individuals or groups who hack into systems to promote political or social causes. They often deface websites, leak sensitive information or disrupt targeted services.

4. **Insiders:** Employees or insiders with privileged access can pose a significant threat to organizations. They may intentionally or inadvertently leak sensitive data, compromise systems, or facilitate unauthorized access.

5. **Advanced Persistent Threats (APTs):** APTs are highly sophisticated and stealthy attackers often associated with nation-state or state-sponsored actors. They focus on prolonged infiltration of targeted organizations to gain unauthorized access and gather sensitive data.

Understanding these threat actors is essential to developing effective cybersecurity strategies.

Cybersecurity Threats

The cybersecurity landscape is dominated by a wide range of threats, which continue to evolve and become more sophisticated. Some of the prominent cybersecurity threats are:

1. **Malware:** Malicious software is a common cyber threat that can infiltrate systems through various means, including email attachments, infected websites, or compromised software. Malware includes viruses, worms, ransomware, and spyware, among others.

2. **Phishing and Social Engineering:** Phishing attacks use deceptive techniques, such as fraudulent emails or websites, to trick individuals into revealing sensitive information. Social engineering involves manipulating people to gain unauthorized access to systems or divulge confidential information.

3. **Data Breaches:** Data breaches involve unauthorized access to sensitive data, leading to its exposure or theft. This can result in severe consequences, including financial loss, reputational damage, and regulatory penalties.

4. **Distributed Denial of Service (DDoS) Attacks:** DDoS attacks overwhelm a target system with a flood of traffic, rendering it inaccessible to legitimate users. These attacks are often launched using botnets, which are networks of compromised devices.

5. **Insider Threats:** Insider threats refer to attacks or data breaches caused by employees, contractors, or other individuals with authorized access to an organization's systems. These threats can be intentional or accidental, and organizations must implement measures to detect and mitigate them.

Cybersecurity Trends

The landscape of cybersecurity is shaped by several emerging trends that are expected to have a significant impact in the coming years. Some of these trends include:

1. **Artificial Intelligence and Machine Learning:** The use of AI and machine learning techniques is becoming increasingly prevalent in cybersecurity. These technologies can enhance threat detection, automate incident response, and improve overall security posture.

2. **Internet of Things (IoT) Security:** The proliferation of IoT devices introduces new security challenges. Securing these devices and the data they collect is crucial to mitigate potential risks associated with their deployment.

3. **Cloud Security:** As organizations increasingly rely on cloud services, securing cloud environments becomes critically important. Effective security measures need to be implemented to protect data, applications, and infrastructure hosted in the cloud.

4. **Securing Critical Infrastructure:** Critical infrastructure, including power grids, transportation systems, and healthcare facilities, faces persistent cyber threats. Securing these systems requires a combination of robust cybersecurity practices and collaboration between the public and private sectors.

5. **Privacy and Data Protection:** With the growing concerns around data privacy, regulations such as the General Data Protection Regulation (GDPR) have been implemented to protect individuals' personal data. Organizations must ensure compliance with these regulations and implement appropriate privacy measures.

6. **Mobile Device Security:** Mobile devices are increasingly targeted by cybercriminals due to their widespread use and the amount of sensitive data they store. Protecting mobile devices against malware, data breaches, and unauthorized access is crucial.

These trends have significant implications for the future of cybersecurity and require organizations to adapt their strategies accordingly.

Cybersecurity Challenges

The current cybersecurity landscape is fraught with various challenges that organizations need to address proactively. Some of the key challenges include:

1. **Skills Gap:** The cybersecurity industry faces a shortage of skilled professionals, making it challenging to meet the demand for cybersecurity expertise.

2. **Rapidly Evolving Threat Landscape:** Cyber threats are constantly evolving, making it difficult for organizations to keep up with the latest attack techniques and vulnerabilities.

3. **Complexity of IT Environments:** Modern IT infrastructures are complex, comprising a diverse range of systems, networks, and applications. Securing such environments requires a comprehensive and integrated approach.

4. **Third-Party Risk:** Organizations often rely on third-party vendors and partners, introducing additional cybersecurity risks. Managing and mitigating these risks is crucial to maintaining a robust security posture.

5. **Compliance and Regulations:** Organizations must comply with a range of cybersecurity regulations and industry standards. Meeting these requirements while maintaining efficient security operations can be a significant challenge.

Effectively addressing these challenges requires a holistic approach involving technology, people, processes, and governance.

Tools and Technologies

The cybersecurity landscape is supported by a range of tools and technologies to detect, prevent, and respond to cyber threats. Some of the key tools and technologies include:

1. **Firewalls and Intrusion Detection Systems:** These technologies monitor network traffic, identify potential threats, and block unauthorized access attempts.

2. **Antivirus and Malware Detection Software:** These tools scan systems for known malware signatures, detect and remove malicious software to protect against a wide range of threats.

3. **Security Information and Event Management (SIEM):** SIEM solutions collect and analyze log data from various sources to identify potential security incidents and provide detailed insights for incident response.

4. **Encryption and Cryptography:** Encryption technologies protect data by converting it into an unreadable format, ensuring that only authorized entities can decrypt and access the data.

5. **Multi-Factor Authentication (MFA):** MFA adds an additional layer of security by requiring users to verify their identity using multiple credentials, such as passwords, biometrics, or security tokens.

These tools and technologies play a crucial role in building resilient cybersecurity defenses.

Conclusion

The current cybersecurity landscape presents a range of challenges and opportunities for organizations across various industries. Understanding the threat actors, cybersecurity threats, trends, and technologies is essential for developing effective strategies to protect data, systems, and infrastructure. By staying informed and adapting to the evolving landscape, organizations can enhance their cyber resilience and mitigate potential risks.

Trends in Cybersecurity Attacks

In today's interconnected world, the frequency and sophistication of cybersecurity attacks are on the rise. Cybercriminals are continuously finding new ways to exploit vulnerabilities, steal sensitive information, disrupt services, and cause financial and reputational damage. Understanding the trends in cybersecurity attacks is crucial for organizations to develop effective defense strategies. In this section, we will explore some of the key trends in cybersecurity attacks and discuss the challenges they pose.

Rise of Ransomware Attacks

Ransomware attacks have emerged as one of the most significant cybersecurity threats in recent years. This type of attack involves encrypting valuable data or locking users out of their systems and demanding a ransom for its release. Ransomware attacks are often carried out through phishing emails, malicious links, or exploit kits. The attackers target individuals, businesses, and even critical infrastructure, causing widespread disruption and financial losses.

One notable example of a ransomware attack is the WannaCry attack in 2017. This global attack impacted hundreds of thousands of computers across more than 150 countries, encrypting files and demanding ransom payments in Bitcoin. The attack exploited a vulnerability in the Windows operating system, highlighting the importance of timely patching and updates.

To mitigate the risk of ransomware attacks, organizations should regularly backup their data, educate users about phishing scams, and keep software and systems up to date with the latest security patches.

Expansion of DDoS Attacks

Distributed Denial of Service (DDoS) attacks are designed to overwhelm a target system or network with a flood of traffic, rendering it inaccessible to legitimate users. DDoS attacks have become more powerful and widespread, posing significant challenges for organizations.

In recent years, attackers have harnessed the power of botnets to amplify the scale of DDoS attacks. Botnets are networks of compromised computers or devices that are controlled by attackers, often without the knowledge of the owners. By leveraging the combined bandwidth of these devices, attackers can launch massive DDoS attacks capable of crippling even the most well-protected systems.

The emergence of Internet of Things (IoT) devices has further expanded the attack surface for DDoS attacks. Inadequately secured IoT devices can be easily compromised and used as part of botnets. This was evidenced in the Mirai botnet attack in 2016, where IoT devices were exploited to launch one of the largest DDoS attacks to date.

To defend against DDoS attacks, organizations should implement robust network security measures, such as traffic filtering, rate limiting, and intrusion detection systems. Additionally, organizations should ensure that their IoT devices are properly configured and updated with the latest security patches.

Targeted Attacks and Advanced Persistent Threats

Targeted attacks, also known as advanced persistent threats (APTs), are sophisticated and stealthy attacks aimed at specific organizations or individuals. These attacks typically involve a combination of advanced techniques, including social engineering, malware, and zero-day exploits.

Targeted attacks often start with reconnaissance, with attackers gathering information about their intended targets to tailor their attack strategies. They may send spear-phishing emails or execute watering hole attacks, where legitimate websites frequented by the target are compromised to deliver malware. Once inside the target network, attackers can remain undetected for long periods, exfiltrating data or gathering intelligence.

The motivations behind targeted attacks vary, ranging from state-sponsored espionage to corporate espionage or financial gain. Notable examples include the breach of the U.S. Office of Personnel Management in 2015, where sensitive personnel data of millions of government employees were stolen, and the Stuxnet worm attack on an Iranian nuclear facility in 2010.

Defending against targeted attacks requires a multi-layered approach, including user awareness training, strong access controls, network segmentation, and robust endpoint protection. Organizations should also implement intrusion detection and prevention systems that can detect and respond to suspicious activities.

Emergence of Insider Threats

Insider threats refer to attacks perpetrated by individuals within an organization who have authorized access to systems, networks, or data. Insider threats can be accidental or malicious. Accidental insider threats are often a result of negligence, while malicious insider threats involve individuals purposely stealing data, leaking information, or sabotaging systems.

Insider threats can be particularly challenging to detect and mitigate due to the inherent trust placed in authorized employees. Insiders may have legitimate access to sensitive information, making it difficult to distinguish between normal and malicious activities.

To address insider threats, organizations should implement strong access controls, employee monitoring systems, and robust security awareness training programs. It is also important for organizations to foster a culture of security and vigilance, encouraging employees to report suspicious activities and potential security incidents.

Mobile and IoT Security Challenges

As the use of smartphones, tablets, and IoT devices continues to grow, so does the risk of security breaches. Mobile devices and IoT devices often have weaker security controls compared to traditional computing devices, making them attractive targets for cybercriminals.

Mobile devices face various security challenges, including unpatched vulnerabilities, malicious apps, and network-based attacks. Malware targeting mobile devices, such as banking Trojans and ransomware, can compromise sensitive information and even hijack devices for malicious purposes.

IoT devices, on the other hand, often lack security-by-design principles and may have default credentials, outdated software, or weak encryption protocols. This makes them vulnerable to exploitation, as seen in the Mirai botnet attack mentioned earlier.

To enhance mobile and IoT security, organizations should implement strong authentication measures, secure application development practices, and regular updates. Users should be educated about the risks associated with mobile and IoT devices, including the need to install updates and only download apps from trusted sources.

Conclusion

The trends in cybersecurity attacks indicate that organizations face an evolving and complex threat landscape. Ransomware attacks, DDoS attacks, targeted attacks, insider threats, and vulnerabilities in mobile and IoT devices pose significant challenges. It is imperative for organizations to stay informed about the latest attack trends, implement robust security measures, and educate employees about potential risks. By taking a proactive approach towards cybersecurity, organizations can mitigate the impact of attacks and ensure the sustainability of their systems and data.

Cybersecurity Policies and Regulations

In today's digital age, the growing reliance on information technology has made businesses and organizations vulnerable to cyber threats. To protect against these threats and ensure the security of information systems, cybersecurity policies and regulations play a critical role. These policies and regulations provide guidelines, standards, and legal frameworks to prevent, detect, respond to, and recover from cyber attacks.

Importance of Cybersecurity Policies and Regulations

Cybersecurity policies and regulations are essential for several reasons:

- **Protecting sensitive data:** Cybersecurity policies and regulations help safeguard sensitive data, including personal information, financial records, intellectual property, and trade secrets. By enforcing strict security measures, organizations can reduce the risk of data breaches and unauthorized access.

- **Mitigating cyber threats:** Policies and regulations provide a framework for identifying and addressing potential cyber threats. They outline preventive measures, such as strong password requirements, encryption, regular software updates, and employee training, to reduce the likelihood of successful attacks.

- **Promoting a culture of security:** Regulations require organizations to prioritize cybersecurity and allocate resources to protect their systems and networks. This encourages a culture of security awareness and proactive risk management.

- **Ensuring legal compliance:** Cybersecurity policies and regulations are essential to ensure an organization's compliance with applicable laws and industry standards. Failure to comply can result in legal penalties, reputation damage, and loss of business.
- **Facilitating information sharing:** Policies and regulations promote information sharing among stakeholders, including government agencies, private organizations, and industry sectors. This collaboration improves threat intelligence, enhances incident response capabilities, and strengthens overall cybersecurity posture.

Types of Cybersecurity Policies and Regulations

There are various types of cybersecurity policies and regulations that organizations should be familiar with:

- **National cybersecurity strategies:** Governments develop national cybersecurity strategies to outline their approach to protecting critical national infrastructure and combating cyber threats. These strategies provide a high-level framework for public-private partnerships, international cooperation, research and development, and capacity building initiatives.
- **Data protection and privacy laws:** Privacy laws, such as the General Data Protection Regulation (GDPR) in the European Union, enforce rules regarding the collection, storage, and processing of personal data. These laws mandate organizations to obtain user consent, implement appropriate security measures, and notify individuals in the event of a data breach.
- **Industry-specific regulations:** Certain industries have specific cybersecurity regulations tailored to their unique risks. For example, the Health Insurance Portability and Accountability Act (HIPAA) in the healthcare sector and the Payment Card Industry Data Security Standard (PCI DSS) for organizations that handle credit card information.
- **Employee cybersecurity policies:** Organizations should establish internal policies that outline acceptable use of company resources, password hygiene, handling and sharing of sensitive information, and reporting security incidents. These policies educate employees about their role in maintaining

cybersecurity and prevent accidental or negligent actions that could compromise security.

- **Incident response and breach notification requirements:** Regulations often require organizations to have an incident response plan in place and specify reporting timelines in the event of a security breach. These requirements ensure a swift and coordinated response to cyber incidents, limiting the impact and facilitating investigations.

Challenges and Considerations

Implementing cybersecurity policies and regulations can pose several challenges for organizations:

- **Rapidly evolving threat landscape:** Cyber threats continuously evolve, requiring policies and regulations to adapt accordingly. It is crucial for organizations to maintain an up-to-date understanding of emerging threats and adjust their security measures promptly.

- **Complex regulatory landscape:** Organizations may operate in multiple jurisdictions, each with its own set of regulations. Compliance with these diverse requirements can be challenging, necessitating robust governance frameworks and cross-functional collaboration.

- **Costs and resource allocation:** Implementing effective cybersecurity policies and regulations often requires significant financial investment and resource allocation. Small and medium-sized enterprises, in particular, may face challenges in dedicating the necessary resources to ensure compliance and maintain a strong security posture.

- **Balancing security and usability:** Policies and regulations must strike a balance between security measures and user convenience. Excessive security controls may hinder user productivity, while lax controls can compromise security. Finding the right balance is crucial in maintaining both security and usability.

- **Emerging technologies and regulatory gaps:** Rapid advances in technologies such as artificial intelligence, Internet of Things (IoT), and blockchain pose challenges for policymakers to keep up with the regulatory framework. Addressing potential risks and vulnerabilities associated with emerging technologies is a complex task that requires ongoing collaboration among industry, academia, and regulators.

Resources and Best Practices

To effectively navigate the complex landscape of cybersecurity policies and regulations, organizations can follow the following best practices:

- **Stay updated:** Regularly monitor and stay informed about changes in relevant laws and regulations. Subscribe to updates from regulatory bodies and industry associations to ensure compliance with the latest requirements.
- **Engage legal counsel:** Seek legal advice to understand the legal implications of cybersecurity policies and regulations specific to your industry and jurisdiction. Legal professionals can provide guidance on compliance requirements and help develop appropriate policies and procedures.
- **Adopt a risk-based approach:** Assess cybersecurity risks specific to your organization and prioritize mitigation efforts based on the potential impact. Tailor policies and controls to your risk profile, focusing on areas of critical importance.
- **Establish a cybersecurity governance framework:** Develop a comprehensive governance framework that defines roles and responsibilities, establishes accountability, and ensures ongoing compliance with policies and regulations. Regularly assess the effectiveness of your governance framework and make necessary improvements.
- **Implement security awareness training:** Educate employees about cybersecurity best practices, their role in maintaining security, and how to identify and report potential threats. Foster a culture of security awareness and ongoing learning within the organization.
- **Collaborate and share information:** Engage in information sharing initiatives with industry peers, government agencies, and relevant cybersecurity networks. Sharing best practices, threat intelligence, and lessons learned helps strengthen overall cybersecurity capabilities.

Case Study: General Data Protection Regulation (GDPR)

The General Data Protection Regulation (GDPR), implemented by the European Union in 2018, is a landmark data protection and privacy regulation. It aims to enhance the protection of individuals' personal data and harmonize data protection laws across EU member states. The GDPR applies to organizations that process personal data of EU citizens, regardless of their location.

The key principles and requirements of the GDPR include:

- **Lawful processing of personal data:** Organizations must have a lawful basis for processing personal data and inform individuals about the purpose, duration, and recipients of the data.
- **Individual rights:** The GDPR grants individuals several rights, including the right to access their data, rectify inaccuracies, erase data under certain conditions ("right to be forgotten"), and object to processing.
- **Privacy by design and default:** Organizations must implement privacy measures at the design stage of systems or processes and ensure that default settings prioritize privacy.
- **Data breach notification:** Organizations must report personal data breaches to the relevant supervisory authority within 72 hours of becoming aware of the breach, unless it is unlikely to result in a risk to individuals' rights and freedoms.
- **Data protection impact assessments:** Organizations must conduct assessments to identify and mitigate risks associated with processing activities that may pose high risks to individuals' rights and freedoms.
- **Data protection officer (DPO):** Some organizations are required to appoint a data protection officer who is responsible for overseeing GDPR compliance, advising on data protection matters, and acting as a point of contact for individuals and supervisory authorities.

The GDPR has significantly impacted how organizations handle personal data, emphasizing the importance of privacy and data protection. Non-compliance with the GDPR can result in substantial fines, underscoring the need for organizations to understand and abide by its requirements.

Conclusion

Cybersecurity policies and regulations are vital components of an organization's cybersecurity strategy. By providing guidelines and legal frameworks, they help protect sensitive data, mitigate cyber threats, promote a culture of security, ensure legal compliance, and facilitate information sharing. Organizations must be aware of the various types of policies and regulations relevant to their industry and region, and adopt best practices to effectively navigate the challenges associated with regulatory compliance. Compliance with policies and regulations not only enhances cybersecurity but also builds trust with stakeholders and strengthens the overall resilience of the organization.

Cybersecurity Compliance and Standards

In the field of cybersecurity, compliance with regulations and adherence to standards is crucial for organizations to effectively protect their information systems and sensitive data. Cybersecurity compliance refers to the process of complying with industry-specific regulations, laws, and guidelines, while cybersecurity standards are a set of best practices and guidelines recommended by industry organizations and regulatory bodies. This section will discuss the importance of cybersecurity compliance and standards, various compliance frameworks and regulations, and their implications for organizations.

Importance of Cybersecurity Compliance and Standards

Cybersecurity compliance and standards provide a framework for organizations to assess, improve, and maintain the security of their information systems. They help organizations establish a baseline level of security and ensure that appropriate controls are in place to protect sensitive information. Compliance and standards also play a significant role in building trust and confidence among customers, partners, and stakeholders by demonstrating a commitment to cybersecurity best practices.

Furthermore, compliance with cybersecurity regulations is often mandated by law and failure to comply can result in significant penalties, damage to reputation, and legal consequences. Organizations that operate in highly regulated industries such as finance, healthcare, and government must comply with specific cybersecurity requirements to protect their customers' data and ensure the integrity of their systems.

Cybersecurity Compliance Frameworks

Various cybersecurity compliance frameworks exist to guide organizations in implementing effective security controls and achieving compliance with industry-specific regulations. These frameworks provide organizations with a structured approach to assess and mitigate risks, as well as to demonstrate compliance to auditors and regulators. Let's take a closer look at some of the widely adopted cybersecurity compliance frameworks:

1. **ISO/IEC 27001:** The International Organization for Standardization (ISO) and International Electrotechnical Commission (IEC) developed the ISO/IEC 27001 standard to provide a systematic approach to managing and securing sensitive information. It sets out the criteria for establishing, implementing, maintaining, and continually improving an information security management system (ISMS).

2. **NIST Cybersecurity Framework:** The National Institute of Standards and Technology (NIST) Cybersecurity Framework offers a guideline for organizations to manage and reduce cybersecurity risks. It provides a common language for organizations to communicate about, assess, and manage cybersecurity risks and aims to foster a culture of cybersecurity awareness and preparedness.

3. **Payment Card Industry Data Security Standard (PCI DSS):** PCI DSS is a set of security standards designed to protect credit card and cardholder data. Developed by the Payment Card Industry Security Standards Council (PCI SSC), PCI DSS provides a framework for organizations that handle cardholder information to implement robust security measures, detect and prevent security breaches, and ensure secure card transactions.

4. **General Data Protection Regulation (GDPR):** GDPR is a comprehensive data protection regulation that applies to all organizations processing and storing the personal data of individuals residing within the European Union (EU). It sets out requirements for the lawful collection, use, storage, and disposal of personal data and imposes strict penalties for non-compliance.

Each compliance framework has its own set of requirements and guidelines, and organizations must select the appropriate framework based on their industry, jurisdiction, and the type of data they handle. It is common for organizations to adopt multiple frameworks to address various compliance requirements.

Implications of Cybersecurity Compliance and Standards

Compliance with cybersecurity regulations and adherence to standards have several implications for organizations, including:

1. **Risk Mitigation:** Cybersecurity compliance helps organizations identify and mitigate risks that could lead to security breaches, data loss, or unauthorized access. By implementing the required controls and following best practices

outlined in compliance frameworks, organizations can reduce the likelihood and impact of security incidents.

2. **Data Protection:** Compliance frameworks often emphasize the protection of sensitive data. Organizations are required to implement measures such as encryption, access controls, secure transmission, and secure data storage to safeguard sensitive information from unauthorized access and disclosure.

3. **Legal and Regulatory Requirements:** Compliance with cybersecurity regulations is not only essential for protecting sensitive data but also for meeting legal and regulatory requirements. Failure to comply with applicable regulations can lead to severe penalties, fines, and legal consequences.

4. **Reputation and Trust:** Compliance with cybersecurity standards and regulations helps organizations build trust among their customers, partners, and stakeholders. Demonstrating a commitment to cybersecurity best practices can enhance an organization's reputation and differentiate it from competitors.

5. **Business Continuity:** Compliance frameworks often require organizations to have robust incident response plans, disaster recovery procedures, and business continuity strategies in place. This ensures that organizations can effectively respond to security incidents, minimize downtime, and maintain essential business operations.

6. **Competitive Advantage:** Adhering to cybersecurity compliance and standards can provide organizations with a competitive advantage. It demonstrates that an organization has implemented appropriate security measures, effectively managing risks, and protecting its assets and stakeholders.

Organizations must regularly assess their compliance posture, conduct audits, and perform gap analyses to identify areas of improvement and ensure ongoing compliance with cybersecurity regulations and standards. Compliance is not a one-time effort but an ongoing process that requires continuous monitoring, evaluation, and adaptation to evolving threats and changing regulatory landscapes.

Challenges and Considerations in Cybersecurity Compliance

While compliance with cybersecurity regulations and standards is critical, organizations often face various challenges and considerations in achieving and maintaining compliance. These include:

1. **Complexity and Technical Debt:** Achieving compliance can be complex, especially for organizations with legacy systems and technical debt. Implementing the necessary controls, conducting regular audits, and ensuring ongoing compliance can be time-consuming and resource-intensive.

2. **Evolving Regulatory Landscape:** Cybersecurity regulations and standards are continually evolving to address emerging threats and technological advancements. Organizations must stay updated with the latest regulations, interpret their applicability, and adapt their cybersecurity programs accordingly.

3. **Interoperability and Integration:** Organizations often use a combination of hardware, software, and services from different vendors. Ensuring interoperability and integration between various components while maintaining compliance can be a challenge.

4. **Third-Party Risk Management:** Organizations often rely on third-party vendors and service providers to handle critical operations or process sensitive data. Managing the cybersecurity risks associated with these third parties and ensuring their compliance with relevant regulations can be a challenge.

5. **Cybersecurity Skills Gap:** The demand for skilled cybersecurity professionals often exceeds the supply. Organizations may face challenges in finding and retaining qualified personnel to manage and ensure compliance.

6. **Monitoring and Reporting:** Compliance requires continuous monitoring and reporting of security controls and incidents. Organizations must have robust monitoring mechanisms in place to detect and respond promptly to security events, as well as report incidents as required by regulations.

7. **Costs and Resource Constraints:** Achieving and maintaining compliance can be costly, especially for small and medium-sized enterprises (SMEs) with limited resources. Organizations must carefully allocate budget and resources to meet compliance requirements effectively.

Organizations can mitigate these challenges by developing a comprehensive cybersecurity compliance strategy, establishing clear roles and responsibilities, investing in staff training and development, and leveraging automation and technology to streamline compliance processes.

Summary

In this section, we explored the importance of cybersecurity compliance and standards in ensuring the security and integrity of information systems. Compliance frameworks and regulations provide organizations with a structured approach to managing cybersecurity risks, protecting sensitive data, and meeting legal and regulatory requirements. Compliance brings several benefits, including risk mitigation, data protection, legal compliance, reputation enhancement, and business continuity. However, organizations also face various challenges in achieving and maintaining compliance, such as complexity, evolving regulations, interoperability, third-party risk, skills gap, monitoring, and resource constraints. By understanding these challenges and considerations, organizations can develop effective strategies to achieve and sustain cybersecurity compliance.

Role of Government in Cybersecurity

Governments play a crucial role in ensuring cybersecurity at national and international levels. As cyber threats continue to evolve and become more sophisticated, government intervention is necessary to protect critical infrastructure, national security, and public safety. In this section, we will explore the various ways in which governments contribute to cybersecurity efforts and the challenges they face.

Policy Frameworks for Cybersecurity

One of the primary responsibilities of governments in the field of cybersecurity is the development and implementation of policy frameworks. These frameworks establish the legal and regulatory requirements that organizations and individuals must adhere to in order to safeguard their digital assets.

Government policies outline guidelines for preventing, detecting, responding to, and recovering from cyber incidents. They also define the roles and responsibilities of various stakeholders, including government agencies, private sector organizations, and individual users. Additionally, government policies promote standards and best practices for cybersecurity, which enhance the overall resilience of the nation's digital infrastructure.

To create effective policy frameworks, governments often consult with cybersecurity experts, industry representatives, and legal professionals. A multidisciplinary approach ensures that the policies are comprehensive, up to date, and aligned with the evolving cyber threat landscape.

Legislation and Regulation

Governments enact legislation and regulations to establish legal requirements, penalties, and incentives related to cybersecurity. These laws define the prohibitions against unauthorized access, data breaches, identity theft, and other cybercrimes. They also address issues such as privacy rights, information sharing, and incident reporting.

Legislation and regulation ensure that organizations implement adequate security measures to protect their networks, systems, and data. They lay out the legal framework for prosecuting cybercriminals and enforcing compliance with cybersecurity standards.

Governments also collaborate with international entities to develop frameworks for cybersecurity cooperation and harmonization of laws. Cross-border cybercrimes require coordinated efforts to investigate, apprehend, and extradite offenders. By collaborating with other nations, governments can enhance their ability to combat cyber threats that transcend geographic boundaries.

National Cybersecurity Strategies

National cybersecurity strategies are comprehensive plans developed by governments to address cyber threats and protect the nation's critical infrastructure. These strategies provide a roadmap for the government's cybersecurity initiatives and outline the goals, objectives, and key actions required to achieve them.

Governments formulate national cybersecurity strategies by assessing their current cybersecurity posture, identifying vulnerabilities, and understanding the evolving threat landscape. The strategies aim to strengthen the resilience of the nation's digital infrastructure and ensure the continuous delivery of essential services.

National cybersecurity strategies typically involve collaboration between various government agencies, industry stakeholders, and research institutions. By bringing together expertise from different sectors, governments can leverage the collective knowledge and resources needed to tackle complex cybersecurity challenges.

Public-Private Partnerships

Cybersecurity is a collective responsibility that requires collaboration between the public and private sectors. Governments foster public-private partnerships to share information, resources, and best practices for combating cyber threats.

These partnerships enable governments to leverage industry expertise, technical capabilities, and threat intelligence from private sector organizations. In return, the government provides regulatory guidance, incentives, and a platform for information exchange.

Public-private partnerships facilitate the development of cybersecurity standards, certification programs, and research initiatives. They also foster innovation by encouraging collaboration between government research institutions, universities, and private sector companies.

Capacity Building and Awareness

Governments play a crucial role in building and enhancing the cybersecurity capabilities of their workforce and citizens. They invest in education and training programs to develop a skilled cybersecurity workforce equipped with the necessary knowledge and expertise to tackle the evolving threat landscape.

Government initiatives include cybersecurity awareness campaigns targeting individuals, businesses, and organizations. These campaigns aim to educate the public about safe online practices, promote cybersecurity hygiene, and raise awareness about emerging threats.

Furthermore, governments provide funding and support for cybersecurity research and development. This investment enables the development of cutting-edge technologies, tools, and techniques to enhance cybersecurity defenses and response capabilities.

Challenges and Future Considerations

Despite their crucial role, governments face several challenges in the realm of cybersecurity. The rapidly evolving nature of cyber threats requires governments to continuously update their policies, regulations, and strategies. Cybercriminals are constantly finding new ways to exploit vulnerabilities, and governments must remain agile and adaptive in their response.

International cooperation is also vital in addressing cyber threats that transcend national borders. Governments need to strengthen collaboration and information sharing mechanisms to effectively respond to cyber incidents and prosecute cybercriminals.

Moreover, privacy concerns and civil liberties must be carefully balanced with the need for enhanced cybersecurity measures. Governments must navigate the complexities of protecting the nation's digital infrastructure while respecting individual privacy rights.

Looking ahead, governments must also consider the impact of emerging technologies on cybersecurity. The widespread adoption of artificial intelligence, internet of things, and quantum computing presents new challenges and opportunities for cybersecurity. Governments need to invest in research and innovation to stay ahead of the evolving threat landscape.

In conclusion, the role of government in cybersecurity is essential for ensuring the security, resilience, and sustainability of digital infrastructures. Through the development of policy frameworks, legislation, and national strategies, governments provide the necessary guidance and regulation to protect critical assets. Public-private partnerships, capacity building, and awareness initiatives further strengthen cybersecurity efforts. However, governments must overcome various challenges and adapt to emerging technologies to effectively address the ever-evolving cyber threat landscape.

Future Directions in Cybersecurity

Emerging Technologies in Cybersecurity

In recent years, the field of cybersecurity has witnessed significant advancements, largely driven by the emergence of new technologies. These technologies have not only brought about new opportunities but have also posed new challenges. In this section, we will explore some of the key emerging technologies in cybersecurity and discuss their impact on the field.

Artificial Intelligence (AI) and Machine Learning (ML)

Artificial Intelligence (AI) and Machine Learning (ML) have gained tremendous attention across various domains, including cybersecurity. AI refers to the development of computer systems capable of performing tasks that typically require human intelligence, such as problem-solving and decision-making. On the other hand, ML is a subset of AI that focuses on enabling computers to learn and make predictions from data without explicit programming.

In the context of cybersecurity, AI and ML techniques are being leveraged to enhance various aspects of defense and response. For instance, AI-based algorithms can analyze vast amounts of security data to identify patterns and anomalies, allowing for the quick detection of potential threats. ML algorithms can also help in identifying new and emerging attack patterns, even if they have not been encountered before.

However, it is important to note that AI and ML also present new challenges in cybersecurity. Adversarial attacks, where hackers infiltrate AI systems to manipulate their behavior, can pose significant risks. Additionally, the use of biased or incomplete training data can lead to incorrect or biased decisions. Therefore, careful consideration and ongoing research are necessary to ensure the security and reliability of AI and ML applications in cybersecurity.

Blockchain and Distributed Ledger Technology (DLT)

Blockchain, which is the underlying technology for cryptocurrencies like Bitcoin, is gaining attention as a potential game-changer in cybersecurity. Blockchain is a decentralized and immutable ledger system that provides transparency, integrity, and security to a wide range of transactions. It uses cryptographic techniques to ensure the authenticity and integrity of data.

In the context of cybersecurity, blockchain can have several applications. One such application is identity management, where blockchain can provide a secure and tamper-proof system for verifying and managing identities. This can help prevent identity theft and enhance authentication mechanisms.

Additionally, blockchain can be used for secure data storage and sharing, as it eliminates the need for intermediaries and provides a transparent and tamper-proof record of transactions. This can significantly enhance data integrity and resilience against attacks.

However, blockchain also poses certain challenges. For instance, scalability and energy consumption are important considerations when implementing blockchain-based solutions. Furthermore, the reliance on consensus mechanisms introduces new vulnerabilities and attack vectors that need to be carefully addressed.

Quantum Computing

Quantum Computing is an emerging field that deals with the development of computers based on quantum mechanics principles. Unlike classical computers, which use bits to represent information as either 0 or 1, quantum computers use quantum bits or qubits, which can exist in multiple states simultaneously, thanks to phenomena such as superposition and entanglement.

Quantum computing has the potential to revolutionize various fields, including cybersecurity. Unfortunately, it also poses significant risks to existing cryptographic systems. Some of the commonly used cryptographic algorithms, such as RSA and ECC, rely on the difficulty of factoring large numbers. However, quantum computers have the potential to efficiently solve such problems, rendering these algorithms insecure.

To address this challenge, researchers are exploring the field of post-quantum cryptography, which focuses on developing encryption algorithms that are resistant to attacks from quantum computers. Several promising post-quantum cryptographic algorithms have been proposed, and ongoing research is being conducted to ensure the security of cryptographic systems in the age of quantum computing.

Internet of Things (IoT)

The Internet of Things (IoT) refers to the network of interconnected physical devices that can communicate and exchange data with each other. IoT devices, such as smart home appliances, wearables, and industrial sensors, have become increasingly prevalent in our daily lives.

While IoT presents numerous benefits and opportunities, it also introduces new cybersecurity challenges. Many IoT devices lack robust security measures, making them vulnerable to attacks. Compromised IoT devices can be leveraged to launch large-scale botnet attacks or gain unauthorized access to critical systems.

To address these challenges, securing IoT systems and networks has become a critical area of focus. This includes implementing robust authentication mechanisms to ensure the integrity of IoT devices, as well as secure communication protocols and encryption algorithms to protect data in transit.

Challenges and Opportunities

As with any emerging technologies, the integration of these technologies in the field of cybersecurity presents both challenges and opportunities. It is essential to carefully assess the limitations, vulnerabilities, and risks associated with these technologies to ensure their secure and reliable implementation.

Moreover, collaboration between researchers, industry professionals, policymakers, and other stakeholders is crucial to addressing these challenges effectively. Continued research and innovation are necessary to develop robust solutions that can keep pace with the evolving cybersecurity landscape.

In conclusion, emerging technologies such as Artificial Intelligence, Blockchain, Quantum Computing, and the Internet of Things offer immense potential to enhance cybersecurity. However, they also introduce new vulnerabilities and risks that need to be addressed. By understanding these technologies and proactively addressing their challenges, we can build a sustainable and secure cybersecurity ecosystem for the future.

Key Takeaways:

- Artificial Intelligence (AI) and Machine Learning (ML) are being utilized to enhance various aspects of cybersecurity, including threat detection and pattern analysis.
- Blockchain and Distributed Ledger Technology (DLT) offer opportunities for secure identity management, data storage, and sharing in the cybersecurity domain.
- Quantum Computing poses risks to existing cryptographic systems, leading to the development of post-quantum cryptography.
- The Internet of Things (IoT) introduces new cybersecurity challenges due to the proliferation of interconnected devices, requiring robust security measures.
- Collaboration, research, and innovation are essential to leverage the potential of emerging technologies effectively while addressing their vulnerabilities and risks in cybersecurity.

Exercises

1. Conduct research on recent advancements in AI-based cybersecurity solutions and discuss their potential advantages and limitations.
2. Explore the use of blockchain in securing healthcare data and analyze its implications for patient privacy and data integrity.
3. Investigate the impact of quantum computing on the security of widely used encryption algorithms and propose potential solutions to mitigate the risks.
4. Research the security challenges faced by IoT devices and propose a framework to enhance the security of IoT systems.

Additional Resources

- Karbab, E., Michailidis, N., & Pacheco-Sanchez, F. (2020). Artificial Intelligence and Machine Learning for Cybersecurity: Trends, Opportunities, and Challenges. arXiv preprint arXiv:2010.13600.

- Tapscott, D., & Tapscott, A. (2016). Blockchain revolution: how the technology behind bitcoin is changing money, business, and the world. Penguin.

- Mosca, M., & Stebila, D. (2018). Post-Quantum Cryptography. Nature, 22(1), 3-7.

- Gubbi, J., Buyya, R., Marusic, S., & Palaniswami, M. (2013). Internet of Things (IoT): A vision, architectural elements, and future directions. Future Generation Computer Systems, 29(7), 1645-1660.

Artificial Intelligence and Machine Learning in Cybersecurity

Artificial Intelligence (AI) and Machine Learning (ML) have emerged as powerful tools in the field of cybersecurity. With the increasing complexity and frequency of cyber threats, traditional security measures alone are no longer sufficient to protect systems and data. AI and ML technologies provide advanced capabilities to detect, prevent, and respond to cyber attacks in real-time. This section explores the applications of AI and ML in cybersecurity and highlights their potential benefits and challenges.

Introduction to Artificial Intelligence and Machine Learning

Artificial Intelligence refers to the development of computer systems that can perform tasks that would typically require human intelligence. Machine Learning, a subfield of AI, focuses on enabling computers to learn from data and improve performance without explicit programming. ML algorithms analyze vast amounts of data, identify patterns, and make predictions or decisions based on the acquired knowledge.

In the context of cybersecurity, AI and ML algorithms can be trained to process enormous amounts of data, detect suspicious activities, and identify patterns indicative of cyber threats. These technologies can enhance the efficiency and accuracy of cybersecurity measures. By continuously analyzing new data, AI and ML-powered systems can adapt and evolve to defend against emerging threats.

Applications of Artificial Intelligence and Machine Learning in Cybersecurity

1. **Threat Detection and Prevention:** AI and ML algorithms can analyze network traffic, system logs, and user behavior to identify malicious activities. By learning from historical data, these algorithms can detect anomalies and patterns associated with potential threats. For example, ML algorithms can detect abnormal network traffic that may indicate a Distributed Denial of Service (DDoS) attack or identify patterns indicative of malware infections.

2. **Vulnerability Management:** AI and ML techniques can assist in identifying and prioritizing vulnerabilities in software and systems. These techniques can analyze code, security configurations, and other relevant data to determine potential weaknesses. By automating vulnerability scanning and assessment, AI and ML can help organizations proactively address vulnerabilities before they are exploited by attackers.

3. **User and Entity Behavior Analytics (UEBA):** AI and ML algorithms can analyze user behavior and identify deviations from normal patterns. This can help organizations detect insider threats or compromised user accounts. By continuously monitoring user activities, AI and ML-powered systems can alert security teams when suspicious behavior is detected.

4. **Automated System Response:** AI and ML technologies can enable automated responses to cyber threats. For example, AI algorithms can analyze network traffic and automatically block suspicious IP addresses or quarantine infected systems. ML algorithms can also assist in developing predictive models to anticipate and mitigate cyber attacks.

5. **Malware Analysis and Detection:** AI and ML techniques can aid in the classification and detection of malware. By analyzing the characteristics and behavior of known malware samples, these techniques can identify new and previously unseen variants. AI algorithms can also analyze code patterns and determine if software is malicious or contains vulnerabilities.

6. **Security Operations and Incident Response:** AI and ML algorithms can streamline security operations by automating repetitive tasks, such as log analysis and incident triage. These technologies can reduce the manual effort required for incident detection and response, allowing security teams to focus on more complex and critical tasks.

Challenges and Limitations

While AI and ML offer significant potential in cybersecurity, there are several challenges and limitations to consider:

1. **Data Quality and Bias:** AI and ML algorithms heavily rely on the quality and diversity of data. Biased or incomplete datasets can lead to inaccurate predictions or decisions. It is crucial to ensure that the training data is representative of the target population and that potential biases are identified and addressed.

2. **Adversarial Attacks:** Attackers can exploit vulnerabilities in AI and ML models to bypass security mechanisms or manipulate the system's output. Adversarial attacks aim to deceive AI and ML algorithms by injecting malicious data or exploiting model vulnerabilities. Ongoing research is needed to develop robust defenses against such attacks.

3. **Interpretability and Explainability:** The opaque nature of AI and ML algorithms can make it challenging to understand the reasoning behind their decisions. In cybersecurity, it is important to be able to explain why a certain action was taken or provide evidence for attribution. Research efforts are focusing on developing interpretable and explainable AI and ML models.

4. **Overreliance and False Positives:** AI and ML algorithms may generate false positives or false negatives, leading to unnecessary alerts or missed detections. It is crucial to strike a balance between achieving high detection rates and minimizing false alarms. Continuous monitoring and fine-tuning of algorithms are necessary to improve accuracy.

Ethical Considerations

The use of AI and ML in cybersecurity raises important ethical considerations that need to be addressed:

1. **Privacy and Data Protection:** The collection and analysis of large amounts of data for AI and ML may raise privacy concerns. Organizations must ensure compliance with applicable privacy laws and regulations and implement appropriate safeguards to protect user data.

2. **Bias and Discrimination:** Biased or discriminatory outcomes can arise from AI and ML models if the training data reflects existing biases. Careful attention must be given to the fairness and transparency of these models to avoid perpetuating social, gender, or racial biases.

3. **Accountability and Transparency:** In critical cybersecurity decisions made by AI and ML systems, it is important to identify the parties responsible and

maintain transparency in the decision-making process. Organizations should provide explanations and justifications for automated decisions.

4. **Human Oversight:** It is crucial to strike a balance between automation and human judgment in cybersecurity. Human oversight and intervention remain essential in complex decision-making processes to ensure ethical and responsible outcomes.

Resources and Further Reading

For those interested in delving deeper into the applications of AI and ML in cybersecurity, the following resources may be useful:

1. Book: "Artificial Intelligence in Cybersecurity" by Cem Gurkok and Charles Crowell 2. Book: "Machine Learning and Security" by Clarence Chio and David Freeman 3. Whitepaper: "Artificial Intelligence for Cybersecurity" by the World Economic Forum 4. Research Paper: "Adversarial Attacks on Machine Learning Systems for Cybersecurity Applications" by Battista Biggio et al. 5. Research Paper: "Interpretability of Machine Learning in Secure Execution Environments" by Anne Edmundson et al.

Conclusion

Artificial Intelligence and Machine Learning are revolutionizing the field of cybersecurity by providing advanced capabilities in threat detection, vulnerability management, and incident response. As the cybersecurity landscape continues to evolve, organizations must leverage AI and ML technologies to enhance their defense mechanisms. However, addressing the challenges and ethical considerations associated with AI and ML is crucial to ensure responsible and secure deployment. By embracing these technologies responsibly, organizations can strengthen their security posture in the face of escalating cyber threats.

Blockchain and Distributed Ledger Technology in Cybersecurity

Blockchain and distributed ledger technology (DLT) are increasingly being recognized as powerful tools in the realm of cybersecurity. With their decentralized and transparent nature, these technologies offer significant potential in enhancing the security and integrity of digital transactions and data storage. In this section, we will explore the fundamentals of blockchain and DLT, their applications in cybersecurity, and the challenges and opportunities they present.

Fundamentals of Blockchain and DLT

At its core, a blockchain is a decentralized and distributed digital ledger that records and verifies transactions across multiple computers or nodes. It consists of a chain of blocks, where each block contains a set of data (transactions) and a reference to the previous block. The data in the blocks, once added, becomes immutable and tamper-resistant.

The key characteristics of blockchain and DLT include:

- **Decentralization:** The ledger is not controlled by a single entity but is distributed among multiple participants, making it resistant to single points of failure and unauthorized manipulations.

- **Transparency:** The ledger is publicly accessible, allowing anyone to view the transactions. Transparency ensures accountability and helps in detecting and preventing fraudulent activities.

- **Immutability:** Once a block is added to the blockchain, its data cannot be altered or deleted, providing a high degree of trust in the integrity of the information recorded.

- **Consensus Mechanism:** To validate and add blocks to the chain, participants in the blockchain network must agree on the validity of transactions through a consensus mechanism such as Proof of Work (PoW) or Proof of Stake (PoS).

- **Smart Contracts:** Blockchain platforms often support the execution of self-executing smart contracts, which are programmable agreements that automatically execute predefined conditions when certain events are met.

Applications in Cybersecurity

Blockchain and DLT have several applications in the field of cybersecurity, providing innovative solutions to some of the existing challenges. Let's explore a few key areas where the technology can be leveraged:

1. **Secure Data Storage:** Blockchain's decentralized architecture makes it an ideal candidate for secure and tamper-proof storage of sensitive data. By distributing encrypted data across multiple nodes, it becomes extremely difficult for attackers to compromise the integrity of the information.

2. **Identity and Access Management (IAM):** Blockchain can enhance IAM systems by providing a decentralized and trustless environment for managing digital identities and controlling access. Through blockchain-based identity solutions, users can retain ownership of their identity data and have better control over its usage.

3. **Secure Supply Chain Management:** Blockchain can be used to create an immutable record of a product's journey throughout the supply chain, ensuring authenticity and preventing counterfeiting. With transparent and verifiable information, stakeholders can easily trace the origin and authenticity of products.

4. **Internet of Things (IoT) Security:** As IoT devices continue to proliferate, their security becomes a critical concern. Blockchain's decentralized and transparent nature can help in securing IoT networks by enabling secure device authentication, data integrity, and decentralized consensus.

5. **Threat Intelligence Sharing:** Blockchain can facilitate secure and anonymous sharing of threat intelligence among organizations and security researchers. By leveraging blockchain, sensitive threat data can be shared without compromising the privacy of the parties involved.

6. **Digital Rights Management:** Blockchain-based solutions can enable secure and transparent management of digital rights, ensuring proper licensing, ownership, and distribution of digital assets such as music, videos, and artwork.

Challenges and Opportunities

While blockchain and DLT offer promising solutions to cybersecurity challenges, they also bring their own set of challenges and opportunities. Some key considerations include:

- **Scalability:** The current scalability limitations of blockchain platforms pose a challenge when it comes to processing a large number of transactions. Efforts are underway to develop scalable solutions that can handle high transaction volumes without compromising security and decentralization.

- **Regulatory and Legal Frameworks:** The legal and regulatory landscape surrounding blockchain and DLT is still evolving. It is crucial to address issues related to data privacy, data protection, and compliance with existing regulations while leveraging the technology for cybersecurity purposes.

- **Interoperability:** The lack of interoperability between different blockchain platforms and legacy systems can hinder the adoption and integration of blockchain-based solutions. Standards and protocols need to be established to ensure seamless interoperability and information exchange.

- **Energy Consumption:** Blockchain-based consensus mechanisms such as PoW require substantial computational power, leading to concerns about the environmental impact and energy consumption. Research and innovation are needed to develop more energy-efficient consensus algorithms.

In conclusion, blockchain and distributed ledger technology have the potential to revolutionize the field of cybersecurity. Their decentralized and transparent nature can significantly enhance the security and integrity of digital transactions and data storage. However, challenges related to scalability, regulatory frameworks, interoperability, and energy consumption need to be addressed for widespread adoption and realization of the full potential of blockchain in cybersecurity.

Quantum Computing and its Implications for Cybersecurity

Quantum computing is a groundbreaking technology that has the potential to revolutionize many aspects of our lives, including cybersecurity. In this section, we will explore the principles of quantum computing and its implications for the field of cybersecurity.

Introduction to Quantum Computing

Quantum computing is a field that harnesses the principles of quantum mechanics to process information in a fundamentally different way than classical computing. While classical computers rely on bits that represent either a 0 or a 1, quantum computers use quantum bits or qubits, which can exist in a superposition of both 0 and 1 states.

One of the most fascinating aspects of quantum computing is the concept of quantum entanglement. This phenomenon allows qubits to become interconnected in such a way that the state of one qubit depends on the state of another, regardless of the physical distance between them. This property gives quantum computers the potential to perform certain computations exponentially faster than classical computers.

Quantum Computing and Cryptography

The development of practical quantum computers poses a significant threat to modern cryptographic systems. Many of the encryption algorithms used today, such as RSA and ECC, rely on the difficulty of certain mathematical problems that are believed to be computationally infeasible to solve using classical computers. However, quantum computers have the potential to break these cryptographic algorithms using powerful quantum algorithms.

One such algorithm is Shor's algorithm, which can efficiently factor large integers and solve the discrete logarithm problem. These problems are the foundation of many cryptographic algorithms used for secure communication, such as the RSA and Diffie-Hellman key exchange protocols. Once a large number is factored or a discrete logarithm is solved, the security of these algorithms is compromised.

Post-Quantum Cryptography

To address the impending threat of quantum computers on cryptography, researchers have been developing and studying post-quantum cryptography.

Post-quantum cryptography refers to cryptographic algorithms that are resistant to attacks by quantum computers.

There are several families of post-quantum cryptographic algorithms being explored, including lattice-based, code-based, and multivariate polynomials. These algorithms are designed to withstand attacks from both classical and quantum computers, ensuring long-term security in the presence of quantum threats.

The National Institute of Standards and Technology (NIST) has initiated a process to standardize post-quantum cryptographic algorithms. This effort involves evaluating the performance, security, and practicality of various post-quantum algorithms to establish a set of recommended standards for the industry.

Quantum Key Distribution

While quantum computers pose a threat to traditional cryptographic systems, quantum technologies can also provide new opportunities for secure communication. Quantum key distribution (QKD) is a cryptographic technique that uses quantum properties to establish secure cryptographic keys between two parties.

QKD relies on the principles of quantum entanglement and the uncertainty principle to ensure the security of key exchange. By transmitting quantum states over a secure channel, any attempt to intercept or measure these states will disturb the system, alerting the parties to the presence of an eavesdropper. This allows for the detection of potential attacks and the establishment of secure keys.

QKD provides a method for secure key exchange that is resistant to attacks from both classical and quantum computers. It offers a promising alternative to traditional key exchange protocols and has the potential to enhance the security of future communication networks.

Quantum-resistant Cryptography

While post-quantum cryptography and quantum key distribution provide solutions to mitigate the impact of quantum computers, there is ongoing research into developing quantum-resistant cryptography. Quantum-resistant cryptography refers to cryptographic algorithms that are secure against attacks from both classical and quantum computers.

One example of a quantum-resistant algorithm is the lattice-based learning with errors (LWE) problem. LWE-based cryptographic schemes rely on the hardness of solving certain lattice problems, which is believed to be resistant to attacks from both classical and quantum computers.

Research in quantum-resistant cryptography is still evolving, and it is essential to continue developing and evaluating new algorithms to ensure the long-term security of sensitive information in the presence of powerful quantum computers.

Challenges and Opportunities

The development and widespread adoption of quantum computers present both challenges and opportunities for the field of cybersecurity. On the one hand, the threat of quantum computers breaking current cryptographic systems requires the development and implementation of post-quantum cryptographic algorithms.

On the other hand, the advancements in quantum technologies, such as quantum key distribution, provide new possibilities for secure communication. Quantum-resistant cryptography also offers the opportunity to enhance the security of sensitive information in a post-quantum world.

However, there are various challenges that need to be addressed. One of the significant challenges is the efficient implementation of quantum-resistant algorithms, as they can be computationally intensive. Additionally, quantum technologies are still in their nascent stages, and more research is needed to overcome technical limitations and ensure their practicality.

Conclusion

Quantum computing has the potential to disrupt the field of cybersecurity by breaking many of the encryption algorithms used today. However, it also offers the opportunity to develop new cryptographic systems and secure communication protocols.

As quantum technologies continue to advance, it is crucial for researchers, policymakers, and the industry to collaborate and invest in the development of post-quantum cryptography and quantum-resistant cryptographic algorithms. This proactive approach will ensure the long-term security of sensitive information in a world where quantum computers are a reality.

Internet of Things (IoT) and Cybersecurity

The Internet of Things (IoT) is a rapidly growing network of interconnected physical devices, vehicles, appliances, and other objects that are embedded with sensors, software, and network connectivity, enabling them to collect and exchange data. The proliferation of IoT devices has revolutionized various domains such as healthcare, transportation, manufacturing, and smart homes. However, this interconnectedness also introduces significant cybersecurity challenges. In this section, we will explore the unique security considerations associated with the IoT and discuss strategies to enhance cybersecurity in this context.

Introduction to IoT Security

The security of IoT devices is crucial as they often handle sensitive data and control critical infrastructure. The distributed nature of IoT networks, large attack surface, resource constraints, and diverse device landscape make securing IoT environments exceptionally challenging. Here are some key aspects to consider when addressing IoT security:

- **Device Authentication:** IoT devices must be securely authenticated to ensure that only authorized devices can access the network. Robust authentication mechanisms, such as digital certificates, unique device identifiers, or biometrics, can help prevent unauthorized access and device impersonation.

- **Data Encryption:** Confidentiality and integrity of data transmitted between IoT devices is vital. Encryption algorithms, such as Advanced Encryption Standard (AES), can be employed to protect data at rest and in transit, minimizing the risk of eavesdropping and tampering.

- **Secure Communication:** Ensuring the security of IoT communications is crucial to prevent data interception and unauthorized access. Implementing secure protocols like Transport Layer Security (TLS) or Secure Shell (SSH) can establish secure communication channels between devices, gateways, and cloud platforms.

- **Firmware and Software Updates:** Continuous monitoring and updating of IoT device firmware and software is essential to address vulnerabilities and counter emerging threats. Robust update mechanisms and regular patch management must be implemented to ensure the security of IoT devices throughout their lifecycle.

IoT Threat Landscape

The IoT ecosystem faces a wide range of threats that exploit vulnerabilities in poorly secured devices and networks. Understanding these threats is critical for developing effective countermeasures. Let's discuss some prominent threat vectors in the IoT landscape:

- **Device Compromise:** Insecure default configurations, weak passwords, and lack of security updates make IoT devices attractive targets for hackers. Compromised devices can be enlisted in botnets for conducting large-scale attacks, such as Distributed Denial of Service (DDoS) attacks.

- **Data Privacy and Unauthorized Access:** IoT devices often collect sensitive personal data. Unauthorized access to this data can lead to privacy breaches, identity theft, and blackmail. It is crucial to implement access controls, data anonymization techniques, and encryption to protect sensitive information.

- **Physical Tampering:** Physical access to IoT devices can enable an attacker to manipulate sensors, alter device behavior, or extract sensitive information. Securing physical access points and implementing tamper-resistant designs can mitigate this threat.

- **Interoperability Issues:** The interconnected nature of IoT devices allows for complex interactions. However, vulnerabilities in device protocols and inadequate authentication mechanisms can be exploited to compromise entire IoT ecosystems. Secure network segmentation, traffic monitoring, and protocol hardening are essential to mitigate this risk.

Securing the IoT

Securing the IoT requires a holistic approach that encompasses device security, network security, and cloud security. Here are some strategies to enhance IoT security:

- **Security by Design:** IoT security should be integrated into the design and development process from the outset. Implementing security best practices, conducting rigorous threat modeling, and adhering to industry standards can significantly reduce vulnerabilities in IoT devices.

- **Access Control and Authorization:** Implementing strong access control mechanisms, such as two-factor authentication, role-based access control, and least privilege principles, can prevent unauthorized access to IoT devices and protect sensitive data.

- **Network Segmentation:** Segregating IoT devices into separate network segments or VLANs can limit the propagation of compromises and restrict lateral movement by attackers. Implementing firewalls, intrusion detection systems, and network segregation techniques can enhance the security of IoT networks.

- **Continuous Monitoring and Intrusion Detection:** Implementing robust monitoring and intrusion detection systems can help identify suspicious activities, anomalous behavior, and potential security breaches. Intrusion detection mechanisms can include anomaly detection, behavior-based analysis, and signature-based detection.

Challenges and Future Directions

Securing the IoT ecosystem is a complex task that requires collaboration among various stakeholders, including device manufacturers, service providers, regulators, and end-users. While significant progress has been made in IoT security, several challenges remain:

- **Resource Constraints:** Many IoT devices have limited computational power, memory, and battery life, making it challenging to implement robust security measures. Efficient security protocols and lightweight cryptography techniques are necessary to address these constraints.

- **Standardization and Interoperability:** Ensuring interoperability and security across diverse IoT devices and platforms is a significant challenge. Industry-wide standards, protocols, and frameworks can facilitate secure and seamless integration of IoT devices.

- **Privacy and Ethical Concerns:** IoT devices collect vast amounts of personal data, raising concerns about privacy and potential misuse. Striking a balance between data collection for IoT functionality and protecting user privacy requires comprehensive privacy frameworks, transparent data handling practices, and user consent mechanisms.

The evolving landscape of the IoT necessitates continuous research, innovation, and collaboration to address emerging threats and enhance cybersecurity. Stay informed about the latest developments, engage in continuous learning, and adopt best practices to navigate the rapidly changing IoT security landscape effectively.

Summary

The Internet of Things (IoT) presents both opportunities and challenges for cybersecurity sustainability. Securing the IoT ecosystem requires robust device authentication, data encryption, secure communication, and firmware updates. Understanding the IoT threat landscape is essential to develop effective countermeasures. Strategies such as security by design, access control, network segmentation, and continuous monitoring can enhance IoT security. Nevertheless, challenges such as resource constraints, standardization, and privacy concerns persist. Continuous research, innovation, and collaboration are crucial to ensure the security and sustainability of the IoT.

Challenges and Opportunities in Securing Future Technologies

In the ever-evolving landscape of cybersecurity, securing future technologies poses unique challenges and opportunities. As novel technologies emerge, so do the accompanying threats that require robust security measures. This section will explore the challenges faced in securing future technologies and the potential opportunities that arise from addressing these challenges.

1. Complexity of Emerging Technologies

Emerging technologies such as artificial intelligence (AI), quantum computing, and the Internet of Things (IoT) bring about unprecedented complexity. AI, for example, can enhance cybersecurity by automating threat detection and response. However, it also introduces new vulnerabilities, such as adversarial attacks that exploit AI algorithms. Securing AI systems requires designing robust models, ensuring data integrity, and addressing ethical considerations.

Quantum computing poses another challenge due to its potential to break existing encryption algorithms that protect sensitive data. Quantum-resistant cryptography methods are being developed to safeguard against this threat. Additionally, the IoT, with its extensive network of interconnected devices, presents difficulties in terms of securing data transmission and ensuring device authenticity. Strengthening device authentication and implementing secure communication protocols are critical in securing the IoT.

Addressing the complexity of emerging technologies requires collaboration among various stakeholders, including researchers, industry professionals, policymakers, and end-users. Interdisciplinary approaches that integrate cybersecurity into the design and development of these technologies can mitigate potential threats and enhance their security.

2. Lack of Standards and Regulations

As new technologies emerge, there is often a lag in the establishment of comprehensive standards and regulations. This gap creates an environment where security practices vary widely, leaving room for vulnerabilities to be exploited. It is crucial to develop industry-wide standards and regulations that address the security needs of future technologies.

Standardization efforts should encompass all aspects of technology design, implementation, and operation. This includes defining secure coding practices, encryption standards, network protocols, and authentication mechanisms. Collaborative initiatives involving industry leaders, government bodies, and cybersecurity experts are necessary to ensure the development and adoption of robust standards.

Regulations play a vital role in setting minimum security requirements and holding organizations accountable for safeguarding user data. Regulatory frameworks need to adapt to evolving technologies and address emerging threats effectively. Balancing innovation with security requires a proactive approach to regulation that fosters technological advancements while prioritizing user protection.

3. Security-by-Design Approach

To ensure robust security in future technologies, a security-by-design approach needs to be ingrained throughout the development lifecycle. This involves considering security aspects from the initial design phase and continuously assessing and mitigating risks throughout the system's lifespan.

Integrating security into the design process requires collaboration between cybersecurity experts and technology developers. Threat modeling techniques can be employed to identify potential vulnerabilities early on and implement appropriate countermeasures. Secure coding practices, such as input validation and proper error handling, should be enforced to minimize the risk of exploits.

Furthermore, organizations must prioritize ongoing security assessments, including penetration testing and vulnerability scanning, to identify and remediate any weaknesses. Regular updates and patch management should be enforced to address newly discovered vulnerabilities.

4. Privacy and Ethical Considerations

Securing future technologies goes beyond technical aspects. Privacy and ethical considerations play a crucial role in building trust and ensuring user acceptance. Data protection and privacy are particularly important in the context of emerging technologies, where vast amounts of personal information are collected and processed.

Organizations must adopt privacy-by-design principles to embed privacy protections into their products and services. This includes implementing robust data encryption, obtaining informed user consent, and providing transparency in data handling practices. Privacy impact assessments can help identify potential risks and guide the implementation of privacy safeguards.

Ethical considerations are also central to securing future technologies. AI systems, for example, raise important ethical dilemmas, such as the responsible use of data and potential bias in decision-making algorithms. Organizations should establish ethical guidelines and frameworks to govern the development and deployment of such technologies.

5. Capacity Building and Collaboration

Addressing the challenges of securing future technologies requires a skilled workforce and collaborative efforts. Capacity building initiatives play a vital role in developing the necessary expertise in both technical and non-technical aspects of cybersecurity.

Educational institutions need to offer comprehensive cybersecurity curricula that cover emerging technologies, threat intelligence, risk management, and privacy. Continuous learning programs and professional certifications should be provided to enable cybersecurity professionals to stay updated with the latest trends and best practices.

Collaboration between academia, industry, and government entities is crucial in sharing knowledge, resources, and threat intelligence. Public-private partnerships can facilitate the exchange of information and help shape effective cybersecurity strategies. International cooperation is also essential to tackle global cybersecurity challenges and establish harmonized standards and regulations.

Conclusion

Securing future technologies presents both challenges and opportunities. By addressing the complexity of emerging technologies, establishing standards and regulations, adopting a security-by-design approach, considering privacy and ethical considerations, and promoting capacity building and collaboration, organizations and stakeholders can mitigate risks and ensure a secure technological landscape.

As the cybersecurity landscape continues to evolve, it is imperative to adopt a proactive approach and remain vigilant in safeguarding future technologies. By embracing these challenges and opportunities, we can build a resilient and secure cyberspace for the technologies of tomorrow.

Cybersecurity Governance and Risk Management

Principles of Cybersecurity Governance

Board of Directors' Responsibility in Cybersecurity Governance

In today's digital age, cybersecurity has become a critical aspect of business operations. Organizations face constant threats from cyber attacks, which can lead to financial losses, reputational damage, and legal liabilities. As the governing body of an organization, the board of directors plays a crucial role in ensuring effective cybersecurity governance. In this section, we will discuss the responsibilities of the board of directors in cybersecurity governance and the principles they should adhere to.

Understanding the Board's Role

The board of directors is responsible for overseeing the strategic direction and management of an organization. Regarding cybersecurity, their role extends beyond just approving the budget for cybersecurity initiatives. The board must understand the potential risks associated with cyber threats, identify the value of information assets, and make informed decisions to protect the organization's interests.

Establishing a Cybersecurity Governance Framework

To fulfill their responsibilities in cybersecurity governance, the board should establish a robust framework that guides the organization's cybersecurity efforts. The framework should include the following key elements:

1. **Cybersecurity Policies:** The board should ensure that comprehensive cybersecurity policies are in place. These policies should define the roles and responsibilities of all employees, contractors, and stakeholders in protecting the organization's information assets.

2. **Risk Management:** The board should oversee the implementation of a risk management process that identifies, assesses, and manages cybersecurity risks. This includes conducting regular risk assessments, implementing risk mitigation strategies, and monitoring risk controls.

3. **Compliance and Assurance:** The board should ensure that the organization complies with relevant cybersecurity regulations, standards, and industry best practices. They should also establish mechanisms for cybersecurity audits and assurance to evaluate the organization's adherence to these requirements.

4. **Incident Response Planning:** The board should oversee the development and testing of an incident response plan. This plan should outline the steps to be taken in the event of a cybersecurity incident and ensure effective communication and coordination among relevant stakeholders.

5. **Training and Awareness:** The board should advocate for cybersecurity training and awareness programs for all employees. It is crucial to foster a culture of cybersecurity awareness throughout the organization to prevent and respond to cyber threats effectively.

Collaboration and Communication

The board of directors should foster collaboration and open communication between the board, executive management, and the organization's cybersecurity professionals. This collaboration ensures that the board is well-informed about the organization's cybersecurity posture and allows for effective decision-making.

Keeping Abreast of Emerging Cybersecurity Trends

Cybersecurity is a rapidly evolving field, with new threats and technologies continually emerging. The board of directors should proactively stay informed about the latest cybersecurity trends, such as emerging threats, regulatory changes, and technological advancements. This knowledge enables the board to steer the organization in the right direction and make informed decisions regarding cybersecurity.

Engaging External Expertise

Given the complex nature of cybersecurity, the board may need to engage external experts, such as cybersecurity consultants or legal advisors, to provide the necessary expertise. External experts can assist the board in understanding the evolving threat landscape, assessing the organization's cybersecurity readiness, and identifying areas for improvement.

Ensuring Accountability

The board of directors should establish clear lines of accountability for cybersecurity within the organization. This includes assigning responsibility for cybersecurity governance at the executive level, ensuring reports on cybersecurity issues are provided to the board regularly, and holding individuals accountable for compliance with cybersecurity policies and procedures.

Ethical Considerations

In the context of cybersecurity governance, ethical considerations are of utmost importance. The board of directors should adhere to ethical principles, such as promoting transparency, fairness, and respect for privacy rights. Ethical decision-making ensures that cybersecurity measures are implemented in a manner that upholds the integrity and reputation of the organization.

Conclusion

The board of directors' responsibility in cybersecurity governance is essential to protect the organization from cyber threats. By establishing a cybersecurity governance framework, fostering collaboration, staying informed about emerging trends, engaging external expertise, ensuring accountability, and considering ethical implications, the board can effectively fulfill their role and safeguard the organization's interests in the digital age. It is crucial for boards to recognize the significance of cybersecurity and prioritize it on their agenda to ensure long-term sustainability and resilience.

Establishing a Cybersecurity Governance Framework

Establishing a cybersecurity governance framework is a critical step in managing and mitigating cybersecurity risks within an organization. A cybersecurity governance framework provides a structured approach to defining, implementing, and monitoring cybersecurity policies, procedures, and controls. This framework helps organizations align their cybersecurity efforts with their overall business objectives and ensures that cybersecurity is considered throughout the organization.

The Need for a Cybersecurity Governance Framework

Cybersecurity governance is essential for organizations to effectively manage and address the evolving cyber threats. A comprehensive cybersecurity governance framework helps organizations establish a clear direction for their cybersecurity program, enables the identification and prioritization of cybersecurity risks, and provides a basis for making informed decisions on resource allocation.

Without a cybersecurity governance framework, organizations may struggle to effectively manage cybersecurity risks. They may lack clear roles and responsibilities, leading to confusion and ineffective coordination. Inadequate governance can result in a reactive approach to cybersecurity, where organizations only respond to incidents instead of proactively identifying and addressing vulnerabilities.

Additionally, a cybersecurity governance framework helps organizations comply with relevant laws, regulations, and industry standards. It ensures that the organization's cybersecurity program aligns with the requirements and expectations of stakeholders, including customers, partners, and regulatory bodies.

Key Components of a Cybersecurity Governance Framework

A cybersecurity governance framework typically consists of the following key components:

1. **Leadership and Oversight:** This component involves the establishment of clear roles and responsibilities for cybersecurity within the organization. It includes the appointment of a cybersecurity steering committee or board, responsible for providing guidance and oversight to the cybersecurity program. The leadership team ensures that cybersecurity is integrated into the organization's strategic goals and objectives.

2. **Policies and Procedures:** Policies and procedures form the foundation of a cybersecurity governance framework. They provide guidance on how the organization will secure its information assets and protect against cyber threats. Policies define the organization's risk tolerance, while procedures outline the specific steps to be followed for implementing and enforcing cybersecurity controls.

3. **Risk Assessment and Management:** Risk assessment is a critical component of cybersecurity governance. It involves identifying and evaluating cybersecurity risks, including threats, vulnerabilities, and potential impacts. Risk management activities include risk mitigation through the implementation of appropriate controls, risk transfer through insurance, and regular monitoring and reassessment of risks.

4. **Control Framework:** The control framework consists of the specific cybersecurity controls and measures that are implemented to protect assets and mitigate risks. These controls can include technical controls (such as firewalls, intrusion detection systems, and encryption), operational controls (such as incident response and business continuity planning), and administrative controls (such as training and awareness programs).

5. **Compliance and Auditing:** Compliance with laws, regulations, and industry standards is a critical component of cybersecurity governance. Organizations need to establish processes to monitor and ensure compliance with applicable requirements. Regular audits and assessments are conducted to evaluate the effectiveness of controls and identify areas for improvement.

Implementing a Cybersecurity Governance Framework

Implementing a cybersecurity governance framework requires a systematic approach. Here are some key steps to consider:

1. **Identify the Governance Framework:** Organizations can choose from various governance frameworks, such as the NIST Cybersecurity Framework, ISO 27001, or COBIT. The selected framework should align with the organization's objectives, industry requirements, and risk tolerance.

2. **Establish the Governance Structure:** Define the roles and responsibilities of key stakeholders, such as the cybersecurity steering committee, executive management, IT department, and legal department. Ensure clear lines of communication and accountability.

3. **Develop Policies and Procedures:** Develop comprehensive cybersecurity policies and procedures that align with the organization's risk appetite. Policies should cover areas such as access control, incident response, data protection, and employee awareness. Procedures should provide step-by-step instructions for implementing and enforcing controls

4. **Conduct a Risk Assessment:** Identify and assess cybersecurity risks specific to the organization. Evaluate the potential impact of these risks on the organization's objectives and develop risk mitigation strategies. This step helps prioritize cybersecurity investments and efforts.

5. **Implement Control Measures:** Based on the identified risks, implement appropriate cybersecurity controls. These controls may include technical measures (such as firewalls and encryption), operational measures (such as incident response and monitoring), and administrative measures (such as training and awareness programs).

6. **Monitor, Measure, and Adapt:** Regularly monitor and measure the effectiveness of the implemented controls. Conduct periodic audits to assess compliance with policies and procedures. Use metrics to track key performance indicators and make informed decisions on cybersecurity improvements.

7. **Continual Improvement:** Cybersecurity governance is an ongoing process. Continually assess the effectiveness of the governance framework and make improvements as needed. Stay up-to-date with emerging threats and technologies and adapt the framework accordingly.

Challenges in Establishing a Cybersecurity Governance Framework

Implementing a cybersecurity governance framework can come with various challenges. Organizations may face resistance to change, lack of awareness, or limited resources. Here are some common challenges and strategies to overcome them:

1. **Lack of Top Management Support:** Without leadership buy-in, implementing a cybersecurity governance framework can be difficult. To overcome this challenge, educate top management on the importance of cybersecurity and its impact on the organization's reputation and bottom line. Communicate the business value of cybersecurity and the potential consequences of not taking action.

2. **Resource Constraints:** Limited budget and resources can hinder the implementation of a robust governance framework. To address this challenge, prioritize cybersecurity investments based on risk assessment and business impact. Leverage open-source and cost-effective security solutions. Explore partnerships with other organizations or industry groups to pool resources and share best practices.

3. **Lack of Awareness and Skills:** Many organizations struggle with a lack of cybersecurity awareness and skills. To tackle this challenge, provide regular training and awareness programs to employees. Invest in professional development and cybersecurity certifications for the IT team. Foster a culture of cybersecurity throughout the organization.

4. **Evolving Threat Landscape:** The cybersecurity landscape is constantly evolving, with new threats and vulnerabilities emerging regularly. Stay updated with the latest industry trends and threat intelligence. Engage in information

sharing and collaboration forums to stay ahead of evolving threats. Conduct regular risk assessments and adapt controls accordingly.

Real-World Example

Consider a financial institution that wants to establish a cybersecurity governance framework. The institution begins by selecting the NIST Cybersecurity Framework as their governance framework. They form a cybersecurity steering committee comprising senior leadership, IT experts, and legal professionals.

The committee develops comprehensive cybersecurity policies and procedures that address areas such as customer data protection, secure software development, and incident response. They conduct a risk assessment to identify cybersecurity risks, analyze the potential impact, and prioritize their mitigation efforts.

Based on the risk assessment, the institution implements a range of cybersecurity controls, including firewalls, intrusion detection systems, encryption, and employee training programs. They establish a monitoring and measurement system to evaluate the effectiveness of these controls and conduct regular audits to assess compliance.

The financial institution continually monitors the evolving threat landscape and adjusts their cybersecurity governance framework accordingly. They promote a culture of cybersecurity awareness among employees, encouraging them to report potential security incidents and stay vigilant.

By establishing a cybersecurity governance framework, the financial institution is better positioned to protect customer data, prevent cyber-attacks, and comply with industry regulations. They can confidently operate in a secure and resilient manner, mitigating cybersecurity risks.

Conclusion

Establishing a cybersecurity governance framework is essential for organizations to effectively manage and mitigate cybersecurity risks. It provides a structured approach to align cybersecurity efforts with business objectives, ensure compliance, and enhance overall security posture. By following a systematic process and addressing potential challenges, organizations can establish a robust cybersecurity governance framework that protects critical assets and enables business growth.

Role of CIO and CISO in Cybersecurity Governance

In today's digital landscape, cybersecurity has become a critical concern for organizations across the globe. With the growing number and severity of cyber threats, it has become essential for organizations to establish effective cybersecurity governance frameworks. The Chief Information Officer (CIO) and Chief Information Security Officer (CISO) play pivotal roles in ensuring the success of these frameworks and mitigating cyber risks.

Understanding the Role of CIO

The CIO is responsible for the overall management and strategic use of information technology (IT) within an organization. In the context of cybersecurity governance, the CIO plays a crucial role in aligning the organization's IT strategy with its overall business objectives and risk management framework. Some key responsibilities of the CIO in cybersecurity governance include:

- **Setting the cybersecurity strategy:** The CIO is responsible for formulating the organization's cybersecurity strategy, which outlines the approach, goals, and objectives for protecting the organization's digital assets. This involves assessing the organization's risk appetite, evaluating emerging cybersecurity threats and technologies, and aligning the strategy with industry best practices and regulatory requirements.

- **Establishing security policies and standards:** The CIO is responsible for developing and implementing comprehensive security policies and standards that govern the organization's IT infrastructure, systems, and processes. This includes defining rules for data classification, access controls, incident response, and business continuity. These policies and standards should be communicated effectively to all stakeholders and regularly reviewed and updated to keep pace with evolving cyber threats.

- **Ensuring technology infrastructure security:** The CIO is responsible for overseeing the implementation and maintenance of secure technology infrastructure. This involves assessing the security posture of the organization's hardware, software, networks, and cloud-based services. The CIO collaborates with technology teams to ensure that security controls and measures are in place to protect the organization's critical assets from unauthorized access, data breaches, and other security incidents.

- **Managing cybersecurity risks:** The CIO plays a critical role in identifying, assessing, and managing cybersecurity risks within the organization. This involves conducting regular risk assessments, vulnerability scanning, and penetration testing to identify and mitigate potential threats. The CIO works closely with the CISO and other stakeholders to develop risk mitigation strategies, implement security controls, and ensure compliance with applicable laws, regulations, and industry standards.

- **Building and managing a skilled cybersecurity workforce:** The CIO is responsible for attracting, developing, and retaining skilled cybersecurity professionals within the organization. This involves identifying the necessary skill sets, developing training and education programs, and fostering a culture of cybersecurity awareness and accountability. The CIO also collaborates with human resources to recruit external talent and establish partnerships with educational institutions and professional organizations to enhance the organization's cybersecurity capabilities.

Understanding the Role of CISO

The CISO is responsible for overseeing the organization's cybersecurity program and ensuring the confidentiality, integrity, and availability of its information assets. The CISO works closely with the CIO and other stakeholders to establish and maintain a robust cybersecurity governance framework. Some key responsibilities of the CISO in cybersecurity governance include:

- **Developing and implementing cybersecurity policies and procedures:** The CISO is responsible for developing, implementing, and maintaining comprehensive cybersecurity policies, procedures, and guidelines. These documents provide clear instructions on how to handle security incidents, manage access controls, monitor network traffic, and enforce security controls. The CISO ensures that these policies and procedures are well-communicated, understood, and followed by employees at all levels of the organization.
- **Conducting risk assessments and vulnerability management:** The CISO is responsible for conducting regular risk assessments to identify potential vulnerabilities and threats to the organization's information assets. This involves assessing the effectiveness of security controls, identifying gaps and weaknesses, and recommending appropriate risk mitigation strategies. The CISO collaborates with technical teams to implement vulnerability management programs, which include processes for vulnerability scanning, patch management, and remediation of security issues.
- **Monitoring and incident response:** The CISO oversees the establishment of a robust security monitoring program, which includes real-time

monitoring of network traffic, log analysis, and security event correlation. The CISO is responsible for the timely detection, analysis, and response to security incidents. This involves establishing incident response plans, defining incident management procedures, and coordinating incident response activities across different teams within the organization. The CISO also interacts with external stakeholders, such as law enforcement agencies and incident response providers, when necessary.

- **Ensuring regulatory compliance:** The CISO ensures that the organization complies with relevant cybersecurity laws, regulations, and industry standards. This involves staying up-to-date with changes in the regulatory environment, conducting regular compliance assessments, and implementing necessary controls and measures to address compliance requirements. The CISO also collaborates with legal and compliance teams to establish effective processes for incident reporting, data breach notification, and evidence preservation in case of legal investigations or litigation.

- **Cybersecurity awareness and training:** The CISO is responsible for promoting cybersecurity awareness and building a strong cybersecurity culture within the organization. This includes designing and delivering security awareness and training programs for employees at all levels. The CISO raises awareness about common cyber threats, best practices for cybersecurity hygiene, and the importance of reporting security incidents. The CISO also ensures that employees are aware of their roles and responsibilities in safeguarding the organization's information assets.

Building Effective Collaboration

To ensure the success of cybersecurity governance, it is crucial for the CIO and CISO to collaborate closely and establish effective communication channels. By working together, they can leverage their respective expertise and perspectives to address cybersecurity risks, align cybersecurity strategies with business goals, and drive a culture of cybersecurity throughout the organization. Some key considerations for building effective collaboration between the CIO and CISO include:

- **Regular communication and reporting:** The CIO and CISO should establish regular communication channels to discuss cybersecurity matters, share updates, and address any issues or concerns. This includes regular reporting on cybersecurity incidents, risk assessments, compliance status, and progress on cybersecurity initiatives. Transparent and timely communication enables both the CIO and CISO to make informed decisions and take appropriate actions.

- **Shared responsibility and accountability:** Cybersecurity governance is a shared responsibility between the CIO and CISO. Both roles should work together to establish clear roles and responsibilities, ensuring there is no ambiguity in decision-making and accountability. Collaboration should extend beyond the CIO and CISO to include other stakeholders such as the board of directors, executive management, legal, compliance, and HR teams to ensure a holistic and coordinated approach to cybersecurity governance.

- **Mutual understanding and respect:** The CIO and CISO should have a solid understanding of each other's roles, challenges, and priorities. This helps in fostering mutual respect and empathy, enabling effective collaboration and decision-making. The CIO should appreciate the technical expertise and specialized knowledge of the CISO, while the CISO should understand the business objectives and constraints that the CIO operates within.

- **Continuous learning and professional development:** The cybersecurity landscape is constantly evolving, and both the CIO and CISO need to stay updated with the latest trends, threats, and technologies. They should engage in continuous learning and professional development activities such as attending conferences, participating in industry forums, and pursuing relevant certifications. This equips them with the knowledge and skills necessary to address emerging cyber risks and challenges effectively.

Case Study: Collaborative Incident Response

To illustrate the importance of collaboration between the CIO and CISO in cybersecurity governance, let's consider a real-world case study. Imagine a large financial institution that detects a sophisticated cyber attack targeting its customer data. The CIO and CISO of the organization need to work together to respond effectively to the incident.

The CIO, with their knowledge of the organization's technology infrastructure, can assess the extent of the attack, identify the affected systems, and coordinate with technical teams to isolate and contain the threat. They can also ensure that appropriate backup and disaster recovery mechanisms are in place to restore services as quickly as possible.

At the same time, the CISO takes charge of incident response coordination, working closely with the CIO and other stakeholders. The CISO leads the investigation to determine the source and nature of the attack, collects evidence for potential legal proceedings, and oversees the communication with external stakeholders, such as regulatory bodies and affected customers. The CISO also coordinates the implementation of additional security controls to prevent similar incidents in the future.

Through their collaboration, the CIO and CISO are able to effectively manage the incident, minimize the impact on the organization and its customers, and learn from the incident to improve the organization's cybersecurity posture.

Conclusion

The role of the CIO and CISO in cybersecurity governance is critical for organizations aiming to safeguard their digital assets and mitigate cyber risks. By working in collaboration, they can establish effective cybersecurity strategies, manage risks, and build a resilient cybersecurity culture. The ongoing learning and adaptability of the CIO and CISO to the ever-changing cybersecurity landscape is paramount to ensuring the long-term success of the organization's cybersecurity governance framework.

Integrating Cybersecurity Governance with Enterprise Risk Management

In today's digital landscape, cybersecurity governance and enterprise risk management play crucial roles in ensuring the protection and sustainability of organizations. Cybersecurity governance refers to the framework, policies, and processes that guide an organization's approach to managing and mitigating cyber risks, while enterprise risk management (ERM) involves identifying, assessing, and managing risks at the organizational level. To effectively protect against cyber threats, it is essential to integrate cybersecurity governance with ERM.

The Need for Integration

The integration of cybersecurity governance with ERM is imperative due to the interconnected nature of cybersecurity and overall risk management. Cybersecurity risks can have significant impacts on an organization's overall risk profile and can disrupt critical business operations, damage reputation, and lead to financial losses. By integrating cybersecurity governance with ERM, organizations can ensure that cyber risks are adequately considered within the broader risk management framework.

Benefits of Integration

Integrating cybersecurity governance with ERM offers several benefits to organizations:

- **Holistic Risk View:** Integration provides a holistic view of risks by considering cyber risks alongside other operational, financial, and strategic risks.
- **Effective Risk Prioritization:** Integration helps in effectively prioritizing risks based on their potential impact on the enterprise. It enables organizations to identify and allocate resources to critical areas of vulnerability, reducing the overall risk exposure.
- **Optimized Resource Allocation:** By understanding the interdependencies between cybersecurity risks and other risks, organizations can allocate resources strategically to minimize the impact of cyber threats on their operations.
- **Enhanced Incident Response:** Integration facilitates a coordinated incident response across the organization. It enables timely detection, analysis, and containment of cybersecurity incidents, minimizing their impact on business operations.
- **Risk-Informed Decision Making:** Integrating cybersecurity governance with ERM ensures that cybersecurity considerations are embedded in the decision-making processes across all levels of the organization. This allows for informed decisions that consider potential cyber risks and their implications.

Key Considerations for Integration

To successfully integrate cybersecurity governance with ERM, organizations should consider the following key aspects:

1. **Board and Executive Leadership Involvement:** The board and executive leadership should actively participate in the integration process and set the

tone for a risk-aware culture. They should understand the importance of cybersecurity and provide the necessary resources and support to ensure effective integration.

2. **Risk Assessment and Identification:** Organizations should conduct comprehensive risk assessments to identify and assess cybersecurity risks in the context of the broader risk landscape. This involves identifying the potential threats, vulnerabilities, and impacts associated with cyber risks.

3. **Risk Mitigation Strategies:** Integration requires developing risk mitigation strategies that address cybersecurity risks alongside other organizational risks. This may include implementing appropriate security controls, developing incident response plans, and conducting regular vulnerability assessments.

4. **Clear Roles and Responsibilities:** Organizations should define clear roles and responsibilities for cybersecurity governance and ERM within the organizational structure. This includes designating individuals responsible for managing cybersecurity risks and establishing effective communication channels between different stakeholders.

5. **Continuous Monitoring and Evaluation:** Integration is an ongoing process that requires continuous monitoring and evaluation of cybersecurity controls and risk management practices. Regular audits and assessments help identify areas for improvement and ensure the effectiveness of integrated governance mechanisms.

Case Study: Integrating Cybersecurity Governance with ERM

To illustrate the practical implementation of integrating cybersecurity governance with ERM, let's consider a hypothetical case study of a financial institution.

The financial institution, ABC Bank, recognized the need to strengthen its cybersecurity governance and integrate it with enterprise risk management. To achieve this, ABC Bank took the following steps:

1. Senior Leadership Commitment: The CEO and the board of directors emphasized the importance of cybersecurity governance and provided the necessary resources to integrate cybersecurity with ERM. They appointed a Chief Information Security Officer (CISO) responsible for overseeing cybersecurity initiatives.

2. Risk Assessment: ABC Bank conducted a comprehensive risk assessment to identify cybersecurity risks. The assessment included a thorough analysis of potential threats, vulnerabilities, and impacts associated with cyber threats, taking into account regulatory requirements and industry best practices.

3. Risk Mitigation Strategies: Based on the risk assessment findings, ABC Bank developed risk mitigation strategies that accounted for cybersecurity risks. This involved implementing multi-factor authentication for customer accounts, conducting regular penetration testing, and implementing intrusion detection and prevention systems.

4. Collaboration and Communication: ABC Bank ensured effective collaboration and communication between different departments and stakeholders. The cybersecurity team actively engaged with the risk management team to share threat intelligence and align risk mitigation efforts.

5. Monitoring and Evaluation: ABC Bank established a robust monitoring and evaluation mechanism to ensure the effectiveness of integrated cybersecurity governance and ERM. This included regular audits, incident response drills, and continuous monitoring of security controls.

By integrating cybersecurity governance with ERM, ABC Bank was able to enhance its overall risk management practices, strengthen its cybersecurity defenses, and minimize the impact of cyber threats on its operations.

Conclusion

Integrating cybersecurity governance with enterprise risk management is essential for organizations to effectively manage cybersecurity risks and safeguard their critical assets. By taking a holistic approach to risk management and considering cyber risks alongside other organizational risks, organizations can prioritize cybersecurity efforts, allocate resources strategically, and make informed decisions. The integration process requires commitment and collaboration from senior leadership, clear roles and responsibilities, continuous monitoring, and evaluation. Ultimately, integrating cybersecurity governance with ERM enables organizations to build resilience in the face of evolving cyber threats and ensures the long-term sustainability of their operations.

Risk Assessment and Management Frameworks

Risk assessment and management are crucial components of an effective cybersecurity strategy. Organizations need to identify and mitigate potential risks to their information systems and data in order to protect themselves from cyber threats. In this section, we will explore various risk assessment and management frameworks that can be used to evaluate and address cybersecurity risks.

Importance of Risk Assessment

Before delving into risk assessment frameworks, it is important to understand why risk assessment is a critical aspect of cybersecurity. Risk assessment helps organizations identify and prioritize potential risks, allowing them to allocate necessary resources for risk mitigation. By conducting a thorough risk assessment, organizations can:

- Identify vulnerabilities and threats to their information systems and data.
- Determine the potential impact of a cybersecurity incident on their operations and reputation.
- Evaluate the likelihood of various threats occurring.
- Prioritize and allocate resources effectively to manage these risks.
- Establish a baseline for monitoring and measuring the effectiveness of their risk management efforts.

Now let's explore some popular risk assessment and management frameworks that organizations can use to evaluate and address cybersecurity risks.

NIST Risk Management Framework

The National Institute of Standards and Technology (NIST) has developed a comprehensive risk management framework that provides organizations with a structured approach to identify, assess, and manage cybersecurity risks. The NIST Risk Management Framework consists of five stages:

1. **Categorize:** This stage involves identifying and categorizing the information systems and data within an organization. It helps determine the criticality of these assets and their impact on the organization's mission and objectives.

2. **Select:** In this stage, organizations select and implement appropriate security controls based on the categorization determined in the previous stage. The selection of security controls should align with the organization's risk tolerance and compliance requirements.

3. **Implement:** The selected security controls are implemented throughout the organization's information systems and processes. This stage focuses on integrating security measures into the organization's operations.

4. **Assess:** Organizations conduct regular assessments to determine the effectiveness of the implemented security controls. This involves evaluating the actual performance of the controls and identifying any gaps or vulnerabilities.

5. **Authorize:** Based on the assessment results, organizations make risk-based decisions regarding the authorization of their information systems. This stage involves management reviewing the assessment findings and deciding whether to accept the identified risks or take additional actions to mitigate them.

6. **Monitor:** The final stage of the NIST Risk Management Framework involves continuous monitoring of the implemented security controls. Organizations should regularly review and update their risk management strategies to address evolving threats and vulnerabilities.

The NIST Risk Management Framework provides a systematic and structured approach to managing cybersecurity risks. It aligns with other NIST cybersecurity publications and frameworks, such as the Cybersecurity Framework (CSF) and Special Publication (SP) series. It is widely adopted by government agencies and organizations seeking a robust risk management methodology.

ISO 27001 and 27005

The International Organization for Standardization (ISO) has developed two important standards for risk assessment and management in the cybersecurity domain: ISO 27001 and ISO 27005.

ISO 27001 provides guidelines for establishing, implementing, maintaining, and continuously improving an information security management system (ISMS) within an organization. The standard emphasizes the importance of risk assessment and treatment as a key component of the ISMS. It provides a structured and systematic approach to identifying and managing information security risks.

ISO 27005, on the other hand, focuses specifically on risk management in the context of information security. It provides practical guidance on how to assess information security risks and select appropriate control measures to mitigate those risks. The standard covers the entire risk management process, including risk identification, analysis, evaluation, treatment, and monitoring.

Organizations that adopt ISO 27001 and ISO 27005 can benefit from a comprehensive and internationally recognized approach to risk assessment and management.

COSO Enterprise Risk Management Framework

While not specific to cybersecurity, the Committee of Sponsoring Organizations of the Treadway Commission (COSO) Enterprise Risk Management (ERM) framework provides a holistic approach to managing risks within an organization. It can be used as a foundation for integrating cybersecurity risk management into the overall enterprise risk management strategy.

The COSO ERM framework consists of eight components:

1. Internal Environment: This component sets the tone for the organization's risk management culture and establishes the foundation for effective risk management.

2. Objective Setting: Organizations need to establish clear objectives to align their risk management efforts with their strategic goals and priorities.

3. Event Identification: This component involves identifying potential events that could impact the achievement of organizational objectives. In the context of cybersecurity, this would include identifying potential cyber threats, vulnerabilities, and potential impacts.

4. Risk Assessment: Organizations assess the significance of identified risks in terms of likelihood and impact. This helps prioritize risk management efforts and allocate resources effectively.

5. Risk Response: Based on the assessment results, organizations develop and implement risk response plans. These plans define how the organization will avoid, accept, mitigate, or transfer the identified risks.

6. Control Activities: This component focuses on implementing control activities to ensure the effectiveness of the risk response plans. In the cybersecurity context, control activities would involve implementing security controls and measures to mitigate identified risks.

7. Information and Communication: Effective communication and information sharing are essential for risk management. This component emphasizes the importance of accurate and timely information for making informed risk management decisions.

8. Monitoring: The final component involves monitoring and continuously assessing the effectiveness of the organization's risk management efforts. Regular monitoring helps identify changes in the risk landscape and ensures the ongoing relevance and effectiveness of risk management strategies.

The COSO ERM framework provides a comprehensive and integrated approach to risk management that can be applied to various domains, including cybersecurity.

Practical Application: Quantitative vs. Qualitative Risk Assessment

One of the key decisions organizations face during the risk assessment process is whether to conduct a quantitative or qualitative risk assessment. Both approaches have their advantages and disadvantages, and the choice depends on various factors, including available data, resources, and organizational goals.

Quantitative risk assessment involves assigning numerical values to the likelihood and impact of identified risks. This approach relies on quantitative data and statistical analysis to estimate the probability of a risk occurring and the potential monetary loss associated with it. The output of a quantitative risk assessment is typically a risk score or metric that helps prioritize risks based on their severity.

Qualitative risk assessment, on the other hand, does not rely on numerical data and focuses more on subjective judgments and expert opinions. It involves assessing risks based on their qualitative characteristics, such as high, medium, or low likelihood and impact. Qualitative risk assessment provides a broader understanding of risks and can be conducted when quantitative data is scarce or unreliable.

Both quantitative and qualitative risk assessments have their strengths and weaknesses. A quantitative approach provides a more objective and quantitative measure of risk, allowing for better prioritization and resource allocation.

However, it requires comprehensive and accurate data, which may not always be available. Qualitative risk assessment, on the other hand, provides a more holistic view of risks but may lack the precision and objectivity of a quantitative approach.

In practice, organizations often use a combination of both approaches. They may start with a qualitative assessment to identify and prioritize risks based on expert judgment and then conduct a quantitative assessment for high-priority risks where reliable data is available.

Conclusion

Risk assessment and management frameworks provide organizations with structured approaches to identify, assess, and manage cybersecurity risks. The NIST Risk Management Framework, ISO 27001 and 27005, and the COSO ERM framework are just a few examples of frameworks that can be used to guide organizations through the risk management process.

Organizations should carefully evaluate their specific needs and requirements when selecting a risk assessment framework. It is also important to regularly review and update risk management strategies to address emerging threats and changes in the risk landscape. By adopting a systematic and comprehensive approach to risk assessment and management, organizations can enhance their cybersecurity posture and better protect their information systems and data.

Cybersecurity Risk Management

Identifying Cybersecurity Risks

Identifying cybersecurity risks is a crucial step in safeguarding an organization's digital assets and sensitive information. By understanding the potential threats and vulnerabilities, organizations can develop effective strategies to mitigate these risks. This section will discuss the principles and techniques for identifying cybersecurity risks, including the use of risk assessments, threat intelligence, and vulnerability assessments.

Risk Assessment

A risk assessment is the process of evaluating and analyzing the potential risks to an organization's information assets. It involves identifying assets, assessing their value, and determining the likelihood and impact of potential threats. The following steps can guide organizations in conducting a comprehensive risk assessment:

Step 1: Asset Identification The first step in a risk assessment is to identify and categorize the organization's information assets. These assets can include hardware, software, data, processes, and personnel. By identifying assets, organizations can prioritize their protection efforts based on their value and criticality.

Step 2: Threat Identification After identifying assets, organizations need to identify the potential threats that can exploit vulnerabilities and compromise these assets. Threats can come from various sources, such as malicious insiders, hackers, or natural disasters. Organizations should consider both internal and external threats during this process.

Step 3: Vulnerability Assessment Once threats are identified, organizations should assess the vulnerabilities within their systems and networks. Vulnerabilities can include software bugs, misconfigurations, weak passwords, or outdated security controls. Conducting vulnerability assessments can help identify weaknesses that can be exploited by attackers.

Step 4: Risk Analysis In risk analysis, organizations evaluate the likelihood and impact of potential threats exploiting vulnerabilities. Likelihood refers to the probability of a threat occurring, while impact relates to the potential harm or damage that could result from the exploitation. By analyzing the risks, organizations can prioritize their mitigation efforts and allocate resources effectively.

Step 5: Risk Evaluation In this step, organizations evaluate the calculated risks based on predefined risk acceptance criteria. By determining the organization's risk tolerance level, they can determine whether the identified risks are acceptable or require further actions. This evaluation enables organizations to make informed decisions about the allocation of resources and the implementation of controls.

Step 6: Risk Mitigation The final step in a risk assessment is to develop and implement risk mitigation strategies. These strategies aim to reduce the identified risks to an acceptable level. Mitigation measures can include implementing security controls, updating software, providing employee training, or adopting industry best practices.

Threat Intelligence

Threat intelligence involves gathering and analyzing information about potential cybersecurity threats to an organization. By understanding the threat landscape, organizations can proactively identify and respond to emerging threats. The following techniques can assist in gathering threat intelligence:

External Threat Monitoring Organizations can monitor various external sources, such as cybersecurity blogs, forums, and news websites, to stay updated on the latest threats. This approach helps organizations gain insights into new attack techniques, vulnerabilities, and malware campaigns.

Information Sharing and Collaboration Sharing threat intelligence with other organizations, industry groups, and government agencies can enhance an organization's ability to identify and respond to emerging threats. Collaborative platforms enable the exchange of real-time information about cyber threats, enabling faster response and mitigation.

Dark Web Monitoring The dark web, a hidden part of the internet, is a hub for criminal activities, including the buying and selling of sensitive information. Organizations can monitor the dark web to identify potential threats and monitor if any of their proprietary information is being sold or traded illicitly.

Vulnerability Assessments

Vulnerability assessments focus on identifying weaknesses in an organization's IT infrastructure, applications, and systems. This assessment helps organizations understand their security posture and identify vulnerabilities that can be exploited by attackers. The following techniques can be utilized during vulnerability assessments:

Network Scanning Network scanning involves using automated tools to identify open ports, services running on those ports, and potential vulnerabilities within the network. By scanning the network, organizations can identify security gaps and take appropriate measures to mitigate them.

Penetration Testing Penetration testing, commonly known as ethical hacking, involves simulating real-world attacks to identify vulnerabilities in systems and applications. Qualified professionals simulate various attack scenarios to identify weaknesses that could be exploited by malicious actors. Penetration testing helps organizations validate the effectiveness of their security controls and identify areas for improvement.

Web Application Assessment Web applications are often vulnerable to attacks due to coding errors or misconfigurations. Web application assessments involve analyzing the source code, configuration settings, and potential attack vectors in web applications. This assessment helps organizations identify vulnerabilities specific to their web applications and implement appropriate security controls.

Security Configuration Review Security configuration reviews involve evaluating the configuration settings of an organization's IT infrastructure, including firewalls, routers, and servers. This review helps identify misconfigurations, weak access controls, or other configuration issues that can lead to vulnerabilities. By addressing these issues, organizations can reduce the likelihood of successful attacks.

In conclusion, identifying cybersecurity risks is a critical step in protecting an organization's valuable information assets. This section discussed the importance of conducting risk assessments, using threat intelligence, and performing vulnerability assessments. By applying these principles and techniques, organizations can enhance their cybersecurity posture and reduce the potential impact of cyber threats. It is essential to regularly update and revisit risk identification processes to align with the evolving threat landscape. Continuous improvement and proactive measures will ensure that organizations are well-prepared to address cybersecurity risks effectively.

Assessing and Prioritizing Cybersecurity Risks

In order to effectively manage cybersecurity risks, organizations need to have a systematic approach to assess and prioritize these risks. This involves identifying potential threats, determining the likelihood of those threats occurring, assessing the potential impact, and prioritizing the risks based on their level of severity.

Identifying Cybersecurity Risks

The first step in assessing cybersecurity risks is to identify the potential threats that could impact an organization. This involves understanding the various types of cyber attacks and vulnerabilities that exist. Some common sources of cybersecurity risks include:

- External threats: These include attacks from hackers, cybercriminals, and state-sponsored actors. Examples of external threats include phishing attacks, malware infections, denial of service attacks, and Advanced Persistent Threats (APTs).

- Internal threats: These refer to risks that come from within the organization. These can include insider threats, such as malicious employees or contractors, as well as unintentional mistakes made by employees that can lead to security breaches.

- Third-party risks: Organizations often rely on third-party vendors, suppliers, and partners to provide various services and technologies. However, these third parties can also introduce potential risks if they do not have robust cybersecurity measures in place.

- Technical vulnerabilities: These are weaknesses or flaws in hardware, software, or network infrastructure that can be exploited by attackers. Examples include outdated software, misconfigured systems, or insecure network protocols.

- Regulatory compliance risks: Failure to comply with relevant cybersecurity regulations and industry standards can expose organizations to legal and financial penalties, as well as reputational damage.

By thoroughly understanding the potential threats and risks that an organization faces, it becomes possible to prioritize efforts and allocate resources effectively.

Assessing and Quantifying Cybersecurity Risks

Once the potential risks have been identified, the next step is to assess and quantify these risks. This involves evaluating the likelihood of a threat occurring and the potential impact it could have on the organization. There are several approaches and techniques that can be used to assess cybersecurity risks:

- Risk likelihood: This involves estimating the probability of a specific threat occurring. This can be based on historical data, industry trends, or expert judgment. It is important to consider both the frequency and the severity of the threat when assessing the likelihood.

- Impact assessment: This involves evaluating the potential consequences of a successful attack or breach. The impact could include financial losses, operational disruptions, damage to reputation, legal and regulatory consequences, or harm to individuals' privacy and data.
- Risk scoring: A risk scoring framework can be used to assign numerical values to the assessed likelihood and impact of each risk. This allows for the prioritization of risks based on their overall risk score. Different organizations may use different approaches, such as qualitative scales (e.g., low, medium, high) or quantitative scales (e.g., assigning numerical values).

It is important to note that the assessment of cybersecurity risks is not a one-time exercise. Risks need to be assessed on an ongoing basis, as the threat landscape evolves and as organizations introduce new technologies, processes, or partnerships.

Prioritizing Cybersecurity Risks

Once the risks have been assessed and quantified, it is necessary to prioritize them based on their level of severity. This helps organizations allocate resources effectively and focus on addressing the most critical risks first. Several factors can be taken into consideration when prioritizing cybersecurity risks:

- Risk severity: Risks with higher potential impact and likelihood should be prioritized over those with lower severity. This ensures that resources are allocated to addressing the risks that pose the greatest threat to the organization.
- Risk appetite: Each organization has its own risk appetite, which refers to the level of risk that the organization is willing to accept. Risks that exceed the organization's risk appetite should be given higher priority.
- Cost and feasibility: It is important to consider the cost and feasibility of mitigating each risk. Risks that can be addressed at a reasonable cost and within a reasonable timeframe should be prioritized over those that require significant resources or are difficult to mitigate.
- Legal and regulatory requirements: Organizations must also consider any legal or regulatory requirements related to cybersecurity. Risks that would result in non-compliance with these requirements should be given high priority.

It is essential for organizations to regularly review and update the prioritization of cybersecurity risks based on changes in the threat landscape, the organization's risk posture, and the availability of new mitigation techniques or technologies.

Risk Mitigation Strategies

Once cybersecurity risks have been assessed and prioritized, organizations can develop and implement risk mitigation strategies. The goal of these strategies is to reduce the likelihood and impact of potential risks. Some common risk mitigation strategies include:

- Implementing technical controls: This involves deploying various cybersecurity solutions, such as firewalls, intrusion detection systems, and anti-malware software, to protect against potential threats.

- Enhancing employee awareness and training: Educating employees about cybersecurity risks and best practices is crucial in preventing successful attacks. This can include training programs, awareness campaigns, and simulated phishing exercises.

- Establishing incident response procedures: Having a well-defined incident response plan in place enables organizations to respond quickly and effectively to security incidents. This includes processes for detection, containment, eradication, and recovery.

- Regular vulnerability assessments and penetration testing: Conducting regular assessments of the organization's systems, applications, and networks can help identify vulnerabilities that could be exploited by attackers. Penetration testing can be used to simulate real-world attacks and identify weaknesses.

- Implementing access controls and authentication mechanisms: Strong access controls, such as multi-factor authentication and role-based access control, can help prevent unauthorized access to systems and data.

It is important to note that risk mitigation strategies should be based on the specific risks identified and the organization's unique requirements. A comprehensive and layered approach should be employed, as no single solution can provide complete protection against all cybersecurity risks.

Continuous Monitoring and Review

Assessing and prioritizing cybersecurity risks is an ongoing process. It is crucial for organizations to continuously monitor the threat landscape and their own risk posture to ensure that risks are identified, assessed, and prioritized effectively. This involves regular review and updating of risk assessments, as well as adapting risk mitigation strategies to address emerging threats. Organizations should also incorporate lessons learned from security incidents and breaches into their risk assessment and mitigation processes.

Summary

Assessing and prioritizing cybersecurity risks is a critical component of effective cybersecurity governance and risk management. By identifying and quantifying potential risks, organizations can prioritize their efforts and allocate resources accordingly. This involves assessing the likelihood and impact of threats, as well as considering factors such as risk severity, risk appetite, cost, feasibility, and legal/regulatory requirements. Risk mitigation strategies should be developed based on the prioritized risks, and continuous monitoring and review should be conducted to ensure that risks are managed effectively. By taking a proactive and systematic approach to assessing and prioritizing cybersecurity risks, organizations can better protect their assets, systems, and data from potential threats.

Developing Risk Mitigation Strategies

In the constantly evolving landscape of cybersecurity, organizations face numerous potential risks that can compromise the confidentiality, integrity, and availability of their information and systems. These risks can come from both internal and external sources, such as malicious attacks, human errors, hardware failures, or natural disasters. To effectively manage these risks, organizations must develop robust risk mitigation strategies that aim to minimize the impact of potential threats.

Identifying Risks

The first step in developing risk mitigation strategies is to identify potential risks that an organization may face. This involves conducting a comprehensive risk assessment, which includes but is not limited to:

- **Asset Identification:** Determining the critical assets of an organization, including information assets, systems, infrastructure, and personnel.

- **Threat Assessment:** Identifying potential threats and vulnerabilities that could exploit the organization's assets. This includes external threats like hackers, malware, and social engineering, as well as internal threats like employee negligence or malicious actions.

- **Impact Analysis:** Assessing the potential impact of identified threats on the organization's assets, including financial, operational, reputational, and legal consequences.

- **Likelihood Assessment:** Evaluating the likelihood of each identified threat occurring based on historical data, trends, and expert knowledge.

By conducting a thorough risk assessment, organizations can gain a comprehensive understanding of the risks they face and prioritize them based on their likelihood and potential impact.

Assessing and Prioritizing Risks

Once the risks have been identified, organizations need to assess and prioritize them to allocate appropriate resources and develop tailored risk mitigation strategies. This involves considering the likelihood and potential impact of each risk and categorizing them into different risk levels. Common risk levels include low, medium, and high, or can be further categorized based on bespoke risk matrices developed by the organization.

To prioritize risks, organizations can use various techniques such as risk scoring or risk ranking. Risk scoring assigns a numerical value to each risk based on factors like likelihood, potential impact, and vulnerability. Risks with higher scores are given higher priority for mitigation. Risk ranking, on the other hand, involves comparing risks based on their relative importance and classifying them accordingly. This allows organizations to focus their efforts on addressing the most critical risks first.

Developing Risk Mitigation Strategies

Once risks have been assessed and prioritized, organizations can start developing risk mitigation strategies. The goal is to reduce the likelihood and impact of identified risks through a combination of preventive, detective, and corrective controls. Here are some key steps to consider when developing risk mitigation strategies:

1. **Risk Avoidance:** Organizations can choose to avoid certain risks altogether by eliminating or discontinuing activities that pose significant risks. This may involve shutting down high-risk systems, discarding outdated technology, or ending business relationships with unreliable partners.

2. **Risk Transfer:** Organizations can transfer the financial impact of risks to external entities by purchasing insurance policies or outsourcing certain activities to third-party vendors who assume the associated risks. This can help mitigate financial losses and provide additional expertise in managing specific risks.

3. **Risk Mitigation:** Risk mitigation involves implementing controls and safeguards to reduce the likelihood and impact of identified risks. This can include the use of firewalls, antivirus software, intrusion detection systems, encryption, access controls, and employee training programs. These measures aim to prevent or minimize the damage caused by potential threats.

4. **Risk Acceptance:** In certain cases where the cost of implementing risk mitigation measures outweighs the potential impact of the risk, organizations may choose to accept the risk. This decision should be made based on a thorough risk assessment and cost-benefit analysis to ensure that the organization's overall objectives are not compromised.

5. **Risk Monitoring and Review:** Risk mitigation strategies should include regular monitoring and review processes to ensure their effectiveness. This involves ongoing assessment of risks, periodic testing of control effectiveness, reviewing security incidents and lessons learned, and updating risk mitigation strategies as needed. This iterative process helps organizations adapt to emerging threats and changes in their risk landscape.

It is important for organizations to develop risk mitigation strategies that are aligned with their overall risk appetite, business objectives, and legal and regulatory requirements. These strategies should be regularly reviewed, updated, and communicated to relevant stakeholders to ensure their effectiveness and that they remain relevant in the face of evolving cyber threats.

Example: Developing Risk Mitigation Strategies for a Financial Institution

Consider a financial institution that has identified the following risks:

- **Risk 1:** Cyber-attacks targeting customer data and financial transactions.
- **Risk 2:** Insider threats, such as employees mishandling sensitive information or engaging in fraudulent activities.
- **Risk 3:** System failures causing disruptions in banking services.

The institution conducts a risk assessment and assigns risk levels to each identified risk based on likelihood and potential impact. Risk 1 is classified as high due to the increasing sophistication of cyber-attacks in the financial industry. Risk 2 is categorized as medium, considering the institution's strong employee screening and monitoring processes. Risk 3 is also classified as medium, given the institution's robust disaster recovery and business continuity measures.

To develop risk mitigation strategies, the financial institution follows these steps:

1. **Risk Avoidance:** To address Risk 1, the institution implements strict access controls, encryption, and multi-factor authentication to protect customer data and transactions. They also conduct regular security audits to identify and address vulnerabilities. By mitigating this risk, the institution aims to avoid significant financial and reputational damage caused by successful cyber-attacks.

2. **Risk Transfer:** The institution purchases comprehensive cyber insurance coverage that provides financial protection in case of a major security breach. This allows them to transfer a portion of the financial risk associated with Risk 1 to the insurance provider.

3. **Risk Mitigation:** To address both Risk 2 and Risk 3, the institution implements a combination of technical controls and human resource management practices. They regularly train employees on cybersecurity best practices to minimize the risk of insider threats. Additionally, they deploy redundant systems, backup power supplies, and off-site data storage to mitigate the risks associated with system failures.

4. **Risk Acceptance:** The institution accepts residual risks in cases where the cost of further mitigation measures outweighs the potential impact. For example, they may accept that a minimal risk of system downtime still exists even after implementing robust disaster recovery measures.

5. **Risk Monitoring and Review:** The financial institution establishes a dedicated cybersecurity team responsible for continuously monitoring and

reviewing the effectiveness of their risk mitigation strategies. This includes actively monitoring security logs, conducting periodic vulnerability assessments and penetration tests, and staying up to date with the latest cybersecurity trends and threats.

By following these risk mitigation strategies, the financial institution can enhance its cybersecurity posture, protect customer assets, and minimize potential financial losses caused by cyber-attacks and system failures.

Conclusion

Developing risk mitigation strategies is a critical aspect of cybersecurity sustainability. By identifying, assessing, and prioritizing risks, organizations can focus on addressing the most significant threats to their information and systems. The development of risk mitigation strategies involves a combination of risk avoidance, risk transfer, risk mitigation, risk acceptance, and ongoing risk monitoring and review. These strategies should be tailored to the organization's specific risk landscape and aligned with its risk appetite, business objectives, and legal and regulatory requirements. Regularly reviewing and updating risk mitigation strategies is essential to ensure their continued relevance and effectiveness in the face of evolving cyber threats.

Monitoring and Reviewing Cybersecurity Risk Controls

Monitoring and reviewing cybersecurity risk controls is a crucial aspect of maintaining an effective cybersecurity program. It involves continuously assessing and evaluating the effectiveness of implemented controls to ensure that they are adequate in mitigating risks and protecting the organization's assets. This section will discuss the importance of monitoring and reviewing cybersecurity risk controls, the key activities involved in this process, and some best practices to follow.

Importance of Monitoring and Reviewing Cybersecurity Risk Controls

Effective monitoring and reviewing of cybersecurity risk controls play a vital role in identifying potential vulnerabilities and weaknesses in an organization's security posture. By regularly assessing the implemented controls, organizations can detect any gaps or deficiencies in their cybersecurity measures and take appropriate actions to address them. This proactive approach helps in preventing security incidents and minimizing the potential impact of any breaches.

Moreover, monitoring and reviewing cyber risk controls provide valuable insights into the overall effectiveness of an organization's cybersecurity strategy. It allows stakeholders to measure the return on investment (ROI) of their security initiatives and make informed decisions about allocating resources for further improvements. By regularly monitoring and reviewing controls, organizations can continuously adapt and enhance their cybersecurity posture to keep up with the evolving threat landscape.

Key Activities in Monitoring and Reviewing Cybersecurity Risk Controls

The process of monitoring and reviewing cybersecurity risk controls involves several key activities to ensure comprehensive coverage and thorough evaluation. These activities can be categorized into the following steps:

1. **Establishing a Monitoring Framework** The first step in monitoring and reviewing cybersecurity risk controls is to establish a monitoring framework. This framework defines the key metrics, indicators, and monitoring tools that will be used to assess the effectiveness of controls. It should outline the frequency and scope of monitoring activities and provide clear guidelines for reporting and escalation of any identified issues.

2. **Regular Monitoring and Assessment** Once the monitoring framework is in place, organizations should conduct regular monitoring and assessment of their cybersecurity risk controls. This involves collecting and analyzing data from various sources, such as security logs, intrusion detection systems, vulnerability scans, and user activity reports. The goal is to detect any unusual or suspicious patterns that may indicate a potential security risk.

3. **Evaluating Control Effectiveness** During the monitoring process, organizations need to evaluate the effectiveness of their implemented controls. This evaluation involves comparing actual performance against predefined benchmarks or industry best practices. It helps in identifying whether the controls are functioning as intended and providing the desired level of protection.

4. **Incident Response and Remediation** In the event of a security incident or breach, organizations should have a well-defined incident response plan in place. The monitoring and review process play a crucial role in detecting and responding to incidents promptly. When an incident is detected, the organization should

follow the established procedures to mitigate the impact, investigate the root cause, and take appropriate actions to prevent recurrence.

5. **Continuous Improvement** Monitoring and reviewing cybersecurity risk controls should not be a one-time activity. It is an ongoing process that requires continuous improvement. Organizations should regularly review their monitoring frameworks, update control benchmarks, and incorporate lessons learned from past incidents to enhance their cybersecurity posture continuously.

Best Practices for Monitoring and Reviewing Cybersecurity Risk Controls

To ensure the effectiveness of the monitoring and review process, organizations should follow some best practices:

1. **Define Clear Objectives and Metrics** Clearly define the objectives of control monitoring and establish measurable metrics to track the effectiveness of controls. This helps in aligning monitoring activities with the organization's overall cybersecurity strategy and enables meaningful analysis of data.

2. **Automate Monitoring Processes** Utilize automated tools and technologies to streamline monitoring and data collection processes. Automation can help in handling large volumes of data, detecting anomalies, and generating alerts in real-time, enabling timely response to potential threats.

3. **Establish Key Performance Indicators (KPIs)** Develop KPIs that reflect the goals and objectives of the cybersecurity program. These KPIs should be regularly monitored and reported to management to demonstrate the effectiveness of the controls and identify areas for improvement.

4. **Conduct Regular Audits** Periodically conduct independent audits to validate the effectiveness of monitoring and review processes. Audits can identify any gaps or weaknesses and provide recommendations for enhancing the control environment.

5. **Foster Collaboration and Communication** Promote collaboration and open communication between different stakeholders involved in the monitoring and review process. This includes IT teams, management, internal audit, and external partners. Effective communication ensures that issues are identified and addressed promptly.

6. Stay Updated with Emerging Threats Keep abreast of the latest cybersecurity threats and trends. Regularly review and update control benchmarks to align with the evolving threat landscape. This helps in adapting controls to new and emerging risks.

7. Provide Continuous Training and Education Invest in training and education programs for employees involved in the monitoring and review process. This ensures that they have the necessary skills and knowledge to effectively identify, assess, and respond to security risks.

In conclusion, monitoring and reviewing cybersecurity risk controls are critical processes for maintaining a robust security posture. By establishing a monitoring framework, regularly assessing control effectiveness, and implementing best practices, organizations can proactively identify security vulnerabilities and take appropriate actions to prevent incidents. Continuous monitoring and improvement are essential for adapting controls to evolving threats and ensuring the long-term sustainability of cybersecurity measures.

Continuous Improvement in Cybersecurity Risk Management

Continuous improvement is a fundamental aspect of effective cybersecurity risk management. As the threat landscape evolves and new vulnerabilities emerge, organizations must continuously adapt their security measures to mitigate risks. This section explores the importance of continuous improvement in cybersecurity risk management, outlines the key steps involved, and provides practical strategies to achieve continuous improvement.

Importance of Continuous Improvement

In today's rapidly changing digital world, cyber threats are becoming more sophisticated and diverse. Adversaries constantly develop new attack techniques, exploit emerging technologies, and identify vulnerabilities in software and systems. To effectively manage cybersecurity risks, organizations must adopt a proactive approach that allows for ongoing assessment and enhancement of their security posture.

Continuous improvement in cybersecurity risk management is important for several reasons. Firstly, it enables organizations to stay ahead of emerging threats by identifying and addressing vulnerabilities before they are exploited. By regularly reviewing and updating security controls, organizations can build resilience and reduce the likelihood and impact of security breaches.

Secondly, continuous improvement helps organizations align their security measures with changing business objectives and technological advancements. As organizations introduce new technologies, such as cloud computing or IoT devices, their risk landscape evolves. Continuous improvement ensures that security controls adapt accordingly to protect these new assets, data, and systems.

Lastly, continuous improvement is essential for maintaining regulatory compliance and meeting industry standards. Many regulatory frameworks, such as the General Data Protection Regulation (GDPR) and Payment Card Industry Data Security Standard (PCI DSS), require organizations to implement effective cybersecurity risk management practices and regularly assess and improve their security controls.

Key Steps in Continuous Improvement

Continuous improvement in cybersecurity risk management involves a cyclical process that consists of several key steps:

1. **Risk Assessment:** The first step in continuous improvement is to conduct a comprehensive risk assessment. This involves identifying and assessing cybersecurity risks, determining their potential impact on the organization, and prioritizing them based on their likelihood and severity. Risk assessment should be performed regularly and whenever significant changes occur in the organization's environment.

2. **Gap Analysis:** Once risks are identified, a gap analysis should be conducted to identify deficiencies and areas for improvement in the current security controls. This involves comparing the existing security measures against industry best practices, regulatory requirements, and organizational objectives. The gap analysis helps identify areas where additional controls or enhancements are needed.

3. **Action Plan:** Based on the results of the risk assessment and gap analysis, an action plan should be developed. This plan outlines the specific steps required to address the identified gaps and improve the organization's security posture. The action plan should include clear goals, timelines, and responsibilities for each action item.

4. **Implementation:** The identified security improvements from the action plan should be implemented according to the established timelines. This may involve deploying new security technologies, enhancing existing controls, providing training to employees, or updating policies and procedures. Effective implementation requires coordination and collaboration among various stakeholders, including IT teams, security professionals, and senior management.

5. **Monitoring and Evaluation:** Continuous monitoring and evaluation are crucial to ensure that the implemented improvements are effective in mitigating risks. This involves regularly monitoring security controls, analyzing security incidents and vulnerabilities, and measuring the effectiveness of the implemented measures. Key performance indicators (KPIs) and metrics should be defined to assess the performance of the security controls and measure the organization's overall security posture.

6. **Feedback and Learning:** Feedback mechanisms should be established to gather input from various stakeholders and learn from security incidents and near misses. This feedback can help identify areas where further improvements are needed and allow the organization to continuously enhance its security measures. Lessons learned should be documented and shared with relevant teams and integrated into future risk assessments and improvement plans.

Strategies for Continuous Improvement

Achieving continuous improvement in cybersecurity risk management requires a structured and proactive approach. Here are some key strategies that can help organizations foster continuous improvement:

1. **Stay Informed:** To effectively manage cybersecurity risks, organizations must stay current with the evolving threat landscape. This involves keeping up-to-date with the latest vulnerabilities, attack techniques, and industry best practices. Regularly monitoring cybersecurity information sources, such as threat intelligence feeds, industry forums, and government advisories, can provide valuable insights to inform risk assessments and improvement plans.

2. **Foster a Culture of Security:** Building a strong security culture is essential for driving continuous improvement. Organizations should promote security awareness and provide ongoing training to employees to ensure they understand their roles and responsibilities in safeguarding critical assets and data. Training should cover topics such as phishing awareness, secure coding practices, and incident reporting procedures.

3. **Engage Stakeholders:** Continuous improvement is a collective effort that involves engagement from various stakeholders, including top management, IT teams, end-users, and third-party vendors. Regular communication, coordination, and collaboration among these stakeholders are crucial for identifying and addressing security gaps and implementing effective security measures.

4. **Regularly Assess and Test Controls:** Organizations should establish periodic assessments and tests of their security controls to ensure their effectiveness. Vulnerability assessments and penetration testing can help identify

weaknesses and vulnerabilities in systems and networks. Regular security audits and compliance assessments can also provide valuable insights for continuous improvement.

5. **Adopt Security Frameworks and Standards:** Implementing recognized security frameworks and standards, such as ISO 27001 or NIST Cybersecurity Framework, can provide a structured approach for continuous improvement. These frameworks provide guidelines, best practices, and control objectives that organizations can align their security measures with. They also offer a roadmap for ongoing assessment, improvement, and compliance.

6. **Learn from Incidents:** Security incidents and breaches offer valuable opportunities to learn and improve. Organizations should conduct thorough investigations and post-mortems following incidents to identify root causes, understand the impact, and implement corrective actions to prevent future occurrences. Lessons learned should be shared with relevant teams and integrated into risk assessments and improvement plans.

Example: Continuous Improvement in Patch Management

Patch management is a critical aspect of cybersecurity risk management. Vulnerabilities in operating systems, applications, and firmware can be exploited by attackers to gain unauthorized access or launch attacks. Continuous improvement in patch management can significantly enhance an organization's security posture. Here's an example of how continuous improvement can be applied to patch management:

- **Risk Assessment:** Conduct a risk assessment to identify the vulnerabilities that pose the highest risk to the organization based on the potential impact and likelihood of exploitation.

- **Gap Analysis:** Perform a gap analysis to evaluate the effectiveness of the current patch management process. Identify areas for improvement, such as delays in patch deployment, inconsistent patching across systems, or lack of visibility into patch status.

- **Action Plan:** Develop an action plan that outlines specific steps to address the identified gaps. This may include implementing a centralized patch management system, defining patch management policies and procedures, and establishing clear roles and responsibilities.

- **Implementation:** Implement the planned improvements, including the deployment of a patch management system, establishment of patch deployment schedules, and automation of patching processes where possible.

- **Monitoring and Evaluation:** Continuously monitor the patch management process to ensure patches are being deployed in a timely manner. Measure key metrics such as patch deployment success rate, time to deploy patches, and the number of unpatched systems.

- **Feedback and Learning:** Gather feedback from system administrators and end-users regarding the patch management process. Regularly review incident reports and vulnerability assessments to identify any recurring issues or patterns and take corrective actions as necessary.

By following this continuous improvement process, organizations can enhance their patch management process, reduce the window of exposure to vulnerabilities, and improve their overall security posture.

Conclusion

Continuous improvement is an essential component of effective cybersecurity risk management. By continuously assessing, enhancing, and adapting security measures, organizations can mitigate risks and stay resilient in an ever-evolving threat landscape. This section discussed the importance of continuous improvement, outlined the key steps involved, and provided practical strategies for achieving continuous improvement. Applying these principles and strategies can help organizations build robust cybersecurity programs and protect their valuable assets and information from emerging threats. It is important to remember that continuous improvement is an ongoing process and should be embedded in the organization's culture to ensure the effectiveness and sustainability of cybersecurity risk management efforts.

Incident Response and Business Continuity Planning

Incident response and business continuity planning are crucial components of an effective cybersecurity program. In this section, we will explore the principles and practices of incident response and business continuity planning, highlighting their importance in mitigating the impact of cybersecurity incidents and ensuring the resilience of an organization.

Incident Response

Incident response refers to the process of handling and managing a cybersecurity incident in a timely and effective manner. It involves detecting, analyzing, and responding to security incidents to minimize the damage caused and restore normal operations as quickly as possible. The goal of incident response is to contain the incident, investigate its cause, and prevent similar incidents from occurring in the future.

Incident Response Lifecycle The incident response lifecycle consists of several phases that guide the actions and activities of the incident response team. These phases include:

1. **Preparation:** This phase involves the development and implementation of an incident response plan. It includes defining roles and responsibilities, establishing communication channels, and creating a framework for incident reporting and escalation.
2. **Detection and Analysis:** In this phase, security monitoring systems and tools are used to detect and analyze potential incidents. This may involve analyzing log files, network traffic, or system behavior to identify suspicious activities or indicators of compromise.
3. **Containment and Eradication:** Once an incident is confirmed, the focus shifts to containing the incident to prevent further damage. This may involve isolating affected systems, disabling compromised accounts, or blocking malicious IP addresses. After containment, the incident response team works to eradicate the root cause of the incident and restore affected systems.
4. **Recovery:** The recovery phase involves restoring normal operations and recovering any lost data or functionality. This may include rebuilding systems, restoring backups, or implementing additional security measures to prevent future incidents.
5. **Lessons Learned:** After the incident is resolved, it is essential to conduct a thorough post-incident analysis to identify lessons learned and improve the organization's incident response capabilities. This includes documenting the incident, evaluating the effectiveness of the response, and updating the incident response plan accordingly.

Roles and Responsibilities Effective incident response requires clear roles and responsibilities within the organization. The following roles are typically involved in incident response:

1. **Incident Response Team (IRT):** This team is responsible for coordinating and executing the incident response plan. It includes members from various departments, such as IT, security, legal, and communications.

2. **Incident Coordinator:** The incident coordinator is responsible for overall coordination and management of the incident response process. They ensure that appropriate actions are taken, resources are allocated, and stakeholders are informed.

3. **Technical Analysts:** Technical analysts investigate and analyze security incidents. They gather evidence, perform forensic analysis, and identify the root cause of the incident.

4. **Communications Coordinator:** The communications coordinator handles the communication aspects of the incident response process. They are responsible for notifying stakeholders, managing public relations, and ensuring consistent messaging.

5. **Legal and Compliance:** Legal and compliance personnel provide guidance on legal and regulatory requirements during an incident. They ensure that the response process aligns with legal obligations and assists with any reporting or notification requirements.

Incident Response Tools Various tools and technologies support the incident response process. These tools aid in incident detection, analysis, containment, and recovery. Some essential incident response tools include:

1. **Security Information and Event Management (SIEM):** SIEM tools collect and analyze log data from various sources to detect and alert on security events.

2. **Endpoint Detection and Response (EDR):** EDR tools provide real-time visibility into endpoint activities and detect suspicious or malicious behavior.

3. **Forensic Tools:** Forensic tools help gather and analyze digital evidence during an incident investigation. They assist in identifying the source and impact of the incident.

4. **Threat Intelligence Platforms:** Threat intelligence platforms provide real-time information about known threats and vulnerabilities, enhancing incident detection and response.

Business Continuity Planning

Business continuity planning (BCP) aims to ensure the availability of critical business processes and services during and after a disruptive event, including cybersecurity incidents. BCP focuses on developing strategies and procedures to minimize the impact of incidents and facilitate the recovery of business operations.

Business Impact Analysis A business impact analysis (BIA) is a critical component of business continuity planning. It assesses the potential impact of disruptions on business operations and identifies the necessary recovery strategies. The BIA helps prioritize critical processes, resources, and systems, ensuring effective allocation of resources during incident response.

The BIA includes the following steps:

1. **Identify Critical Business Processes:** Identify and define the organization's critical business processes, which are essential for its survival and must be quickly restored after an incident.
2. **Assess Impact and Dependencies:** Determine the impact of disruptions to critical processes and identify their dependencies on systems, resources, and personnel.
3. **Establish Recovery Time Objectives (RTO) and Recovery Point Objectives (RPO):** Define the acceptable time frame for restoring critical processes (RTO) and the maximum amount of data loss acceptable (RPO) for each process.
4. **Identify Recovery Strategies:** Develop recovery strategies to minimize downtime and restore critical processes within the defined RTO and RPO. This may involve having redundant systems, backup data, or alternative work locations.
5. **Plan Development:** Document the recovery strategies and procedures in a business continuity plan. The plan should include detailed instructions, roles and responsibilities, communication procedures, and testing/validation procedures.

Testing and Validation Regular testing and validation of the business continuity plan are essential to ensure its effectiveness. Testing allows organizations to identify and address gaps or weaknesses in the plan, validate recovery strategies, and train personnel in their roles and responsibilities.

Common testing methodologies include:

1. **Tabletop Exercises:** Tabletop exercises involve scenario-based discussions and decision-making to test the effectiveness and coordination of the business continuity plan. It helps identify gaps in knowledge, coordination, or procedures.
2. **Functional Exercises:** Functional exercises simulate a partial disruption to test specific elements of the business continuity plan. It involves executing specific recovery strategies and validating their effectiveness.
3. **Full-Scale Exercises:** Full-scale exercises simulate a complete disruption and test the end-to-end functionality of the business continuity plan. It involves activating the plan, mobilizing resources, and recovering critical processes.

Regular testing and validation ensure that the business continuity plan remains up to date, aligned with organizational changes, and capable of effectively responding to incidents.

Conclusion

Incident response and business continuity planning are critical aspects of a robust cybersecurity program. They enable organizations to respond swiftly and effectively to security incidents, minimize the impact of disruptions, and ensure the continuity of critical business operations. By understanding and implementing the principles and practices of incident response and business continuity planning, organizations can enhance their resilience against cybersecurity threats and maintain their competitive edge in a rapidly evolving threat landscape.

In the next section, we will delve into the privacy and legal aspects of cybersecurity, exploring the laws, regulations, and considerations organizations must navigate to protect the privacy of individuals and ensure compliance with legal requirements.

Cybersecurity Assurance and Compliance

Cybersecurity Audit and Assurance

In the ever-evolving landscape of cybersecurity, organizations face numerous threats and challenges that test the integrity and security of their information systems. To ensure that their systems are adequately protected, organizations must take proactive measures to assess and mitigate risks. One such measure is conducting cybersecurity audits and implementing assurance practices. In this section, we will explore the concept of cybersecurity audit and assurance, its purpose, process, and key considerations.

Definition of Cybersecurity Audit and Assurance

Cybersecurity audit and assurance is a systematic and independent examination of an organization's cybersecurity controls, policies, and practices to determine their effectiveness and adherence to established standards, regulations, and best practices. The goal of cybersecurity audit and assurance is to assess the organization's ability to protect its information assets from unauthorized access, disclosure, alteration, destruction, and disruption. It involves evaluating the organization's cybersecurity governance, risk management, compliance with regulations, and overall security posture.

Purpose of Cybersecurity Audit and Assurance

Cybersecurity audit and assurance serve multiple purposes within an organization. Some of the key objectives are:

1. **Assessing the effectiveness of cybersecurity controls:** Audits help identify any vulnerabilities or weaknesses in an organization's cybersecurity controls and provide recommendations for improvement. This enables the organization to strengthen its defense mechanisms and reduce the risk of cybersecurity incidents.

2. **Ensuring compliance with regulations and standards:** Audits help ensure that the organization is compliant with relevant cybersecurity regulations and standards. Compliance is essential to protect the organization from legal and financial consequences resulting from non-compliance.

3. **Identifying gaps in cybersecurity governance:** Audits evaluate the organization's cybersecurity governance practices, including the roles and responsibilities of key stakeholders, to ensure that cybersecurity is integrated into the organization's overall governance framework effectively.

4. **Enhancing stakeholder trust:** Organizations that undergo cybersecurity audits and provide assurance to stakeholders demonstrate their commitment to protecting sensitive information, which builds trust and confidence among customers, partners, and shareholders.

Cybersecurity Audit Process

The cybersecurity audit process typically involves the following stages:

1. **Planning and scoping:** This stage involves defining the scope of the audit, determining the objectives, and developing a detailed plan. The scope may include specific systems, processes, or areas within the organization that are most critical or vulnerable to cybersecurity risks.

2. **Risk assessment:** The next step is to assess the organization's cybersecurity risks. This involves identifying potential threats, vulnerabilities, and their impact on the organization's information assets. Risk assessment enables auditors to prioritize their audit activities and focus on the areas of highest risk.

3. **Control evaluation:** In this stage, auditors examine the organization's cybersecurity controls to determine their effectiveness. This may involve reviewing security policies, procedures, technical controls, and operational practices. Auditors may conduct interviews, review documentation, and perform testing to gather evidence and assess the controls' adequacy.

4. **Findings and recommendations:** Based on the control evaluation, auditors identify any deficiencies or weaknesses in the organization's cybersecurity controls. They provide detailed findings and recommendations to address these issues, improve security, and mitigate identified risks. Recommendations may include implementing additional controls, enhancing existing controls, or revising policies and procedures.

5. **Reporting and follow-up:** The final stage involves preparing an audit report that summarizes the findings, recommendations, and overall assessment of the organization's cybersecurity posture. The report is shared with management and stakeholders, highlighting areas of improvement and providing guidance for remediation actions. Auditors may also follow up to ensure that recommended actions are implemented appropriately.

Key Considerations in Cybersecurity Audit and Assurance

When conducting a cybersecurity audit, there are several key considerations that auditors should keep in mind:

1. **Relevance of cybersecurity standards and frameworks:** Auditors should be familiar with relevant cybersecurity standards and frameworks, such as ISO 27001, NIST Cybersecurity Framework, and CIS Controls. These provide guidance on best practices and help assess the adequacy of cybersecurity controls.

2. **Engagement with stakeholders:** Effective communication and collaboration with key stakeholders are crucial throughout the audit process. This ensures that all relevant perspectives are considered, that audit objectives align with organizational goals, and that findings and recommendations are clearly understood.

3. **Technical expertise:** Cybersecurity audits often involve assessing complex technical controls and systems. Auditors should possess the necessary technical expertise to understand and evaluate these controls effectively.

This may require specialized knowledge in areas such as network security, encryption, access controls, and vulnerability management.

4. **Continuous monitoring and improvement:** Cybersecurity threats and risks are constantly evolving. Auditors should emphasize the importance of continuous monitoring and improvement as part of the audit process. This includes regular reassessment of controls, staying updated on emerging threats and technologies, and adapting audit practices to address new challenges.

Real-world Example: Cybersecurity Audit in a Financial Institution

Consider a financial institution that wants to enhance its cybersecurity posture through an audit. The institution collaborates with an external audit firm to conduct a comprehensive cybersecurity audit. The audit firm follows a systematic approach, starting with scoping the audit to cover critical systems, processes, and regulatory requirements relevant to the financial industry.

During control evaluation, the audit firm reviews the institution's cybersecurity policies, access controls, data encryption practices, incident response procedures, and third-party risk management protocols. They conduct interviews with key stakeholders, examine technical configurations, and analyze security logs. Through this evaluation, the auditors identify several areas for improvement, including outdated controls, inadequate patch management processes, and insufficient user awareness training.

Based on the findings, the audit firm prepares a detailed report, including specific recommendations for the institution. These recommendations include implementing multi-factor authentication, enhancing network monitoring capabilities, conducting regular vulnerability assessments, and providing ongoing cybersecurity training to employees. The institution then takes action by implementing the recommended controls and addressing the identified gaps, thereby strengthening its cybersecurity defenses.

Conclusion

Cybersecurity audit and assurance play a vital role in assessing and enhancing an organization's cybersecurity posture. By evaluating cybersecurity controls, ensuring compliance with regulations, and identifying areas for improvement, audits help organizations protect their information assets from evolving cyber threats. Effective cybersecurity audit practices require a comprehensive approach, technical expertise, engagement with stakeholders, and a focus on continuous monitoring and improvement.

Compliance with Cybersecurity Regulations and Standards

Compliance with cybersecurity regulations and standards is an essential component of an effective cybersecurity program. In this section, we will explore the importance of compliance, discuss key regulations and standards in the field, and provide guidance on achieving and maintaining compliance.

Importance of Compliance

Compliance with cybersecurity regulations and standards is crucial for several reasons. First and foremost, it helps organizations protect their sensitive data and systems from security breaches and cyber attacks. Compliance requirements often include specific security controls, practices, and procedures that are designed to mitigate known vulnerabilities and protect against emerging threats.

Secondly, compliance helps build trust and confidence among stakeholders. Organizations that demonstrate a commitment to cybersecurity by meeting regulatory requirements and following industry best practices are seen as more reliable and trustworthy by customers, partners, and investors. Compliance can also help organizations avoid legal and financial consequences associated with non-compliance.

Furthermore, compliance with cybersecurity regulations and standards promotes a proactive and risk-based approach to cybersecurity. By aligning their cybersecurity practices with established frameworks, organizations can identify and prioritize security risks, implement appropriate controls, and continuously monitor and improve their security posture.

Key Regulations and Standards

There are numerous cybersecurity regulations and standards that organizations need to be aware of and comply with. Here, we will discuss some of the most important ones:

1. **General Data Protection Regulation** (GDPR): GDPR is a European Union regulation that sets guidelines for the collection, processing, and protection of personal data of EU residents. It applies to all organizations that handle EU citizens' data, regardless of their location. GDPR emphasizes the protection

of individual privacy rights and imposes strict penalties for non-compliance, including fines up to €20 million or 4

2. **Payment Card Industry Data Security Standard (PCI DSS):** PCI DSS is a set of security standards enforced by the major card brands (Visa, Mastercard, etc.) to protect credit cardholder data. Organizations that handle payment card transactions are required to comply with PCI DSS. The standard includes requirements related to network security, access control, and encryption, among others. Non-compliance with PCI DSS can result in significant fines and the loss of the ability to process credit card transactions.

3. **Health Insurance Portability and Accountability Act (HIPAA):** HIPAA sets standards for the protection of individually identifiable health information. It applies to healthcare providers, health plans, and other entities that handle health information. HIPAA requires the implementation of administrative, physical, and technical safeguards to protect the privacy and security of health data. Non-compliance with HIPAA can lead to substantial penalties and reputational damage.

4. **ISO 27001:** ISO 27001 is an international standard that provides a framework for establishing, implementing, maintaining, and continually improving an information security management system (ISMS). Compliance with ISO 27001 ensures that an organization has implemented a comprehensive set of controls to manage information security risks.

5. **National Institute of Standards and Technology (NIST) Cybersecurity Framework:** The NIST Cybersecurity Framework is a voluntary framework developed by the U.S. government to help organizations manage and reduce cybersecurity risks. It provides a common language for organizations to communicate about cybersecurity and a framework for assessing and improving their cybersecurity practices.

It is important to note that compliance requirements may vary based on the industry, geographical location, and specific business operations of an organization. Therefore, it is essential for organizations to identify and understand the regulations and standards that are applicable to their specific circumstances.

Achieving and Maintaining Compliance

Achieving and maintaining compliance with cybersecurity regulations and standards requires a systematic and proactive approach. Here are some key steps to consider:

1. **Assessing Regulatory Requirements:** Start by identifying the specific regulations and standards that are applicable to your organization. Conduct a thorough assessment to understand the requirements and determine the gaps between your current practices and the compliance requirements.

2. **Developing a Compliance Program:** Establish a formal compliance program that outlines the policies, procedures, and controls to meet the regulatory requirements. The program should clearly define roles and responsibilities, establish accountability, and provide guidance on implementing and maintaining compliance.

3. **Implementing Controls:** Implement the necessary technical and organizational controls to meet the compliance requirements. This may include measures such as access controls, encryption, incident response procedures, and employee training programs. Ensure that the controls are regularly tested and audited to ensure their effectiveness.

4. **Monitoring and Reporting:** Establish a process for ongoing monitoring and reporting of compliance activities. Regularly review security logs, conduct internal and external audits, and generate compliance reports to identify any deviations and take appropriate corrective actions.

5. **Continuous Improvement:** Compliance is not a one-time effort but an ongoing process. Continuously monitor the regulatory landscape, stay updated on emerging threats and vulnerabilities, and adapt your cybersecurity program accordingly. Regularly review and update your compliance program to reflect changes in regulations and standards.

Challenges and Considerations

Compliance with cybersecurity regulations and standards can be challenging for organizations. Here are some common challenges and considerations to keep in mind:

1. **Complexity of Regulatory Requirements:** Regulations and standards can be complex and sometimes difficult to interpret. It is essential to invest time and

resources in understanding the specific requirements and seeking guidance from experts if needed.

2. **Evolution of Threat Landscape:** The cybersecurity threat landscape is constantly evolving, with new threats and vulnerabilities emerging regularly. Compliance programs need to be flexible and adaptable to address emerging risks and incorporate new security controls as needed.

3. **Resource Constraints:** Compliance efforts often require significant resources, including financial investments, skilled personnel, and dedicated time and effort. Organizations need to allocate appropriate resources to ensure effective compliance management.

4. **Third-party Compliance:** Organizations often rely on third-party vendors and service providers to handle critical data and systems. It is important to ensure that these third parties also adhere to relevant compliance requirements and have appropriate security measures in place.

5. **Audits and Assessments:** Compliance often involves audits and assessments by external parties. Organizations should be prepared for these audits and maintain proper documentation and evidence to demonstrate compliance with the relevant regulations and standards.

In conclusion, compliance with cybersecurity regulations and standards is essential for organizations to protect sensitive data, build trust, and ensure a proactive approach to cybersecurity. By understanding the requirements, implementing appropriate controls, and continuously monitoring and improving their security posture, organizations can successfully achieve and maintain compliance, effectively mitigating cyber risks and protecting their assets.

Security Metrics and Key Performance Indicators

In the field of cybersecurity, measuring the effectiveness of security measures is crucial for organizations to assess their overall security posture and make informed decisions about resource allocation and risk management. Security metrics and key performance indicators (KPIs) play a vital role in this process by providing quantifiable measures of security performance and helping organizations track their progress towards security goals.

Importance of Security Metrics and KPIs

Security metrics and KPIs provide objective and measurable data that can be used to evaluate the effectiveness of security controls, identify vulnerabilities and threats, and measure the impact of security initiatives. They enable organizations to:

- Assess the overall security posture: Security metrics provide a snapshot of an organization's security posture by measuring the performance of security controls, the effectiveness of incident response processes, and the level of compliance with security policies and regulations.

- Identify security weaknesses and trends: By continuously monitoring and analyzing security metrics, organizations can identify patterns, trends, and vulnerabilities in their security infrastructure. This information is invaluable for making proactive decisions and implementing necessary improvements to mitigate risks.

- Prioritize security investments: Security metrics help organizations prioritize investments in security tools, technologies, and resources. By analyzing the impact of security initiatives and measuring their return on investment, organizations can allocate resources effectively and focus on areas that need improvement.

- Demonstrate security performance: Security metrics provide a way to communicate security performance both internally and externally. Organizations can use these metrics to demonstrate compliance with regulations, assure stakeholders, and build trust with customers and partners.

Common Security Metrics and KPIs

There are various types of security metrics and KPIs that organizations can use to measure different aspects of their cybersecurity program. Let's explore some common security metrics and KPIs:

- **Number of security incidents:** This metric measures the total number of security incidents over a specific period. It provides an overview of the organization's security incident response effectiveness and helps identify trends or patterns that need attention.

- **Mean time to detect** (MTTD): MTTD measures the average time it takes for an organization to detect a security incident or breach. A lower MTTD indicates a more efficient detection and monitoring capability, enabling swift response to mitigate the impact of the incident.

- **Mean time to respond** (MTTR): MTTR measures the average time it takes for an organization to respond to a security incident after detection. A lower MTTR indicates a more effective incident response process, reducing the overall impact and consequences of security incidents.

- **Percentage of vulnerabilities patched:** This metric assesses the organization's ability to patch security vulnerabilities within a specified timeframe. It helps identify potential weaknesses in the patch management process and highlights areas where improvements are necessary.

- **Security awareness training completion rate:** This metric measures the percentage of employees who have completed security awareness training. It provides insights into the organization's efforts to educate and empower employees to contribute to a secure work environment.

- **Compliance with security policies:** This metric evaluates the organization's adherence to established security policies and standards. It measures the degree to which employees and systems comply with security controls and processes.

- **Number of unauthorized access attempts:** This metric represents the total number of unauthorized attempts to access the organization's systems or data. It helps gauge the effectiveness of access controls and detect potential security breaches.

Challenges and Considerations

While security metrics and KPIs are invaluable in assessing security performance, there are several challenges and considerations that organizations must keep in mind:

- **Relevance and alignment:** The metrics chosen should align with the organization's security goals and objectives. They should be relevant to the specific industry, context, and risk landscape to provide meaningful insights.

- **Data accuracy and availability:** It is crucial to ensure the accuracy, integrity, and availability of the data used to calculate metrics. Organizations should invest in tools and processes that collect and analyze data from reliable sources.

- **Benchmarking:** Comparing security metrics against industry benchmarks can provide organizations with insights into their relative performance. However, obtaining accurate benchmark data can be challenging due to the variability of security environments and the lack of standardized metrics across industries.

- **Avoiding data overload:** While it is important to collect relevant data, organizations should avoid collecting excessive data that may overwhelm the analysis process. Focusing on meaningful and actionable metrics is key.

- **Balancing quantitative and qualitative metrics:** While quantitative metrics provide objective data, qualitative metrics, such as feedback from security awareness programs or expert assessments, can provide additional insights into security performance.

- **Continuous improvement:** Security metrics should be reviewed and updated regularly to ensure that they remain relevant and aligned with the evolving threat landscape and organizational objectives.

Case Study: Measuring Effectiveness of Endpoint Protection

Let's consider a case study to illustrate the use of security metrics and KPIs in measuring the effectiveness of endpoint protection, a critical component of any cybersecurity program.

Scenario: A large financial institution implemented an advanced endpoint protection solution to safeguard their endpoints from malware and other threats. They want to measure the effectiveness of the solution and identify areas for improvement.

Metrics and KPIs: The organization can consider the following metrics:

- **Endpoint infection rate:** This metric measures the number of endpoints infected with malware over a specific period. A lower infection rate indicates the effectiveness of the endpoint protection solution in preventing malware infections.

- **Mean time to remediate (MTTR):** MTTR measures the average time it takes to remediate malware-infected endpoints. A lower MTTR suggests an efficient incident response process and a timely restoration of affected endpoints.
- **Number of false positives:** This metric measures the number of alerts triggered by the endpoint protection solution that are found to be false positives after investigation. A lower number indicates the accuracy and effectiveness of the solution in detecting genuine threats.
- **Endpoint compliance rate:** This metric assesses the percentage of endpoints that are compliant with the organization's security policies and configurations. A higher compliance rate indicates the successful deployment and enforcement of security controls on endpoints.

Conclusion

Security metrics and key performance indicators are essential tools for organizations to evaluate their cybersecurity program's effectiveness, monitor security performance, and make informed decisions. By selecting and analyzing relevant metrics, organizations can identify vulnerabilities, measure the impact of security controls, and prioritize investments in security improvement. However, it is critical to address challenges such as data accuracy, relevance, and avoiding data overload to ensure that security metrics provide valuable insights. Continuously reviewing and refining security metrics will contribute to a robust and sustainable cybersecurity program.

Incident Response and Disaster Recovery Planning

Incident response and disaster recovery planning are critical components of a robust cybersecurity program. In this section, we will explore the concepts, best practices, and key considerations for effectively managing and recovering from cybersecurity incidents and disasters.

Understanding Incident Response

Cybersecurity incidents refer to any unauthorized activity or compromise of computer systems, networks, or data that has the potential to impact the confidentiality, integrity, or availability of information. Incident response is a structured approach to addressing and managing these incidents in a timely and efficient manner.

The Incident Response Lifecycle: Incident response follows a well-defined process that includes the following stages:

1. **Preparation:** This phase involves establishing incident response policies, procedures, and plans. It includes defining roles and responsibilities, deciding on escalation procedures, and identifying the necessary tools and technologies for incident response.
2. **Detection and Analysis:** This stage involves monitoring and detecting potential incidents. It includes analyzing the scope and impact of the incident, identifying the root cause, and classifying the incident based on severity and priority.
3. **Containment and Eradication:** In this phase, the incident is contained to prevent further damage or spread. The focus is on reducing the impact, eliminating the root cause, and eradicating any compromised systems or malware.
4. **Recovery:** The recovery phase involves restoring the affected systems, networks, and data to their normal state. This may include recovering from backups, applying patches and updates, and implementing additional security controls to prevent similar incidents in the future.
5. **Post-Incident Analysis:** After the incident is resolved, a comprehensive post-incident analysis is conducted to understand the lessons learned, identify areas for improvement, and update incident response plans and procedures accordingly.

Creating an Incident Response Plan: An incident response plan serves as a guide for handling cybersecurity incidents effectively. It outlines the necessary steps and procedures to be followed during an incident and ensures a coordinated response across the organization.

A comprehensive incident response plan should include:

1. **Roles and Responsibilities:** Clearly define the roles and responsibilities of individuals involved in the incident response process. This includes designating an incident response team leader, communication coordinator, technical experts, and legal, public relations, and executive contacts.
2. **Communication Procedures:** Establish clear communication channels and protocols for reporting and escalating incidents both internally and externally. This includes contact details for key stakeholders, incident reporting templates, and predefined notification lists.
3. **Detection and Analysis:** Define the tools, technologies, and processes for detecting and analyzing potential incidents. This may include antivirus software, intrusion detection systems, log analysis tools, and incident response playbooks.

4. **Containment and Eradication:** Outline the procedures and steps to be followed to contain the incident, limit its impact, and eradicate the root cause. This may include isolating affected systems, shutting down network segments, or applying patches and updates.

5. **Recovery and Restoration:** Define the processes and methods for recovering from an incident and restoring systems, networks, and data to a normal state. This may involve restoring from backups, reconfiguring systems, or rebuilding compromised environments.

6. **Post-Incident Analysis and Lessons Learned:** Establish a process for conducting a thorough analysis of the incident, identifying the root cause, and capturing lessons learned. This information can be used to update incident response plans, improve security controls, and enhance the overall cybersecurity posture.

Understanding Disaster Recovery Planning

Disaster recovery planning focuses on ensuring business continuity in the event of a major cybersecurity incident or natural disaster. It involves developing strategies, procedures, and technologies to recover critical systems, applications, and data to minimize downtime and ensure the organization can resume its operations as quickly as possible.

Business Impact Analysis (BIA): Before developing a disaster recovery plan, it is essential to conduct a business impact analysis (BIA) to identify critical business processes and their dependencies on IT systems and resources. The BIA helps prioritize recovery efforts and allocate resources effectively.

Key Elements of a Disaster Recovery Plan: A comprehensive disaster recovery plan should include the following key elements:

1. **Recovery Point Objective (RPO):** The RPO is the maximum acceptable amount of data loss that an organization can tolerate in the event of a disaster. It defines the frequency of backups or replication mechanisms required to ensure data can be restored to an acceptable state.

2. **Recovery Time Objective (RTO):** The RTO is the maximum tolerable downtime for critical systems and applications. It defines the timeframe within which systems and applications must be restored to a functioning state after a disaster.

3. **Backup and Recovery Procedures:** Define backup schedules, retention policies, and restoration procedures for critical systems, applications, and data.

This may include regular full backups, incremental backups, offsite storage, and testing of the restoration process.

4. **Infrastructure Redundancy:** Establish redundant systems and infrastructure to ensure high availability and minimize single points of failure. This may include redundant servers, network devices, storage systems, and power and cooling infrastructure.

5. **Data Replication and Failover Mechanisms:** Implement technologies and processes to replicate critical data and applications to a secondary location. This may include disk mirroring, database replication, or virtual machine failover.

6. **Documentation and Procedures:** Document all recovery procedures, including step-by-step instructions, contact details, and required tools and resources. Ensure the documentation is regularly updated, easily accessible, and available to all relevant personnel.

7. **Testing and Maintenance:** Regularly test the disaster recovery plan to ensure its effectiveness and identify any gaps or deficiencies. This may include conducting tabletop exercises, functional exercises, or full-scale simulations. Update the plan based on the test results and lessons learned.

Best Practices and Challenges

To ensure effective incident response and disaster recovery planning, consider the following best practices:

1. **Proactive Approach:** Adopt a proactive stance towards incident response and disaster recovery by implementing robust security controls, regular monitoring, and testing mechanisms. Stay updated with emerging threats and vulnerabilities to be prepared for potential incidents.

2. **Continuous Improvement:** Regularly review and update incident response and disaster recovery plans based on lessons learned, changes in the threat landscape, technology advancements, and regulatory requirements. This ensures the plans remain relevant and effective over time.

3. **Training and Awareness:** Provide comprehensive training and awareness programs to all staff members on incident response procedures, disaster recovery plans, and their roles and responsibilities. Conduct regular drills and tabletop exercises to enhance preparedness.

4. **Collaboration and Communication:** Establish effective communication channels and foster collaboration between the incident response team, IT department, executive management, legal counsel, and external stakeholders. A coordinated and timely response is crucial during incidents and disasters.

5. **Third-Party Relationships:** Consider third-party relationships and dependencies in incident response and disaster recovery planning. Review the incident response capabilities of vendors, service providers, and partners to ensure a cohesive response in case of joint incidents.

Despite the best efforts, incident response and disaster recovery planning face several challenges:

1. **Complexity and Scale:** Incident response and recovery become increasingly complex due to the evolving threat landscape, ever-increasing volumes of data, and the breadth of digital infrastructure. Managing incidents and disasters across large-scale environments can be a daunting task.
2. **Resource Constraints:** Adequate resource allocation in terms of skilled personnel, technology, and budget is imperative for effective incident response and disaster recovery. Resource constraints may hinder the organization's ability to respond and recover promptly.
3. **Changing Regulations and Compliance:** Compliance requirements vary across industries and jurisdictions. Organizations must ensure their incident response and disaster recovery plans align with the relevant regulations, laws, and industry standards.
4. **Emerging Technologies:** The rapid adoption of emerging technologies, such as cloud computing, Internet of Things (IoT), and artificial intelligence (AI), introduces new challenges for incident response and disaster recovery. Organizations must adapt their plans to address these technologies' unique security risks.
5. **Coordination and Collaboration:** Coordinating incident response efforts and collaborating with various stakeholders, including internal teams, external entities, and law enforcement agencies, can be challenging. Effective communication and mutual understanding are crucial for a successful response.

Real-World Example: The Equifax Data Breach

The Equifax data breach, one of the largest cybersecurity incidents in history, serves as an instructive example of the importance of incident response and disaster recovery planning.

In 2017, Equifax, a consumer credit reporting agency, suffered a data breach that exposed the personal information of approximately 147 million individuals. The breach resulted from a vulnerability in Equifax's web application, which allowed hackers to gain unauthorized access to sensitive customer data.

Equifax's response to the breach was heavily criticized due to its lack of preparedness and inadequate incident response. The incident persisted for months, and vital steps, such as timely patching and appropriate detection and containment measures, were not taken promptly. This delayed the response, increased the impact, and eroded public trust.

The Equifax breach highlights the need for organizations to develop and regularly update comprehensive incident response and disaster recovery plans. Inadequate incident response can result in severe consequences, including reputational damage, legal implications, regulatory fines, and financial loss.

Conclusion

Incident response and disaster recovery planning are essential aspects of a holistic cybersecurity program. By establishing well-defined processes, creating incident response plans, and developing robust disaster recovery strategies, organizations can effectively manage and recover from cybersecurity incidents and ensure business continuity. However, these plans must be continuously reviewed, updated, and tested to remain resilient in the face of evolving threats and emerging technologies.

Building a Resilient Cybersecurity Program

Building a resilient cybersecurity program is crucial in today's ever-evolving threat landscape. As the complexity and sophistication of cyber attacks continue to increase, organizations must adopt proactive strategies to protect their assets and ensure the continuity of their operations. In this section, we will explore the key components and best practices for building a resilient cybersecurity program.

Understanding Resilience in Cybersecurity

Resilience in cybersecurity refers to an organization's ability to anticipate, withstand, and recover from cyber attacks or other security incidents. It encompasses the implementation of robust security measures, continuous monitoring and detection of threats, timely incident response, and effective recovery procedures.

To build a resilient cybersecurity program, organizations need to adopt a holistic approach that addresses both technical and non-technical aspects. This involves considering people, processes, and technology and fostering a culture of security awareness throughout the organization.

Key Components of a Resilient Cybersecurity Program

A resilient cybersecurity program consists of several key components that work together to provide comprehensive protection against cyber threats. These components include:

1. **Risk Assessment and Management:** Conducting a thorough risk assessment is essential to identify and prioritize potential cybersecurity risks. This involves assessing both internal and external threats and vulnerabilities and developing a risk management framework to address them. Organizations should regularly review and update their risk management strategies to adapt to changing threat landscapes.

2. **Security Controls and Technologies:** Implementing a layered security approach is crucial to mitigate risks and protect critical assets. This involves deploying a combination of preventive, detective, and corrective security controls such as firewalls, intrusion detection systems, encryption technologies, and endpoint security solutions. Regular security audits should be conducted to ensure the effectiveness of these controls.

3. **Incident Response and Business Continuity:** Establishing an incident response plan is essential to efficiently and effectively respond to security incidents. This includes procedures for incident detection, containment, eradication, and recovery. Additionally, organizations should develop and test business continuity and disaster recovery plans to ensure minimal disruption to operations in the event of a cybersecurity incident.

4. **Continuous Monitoring and Threat Intelligence:** Implementing a robust monitoring system is crucial to detect and respond to threats in real-time. This involves the use of security information and event management (SIEM) tools, intrusion detection systems, and threat intelligence feeds. By continuously monitoring network traffic and analyzing security logs, organizations can quickly identify and mitigate potential security incidents.

5. **Security Awareness and Training:** A resilient cybersecurity program requires a well-informed workforce. Organizations should provide regular cybersecurity awareness training to employees to educate them about common cyber threats, safe computing practices, and the importance of reporting suspicious activities. By

creating a security-conscious culture, organizations can reduce the risk of human error and enhance the overall security posture.

6. **Third-party Risk Management:** Organizations often rely on third-party vendors and service providers for various business functions. It is crucial to assess the security posture of these third parties and establish strong security controls and contract provisions to manage potential risks. Regular audits of the third parties' security practices should be conducted to ensure compliance with security standards.

Best Practices for Building a Resilient Cybersecurity Program

Building a resilient cybersecurity program requires following best practices that align with industry standards and regulatory requirements. The following are some essential best practices to consider:

1. **Adopt a Risk-based Approach:** Prioritize security investments based on the risk levels identified during the risk assessment phase. Allocate resources to address the most critical risks and continuously evaluate the effectiveness of security measures.

2. **Implement Defense-in-Depth Strategy:** Deploy multiple layers of security controls to protect against different attack vectors. This includes perimeter protection, network segmentation, endpoint protection, access controls, and encryption.

3. **Regularly Update and Patch Systems:** Keep all systems, applications, and software up to date with the latest security patches. Regularly review and update security configurations to address new vulnerabilities and emerging threats.

4. **Conduct Security Awareness Training:** Educate employees about security best practices, social engineering techniques, and the importance of reporting security incidents. Regularly reinforce security awareness through training programs and simulated phishing exercises.

5. **Monitor and Analyze Security Logs:** Implement a robust log management and analysis system to detect and investigate security incidents. Regularly review security logs and establish incident response procedures based on identified patterns or anomalies.

6. **Establish Incident Response Procedures:** Develop a well-defined incident response plan that outlines roles, responsibilities, and procedures for different types of security incidents. Conduct regular drills and exercises to test the effectiveness of the plan and identify areas for improvement.

7. **Regularly Test and Update Business Continuity Plans:** Conduct periodic testing of business continuity and disaster recovery plans to ensure their effectiveness. Update the plans based on lessons learned from security incidents and changing business needs.

8. **Maintain an Up-to-Date Inventory of Assets:** Maintain an inventory of all hardware, software, and data assets within the organization. This helps ensure that all assets are adequately protected and facilitates effective incident response and recovery.

9. **Engage in Information Sharing and Collaboration:** Participate in industry forums, threat intelligence-sharing communities, and public-private partnerships to stay informed about emerging threats and best practices. Collaborate with peers and security experts to share knowledge and insights.

Case Study: Resilient Cybersecurity Program Implementation

To better understand the practical implementation of a resilient cybersecurity program, let's consider a case study of a large financial institution.

The financial institution conducted a comprehensive risk assessment to identify its unique cybersecurity risks. It identified external threats such as phishing attacks, malware infections, and distributed denial of service (DDoS) attacks, as well as internal risks such as insider threats and inadequate security controls.

Based on the risk assessment findings, the institution implemented a combination of technical and non-technical controls. This included deploying robust firewalls, intrusion detection and prevention systems, and advanced endpoint protection solutions to safeguard its networks and systems.

Additionally, the institution established an incident response team comprised of representatives from various departments, including IT, legal, and public relations. The team developed an incident response plan that outlined the procedures for reporting, assessing, and responding to security incidents.

Regular security awareness training sessions were conducted for all employees to ensure they were equipped with the knowledge and skills to detect and report potential security threats. Simulated phishing exercises were also conducted periodically to assess the effectiveness of the training program.

Furthermore, the institution engaged in information sharing and collaboration with other financial institutions, regulatory bodies, and cybersecurity organizations. By participating in threat intelligence-sharing communities and sharing best practices, the institution enhanced its ability to detect and respond to emerging threats.

Through the implementation of a resilient cybersecurity program, the financial institution significantly reduced its risk exposure and effectively mitigated security incidents. The program facilitated a proactive approach to cybersecurity, ensuring the continuous protection of critical assets and maintaining customer trust.

Conclusion

Building a resilient cybersecurity program is essential for organizations to effectively protect their assets and mitigate the risks posed by evolving cyber threats. By adopting a holistic approach that encompasses risk assessment and management, security controls and technologies, incident response and business continuity, continuous monitoring and threat intelligence, security awareness and training, and third-party risk management, organizations can build robust and adaptable cybersecurity programs. Following best practices and staying informed about emerging threats and industry standards is crucial in maintaining a resilient cybersecurity posture.

Third-party Risk Management

In today's interconnected digital ecosystem, organizations increasingly rely on third-party vendors and service providers for various business functions. While this collaboration brings many benefits, it also introduces new cybersecurity risks that need to be effectively managed. Third-party risk management (TPRM) is the process of identifying, assessing, and mitigating these risks to protect the organization's sensitive data and critical assets.

Importance of Third-party Risk Management

Third-party risk management is critical for several reasons. First, organizations often share sensitive information with third-party vendors, such as customer data, intellectual property, and financial records. If these vendors have weak cybersecurity controls, it can expose the organization to data breaches, financial loss, and reputational damage.

Second, regulations and industry standards increasingly require organizations to ensure the cybersecurity practices of their third-party vendors. Non-compliance can result in regulatory penalties and legal liabilities. Additionally, organizations may be held responsible for any data breaches or security incidents that occur through their third-party relationships.

Third, the supply chain is a common target for cyberattacks. Sophisticated threat actors may exploit vulnerabilities in third-party systems to gain unauthorized access to the organization's network. Therefore, it is essential for organizations to ensure the security of their supply chain to prevent compromise and maintain business continuity.

Key Steps in Third-party Risk Management

Effective third-party risk management involves a series of steps to identify, assess, mitigate, and monitor risks throughout the vendor lifecycle. The following are the key steps in the TPRM process:

1. **Vendor Onboarding:** Before engaging with a third-party vendor, organizations should conduct due diligence to evaluate the vendor's cybersecurity posture. This includes assessing the vendor's security policies, procedures, and controls, as well as reviewing their security certifications and audit reports.

2. **Risk Assessment:** Once a vendor is onboarded, organizations need to perform a comprehensive risk assessment to identify potential risks associated with the vendor's systems and services. This assessment should consider factors such as the sensitivity of the data shared, the vendor's access privileges, their security controls, and any previous security incidents.

3. **Risk Mitigation:** Mitigating third-party risks involves implementing controls and measures to reduce the likelihood and impact of potential security incidents. This may include contractual obligations, such as specific security requirements, incident response protocols, and data protection clauses. Additionally, organizations should establish regular security audits and assessments to verify the vendor's ongoing compliance with agreed-upon security practices.

4. **Ongoing Monitoring:** Third-party risk management is an ongoing process, and organizations should continuously monitor the security posture of their vendors. This includes regular assessments, vulnerability scanning, and penetration testing to identify any potential security weaknesses. Organizations should also have clear incident response and communication procedures in place to address any security incidents involving third-party vendors.

Challenges in Third-party Risk Management

Managing third-party risks presents several challenges for organizations. Some of the common challenges include:

1. **Lack of Visibility:** Organizations often lack visibility into their third-party vendors' cybersecurity practices and control frameworks. This makes it challenging to assess and monitor the risks associated with these relationships effectively. Limited transparency can also hinder organizations' ability to respond promptly to any security incidents involving third-party vendors.

2. **Complex Vendor Ecosystems:** Large organizations often have complex vendor ecosystems with numerous third-party relationships across different business functions. Managing the cybersecurity risks associated with each vendor becomes a complex task, requiring coordination across various departments and stakeholders.

3. **Limited Resources:** Implementing an effective third-party risk management program requires dedicated resources, including skilled personnel and technology tools. However, many organizations struggle with limited resources, making it difficult to allocate the necessary time and expertise to adequately manage third-party risks.

Best Practices in Third-party Risk Management

To overcome the challenges and enhance the effectiveness of third-party risk management, organizations can follow certain best practices:

1. **Vendor Selection:** A robust vendor selection process is crucial. Organizations should prioritize vendors with strong cybersecurity controls and a proven track record of protecting sensitive data. Evaluating vendors based on their security certifications, audit reports, and references can help ensure the selection of reliable and secure partners.

2. **Clearly Defined Security Requirements:** Organizations should clearly define their security requirements and expectations for third-party vendors in contractual agreements. These requirements should cover areas such as data protection, incident response, security audits, and access controls. Regular security assessments should also be conducted to verify ongoing compliance.

3. **Continuous Monitoring:** Organizations should establish a continuous monitoring program to track the security posture of their third-party vendors. This can include regular assessments, vulnerability scans, and penetration tests. Automated tools can help streamline this process by providing real-time insights into the vendors' security controls.

4. **Incident Response Planning:** Organizations should have well-defined incident response plans that include specific procedures for addressing security incidents involving third-party vendors. This ensures a coordinated response and minimizes the impact of any security breaches.

Case Study: Target Data Breach

The Target data breach in 2013 serves as a prominent example of the consequences of inadequate third-party risk management. Hackers gained access to Target's network through a third-party vendor's compromised credentials, resulting in the theft of credit card and personal information of over 40 million customers. The incident not only led to significant financial losses for Target but also damaged its reputation and customer trust.

This case highlights the importance of thoroughly assessing the cybersecurity practices of third-party vendors, including their access controls and the security of their systems. It also emphasizes the need for ongoing monitoring and regular security audits to ensure that vendors maintain a robust security posture.

Conclusion

As organizations increasingly rely on third-party vendors, effective third-party risk management is essential to safeguard sensitive data and protect critical assets. By following established best practices, organizations can mitigate risks, enhance cybersecurity, and maintain trust in their vendor relationships. However, managing third-party risks is an ongoing process, requiring continuous monitoring and adaptation to address evolving cybersecurity threats.

Cybersecurity Architecture and Design

Fundamentals of Cybersecurity Architecture

Security Frameworks and Models

In order to establish effective cybersecurity measures, organizations often rely on security frameworks and models as guidelines for designing and implementing their security architecture. These frameworks provide a structured approach to managing security risks and ensuring the confidentiality, integrity, and availability of information assets. In this section, we will explore some of the widely used security frameworks and models.

ISO/IEC 27001:2013

The International Organization for Standardization (ISO) and the International Electrotechnical Commission (IEC) jointly developed the ISO/IEC 27001 standard to establish the requirements for an information security management system (ISMS). The ISMS provides a systematic approach for managing and protecting sensitive information within an organization.

ISO/IEC 27001 follows a risk-based approach, where organizations identify and assess the risks to their information assets and implement controls to mitigate those risks. The standard comprises several components, including:

- **Scope and objectives:** Organizations define the scope of their ISMS and establish the objectives for information security management.
- **Risk assessment:** Organizations identify and analyze the risks to their information assets and assess the potential impacts of those risks.

- **Treatment plan:** Organizations develop a treatment plan to address the identified risks and implement appropriate controls.

- **Statement of applicability:** Organizations document which controls from the ISO/IEC 27001 Annex A they have selected and implemented.

- **Performance evaluation:** Organizations monitor and measure the performance of their ISMS to ensure its effectiveness and make improvements as necessary.

- **Management review:** Top management reviews the ISMS to ensure its continuing suitability, adequacy, and effectiveness.

ISO/IEC 27001 provides a flexible framework that can be applied to a wide range of organizations, regardless of their size or industry. It helps organizations establish a systematic and ongoing approach to managing information security risks and demonstrates their commitment to protecting sensitive information.

NIST Cybersecurity Framework

The National Institute of Standards and Technology (NIST) developed the Cybersecurity Framework (CSF) to provide organizations with a set of best practices and standards for managing and mitigating cybersecurity risks. The CSF follows a risk-based approach and focuses on five key functions: Identify, Protect, Detect, Respond, and Recover.

- **Identify:** Organizations identify and prioritize their information assets, assess the risks to those assets, and develop a clear understanding of their cybersecurity posture.

- **Protect:** Organizations implement safeguards to protect their information assets, including access controls, awareness training, and data encryption.

- **Detect:** Organizations establish mechanisms to detect and identify cybersecurity events, including continuous monitoring, intrusion detection systems, and security information and event management (SIEM) tools.

- **Respond:** Organizations develop and implement an incident response plan to effectively respond to cybersecurity incidents, including containment, eradication, and recovery activities.

- **Recover:** Organizations develop and implement strategies to restore their systems and data after a cybersecurity incident, including backups, disaster recovery plans, and business continuity management.

The NIST CSF provides a flexible framework that organizations can adapt to their specific needs and risk profiles. It helps organizations enhance their cybersecurity resilience and facilitates communication and collaboration among stakeholders.

COBIT 2019

The Control Objectives for Information and Related Technologies (COBIT) is a framework developed by the Information Systems Audit and Control Association (ISACA) to help organizations govern and manage their IT environments. COBIT 2019 includes a comprehensive set of management practices and tools that align IT objectives with business goals and enable effective IT governance.

COBIT 2019 is organized around five governance domains, which are further divided into processes and activities:

- **Evaluate, Direct, and Monitor (EDM):** Provides overarching governance and management activities and ensures that IT supports business objectives.

- **Align, Plan, and Organize (APO):** Enables the development of IT strategies, plans, and frameworks to align IT with the business and optimize the use of IT resources.

- **Build, Acquire, and Implement (BAI):** Focuses on the effective and efficient delivery of IT solutions and services, including the management of IT projects and the acquisition of IT assets.

- **Deliver, Service, and Support (DSS):** Ensures the delivery of IT services, including service design, service delivery, and service support activities.

- **Monitor, Evaluate, and Assess (MEA):** Provides a feedback loop to ensure that IT processes and controls are effective, efficient, and aligned with business objectives.

COBIT 2019 helps organizations establish robust IT governance and management practices, ensuring that IT resources are used effectively, risks are managed appropriately, and business objectives are achieved.

MITRE ATT&CK

MITRE ATT&CK (Adversarial Tactics, Techniques, and Common Knowledge) is a knowledge base and framework for understanding and describing the tactics, techniques, and procedures (TTPs) used by attackers during cyber-attacks. It provides a structured taxonomy of adversary behaviors and helps organizations improve their threat detection and response capabilities.

The MITRE ATT&CK framework consists of a matrix that describes adversary behaviors across different stages of a cyber-attack, organized into tactics and techniques. The matrix includes a wide range of techniques used by adversaries, such as initial access, execution, persistence, privilege escalation, and exfiltration.

By mapping their existing defenses and detection capabilities to the MITRE ATT&CK matrix, organizations can identify gaps in their security posture and prioritize their investments in security technologies and threat intelligence. The framework also helps organizations improve their incident response planning and enhance collaboration with industry peers.

Conclusion

Security frameworks and models play a crucial role in guiding organizations to establish effective cybersecurity measures. The ISO/IEC 27001 standard provides a comprehensive approach to managing information security risks, while the NIST Cybersecurity Framework helps organizations align their cybersecurity efforts with business objectives. COBIT 2019 enables organizations to establish robust IT governance and management practices, and the MITRE ATT&CK framework helps organizations understand adversaries' behaviors and enhance their threat detection capabilities.

By implementing these security frameworks and models, organizations can strengthen their cybersecurity defenses, mitigate risks, and protect their critical information assets. However, it is important to note that no framework or model provides a one-size-fits-all solution. Organizations should tailor these frameworks to their specific needs and continuously monitor and adapt their cybersecurity measures to address emerging threats.

Security Architecture Design Principles

In the field of cybersecurity, designing an effective security architecture is crucial for protecting an organization's information assets from various threats and vulnerabilities. A security architecture is a blueprint that outlines the structure, components, and controls required to protect sensitive information and systems. This section discusses the fundamental design principles that should be considered when developing a security architecture.

Defense in Depth

One of the key principles in security architecture design is the concept of defense in depth. Defense in depth refers to the layered approach of implementing multiple security measures throughout an organization's network, systems, and applications. The goal is to create multiple layers of protection to prevent or mitigate the impact of potential security breaches.

A defense in depth strategy includes implementing various security controls at different levels, such as network, host, application, and data. Each layer of defense should be independent and resilient, ensuring that even if one layer is compromised, other layers will provide additional protection.

For example, a defense in depth approach might involve implementing network firewalls, intrusion detection systems, strong authentication mechanisms, encryption, and regular security monitoring. By employing multiple layers of defense, the organization can minimize the risk of a successful attack and reduce the potential impact of breaches.

Least Privilege

The principle of least privilege is another important consideration in security architecture design. Least privilege means granting users or processes only the permissions and access rights necessary for them to perform their specific tasks. This principle ensures that users are not granted excessive privileges that could be exploited by attackers.

Implementing least privilege involves conducting a thorough analysis of user roles and responsibilities within the organization. Based on this analysis, access controls and privileges should be established to limit the exposure of sensitive information and critical systems.

For example, in a financial institution, only authorized employees involved in financial transactions should have access to the banking systems. Other employees, such as human resources or marketing staff, should not be granted unnecessary access to these secured systems.

Enforcing least privilege can significantly reduce the risk of insider threats or unauthorized access to sensitive information. It also helps to minimize the potential impact of a compromised user account or system.

Secure by Design

The principle of secure by design emphasizes the need to incorporate security measures and controls into the early stages of system or application development. This proactive approach aims to address security requirements and considerations from the inception of the design process, rather than attempting to add security as an afterthought.

By integrating security into the design phase, organizations can identify potential vulnerabilities, threats, and mitigation strategies at an early stage. This approach allows for the implementation of secure coding practices, secure configuration settings, and robust authentication and encryption mechanisms.

For example, when developing a web application, secure coding practices, such as input validation, output encoding, and proper error handling, should be followed. Additionally, the application's access controls, authentication mechanisms, and data protection should be designed with security in mind.

Furthermore, secure by design principles also encompass the ongoing maintenance and updating of systems and applications. Regular patching and security updates must be applied to address newly discovered vulnerabilities and mitigate emerging threats.

Simplicity and Usability

While security measures are designed to protect organizations from various threats, it is important to ensure that these measures do not hinder the usability and productivity of the users. Security architecture should aim for a balance between security and usability.

Complex and overly restrictive security controls can lead to user frustrations and workarounds, which can introduce new vulnerabilities or weaken the overall security posture. Therefore, simplicity and usability should be prioritized in security architecture design.

For example, security controls, such as password policies, should strike a balance between complexity and ease of use. Implementing overly complex password requirements can lead to users writing down their passwords or using easily guessable passwords. Similarly, access controls should be designed to minimize the impact on legitimate user workflows, while still enforcing necessary security measures.

Security awareness training and clear guidelines can also contribute to the usability of security measures by ensuring that users understand their responsibilities and how to comply with security policies.

Continuous Monitoring and Improvement

Security architecture design is not a one-time activity; it requires continuous monitoring and improvement to address evolving threats and vulnerabilities. Regular monitoring of security controls and systems is essential to detect any potential breaches or anomalies.

Organizations should establish processes for monitoring and responding to security alerts and incidents. This includes setting up security information and event management (SIEM) systems to collect and analyze security logs, conducting periodic vulnerability assessments and penetration tests, and monitoring network traffic for suspicious activities.

Based on the insights gained from monitoring, organizations can prioritize and implement necessary improvements to enhance their security architecture. Such improvements may include updating security controls, addressing vulnerabilities, or refining incident response procedures.

To continually improve security architecture, organizations should stay informed about emerging security trends, learn from industry best practices, and foster a culture of security awareness.

Example Scenario: Financial Institution

To illustrate the application of security architecture design principles, let's consider a scenario in a financial institution. The organization wants to ensure the security of its online banking system, which allows customers to perform financial transactions.

- Defense in Depth: The organization implements multiple layers of security controls, such as network firewalls, intrusion detection systems, and encryption, to protect the online banking system. Additionally, regular security monitoring and incident response capabilities are established to detect and respond to potential threats.

- Least Privilege: Access controls are enforced to ensure that only authorized bank employees have access to the online banking systems. Least privilege principles are applied to limit employees' access rights based on their roles and responsibilities.

- Secure by Design: The online banking system is designed with security in mind from the early stages of development. Secure coding practices, such as input validation and output encoding, are followed. User authentication and session management follow industry best practices, and multiple layers of encryption are employed to protect sensitive customer data.

- Simplicity and Usability: While ensuring security, the organization designs the online banking system to provide a user-friendly and seamless experience for customers. It avoids overly complicated security measures that could hinder usability and productivity.

- Continuous Monitoring and Improvement: The financial institution regularly monitors the online banking system through automated security tools and manual security assessments. Incident response procedures are regularly reviewed and updated based on lessons learned from previous incidents. The organization stays updated with the latest cybersecurity trends and continuously works on improving the security architecture to address emerging threats.

In conclusion, security architecture design principles, such as defense in depth, least privilege, secure by design, simplicity and usability, and continuous monitoring and improvement, are essential for developing effective security architectures. By considering these principles, organizations can create robust security measures that protect their information assets and mitigate the risks associated with cybersecurity threats.

Defense in Depth and Layered Security Approaches

In order to effectively protect an organization's assets and information from cyber threats, it is essential to implement a comprehensive and layered approach to security. This approach, known as defense in depth, involves the use of multiple layers or barriers to deter, detect, and delay attackers. Each layer is designed to provide a unique level of protection, and in the event that one layer is breached, other layers are still in place to defend against the attack. This section will explore the principles and best practices of defense in depth and layered security approaches.

Principles of Defense in Depth

The concept of defense in depth is rooted in the idea that no single security measure can provide complete protection against all cyber threats. By implementing multiple layers of security, organizations can create overlapping defense mechanisms that increase the overall resilience of their systems. The principles of defense in depth include:

1. Layered Approach: The organization should implement multiple layers of security controls, with each layer providing a different level of protection. These

layers should be designed to work together and collectively provide a strong defense against cyber threats.

2. Defense-In-Depth Strategy: Each layer should be independent and self-sufficient in providing security. This means that even if one layer is compromised, other layers should still be able to detect and block attacks.

3. Redundancy: The organization should deploy redundant security measures to ensure the availability and integrity of critical assets. Redundancy can include backup systems, failover mechanisms, and redundant network connections, among others.

4. Diversity: Each layer of the defense in depth strategy should employ different security measures and technologies, reducing the likelihood that a single vulnerability or attack vector will compromise the entire system.

5. Defense at Multiple Levels: Defense in depth should be implemented at various levels, including the network, application, host, and data levels. This ensures that multiple attack vectors are protected, and no single point of failure exists.

6. Continuous Monitoring and Improvement: To maintain the effectiveness of defense in depth measures, the organization must continually monitor and evaluate their security controls. Regular updates and improvements should be made based on emerging threats and vulnerabilities.

Layers of Defense in Depth

Defense in depth is typically implemented using several layers of security controls. These layers can be categorized into three main categories: preventive, detective, and corrective.

1. Preventive Controls: These controls are designed to stop attacks from occurring. Examples of preventive controls include firewalls, intrusion prevention systems, access controls, and strong authentication mechanisms. These controls act as the first line of defense, preventing unauthorized access and protecting the organization's assets.

2. Detective Controls: Detective controls are used to detect incidents or attacks that have bypassed the preventive controls. Examples of detective controls include security monitoring systems, log analysis tools, and intrusion detection systems. These controls monitor network traffic and system logs to identify potential security breaches or suspicious activities.

3. Corrective Controls: Corrective controls are implemented to mitigate the impact of an incident or attack. Examples of corrective controls include incident response plans, disaster recovery plans, and backup and restoration processes. These

controls are essential for minimizing the damage caused by a successful attack and restoring the affected systems to their normal state.

Applying Layered Security Approaches

Implementing a layered security approach requires careful planning and consideration of the organization's specific needs and risk profile. Here are some key steps to follow when applying layered security approaches:

1. Identify Assets and Vulnerabilities: Conduct a thorough assessment of the organization's assets and identify potential vulnerabilities or weaknesses. This can include hardware, software, network infrastructure, and data assets.

2. Determine the Security Requirements: Based on the assessment, determine the security requirements for each asset and the associated risks. This will help in prioritizing the implementation of security controls.

3. Define Security Layers: Design and implement multiple layers of security controls, considering preventive, detective, and corrective measures. Each layer should complement the others and provide additional protection against potential threats.

4. Implement Security Controls: Deploy the identified security controls, ensuring that they are properly configured and integrated into the organization's infrastructure. This may involve deploying firewalls, intrusion detection systems, access controls, encryption mechanisms, and other security technologies.

5. Monitor and Update: Regularly monitor the effectiveness of the deployed security controls and update them as needed. This includes updating security patches, reviewing logs and alerts, and benchmarking against industry best practices.

6. Educate and Train Personnel: Train employees on the importance of following security policies and procedures. Conduct regular security awareness programs to educate employees about common attack vectors and how to respond to security incidents.

7. Continuously Improve: Cyber threats are constantly evolving, so it is essential to continuously assess and improve the organization's security posture. Stay informed about emerging threats and technologies and adapt the security controls accordingly.

Example: Application of Defense in Depth

To illustrate the application of defense in depth, consider an organization that wants to protect its customer data stored in a web application. The organization can implement the following layers of security:

1. Preventive Controls: - Implement a web application firewall (WAF) to filter and block malicious traffic. - Enforce strong user authentication mechanisms, such as multi-factor authentication. - Apply secure coding practices to the web application to prevent common vulnerabilities.

2. Detective Controls: - Enable logging and monitoring of the web application to detect any suspicious activities. - Implement a Security Information and Event Management (SIEM) system to centralize log analysis and threat detection. - Deploy an intrusion detection system (IDS) to detect and alert on any potential attacks.

3. Corrective Controls: - Develop an incident response plan to guide the organization's response in the event of a security incident. - Regularly back up the customer data and test the restoration process to ensure data integrity. - Conduct vulnerability assessments and penetration tests to identify and address any weaknesses in the web application.

By implementing these layers of security controls, the organization can significantly reduce the risk of unauthorized access to customer data and minimize the potential impact of a security breach.

Conclusion

The adoption of a defense in depth and layered security approach is crucial in today's evolving threat landscape. By implementing multiple layers of security controls, organizations can enhance their overall security posture and better protect their assets and information. However, it is important to regularly assess and update these controls to align with emerging threats and best practices. By following the principles and best practices of defense in depth, organizations can better defend against cyber threats and ensure the sustainability of their cybersecurity efforts.

Security Standards and Best Practices

Ensuring the security of an organization's information assets is of utmost importance in today's digital world. To achieve this, organizations need to follow security standards and best practices that provide guidelines and recommendations for implementing effective security controls. In this section, we will discuss some widely recognized security standards and best practices that can help organizations protect their assets and mitigate risks.

ISO/IEC 27001

ISO/IEC 27001 is an international standard for information security management systems (ISMS). It provides a systematic approach to managing sensitive company information and ensuring its confidentiality, integrity, and availability. The standard provides a framework for implementing security controls based on a risk management approach.

Organizations that achieve ISO/IEC 27001 certification demonstrate their commitment to information security and their ability to effectively manage risks. The standard covers various areas, including asset management, access control, cryptography, physical security, and incident management.

By implementing ISO/IEC 27001, organizations can establish a robust security management system, identify and mitigate security risks, and ensure compliance with legal and regulatory requirements.

NIST Cybersecurity Framework

The National Institute of Standards and Technology (NIST) Cybersecurity Framework is a widely recognized and comprehensive guideline for improving cybersecurity risk management in organizations. It provides a flexible, risk-based approach to managing and reducing cybersecurity risks.

The framework consists of five core functions: Identify, Protect, Detect, Respond, and Recover. Each function is further divided into various categories and subcategories, providing organizations with a structured approach to managing cybersecurity risks.

The NIST Cybersecurity Framework emphasizes the importance of risk assessment, continuous monitoring, incident response planning, and business continuity. It encourages organizations to actively collaborate with stakeholders and share threat information to enhance their cybersecurity posture.

PCI DSS

The Payment Card Industry Data Security Standard (PCI DSS) is a set of requirements designed to ensure the secure handling of credit card information. It applies to any organization that processes, stores, or transmits cardholder data.

PCI DSS provides a framework for securing the cardholder data environment by implementing controls such as network security, access control, encryption, and vulnerability management. Compliance with PCI DSS is mandatory for organizations that accept credit card payments, and non-compliance can result in significant penalties and reputational damage.

To achieve PCI DSS compliance, organizations need to implement and maintain a secure network, regularly monitor and test security systems, and maintain an information security policy.

OWASP Top Ten

The Open Web Application Security Project (OWASP) Top Ten is a list of the most critical web application security risks. It provides guidance on the common vulnerabilities and weaknesses found in web applications, helping organizations prioritize their security efforts.

The OWASP Top Ten includes vulnerabilities such as injection attacks, broken authentication, cross-site scripting (XSS), and insecure direct object references. By addressing these vulnerabilities, organizations can significantly reduce the risk of unauthorized access, data breaches, and other security incidents.

To mitigate the risks identified in the OWASP Top Ten, organizations should adopt secure coding practices, regularly update and patch their applications, and implement robust security testing and validation processes.

Best Practices

In addition to specific security standards, there are several best practices that organizations should follow to enhance their overall security posture. Some of these best practices include:

- Regularly conducting security risk assessments to identify vulnerabilities and potential threats.
- Implementing strong access controls, including user authentication, authorization, and multi-factor authentication.
- Keeping systems and applications up to date with the latest security patches and updates.
- Encrypting sensitive data at rest and in transit to protect it from unauthorized access.
- Implementing secure configurations for systems, networks, and applications. This includes disabling unnecessary services, removing default accounts and passwords, and using strong encryption.
- Training employees on security awareness and best practices, including how to identify and respond to security incidents.

- Establishing an incident response plan that outlines the steps to be taken in the event of a security breach or incident.
- Regularly monitoring and reviewing security controls to ensure their effectiveness and identify any gaps or weaknesses.

By implementing these best practices, organizations can create a strong security foundation and be better prepared to prevent, detect, and respond to security incidents.

Challenges and Considerations

While following security standards and best practices is crucial for ensuring robust cybersecurity, there are challenges and considerations that organizations need to address. Some of these challenges include:

- The rapid pace of technological advancements, which may result in new vulnerabilities and risks that existing standards and practices do not cover.
- Balancing security requirements with usability and business needs, as strict security measures can sometimes hinder productivity and user experience.
- The complex and constantly evolving threat landscape, which requires organizations to stay up to date with emerging threats and adapt their security measures accordingly.
- Limited resources and budget constraints, which may make it challenging for organizations to implement and maintain security controls.
- The need for ongoing training and awareness programs to ensure that employees understand and comply with security standards and best practices.

Organizations need to consider these challenges and tailor their security strategies to address them effectively.

Conclusion

Adhering to security standards and implementing best practices is crucial for organizations aiming to protect their sensitive information and assets from cybersecurity threats. Standards such as ISO/IEC 27001, NIST Cybersecurity Framework, PCI DSS, and best practices provide guidance and a structured approach to managing risks and ensuring compliance. By following these standards and practices, organizations can enhance their security posture, reduce the likelihood of security incidents, and safeguard their reputation and customer trust. However, it is essential to understand that cybersecurity is an ongoing process that requires continuous monitoring, review, and adaptation to address emerging threats and challenges.

Network Security Architecture

Secure Network Design Principles

Secure network design is a critical aspect of cybersecurity as it provides the foundation for protecting an organization's data and resources from cyber threats. In this section, we will explore the key principles of secure network design and discuss various techniques and best practices to ensure the confidentiality, integrity, and availability of network infrastructure.

Defense in Depth

The principle of defense in depth is fundamental to secure network design. It involves layering multiple security controls and measures to create multiple lines of defense against potential cyber threats. By implementing multiple layers of security, organizations can minimize the impact of a single security breach and increase the overall resilience of the network infrastructure.

To apply defense in depth, it is important to consider different levels of security controls, including:

- **Perimeter security:** Implementing firewalls, intrusion detection and prevention systems (IDPS), and network segmentation to control and monitor traffic entering and leaving the organization's network.

- **Network security:** Configuring secure protocols, such as Transport Layer Security (TLS) and IPsec, to encrypt network traffic and protect data in transit. Implementing secure authentication mechanisms, such as two-factor authentication (2FA) and strong passwords, to prevent unauthorized access to the network.

- **Host security:** Ensuring that individual systems and devices within the network are properly hardened, patched, and protected against malware and other malicious activities. This includes regular security updates, antivirus software, and host-based firewalls.

- **Application security:** Implementing secure coding practices, input validation, and robust access controls to protect against common web application vulnerabilities, such as cross-site scripting (XSS) and SQL injection attacks.

- **Data security:** Encrypting sensitive data at rest and in transit, implementing data loss prevention (DLP) measures, and enforcing strong access controls to protect against unauthorized data access or exfiltration.

By implementing layers of security controls at different levels, organizations can significantly reduce the risk of a successful cyber attack.

Least Privilege

The principle of least privilege (PoLP) is a best practice for secure network design that restricts user and system privileges to only what is necessary to perform their specific tasks. This principle ensures that users and systems have the minimum level of access required to carry out their functions, reducing the potential attack surface and limiting the potential impact of a compromised account or system.

To implement the principle of least privilege, organizations should:

- **User access control:** Assign users the minimum set of permissions necessary to perform their roles and responsibilities. Regularly review and update user access privileges based on organizational changes and job functions.

- **System access control:** Apply the principle of least privilege to system accounts and services. Limit administrative access to critical systems, enforce strong authentication mechanisms, and regularly review and audit system access logs.

- **Physical access control:** Restrict physical access to network infrastructure components, such as routers, switches, and servers, to authorized personnel only. Implement measures such as biometric authentication, access cards, and surveillance systems to prevent unauthorized physical access.

By implementing the principle of least privilege, organizations can minimize the potential for privilege escalation attacks and protect sensitive data and resources.

Separation of Duties

The principle of separation of duties (SoD) is another important aspect of secure network design. It involves assigning different tasks and responsibilities to different individuals to ensure a system of checks and balances. By separating duties, organizations can reduce the likelihood of insider threats and unauthorized activities.

To implement the principle of separation of duties, organizations should:

- **Role-based access control (RBAC):** Assign users roles and permissions based on their job functions and responsibilities. Ensure that critical tasks requiring high-level permissions are divided among multiple individuals or groups to prevent any one person from having too much control or access.

- **Two-person integrity (TPI):** Implement TPI for critical tasks or operations where the involvement of multiple authorized individuals is required to complete a task. This reduces the risk of malicious behavior or accidental errors and provides an additional layer of accountability.

- **Audit trails and logging:** Implement comprehensive logging mechanisms to capture and monitor activities performed by users and systems. Regularly review and analyze log data to detect any suspicious or unauthorized activities.

By implementing the principle of separation of duties, organizations can establish a system of checks and balances, reducing the potential for fraud, errors, and unauthorized activities.

Secure Configuration Management

Secure configuration management is a vital principle in network design that focuses on configuring network devices and systems in a secure manner. It involves ensuring that network devices have a minimal and secure configuration, minimizing potential vulnerabilities and reducing the attack surface.

To implement secure configuration management, organizations should:

- **Remove unnecessary services and features:** Disable or remove any unnecessary services, protocols, or features from network devices to reduce the potential attack surface.

- **Regularly update and patch software:** Implement a regular patch management process to keep network devices up to date with the latest security patches and firmware updates. This helps address any known vulnerabilities and ensure that devices have the latest security features.
- **Secure password and authentication settings:** Enforce strong password policies, including minimum complexity requirements and regular password changes. Implement multi-factor authentication wherever possible to enhance the security of authentication mechanisms.
- **Implement secure network device management:** Apply secure management protocols, such as Secure Shell (SSH), and restrict management access to authorized personnel only. Regularly review and update access control rules and implement logging and monitoring for management access.

By implementing secure configuration management practices, organizations can significantly reduce the risk of network device compromise and unauthorized access.

Secure Remote Access

In today's interconnected world, the ability to securely access network resources remotely is crucial. However, remote access introduces additional security risks, making it essential to implement secure remote access controls and mechanisms.

To ensure secure remote access, organizations should:

- **Virtual Private Network (VPN):** Implement VPN technologies to create secure encrypted tunnels for remote access. This allows remote users to securely connect to the organization's network over the internet, while ensuring the confidentiality and integrity of the data transmitted.
- **Strong authentication:** Implement multi-factor authentication to enhance the security of remote access. This can include a combination of passwords, biometric verification, smart cards, or hardware tokens.
- **Access controls and logging:** Implement granular access controls for remote users, limiting access only to the resources required for their specific tasks. Enable logging and monitoring of remote access sessions to detect any suspicious or unauthorized activities.
- **Endpoint security:** Enforce endpoint security policies and ensure remote devices, such as laptops and mobile devices used for remote access, are properly protected with up-to-date antivirus software and security patches.

By implementing secure remote access controls, organizations can enable remote work capabilities while maintaining the security of their network infrastructure.

Conclusion

In this section, we discussed the principles of secure network design, which form the basis for building a resilient and secure network infrastructure. By applying the principles of defense in depth, least privilege, separation of duties, secure configuration management, and secure remote access, organizations can establish a strong network foundation and minimize their exposure to cyber threats. It is essential for organizations to regularly assess and update their network design to address emerging threats and technologies, ensuring the long-term sustainability and effectiveness of their cybersecurity efforts.

Perimeter Security Controls

Perimeter security controls play a crucial role in protecting an organization's network from unauthorized access and external threats. These controls are designed to establish a secure boundary around the network, preventing unauthorized entry and mitigating potential attacks. In this section, we will discuss the fundamentals of perimeter security controls, including the components involved, key principles, and best practices.

Components of Perimeter Security Controls

Perimeter security controls typically consist of various components that collectively work together to safeguard the network. These components include:

- Firewalls: Firewalls form the cornerstone of perimeter security controls. They act as gatekeepers, monitoring and controlling the incoming and outgoing network traffic based on predefined security policies. Firewalls can be hardware or software-based and are essential for filtering malicious traffic and blocking unauthorized access attempts.

- Intrusion Detection and Prevention Systems (IDS/IPS): IDS/IPS are vital components that provide an additional layer of defense against network attacks. IDS monitors network traffic for suspicious activities, while IPS actively blocks and mitigates identified threats. These systems use signature-based and behavior-based detection techniques to identify and respond to potential threats.

- Virtual Private Networks (VPNs): VPNs enable secure communication over public networks by establishing encrypted tunnels between remote users or networks. They facilitate secure remote access and data transfer by encrypting all communication traffic. VPNs are essential for maintaining the confidentiality and integrity of data transmitted over untrusted networks, such as the internet.

- Network Access Control (NAC): NAC solutions ensure that only authorized devices and users can access the network. These solutions authenticate and authorize devices before granting network access, enforcing security policies and ensuring compliance with predefined rules. NAC solutions may include technologies such as port-based authentication, certificate-based authentication, and network segmentation.

- Demilitarized Zone (DMZ): A DMZ is a secure network segment that acts as a buffer zone between the internal network and external entities, such as the internet. It houses systems and services intended for public access, such as web servers and email servers. The DMZ prevents direct access to sensitive internal resources and provides an additional layer of security by isolating publicly accessible services.

Principles of Perimeter Security Controls

Perimeter security controls are designed based on certain key principles. Understanding these principles is crucial for developing an effective and robust perimeter security strategy. The principles include:

1. **Defense in Depth:** Perimeter security controls should be implemented in layers, with each layer providing an added level of protection. By having multiple security layers, even if one layer is breached, the remaining layers can still offer defense against potential threats. This principle ensures that a single point of failure does not compromise the entire network security.

2. **Least Privilege:** Perimeter security controls should enforce the principle of least privilege, granting access rights and permissions only to those who require them for their specific roles and responsibilities. This minimizes the potential impact of a security breach by limiting the access and capabilities of unauthorized users or malicious entities.

3. **Default Deny:** By default, all incoming network traffic should be denied unless specifically allowed based on predefined security policies. This

approach ensures that only authorized and legitimate traffic is permitted, reducing the attack surface and preventing unauthorized access attempts.

4. **Continuous Monitoring:** Perimeter security controls should include mechanisms to monitor network traffic continuously. This allows for prompt detection and response to any anomalies or security breaches. Continuous monitoring ensures that any potential threats or vulnerabilities are identified and mitigated in a timely manner.

5. **Regular Updates and Patching:** Perimeter security controls should be regularly updated with the latest security patches and firmware updates. This helps address any known vulnerabilities and ensures that the controls remain effective against evolving threats. Keeping the controls up-to-date is essential for maintaining the overall security posture of the network.

Best Practices for Perimeter Security Controls

Implementing perimeter security controls effectively requires following best practices that align with industry standards and recommendations. Some of the key best practices include:

- **Network Segmentation:** Properly segmenting the network into different security zones helps minimize the impact of a potential breach. By isolating critical assets from less-trusted areas, the damage caused by a successful attack can be contained. Network segmentation also enhances the efficiency of security controls by allowing for more granular security policies and enforcement.

- **Strong Authentication and Access Controls:** Robust authentication mechanisms, such as user credentials, two-factor authentication, and certificates, should be employed to verify the identity of users and devices attempting to access the network. Access controls should be properly configured, ensuring that only authorized users and devices can gain entry. Audit logs should be maintained to track and monitor access attempts.

- **Regular Security Audits:** Performing regular security audits and vulnerability assessments helps identify weaknesses and potential vulnerabilities in the perimeter security controls. These audits can be conducted internally or by third-party security experts to ensure a comprehensive review of the network's security posture. Identified issues should be promptly addressed to maintain an effective security posture.

- **Security Incident Response Planning:** A robust incident response plan should be developed and tested to ensure an organized and timely response to security incidents. The plan should include predefined steps for incident detection, containment, eradication, and recovery. Regular drills and simulations help validate the effectiveness of the plan and ensure that all stakeholders are well-prepared to handle security incidents.

- **Employee Training and Awareness:** Employees play a critical role in maintaining effective perimeter security. Regular training and awareness programs should be conducted to educate employees about security best practices, such as identifying phishing attempts, using secure passwords, and reporting suspicious activities. This helps create a security-conscious culture within the organization.

Example: Securing the Perimeter

Let's consider an example of how perimeter security controls can be implemented in a corporate network. ABC Corporation, an international financial services company, wants to protect its internal network from potential external threats. They decide to implement a robust perimeter security strategy. Here's an overview of their approach:

- They deploy a next-generation firewall at the network perimeter to filter incoming and outgoing traffic based on pre-defined rules. The firewall is configured to block known malicious IP addresses and applies deep packet inspection for enhanced security.

- An Intrusion Detection and Prevention System (IDS/IPS) is implemented to monitor network traffic for any suspicious activities. The IDS/IPS uses a combination of signature-based and behavior-based detection techniques to detect and mitigate potential threats in real-time.

- The corporate network is segmented into different security zones, separating critical assets from less-trusted areas. This helps limit the impact of a potential breach and allows for more granular security policies and controls.

- VPNs are used for secure remote access to the corporate network. All communication between remote users and the network is encrypted, ensuring the confidentiality and integrity of the data transmitted over untrusted networks.

- Regular security audits and vulnerability assessments are conducted to identify any weaknesses in the perimeter security controls. Any identified vulnerabilities are promptly addressed and patched to maintain an effective security posture.

By implementing these perimeter security controls and following the best practices discussed earlier, ABC Corporation enhances the overall security of its network, protecting sensitive data and minimizing the risk of unauthorized access.

In conclusion, perimeter security controls form a critical component of an organization's overall cybersecurity strategy. By establishing a secure boundary around the network, these controls play a vital role in preventing unauthorized access and mitigating external threats. Understanding the components, principles, and best practices of perimeter security controls is crucial for implementing an effective and robust security solution.

Intrusion Detection and Prevention Systems

Intrusion Detection and Prevention Systems (IDPS) play a crucial role in safeguarding computer networks and systems against various cyber threats. They are designed to detect, prevent, and respond to unauthorized activities and attacks, providing an essential layer of defense for organizations. This section explores the fundamentals of IDPS, their types and components, and their role in network security.

Fundamentals of Intrusion Detection and Prevention Systems

IDPS are security solutions that monitor network and system activities, analyze them for signs of malicious behavior, and take actions to mitigate the threats. They operate by examining network traffic, system logs, and other sources of information to identify potential security breaches. The main goals of IDPS are to detect and prevent unauthorized access, identify anomalous activities, and respond to security incidents promptly.

Types of Intrusion Detection and Prevention Systems

There are two primary types of IDPS: Network-based Intrusion Detection and Prevention Systems (NIDPS) and Host-based Intrusion Detection and Prevention Systems (HIDPS).

Network-based Intrusion Detection and Prevention Systems (NIDPS): NIDPS monitor network traffic and analyze it to detect and prevent intrusions.

They are typically placed at network entry points, such as firewalls or routers, to examine incoming and outgoing traffic. NIDPS can detect various types of attacks, including network scanning, port scanning, and known attack patterns. They can also identify abnormal traffic behavior, such as a sudden increase in data transfer or unusual protocols.

Host-based Intrusion Detection and Prevention Systems (HIDPS): HIDPS are deployed on individual hosts or servers and monitor activities occurring on the host. They examine system logs, file integrity, and other host-centric data to identify suspicious activities. HIDPS can detect attacks that originate internally or target specific hosts. They can also detect unauthorized configuration changes, suspicious file modifications, or abnormal system behavior.

Components of Intrusion Detection and Prevention Systems

The components of an IDPS may vary depending on the specific implementation, but generally include the following:

Sensors: Sensors collect data from various sources, such as network traffic, system logs, or operating system events. They act as the eyes and ears of the IDPS, capturing information needed for analysis.

Analyzers: Analyzers process the data collected by sensors and analyze it for signs of intrusions or suspicious behavior. They use algorithms and predefined rules to identify patterns and indicators of potential threats.

Alerts and Notifications: When an analyzer identifies a potential security incident, it generates an alert or notification to inform system administrators or security personnel. The alert may contain information about the nature of the threat, the affected system, and recommended actions.

Response Mechanisms: IDPS may include various response mechanisms to mitigate detected threats. These mechanisms can range from simple actions like blocking network traffic to more complex responses, such as isolating compromised hosts or initiating incident response workflows.

Intrusion Detection and Prevention Techniques

IDPS utilize various techniques to detect and prevent intrusions. Some common techniques include:

Signature-based Detection: This technique involves comparing observed events or patterns against a database of known attack signatures. If a match is found, the IDPS raises an alert. Signature-based detection is effective for identifying known attacks, but it may miss new or modified attacks that do not match existing signatures.

Anomaly-based Detection: Anomaly-based detection focuses on identifying deviations from normal behavior. The IDPS establishes a baseline of expected activity and flags any deviations as potential intrusions. This technique is useful for detecting novel attacks but can result in false positives due to legitimate changes in network or system behavior.

Heuristic-based Detection: Heuristic-based detection involves using predefined rules or algorithms to identify suspicious patterns or behaviors. Unlike signature-based detection, which relies on exact matches, heuristic-based detection identifies deviations from normal behavior based on predefined thresholds or rules. This technique provides a balance between the accuracy of signature-based detection and the flexibility of anomaly-based detection.

Challenges and Considerations in Intrusion Detection and Prevention Systems

While IDPS are valuable tools in network security, they face several challenges and considerations:

False Positives and Negatives: IDPS can generate false positives, flagging legitimate activities as potential threats, or false negatives, failing to detect actual intrusions. Tuning the systems to reduce false positives without increasing false negatives requires careful configuration and monitoring.

Efficiency and Performance: IDPS must be able to handle large volumes of network traffic without causing significant network latency. They should be optimized for performance to avoid impacting the overall system efficiency.

Continuous Updates and Threat Intelligence: To stay effective, IDPS need to be regularly updated with the latest threat intelligence and signatures. This requires continuous monitoring and collaboration with security researchers and organizations.

Secure Implementation: IDPS themselves can be potential targets for attackers. It is important to ensure their secure deployment and configuration to prevent unauthorized access or tampering.

Real-world Example: IDS and IPS in a Corporate Network

Consider a scenario where a large corporate network is equipped with both an Intrusion Detection System (IDS) and an Intrusion Prevention System (IPS). The

IDS monitors network traffic and system logs, while the IPS actively blocks suspicious activities.

One day, the IDS generates an alert indicating a potential SQL injection attack targeting a web application server. The alert provides details about the attack vector and the affected server. The security team, upon receiving the alert, verifies the validity of the threat by analyzing additional log files and network traffic.

Upon confirming the attack, the IPS automatically updates the firewall rules to prevent further SQL injection attempts, blocking the attacker's IP address. Simultaneously, the security team initiates an incident response workflow to investigate the extent of the compromise and remediate any vulnerabilities in the web application server.

This real-world example highlights the importance of including both IDS and IPS components in an overall IDPS strategy. The IDS detects the attack, while the IPS takes immediate action to prevent further exploitation.

Resources and Further Reading

- Case, John, and Marc Olano. "Intrusion Detection Systems: Principles and Techniques." In Handbook of Information Security, edited by H. Bidgoli, 675-690. John Wiley & Sons, 2006.

- Scarfone, Karen, and Peter Mell. "Guide to Intrusion Detection and Prevention Systems (IDPS)." National Institute of Standards and Technology (NIST), Special Publication 800-94, 2007.

- Northcutt, Stephen, Judy Novak, and Judy Novak. Network Intrusion Detection. New Riders Publishing, 2002.

- "Intrusion Detection Systems." SANS Institute. https://www.sans.org/intrusion-detection/.

Exercises

1. Research and compare different open-source IDPS solutions currently available. 2. Set up a virtual lab to deploy and test an IDPS solution of your choice. Evaluate its effectiveness in detecting common network-based attacks. 3. Investigate recent real-world cyber attacks and analyze how an IDPS could have potentially detected or prevented them. 4. Explore the legal and ethical considerations surrounding the use of IDPS, particularly in terms of privacy and the monitoring of network traffic.

Virtual Private Networks (VPNs)

Virtual Private Networks (VPNs) are a crucial component of modern cybersecurity infrastructure. In an increasingly interconnected world, VPNs serve as a secure method for transmitting data over public networks. This section will explore the fundamental concepts of VPNs, their working principles, and the various protocols and technologies that underpin their functionality.

Introduction to VPNs

A Virtual Private Network (VPN) allows users to create a secure connection over a public network, such as the internet. It acts as a private tunnel through which data can be transmitted securely and privately, protecting it from unauthorized access or interception.

The need for VPNs arises from the inherent security risks associated with transmitting sensitive data over public networks. Without proper encryption and security measures, data can be intercepted, modified, or even stolen. By encrypting the data and encapsulating it within a secure tunnel, VPNs provide a solution for secure communication across untrusted networks.

Working Principles of VPNs

VPNs employ various techniques to ensure secure communication between two endpoints. These techniques involve encryption, tunneling, and authentication protocols.

Encryption: Encryption forms the foundation of VPNs. It entails converting plain text data into an encoded format that can only be decoded with the appropriate decryption key. Common encryption algorithms utilized in VPNs include AES (Advanced Encryption Standard) and RSA (Rivest-Shamir-Adleman).

Tunneling: VPNs use tunneling protocols to encapsulate data packets within another packet, thus creating a secure tunnel. This encapsulation ensures that the data remains protected and hidden from unauthorized parties. Tunneling protocols used in VPNs include Point-to-Point Tunneling Protocol (PPTP), Layer 2 Tunneling Protocol (L2TP), and Internet Protocol Security (IPSec).

Authentication: Authentication protocols are used to verify the identity of both the VPN client and the server. This ensures that only authorized users can establish a connection and access the VPN. Common authentication methods include username and password, digital certificates, and two-factor authentication.

VPN Protocols and Technologies

There are several VPN protocols and technologies available, each with its own strengths and weaknesses. The choice of protocol depends on factors such as the level of security required, network configuration, and available resources.

OpenVPN: OpenVPN is an open-source VPN protocol that is highly configurable and supports various encryption algorithms. It is known for its robust security features, including the use of SSL/TLS for encryption and authentication, making it a popular choice for VPN implementations.

IPSec: Internet Protocol Security (IPSec) is a widely used protocol suite for securing IP communications. It provides authentication and encryption services at the IP layer, ensuring the confidentiality, integrity, and authentication of network data. IPSec can be used in conjunction with other tunneling protocols, such as L2TP, to provide a secure VPN connection.

PPTP: Point-to-Point Tunneling Protocol (PPTP) is one of the oldest VPN protocols. It is easy to set up and widely supported across various platforms. However, PPTP has some security vulnerabilities and is considered less secure than other VPN protocols.

L2TP/IPSec: Layer 2 Tunneling Protocol (L2TP) combined with IPSec provides a secure and reliable VPN connection. L2TP establishes the tunnel, while IPSec provides the encryption and authentication capabilities. L2TP/IPSec is often used in enterprise VPN environments due to its strong security features.

Benefits and Applications of VPNs

VPNs offer numerous benefits and find applications in various domains. Some of the key advantages of using VPNs include:

Enhanced Security: VPNs provide strong encryption and authentication mechanisms, ensuring the confidentiality and integrity of transmitted data.

Privacy and Anonymity: By masking the user's IP address and encrypting their internet traffic, VPNs help safeguard privacy and provide a degree of anonymity.

Remote Access: VPNs enable secure remote access to corporate networks, allowing employees to connect to their organization's internal resources from any location.

Geographical Restrictions Bypass: VPNs can circumvent geographical restrictions and censorship by hiding the user's real location and granting access to restricted content.

Secure File Sharing: VPNs facilitate secure file sharing between geographically dispersed users, making it ideal for collaborative work environments.

Key Considerations and Challenges

While VPNs offer numerous benefits, there are also considerations and challenges to be aware of:

Performance Overhead: VPNs introduce additional processing and encryption/decryption overhead, which can impact network performance.

Security Vulnerabilities: Certain VPN protocols or implementations may have security vulnerabilities that could be exploited. It is crucial to choose reliable and well-vetted solutions.

User Awareness and Training: Users need to be educated about the proper usage and best practices of VPNs to avoid inadvertently compromising security.

Network Infrastructure Compatibility: Not all network infrastructures may be compatible with VPNs, necessitating the implementation of compatible hardware and software.

Case Study: VPNs in Remote Work Environments

The COVID-19 pandemic has led to a shift towards remote work environments, with many organizations relying heavily on VPNs for secure remote access. For instance, a company may use a VPN to allow employees to connect to the corporate network and access sensitive files and applications securely.

However, the rapid adoption of VPNs at such a large scale has presented challenges. Organizations have had to ensure that VPNs can handle increased traffic demands, provide sufficient bandwidth, and maintain security while accommodating a predominantly remote workforce.

Further Resources

To deepen your understanding of VPNs and their applications, the following resources are recommended:

Books:

- "Virtual Private Networks: Technologies and Solutions" by Ruixi Yuan and W. Timothy Strayer
- "Deploying IP and MPLS QoS for Multiservice Networks: Theory and Practice" by John William Evans, Clarence Filsfils, and Francois Le Faucheur

Websites:

- OWASP VPN Security Testing Guide: `https://owasp.org/www-project-vpn-testing/`
- US-CERT Cybersecurity Bulletin: Defending Against VPN-Based Attacks: `https://www.us-cert.gov/ncas/alerts/TA13-024A`

Conclusion

Virtual Private Networks (VPNs) provide a secure and private means of transmitting data over public networks. By employing encryption, tunneling, and authentication protocols, VPNs ensure the confidentiality and integrity of communications. Various protocols, such as OpenVPN, IPSec, PPTP, and L2TP/IPSec, offer different levels of security and functionality. VPNs find applications in remote work environments, secure file sharing, privacy protection, and bypassing geographic restrictions. However, organizations must address considerations and challenges related to performance, security vulnerabilities, user awareness, and network infrastructure compatibility. In the era of remote work, VPNs have become an essential tool for ensuring secure and seamless communication.

Wireless Network Security

Wireless networks have become an integral part of our daily lives, enabling us to connect to the internet and communicate wirelessly with various devices. However, the convenience and ubiquity of wireless networks also come with inherent security risks. In this section, we will explore the fundamental concepts of wireless network security, including threats, vulnerabilities, and countermeasures.

Wireless Network Threats

Wireless networks are vulnerable to a wide range of threats that can compromise the confidentiality, integrity, and availability of data. Understanding these threats is vital for developing effective security measures. Here are some common threats in wireless network environments:

1. Eavesdropping: Attackers can intercept wireless communications and capture sensitive information, such as passwords, credit card numbers, or confidential business data.
2. Unauthorized Access: Attackers can gain unauthorized access to a wireless network by cracking weak encryption, exploiting default or weak passwords, or impersonating legitimate users.

3. Denial of Service (DoS): Attackers can disrupt wireless network services by overwhelming the network with excessive traffic or by exploiting vulnerabilities in network protocols.

4. Man-in-the-Middle (MitM) Attacks: Attackers can intercept and modify wireless communications between devices, allowing them to tamper with data or inject malicious code into the network.

5. Rogue Access Points: Attackers can set up rogue access points that mimic legitimate network infrastructure, tricking users into connecting to them and compromising their data.

Wireless Network Security Measures

To protect wireless networks from these threats, several security measures should be implemented. Here are some essential steps to enhance wireless network security:

1. Strong Encryption: Using strong encryption protocols, such as Wi-Fi Protected Access (WPA2), ensures that wireless communications are encrypted and protected from eavesdropping.

2. Secure Authentication: Implementing strong authentication methods, such as using strong passwords or utilizing two-factor authentication, adds an extra layer of security to wireless networks.

3. Access Control: Employing access control mechanisms, like MAC address filtering or IEEE 802.1X authentication, helps restrict unauthorized access to the wireless network.

4. Regular Firmware Updates: Keeping wireless network devices up to date with the latest firmware patches and security updates is crucial for addressing vulnerabilities and minimizing the risk of attacks.

5. Intrusion Detection and Prevention Systems (IDPS): Deploying IDPS can help detect and prevent unauthorized access attempts, malicious activities, and other network anomalies.

6. Wireless Network Monitoring: Regularly monitoring wireless networks for abnormalities, such as unexpected devices, unusual traffic patterns, or unauthorized connections, can help detect potential security breaches.

7. Physical Security: Protecting the physical infrastructure of wireless networks, such as securing access points and other network devices, prevents unauthorized physical tampering or theft.

Wireless Network Security Best Practices

In addition to implementing security measures, adopting best practices can further enhance the security of wireless networks. Here are some best practices to consider:

1. Change Default Settings: Change default passwords, SSIDs, and other default settings to reduce the risk of unauthorized access.

2. Disable Unnecessary Services: Disable unnecessary services, such as remote administration or guest networks, that could introduce potential vulnerabilities.

3. Network Segmentation: Divide wireless networks into smaller segments using virtual LANs (VLANs) to isolate sensitive data and minimize the impact of potential security breaches.

4. Regular Security Audits: Conduct regular security audits to identify vulnerabilities, assess the effectiveness of security controls, and address any weaknesses promptly.

5. User Awareness and Education: Educate users about wireless network security best practices, such as avoiding connecting to untrusted networks, recognizing phishing attempts, or being cautious when sharing sensitive information over wireless networks.

6. Use VPNs for Remote Access: Encourage the use of Virtual Private Networks (VPNs) when accessing the wireless network remotely to encrypt communications and ensure secure data transmission.

7. Physical Environment Considerations: Consider shielding wireless signals, securing access points in locked areas, and configuring wireless devices to mitigate the risk of unauthorized physical access.

By following these measures and best practices, organizations can significantly enhance the security of their wireless networks and protect sensitive information from unauthorized access or compromise.

Wireless Network Security Challenges

While wireless network security measures are effective, there are ongoing challenges that organizations face in securing their wireless networks. Some of these challenges include:

1. BYOD (Bring Your Own Device): The proliferation of personal devices in the workplace introduces additional security risks, as organizations must manage and secure a wide variety of devices with different security configurations.

2. Wi-Fi Roaming: Seamless roaming between different Wi-Fi networks can expose devices to potential security risks, as devices may automatically connect to untrusted or compromised networks.

3. IoT Devices: The increasing number of Internet of Things (IoT) devices connected to wireless networks introduces new security challenges, as many of these devices lack robust security features.

4. Wi-Fi Phishing: Attackers can set up fake wireless networks (known as "evil twin" networks) to trick users into connecting to them, capturing sensitive information or injecting malware.

5. Legacy Devices: Older devices that cannot support the latest security protocols or firmware updates may pose security risks to wireless networks.

To address these challenges, organizations should regularly assess and update their wireless network security measures to adapt to evolving threats and ensure the ongoing security of their wireless infrastructure.

Wireless Network Security Resources

For further in-depth information and resources on wireless network security, consider the following references:

1. *CWSP Certified Wireless Security Professional Official Study Guide*, by David D. Coleman and David A. Westcott.

2. *Hacking Exposed Wireless: Wireless Security Secrets and Solutions*, by Johnny Cache, Joshua Wright, and Vincent Liu.

3. *Wi-Fi Security: Guide to Wireless Network Security*, by Stewart Miller.

4. The Wi-Fi Alliance website (`www.wi-fi.org`) provides extensive information on Wi-Fi security standards, certifications, and best practices.

5. The NIST (National Institute of Standards and Technology) publication SP 800-153, "Guidelines for Securing Wireless Local Area Networks (WLANs)," offers detailed recommendations for securing wireless networks.

Remember, wireless network security is an ongoing process that requires regular assessment, maintenance, and vigilance to ensure the confidentiality, integrity, and availability of data transmitted over wireless networks.

Application Security Architecture

Secure Application Development Lifecycle

In this section, we will discuss the concept of a secure application development lifecycle (SADLC) and its importance in ensuring the security of software applications. We will explore the key phases of the SADLC and the best practices that developers should follow to minimize vulnerabilities and protect against potential security threats.

Introduction to Secure Application Development Lifecycle

The secure application development lifecycle is a structured approach that integrates security considerations into every phase of the software development process. It is based on the principle that building security into the application from the beginning is far more effective and cost-efficient than attempting to address security issues after the application has been developed.

The SADLC includes a set of processes, methods, and tools that help developers identify, mitigate, and manage security risks throughout the development lifecycle. By incorporating security best practices into each stage, organizations can minimize the potential for security breaches and enhance the overall security posture of their applications.

Phases of the Secure Application Development Lifecycle

The secure application development lifecycle consists of several distinct phases, each with its specific goals and activities. Let's explore each of these phases in detail:

1. **Requirements Gathering and Analysis** During this phase, developers work closely with stakeholders to gather and analyze the functional and non-functional requirements of the application. From a security perspective, the focus is on identifying and understanding the potential security risks and challenges associated with the application. This includes evaluating the sensitivity of the data handled, the potential threat landscape, and any regulatory or compliance requirements.

2. **Threat Modeling** Threat modeling is a critical phase in the SADLC, where developers identify and prioritize potential threats and vulnerabilities in the application. This involves analyzing the application's architecture, design, and implementation to determine potential weaknesses and areas of concern. By identifying threats at an early stage, developers can implement appropriate controls and countermeasures to minimize the risk.

3. **Secure Design and Architecture** In this phase, developers design the application's architecture and define the security controls and mechanisms that will be implemented. The goal is to create a robust and resilient architecture that can withstand potential attacks and protect sensitive data. Security considerations at this stage include secure network and communication protocols, secure data storage, authentication and authorization mechanisms, input validation, and error handling.

4. **Secure Coding** Secure coding practices are crucial to building secure applications. During this phase, developers follow established coding standards and best practices to minimize the introduction of vulnerabilities into the codebase. This includes principles such as input validation, proper error handling, secure coding APIs, and secure coding practices for specific programming languages. Developers should also be knowledgeable about common coding vulnerabilities, such as SQL injection, cross-site scripting, and buffer overflows, and use techniques to mitigate these risks.

5. **Security Testing** Security testing is an essential part of the SADLC, allowing developers to identify and remediate security vulnerabilities before the application is deployed. This includes a combination of manual and automated testing techniques, such as penetration testing, vulnerability scanning, code review, and security-focused quality assurance. Testing should cover various attack vectors and scenarios to ensure the application's resilience against potential threats.

6. **Deployment and Operations** Once the application has been developed and tested, it is deployed to production environments. During this phase, developers and operations teams collaborate to ensure a secure deployment and configuration of the application. This includes secure deployment practices, secure configuration management, and ongoing monitoring and maintenance to detect and respond to any security incidents.

7. **Secure Maintenance and Updates** Software applications require regular maintenance and updates to address security vulnerabilities and bugs. During this phase, developers should follow secure software maintenance practices, including timely patching, vulnerability management, and incident response. This helps to ensure that the application remains secure and protected against emerging threats.

Best Practices for Secure Application Development Lifecycle

To effectively implement the secure application development lifecycle, developers should follow certain best practices to minimize vulnerabilities and enhance the security of their applications. Let's explore some of these best practices:

1. **Security Education and Awareness** Developers should have a strong understanding of secure coding practices, common vulnerabilities, and security principles. Regular security education and training programs should be conducted to keep developers updated on the latest security threats and mitigation techniques.

2. **Use of Secure Development Frameworks** Leveraging secure development frameworks can greatly simplify the implementation of security controls and best practices. These frameworks provide pre-built secure code modules, libraries, and APIs that developers can use to ensure the secure development of their applications.

3. **Code Review and Secure Coding Standards** Regular code reviews should be conducted to identify and remediate security vulnerabilities. Developers should follow secure coding standards and guidelines specific to their programming language to minimize the risk of introducing vulnerabilities during the coding process.

4. **Automated Security Testing** Leveraging automated security testing tools can help identify vulnerabilities early in the development process. Techniques like static analysis, dynamic analysis, and fuzz testing can be used to identify potential security flaws efficiently.

5. **Secure Configuration Management** Developers should pay special attention to the secure configuration of the application and its underlying components. This includes secure default settings, secure communication protocols, secure storage of credentials and sensitive data, and protection against common misconfigurations.

6. **Continuous Monitoring and Incident Response** Implementing continuous monitoring and incident response mechanisms allows organizations to detect and respond to security incidents promptly. This includes setting up security monitoring systems, establishing incident response processes, and conducting regular threat intelligence analysis.

7. **Regular Security Updates** Keeping the application and its underlying components up to date is crucial to addressing newly discovered security vulnerabilities. Regularly applying security patches and updates ensures that the application remains protected against emerging threats.

Case Study: XSS Vulnerability

To illustrate the importance of the secure application development lifecycle, let's consider a real-world example of an XSS (Cross-Site Scripting) vulnerability.

In a web application that allows users to post comments, a developer fails to sanitize user input properly. As a result, an attacker can inject malicious JavaScript code into the comments section, which gets executed when other users view the comment.

By following the principles of the secure application development lifecycle, this vulnerability could have been mitigated. Threat modeling during the requirements gathering phase could have identified the potential for XSS attacks. Secure design and architecture could have included input validation and output encoding to prevent the injection of malicious code. Secure coding practices, such as using appropriate input validation libraries, could have further minimized the risk. Finally, security testing would have included specific XSS attack scenarios to detect and resolve this vulnerability before deployment.

Additional Resources

To delve deeper into secure application development lifecycle practices, consider exploring the following resources:

- "Secure Coding in C and C++" by Robert C. Seacord
- "OWASP Application Security Verification Standard" by OWASP
- "The Web Application Hacker's Handbook: Finding and Exploiting Security Flaws" by Dafydd Stuttard and Marcus Pinto

Conclusion

The secure application development lifecycle is a critical aspect of building secure software applications. By integrating security considerations into every phase of the development process, organizations can significantly reduce the risk of security breaches and protect sensitive data. Implementing best practices, such as security education, secure coding, testing, and continuous monitoring, enhances the overall security posture of applications and helps minimize vulnerabilities.

Secure Coding Practices

Secure coding practices are essential in ensuring the security and integrity of software applications. By following established guidelines and best practices, developers can minimize the risk of vulnerabilities, exploits, and attacks in their code. In this section, we will explore the principles and techniques of secure coding, covering topics such as input validation, secure data handling, and error handling.

Input Validation

Input validation is the process of checking and filtering user input to ensure that it meets the necessary criteria before it is processed by the application. Failure to properly validate input can leave an application vulnerable to various attacks such as injection and buffer overflow. Here are some important techniques for secure input validation:

- **Data Type Validation:** Validate the data type of the input to ensure that it matches the expected format. For example, if the input is expected to be an integer, ensure that it is indeed an integer and not a string or any other data type.
- **Length Validation:** Validate the length of the input to prevent buffer overflow or truncation attacks. Ensure that the input does not exceed the maximum allowed length.
- **Format Validation:** Validate the input against a specific format or pattern. For example, if the input is expected to be an email address, validate it against a regular expression pattern for email validation.
- **Encoding Validation:** Validate that the input is encoded correctly and does not contain any malicious characters or encoding techniques that can be exploited. For example, check for double URL encoding or UTF-8 overlong encoding.
- **Whitelist Validation:** Use a whitelist approach by accepting only known valid inputs and rejecting all others. This approach helps to prevent attacks such as SQL injection and cross-site scripting (XSS) by rejecting any input that does not conform to the expected patterns.

By implementing these input validation techniques, developers can significantly reduce the risk of vulnerabilities and strengthen the overall security of their applications.

Secure Data Handling

Secure data handling involves ensuring the confidentiality, integrity, and availability of sensitive data throughout its lifecycle within an application. By applying secure coding practices to data handling processes, developers can mitigate risks associated with data breaches and unauthorized access. Here are some key considerations for secure data handling:

- **Data Encryption:** Encrypt sensitive data at rest and in transit using strong encryption algorithms. This helps to protect data from unauthorized disclosure or tampering.
- **Password Storage:** Hash and salt passwords before storing them in a database. Utilize strong and adaptive hashing algorithms, such as bcrypt or Argon2, to protect passwords from brute-force attacks.
- **Secure Storage and Transmission:** Ensure that sensitive data, such as financial information or personally identifiable information (PII), is stored and transmitted securely. Use secure protocols, such as HTTPS, and encrypt data with SSL/TLS certificates.
- **Access Control:** Implement proper access controls to restrict data access based on user roles and permissions. Follow the principle of least privilege to ensure that only authorized individuals can access sensitive data.
- **Secure Coding Libraries and APIs:** Utilize trusted and secure coding libraries and APIs for handling sensitive data. Avoid writing custom cryptographic algorithms or using outdated libraries that may have known vulnerabilities.

By adhering to these data handling practices, developers can effectively protect sensitive information and safeguard the privacy of their users.

Error Handling

Error handling is an integral part of secure coding, as it helps to prevent information leakage and avoid potential security vulnerabilities. Proper error handling ensures that the application behaves gracefully and securely in the face of unexpected situations. Here are some important considerations for secure error handling:

- **Information Disclosure:** Avoid exposing sensitive information in error messages that could be exploited by attackers. Error messages should be informative to users but should not reveal any implementation details or sensitive data.
- **Logging:** Implement secure logging practices to capture relevant information about errors and exceptions. Ensure that logs are appropriately protected, stored, and monitored to prevent unauthorized access.

- **Exception Handling:** Implement comprehensive exception handling mechanisms to gracefully handle runtime errors and prevent application crashes. Avoid using generic catch statements and instead handle specific exceptions explicitly.

- **Fail-Safe Design:** Design the application to fail securely in case of critical errors or unexpected situations. Failures should not compromise the security or integrity of the system and should provide a graceful degradation of functionality.

Robust error handling practices can prevent security incidents, aid in debugging, and enhance the overall reliability of the software application.

Secure Coding Resources and Tools

Developers can leverage various resources and tools to enhance their knowledge of secure coding practices and facilitate the implementation of these practices. Here are some valuable resources and tools available for secure coding:

- **Secure Coding Guidelines:** Refer to established secure coding guidelines and best practices such as the OWASP Secure Coding Practices or the CERT Secure Coding Standards. These guidelines provide detailed recommendations for secure coding practices across different programming languages.

- **Security Code Review Tools:** Utilize static code analysis tools such as Fortify, Coverity, or SonarQube to automatically detect security vulnerabilities in the code. These tools can help identify potential security flaws early in the development process.

- **Security Training and Courses:** Attend security training programs and courses to enhance knowledge in secure coding practices. Organizations like the SANS Institute provide comprehensive security training courses for developers.

- **Secure Coding Checklist:** Use a secure coding checklist as a reference to ensure that all necessary security controls and practices are implemented during the development process. The checklist can include items such as input validation, data sanitization, and handling of sensitive data.

- **Security Bug Bounty Programs:** Participate in security bug bounty programs offered by organizations to identify and report security vulnerabilities in their software applications. This allows developers to gain practical experience in secure coding and learn from real-world vulnerabilities.

By utilizing these resources and tools, developers can continuously improve their understanding of secure coding practices and incorporate them effectively in their development processes.

Conclusion

In this section, we explored the principles and techniques of secure coding practices. We discussed the importance of input validation, secure data handling, and error handling in ensuring the security of software applications. By following well-defined guidelines and adopting secure coding practices, developers can significantly reduce the risk of vulnerabilities and protect critical assets from potential attacks. Moreover, we introduced various resources and tools that can assist developers in implementing and maintaining secure coding practices. It is crucial for developers to continually update their knowledge and skills in secure coding to adapt to evolving threats and ensure the resilience of their applications against future attacks.

Authentication and Authorization Mechanisms

Authentication and authorization are fundamental components of cybersecurity that play a crucial role in ensuring the security and privacy of information and resources. In this section, we will explore the concepts of authentication and authorization, discuss various mechanisms used to implement them, and examine their importance in maintaining the integrity and confidentiality of digital systems.

Authentication

Authentication is the process of validating the identity of a user or system entity. It is essential for establishing trust and ensuring that only authorized individuals or entities gain access to resources. There are several authentication mechanisms commonly used in cybersecurity:

1. **Password-based Authentication:** This mechanism involves the use of a secret password or passphrase known only to the user. The user provides this password during the authentication process, and if it matches the stored password, access is granted. However, passwords alone may be vulnerable to

various attacks, such as password cracking and brute-force attacks, if not properly managed.

2. **Multi-factor Authentication (MFA):** MFA adds an extra layer of security by requiring users to provide multiple pieces of evidence to prove their identity. This evidence can be something the user knows (e.g., a password), something the user possesses (e.g., a smart card or token), or something the user is (e.g., biometric traits like fingerprints or iris scans). MFA significantly enhances the security of authentication by reducing the risk of compromised credentials.

3. **Biometric Authentication:** Biometric authentication uses unique physical or behavioral characteristics of individuals, such as fingerprints, facial features, or voice patterns, to verify their identities. This mechanism is particularly effective in preventing password-related attacks and unauthorized access.

4. **Public Key Infrastructure (PKI):** PKI is an asymmetric encryption system that uses cryptographic key pairs consisting of a private key and a corresponding public key. The private key is securely stored by the user, while the public key is made widely available. Users can authenticate themselves by encrypting data with their private key, which can only be decrypted using their corresponding public key. PKI provides a high level of security and enables secure communication over untrusted networks.

5. **Smart Cards and Tokens:** Smart cards and tokens provide a portable and secure means of authentication. They store cryptographic keys and can be used in conjunction with passwords or PKI to provide an additional layer of authentication. Smart cards are especially useful in scenarios where users need to authenticate themselves across different systems or physical locations.

It is important to note that different authentication mechanisms have varying levels of security and usability. Organizations should consider the level of risk, user convenience, and the sensitivity of the information or resources being protected when choosing which authentication mechanisms to implement.

Authorization

Once a user's identity has been successfully authenticated, authorization determines the permissions and privileges granted to that user. Authorization ensures that users only have access to the resources and actions they are entitled to, based on their roles, responsibilities, and the security policies in place. There are several authorization mechanisms commonly used in cybersecurity:

1. **Role-Based Access Control** (RBAC): RBAC is a widely adopted authorization model that assigns permissions to users based on their roles within an organization. Users are given specific roles, and these roles define the scope of their access privileges. RBAC simplifies the management of access control by centralizing permissions and making it easier to grant or revoke access based on changes in user roles.

2. **Attribute-Based Access Control** (ABAC): ABAC is a more flexible authorization model that relies on complex policies and attributes to determine access control decisions. It leverages attributes of users, resources, and environmental conditions to dynamically assign access rights. ABAC allows for fine-grained permissions and can accommodate complex access control requirements.

3. **Mandatory Access Control** (MAC): MAC is a strict form of access control where access decisions are based on security labels associated with users and resources. This mechanism is typically used in highly secure environments where information classification and data integrity are critical. MAC is often implemented in government, military, and intelligence organizations.

4. **Discretionary Access Control** (DAC): DAC allows users to determine access permissions for resources they own. Users have the freedom to assign permissions to other users as they see fit. While DAC provides flexibility and user autonomy, it can also lead to security vulnerabilities if not carefully managed.

5. **Rule-Based Access Control** (RBAC): RBAC is similar to RBAC, but access control is defined based on specific rules or conditions rather than predefined roles. These rules can take into account a wide range of factors, such as time of day, location, user behavior, or resource attributes, to determine access privileges. RBAC can provide more granular authorization control in complex environments.

Authentication and authorization mechanisms work together to ensure that only authenticated users with the necessary permissions can access resources. By implementing robust authentication and authorization mechanisms, organizations can strengthen their overall security posture and protect against unauthorized access and data breaches.

Common Challenges and Best Practices

Implementing effective authentication and authorization mechanisms comes with its own set of challenges. Some common challenges include:

- **Credential management:** Managing passwords, certificates, or biometric data securely is essential to prevent unauthorized access. Organizations must implement strong password policies, enforce proper encryption techniques, and ensure secure storage of sensitive authentication information.

- **User experience:** Authentication mechanisms should strike a balance between security and usability. Complex or cumbersome authentication procedures can lead to user frustration and may encourage workarounds that compromise security. Organizations should prioritize the development of user-friendly authentication methods that do not sacrifice security.

- **Integration with existing systems:** Introducing new authentication and authorization mechanisms into existing systems can be challenging. Legacy systems may not support modern authentication protocols, and migrating to new systems can be time-consuming and costly. Organizations should carefully plan and test the integration process to minimize disruptions and ensure compatibility.

To overcome these challenges, organizations should adopt the following best practices:

- **Implement Multi-factor Authentication (MFA):** MFA adds an extra layer of security and is highly effective in preventing unauthorized access. Organizations should consider implementing MFA whenever possible, especially for critical systems and sensitive data.

- **Regularly Update and Patch Authentication Systems:** Vulnerabilities in authentication systems can be exploited by attackers. Organizations should stay up to date with the latest security patches and updates to protect against known vulnerabilities.

- **Implement Principle of Least Privilege (PoLP):** Applying the principle of least privilege ensures that users only have access to the resources necessary to perform their tasks. This reduces the risk of unauthorized access and helps contain potential damage if a user's credentials are compromised.

- **Monitor User Activity:** Implementing robust monitoring and auditing mechanisms allows organizations to detect suspicious activities and potential security breaches. By analyzing user behavior and access patterns, organizations can quickly identify and respond to unauthorized access attempts.

In conclusion, authentication and authorization mechanisms play a critical role in maintaining the security and integrity of digital systems. By implementing robust authentication mechanisms and employing effective authorization models, organizations can ensure that only authorized individuals or entities gain access to sensitive resources. However, it is important to continually evaluate and update these mechanisms to adapt to emerging threats and evolving cybersecurity landscapes.

Secure Software Testing and Vulnerability Management

Secure software testing and vulnerability management are critical components of an effective cybersecurity program. They play a crucial role in identifying and mitigating security weaknesses in software applications. This section will provide an overview of the principles and best practices involved in secure software testing and vulnerability management.

Importance of Secure Software Testing

Secure software testing is the process of evaluating the security of software applications to identify vulnerabilities and weaknesses that could be exploited by attackers. It is an essential step in the software development life cycle (SDLC) and helps ensure that applications are robust and resilient against security threats.

The importance of secure software testing can be summarized as follows:

1. Early detection of vulnerabilities: By conducting thorough security testing, organizations can identify vulnerabilities early in the development process, allowing them to address and fix these issues before deployment. This helps prevent security breaches and reduces the potential impact of attacks.

2. Enhanced application security: Secure software testing helps identify and address security flaws, such as input validation vulnerabilities, insecure authentication mechanisms, and insecure data storage practices. By addressing these issues, organizations can enhance the overall security of their applications and protect sensitive data.

3. Compliance with regulations and standards: Many industries have specific regulations and standards that require organizations to implement secure software

development practices. By conducting secure software testing, organizations can ensure compliance with these requirements and avoid legal and financial repercussions.

4. Reputation protection: Security breaches and vulnerabilities in software applications can severely damage an organization's reputation and erode customer trust. By proactively testing for vulnerabilities and ensuring the security of their applications, organizations can protect their reputation and maintain customer confidence.

Principles of Secure Software Testing

To effectively conduct secure software testing, organizations should follow a set of principles and best practices. These principles provide a framework for designing and executing comprehensive and reliable security testing processes. Some of the key principles of secure software testing include:

1. Measurable goals: Clearly define the goals and objectives of the security testing process. This helps ensure that the testing activities align with the desired security outcomes and allows for the measurement of progress and results.

2. Comprehensive coverage: Test all aspects of the software application, including its functionality, input validation, access controls, authentication mechanisms, and secure data storage practices. Ensure that all potential attack vectors are considered and tested.

3. Realistic test environments: Create test environments that mimic the production environment as closely as possible. This helps identify vulnerabilities and weaknesses that may only manifest in specific configurations or environments.

4. Threat modeling: Conduct threat modeling exercises to identify potential threats and attack vectors. Use this information to prioritize testing efforts and focus on the most critical and likely security risks.

5. Manual and automated testing: Combine both manual and automated testing approaches to ensure thorough coverage. While automated tools can assist in identifying common vulnerabilities, manual testing is essential for uncovering more complex security issues.

6. Continuous testing: Implement a continuous testing approach throughout the software development life cycle. Regularly test applications as new features are added or changes are made to identify and address potential vulnerabilities in a timely manner.

Vulnerability Management

Vulnerability management is the process of identifying, evaluating, prioritizing, and addressing vulnerabilities in software applications. It encompasses activities such as vulnerability scanning, vulnerability assessment, and vulnerability remediation. Effective vulnerability management helps organizations proactively address security weaknesses and reduce the risk of successful attacks.

The vulnerability management process typically involves the following steps:

1. Vulnerability identification: Use automated tools and manual techniques to identify vulnerabilities in software applications. This may include performing vulnerability scans, code reviews, and penetration testing.

2. Vulnerability assessment: Evaluate the severity and impact of identified vulnerabilities. This involves determining the likelihood of the vulnerability being exploited and the potential damage it could cause.

3. Prioritization: Prioritize the remediation of vulnerabilities based on their severity, potential impact, and the resources available. Focus on addressing high-risk vulnerabilities that pose an immediate threat to the security of the application.

4. Remediation: Develop and implement a plan to address identified vulnerabilities. This may involve patching or updating software components, changing configuration settings, or modifying the codebase.

5. Verification: Validate that the remediation measures have effectively addressed the identified vulnerabilities. Conduct retesting to ensure that the vulnerabilities have been successfully mitigated.

6. Continuous monitoring: Continuously monitor the application for new vulnerabilities and emerging threats. Regularly update and patch software components to address known vulnerabilities.

Secure Software Testing Techniques

Secure software testing employs various techniques to identify vulnerabilities and security weaknesses. Some commonly used techniques include:

1. Static Application Security Testing (SAST): SAST involves analyzing the source code or binary of an application without executing it. This technique helps identify coding errors, insecure coding practices, and known vulnerabilities.

2. Dynamic Application Security Testing (DAST): DAST involves testing the application while it is running to identify vulnerabilities and weaknesses. It simulates real-world attack scenarios and helps identify vulnerabilities that may not be apparent from static analysis.

3. Fuzz Testing: Fuzz testing involves inputting malformed or unexpected data to the application to assess its resilience and ability to handle unexpected inputs. It helps identify vulnerabilities like buffer overflows, format string vulnerabilities, and injection attacks.

4. Penetration Testing: Penetration testing, also known as ethical hacking, involves simulating real-world attacks to identify vulnerabilities and weaknesses in an application. It helps uncover vulnerabilities that may not be detected through automated scanning techniques.

Challenges in Secure Software Testing and Vulnerability Management

Despite the importance of secure software testing and vulnerability management, there are challenges that organizations face in implementing effective practices. These challenges include:

1. Time and resource constraints: Conducting thorough security testing requires time, expertise, and resources. Organizations often face constraints in terms of budget, skilled personnel, and project timelines, making it challenging to prioritize and conduct comprehensive testing activities.

2. Complexity of applications: Modern software applications are complex, with numerous interconnected components and dependencies. Testing these applications requires a deep understanding of their architecture and functionality, making vulnerability detection and assessment challenging.

3. False positives and false negatives: Automated vulnerability scanning tools may produce false positives or false negatives, leading to inefficient use of resources. Proper analysis and validation are required to differentiate real vulnerabilities from false positives.

4. Rapid software development cycles: Agile development methodologies and continuous integration/continuous deployment (CI/CD) practices shorten software development cycles. This poses a challenge for security testing, as there may be limited time to conduct thorough testing before the release of new features or updates.

To address these challenges, organizations should invest in skilled personnel, leverage automated testing tools, integrate security testing into the development process, and adopt a risk-based approach to prioritize testing efforts.

Resources and Further Reading

- OWASP: The Open Web Application Security Project (OWASP) provides a wealth of resources, best practices, and testing guides for secure software development and vulnerability management. Their website (https://www.owasp.org) offers a comprehensive set of tools and guidance for improving application security.

- NIST SP 800-115: The National Institute of Standards and Technology (NIST) Special Publication 800-115 provides a comprehensive guide to implementing secure software testing practices. It includes recommendations for vulnerability identification, assessment, remediation, and verification.

- SANS Institute: The SANS Institute offers various training courses and resources on secure software development, testing, and vulnerability management. Their website (https://www.sans.org) provides valuable insights and educational materials for professionals in the cybersecurity field.

- Secure Coding: Principles and Practices (Robert C. Seacord): This book focuses on secure coding practices and techniques to develop robust and secure software applications. It covers topics such as input validation, buffer overflow prevention, and secure error handling.

Summary

Secure software testing and vulnerability management are crucial elements of an effective cybersecurity program. By identifying and addressing vulnerabilities in software applications, organizations can enhance their overall security posture and protect against potential cyber threats. The principles, techniques, and resources outlined in this section provide a solid foundation for implementing secure software testing and vulnerability management practices.

Web Application Security

Web application security is a critical aspect of cybersecurity. With the increasing reliance on web-based applications for various purposes, it is crucial to ensure that these applications are secure and protected against potential threats and attacks. In this section, we will explore the fundamental principles and techniques of web application security, including common vulnerabilities, best practices, and security measures.

Introduction to Web Application Security

Web applications are software programs that run on a web server and interact with users through a web browser. They have become an integral part of our daily lives, enabling us to perform various tasks such as online shopping, banking, social media interaction, and accessing cloud-based services. However, the very nature of web applications makes them vulnerable to a wide range of security threats.

Web application security encompasses the measures and practices employed to protect web applications from unauthorized access, data breaches, and other malicious activities. It involves identifying and mitigating vulnerabilities, implementing secure coding practices, and deploying security controls to prevent and detect attacks. Let's delve into the key aspects of web application security.

Common Web Application Vulnerabilities

Web applications are susceptible to a variety of vulnerabilities that can be exploited by attackers to gain unauthorized access, steal sensitive data, or disrupt the application's functionality. Understanding these vulnerabilities is essential in designing effective security measures. Some of the most common web application vulnerabilities include:

1. **Injection Attacks:** Injection attacks occur when untrusted data is sent to an interpreter as part of a command or query and manipulated in such a way that it is executed unintentionally. One example is SQL injection, where attackers inject malicious SQL statements into an application's database query, potentially leading to unauthorized data disclosure or modification. Proper input validation, parameter binding, and the use of prepared statements can mitigate injection attacks.

2. **Cross-Site Scripting (XSS):** XSS vulnerabilities occur when an attacker injects malicious scripts into web pages viewed by other users. These scripts can execute arbitrary code, hijack user sessions, or steal sensitive information. Preventing XSS attacks involves input validation, output encoding, and the use of security headers like Content Security Policy (CSP) to restrict the execution of scripts.

3. **Cross-Site Request Forgery (CSRF):** CSRF attacks exploit the trust users have in a particular website by tricking them into executing unwanted actions unknowingly. For example, an attacker can create a malicious webpage that sends a request to modify a user's account on a targeted website where the user is already authenticated. CSRF protection mechanisms, such as unique request tokens, can prevent such attacks.

4. **Authentication and Session Management Issues:** Weak or flawed authentication mechanisms can allow attackers to bypass authentication,

escalate privileges, or hijack user sessions. Common vulnerabilities include weak passwords, brute-force attacks, session fixation, and session hijacking. Secure password policies, multi-factor authentication, session expiry controls, and secure session management can alleviate these risks.

5. **Insecure Direct Object References (IDOR):** IDOR vulnerabilities arise when an application exposes direct references to internal implementation objects, such as database records, without proper authorization checks. Attackers can manipulate these references to access unauthorized data or perform unintended actions. Implementing access controls, securing direct object references, and using indirect object references can mitigate IDOR risks.

6. **Security Misconfigurations:** Security misconfigurations occur when applications, web servers, or frameworks are not properly configured, leaving them vulnerable to attacks. Common misconfigurations include default passwords, unnecessary services, outdated software, and exposed sensitive information. Regular security audits, secure configuration guidelines, and patch management practices can address misconfiguration issues.

These are just a few examples of the many web application vulnerabilities that exist. Addressing these vulnerabilities requires a multi-layered approach that combines secure coding practices, secure configuration, and continuous monitoring.

Secure Coding Practices

One of the fundamental pillars of web application security is secure coding. Secure coding practices involve adopting techniques and guidelines that minimize software vulnerabilities and protect against various types of attacks. Here are some key principles of secure coding for web applications:

1. **Input Validation:** All user inputs should be validated and sanitized before being processed or used in database queries. It ensures that only expected and valid data is accepted, reducing the risk of injection attacks.

2. **Output Encoding:** All user-supplied data that is displayed on web pages or included in dynamic content should be properly encoded to prevent XSS attacks. This includes escaping special characters and using output encoding functions provided by web frameworks or libraries.

3. **Secure Authentication and Session Management:** Implement strong password policies, including password complexity requirements, secure password storage (e.g., using salted hashes), and mechanisms for multi-factor authentication. Additionally, enforce session management best practices, such as unique session IDs, secure cookie attributes, and session expiration controls.

4. **Least Privilege Principle:** Apply the least privilege principle by granting only the necessary permissions and access rights to users, processes, and components. Limit privileges to prevent unauthorized actions and minimize the potential impact of a successful attack.

5. **Secure Error Handling:** Implement proper error handling mechanisms to avoid exposing sensitive information and prevent attackers from exploiting error messages. Display user-friendly error messages without disclosing technical details that could aid attackers.

6. **Secure Configuration:** Ensure that the application's underlying infrastructure, web servers, databases, and frameworks are securely configured. Remove or disable unnecessary services, apply security patches regularly, and follow secure configuration guidelines provided by the vendors.

7. **Secure File and Resource Handling:** Validate and sanitize all file uploads to prevent malicious files from being executed on the server. Restrict file permissions, implement secure file storage mechanisms, and be cautious of path traversal vulnerabilities.

Adhering to secure coding practices significantly improves the security posture of web applications. Developers and software engineers should receive proper training and education on secure coding, and organizations should enforce secure development processes and code reviews.

Web Application Security Measures

In addition to secure coding practices, there are several security measures that organizations can implement to enhance the security of web applications. These measures complement secure coding practices and provide additional layers of protection against potential threats. Here are some key security measures for web application security:

1. **Web Application Firewalls (WAF):** WAFs are security appliances or software solutions that sit between web clients and servers, filtering incoming and outgoing traffic to detect and block malicious activities. They employ various techniques, such as signature-based filtering, anomaly detection, and behavioral analysis, to identify and prevent attacks.

2. **Transport Layer Security (TLS):** TLS, formerly known as SSL, is an encryption protocol that secures the communication between web clients and servers. It ensures the confidentiality and integrity of data in transit, preventing eavesdropping, tampering, and man-in-the-middle attacks. Implementing TLS with strong cipher suites and proper certificate management is essential for securing web applications.

3. **Secure Software Development Lifecycle (SDLC):** Adopting a secure SDLC approach involves integrating security throughout the entire software development process. It includes security requirements analysis, threat modeling, security testing, code reviews, and security-focused quality assurance activities. A secure SDLC ensures that security is considered at every phase of a web application's lifecycle.

4. **Web Application Scanners and Penetration Testing:** Perform regular vulnerability assessments and penetration testing to identify and address potential security weaknesses. Web application scanners automate the process of scanning for known vulnerabilities, while penetration testing involves manual testing and simulated attacks to uncover unknown vulnerabilities.

5. **Secure Session Management:** Implement session management controls, such as secure session identifiers, cookie attributes (e.g., secure and HttpOnly flags), and mechanisms to detect and invalidate sessions upon logout or inactivity. Consider adopting session management best practices, such as session pooling or distributed session management, for scalability and resilience.

6. **Security Headers:** Use security headers to enforce security policies and mitigate specific types of attacks. For example, Content Security Policy (CSP) headers can restrict the execution of malicious scripts, while HTTP Strict Transport Security (HSTS) headers enforce the use of HTTPS for all communication.

These security measures, combined with secure coding practices, help safeguard web applications against a wide range of attacks. It is crucial to implement a defense-in-depth strategy that combines multiple layers of security controls to ensure comprehensive protection.

Example: Securing a Web Application

To illustrate the practical application of web application security principles, let's consider an example of securing an e-commerce web application that handles sensitive customer data. Here are some steps that can be taken to enhance its security:

1. Use a secure coding framework or library, such as OWASP Top 10, to ensure that the web application is developed using secure coding practices. Regularly update the framework/library to leverage the latest security enhancements.

2. Implement input validation and output encoding mechanisms to prevent common vulnerabilities like injection attacks and XSS. Use parameterized queries or prepared statements to prevent SQL injection, and sanitize user inputs to prevent XSS attacks.

3. Enforce strong password policies for user accounts, including complexity requirements and password expiration. Implement multi-factor authentication to add an extra layer of security and protect against credential theft.

4. Apply secure session management practices, including the use of secure session identifiers, session expiration controls, and secure cookie attributes. Invalidate sessions upon logout or inactivity and enforce re-authentication for sensitive actions.

5. Regularly scan the web application for vulnerabilities using automated web application scanning tools. Perform periodic penetration testing to identify and address any security weaknesses that may not be detected by automated scanning.

6. Implement a Web Application Firewall (WAF) to monitor and filter incoming web traffic. Configure the WAF to detect and block suspicious activities, such as SQL injection attempts or malicious file uploads.

7. Use Transport Layer Security (TLS) with strong cipher suites and proper certificate management to encrypt all communication between the web application and users' browsers. Ensure that the TLS configuration adheres to recommended security standards.

8. Keep all software components, including the web server, application framework, and libraries, up to date with the latest security patches. Regularly review configuration settings to eliminate any security vulnerabilities caused by misconfigurations.

9. Educate developers and web application administrators on secure coding practices and security best practices. Conduct periodic security awareness training to ensure that everyone involved understands their roles and responsibilities in maintaining the security of the web application.

By adopting these security measures and following secure coding practices, the e-commerce web application can significantly reduce the risk of security breaches and protect customer data.

Conclusion

Web application security is of paramount importance for organizations as they strive to protect sensitive data and maintain the trust of their users. This section has provided an overview of web application security, including common vulnerabilities, secure coding practices, and security measures. By adhering to these principles and incorporating security into all phases of the software development lifecycle, organizations can build robust and resilient web applications that can withstand the evolving challenges in the cybersecurity landscape. It is crucial to remain vigilant, stay informed about emerging threats, and continuously update security measures to ensure the ongoing protection of web applications.

Cloud Security Architecture

Cloud Computing Fundamentals

Cloud computing is a fundamental concept in modern computing, enabling the delivery of computing services over the internet. In this section, we will explore the basic principles of cloud computing and discuss its significance in the field of cybersecurity sustainability.

Definition of Cloud Computing

Cloud computing refers to the practice of using a network of remote servers, housed in data centers, to store, manage, and process data, rather than using a local server or personal computer. It involves the provision of various services, such as storage, databases, software applications, and infrastructure, over the internet.

Key Characteristics of Cloud Computing

There are several key characteristics that define cloud computing:

- **On-demand self-service:** Users can provision computing resources and services as needed without requiring human intervention from the service provider.
- **Broad network access:** Cloud services can be accessed over the internet using standard devices, such as computers, smartphones, and tablets.
- **Resource pooling:** Multiple users, or tenants, share the same physical and virtual resources of the cloud provider, allowing for efficient resource utilization.
- **Rapid elasticity:** Cloud resources can be easily and rapidly scaled up or down to meet changing demands, providing flexibility and cost savings.
- **Measured service:** Cloud service providers monitor, measure, and control resource usage, enabling transparent and accurate billing and resource allocation.

Service Models of Cloud Computing

Cloud computing offers various service models to cater to different needs and requirements:

- **Infrastructure as a Service (IaaS):** In this model, the cloud service provider offers virtualized computing resources, such as virtual machines, storage, and networks, to users. Users have the flexibility to deploy and manage their applications and can scale resources as needed.
- **Platform as a Service (PaaS):** PaaS provides a complete development and deployment environment to users, including operating systems, programming languages, and development tools. Users can focus on building and deploying applications without worrying about the underlying infrastructure.

- **Software as a Service (SaaS):** SaaS delivers fully functional software applications over the internet, accessible by users through web browsers or client applications. Users do not need to install or maintain the software, as it is managed by the cloud service provider.

Deployment Models of Cloud Computing

Cloud computing can be deployed in different ways, depending on the needs and constraints of the organization:

- **Public Cloud:** Public cloud services are available to the general public or a large industry group and are typically owned and operated by third-party providers. Resources are shared among multiple tenants, and the cloud provider is responsible for maintaining and managing the infrastructure.
- **Private Cloud:** Private cloud services are exclusively used by a single organization and can be located on-premises or hosted by a third-party provider. They offer enhanced security and control but require additional investment in infrastructure and maintenance.
- **Hybrid Cloud:** Hybrid cloud combines public and private cloud environments, allowing organizations to leverage the benefits of both. It provides flexibility and scalability while maintaining control over sensitive data and applications.
- **Community Cloud:** Community cloud is shared by several organizations with common goals, such as government agencies or research institutions. It offers dedicated resources and facilitates collaboration and resource sharing within the community.

Benefits and Challenges of Cloud Computing

Cloud computing offers several benefits for organizations:

- **Scalability and Flexibility:** Cloud resources can be easily scaled up or down to meet fluctuating demands, allowing organizations to optimize costs and improve operational efficiency.
- **Cost Savings:** Cloud computing eliminates the need for upfront infrastructure investments and reduces ongoing maintenance costs, as the responsibility for hardware and software maintenance lies with the cloud service provider.

- **High Availability and Reliability:** Cloud service providers offer redundant infrastructure and data backup, ensuring high availability and reliability of services.

- **Global Accessibility:** Cloud services can be accessed from anywhere at any time, as long as there is an internet connection, enabling remote work and collaboration.

However, cloud computing also presents certain challenges that organizations need to consider:

- **Data Security:** Storing data in the cloud raises concerns about data security, as organizations no longer have full control over their data. Adequate security measures and encryption protocols must be implemented to protect sensitive information.

- **Dependency on Internet Connectivity:** Cloud computing heavily relies on internet connectivity, and any disruption in connectivity can impact access to cloud services.

- **Vendor Lock-in:** Moving to a specific cloud provider may result in vendor lock-in, making it difficult to switch to a different provider or bring services back in-house.

- **Compliance and Regulatory Requirements:** Organizations must ensure that their use of cloud services adheres to relevant industry regulations and compliance standards.

Real-world Example: Dropbox

One of the most well-known cloud computing applications is Dropbox, a file hosting service. Dropbox allows users to store and share files and folders in the cloud, enabling easy collaboration and accessibility from any device with an internet connection. It offers a user-friendly interface and provides various features, such as file synchronization, file versioning, and file sharing permissions. Dropbox utilizes cloud infrastructure to provide reliable and scalable storage services to millions of users worldwide.

Further Reading

For further exploration of cloud computing and its implications for cybersecurity:

- Armbrust, M., et al. (2010). A view of cloud computing. Communications of the ACM, 53(4), 50-58.
- Mell, P., & Grance, T. (2011). The NIST Definition of Cloud Computing. NIST Special Publication, 800(145), 7-26.
- Chandersekaran, S., & Kesavan, S. (2020). Handbook of Research on Cloud Computing and Security: Concepts, Methodologies, Tools, and Applications. IGI Global.

Conclusion

Cloud computing is a transformative technology that has revolutionized the way organizations store, manage, and process data. Understanding the fundamentals of cloud computing is crucial in the context of cybersecurity sustainability, as it provides insights into the challenges and opportunities that arise with the adoption of cloud services. By leveraging the benefits of cloud computing while addressing its associated risks, organizations can enhance their cybersecurity posture and achieve long-term sustainability in the digital age.

Cloud Security Challenges and Considerations

Cloud computing has revolutionized the way organizations store, process, and access data and applications. However, with this shift to the cloud, new security challenges and considerations have emerged. In this section, we will explore some of these challenges and discuss the key considerations that organizations must address to ensure the security of their cloud environments.

Data Confidentiality and Privacy

One of the primary concerns when migrating to the cloud is ensuring the confidentiality and privacy of data. As organizations entrust their sensitive data to cloud service providers (CSPs), they must ensure that appropriate measures are in place to protect against unauthorized access or data breaches. Encryption techniques, such as strong encryption algorithms and secure key management, play a crucial role in safeguarding sensitive data stored in the cloud.

Organizations should also carefully consider the location of their data and the regulatory requirements governing its storage and processing. Laws and regulations related to data privacy vary across different countries and jurisdictions. It is important to choose a CSP that complies with applicable data protection regulations and provides transparency around data residency and data handling practices.

Identity and Access Management

Managing user identities and controlling access to cloud resources is another critical challenge in cloud security. Organizations need to ensure that only authorized users can access their cloud resources and that appropriate controls are in place to prevent unauthorized access or privilege escalation.

Identity and access management (IAM) solutions, such as multi-factor authentication, role-based access control, and privileged access management, can help organizations enforce strong access controls in the cloud environment. It is essential to implement robust authentication mechanisms, regularly review and update user access privileges, and monitor user activities to detect any suspicious or unauthorized behavior.

Data Loss and Availability

Cloud service outages and the potential loss of data can have severe implications for organizations. It is crucial to establish comprehensive backup and disaster recovery strategies to ensure the availability and integrity of data in the cloud.

Organizations should work closely with their CSPs to understand the backup and recovery mechanisms in place and assess how these align with their specific business requirements. Regular backup testing and validation can help identify any potential issues and ensure the recoverability of data in the event of a disruption.

Additionally, organizations should consider implementing redundancy and failover mechanisms to minimize the impact of service interruptions. This may involve using multiple CSPs or implementing a hybrid cloud architecture to distribute resources across different environments.

Cloud Provider Security Measures

When choosing a cloud service provider, organizations must evaluate the security measures implemented by the provider. This includes understanding the physical security controls at data centers, the effectiveness of network security measures, and the availability of security certifications and compliance audits.

Organizations should seek transparency from their CSPs regarding their security practices and should review service level agreements (SLAs) to ensure that the provider meets the necessary security standards. It is important to perform due diligence and regularly monitor the security posture of the chosen CSP to ensure ongoing compliance and a strong security posture.

Data Governance and Compliance

Cloud environments often involve the sharing of data and resources across different entities and geographic regions. This introduces additional complexities in terms of data governance and compliance.

Organizations must address issues related to data ownership, data classification, data handling practices, and regulatory compliance in their cloud environments. Establishing clear data governance policies and procedures can help ensure that data is managed appropriately, regardless of its location.

Organizations should also regularly assess their cloud environment's compliance with relevant regulations and standards, such as the General Data Protection Regulation (GDPR), the Health Insurance Portability and Accountability Act (HIPAA), and industry-specific security frameworks like the Payment Card Industry Data Security Standard (PCI DSS).

Cloud Security Monitoring and Incident Response

Effective security monitoring and incident response capabilities are crucial in a cloud environment. Organizations should implement robust logging and monitoring mechanisms to detect and respond to security incidents in a timely manner.

Security information and event management (SIEM) tools can help consolidate and analyze security logs from different cloud resources, enabling organizations to identify potential security threats. Additionally, organizations should establish an incident response plan that outlines the steps to be taken in the event of a security incident, including incident escalation procedures and communication protocols.

Regular security assessments, vulnerability scanning, and penetration testing should also be performed to identify and remediate any vulnerabilities within the cloud environment.

Conclusion

Embracing cloud computing offers numerous benefits but also poses security challenges that organizations must address. By understanding and proactively addressing these challenges, organizations can ensure the security and integrity of their cloud environments. Through careful planning, implementation of appropriate security controls, and continuous monitoring and improvement, organizations can navigate the complexities of cloud security and leverage the power of the cloud while maintaining the confidentiality, integrity, and availability of their data and applications.

By being aware of the challenges and considerations discussed in this section, organizations can make informed decisions about their cloud security strategies and establish a robust security posture in their cloud environments. It is crucial to prioritize cloud security and adopt a proactive approach to address potential risks and vulnerabilities effectively. Only through a comprehensive and holistic approach to cloud security can organizations maximize the benefits of cloud computing while minimizing the potential security risks.

Cloud Security Services and Technologies

Cloud computing has revolutionized the IT landscape by providing flexible and scalable services to businesses and individuals. However, the shift to the cloud also brings unique security challenges, as sensitive data and critical applications are stored and processed outside of traditional on-premises environments. To address these challenges, various cloud security services and technologies have emerged. This section explores some of the key components of cloud security and how they help safeguard the cloud infrastructure and data.

Cloud Access Security Broker (CASB)

A Cloud Access Security Broker (CASB) is a critical component of cloud security architecture. It acts as an intermediary between cloud service providers and cloud consumers, providing visibility, control, and security enforcement across multiple cloud services. CASBs offer functionalities such as data loss prevention (DLP), threat protection, encryption, and access control. They extend the security perimeter of organizations to cloud environments, helping to mitigate risks associated with unauthorized access, data exposure, and compliance violations.

CASBs use various techniques to enforce security policies and monitor cloud usage. These include real-time monitoring of cloud activity, user behavior analytics, and anomaly detection. By providing a centralized platform for managing and securing cloud services, CASBs enable organizations to apply consistent security policies, regardless of the cloud service provider.

Identity and Access Management (IAM)

Identity and Access Management (IAM) solutions play a crucial role in securing cloud environments by ensuring that only authorized users have access to resources and data. IAM technologies help organizations manage user identities, roles, and permissions across multiple cloud services. They enable centralized administration of user accounts, authentication, and authorization, reducing the risk of unauthorized access and identity theft.

IAM solutions typically provide features such as Single Sign-On (SSO), multi-factor authentication (MFA), and role-based access control (RBAC). SSO allows users to authenticate once and access multiple cloud services without re-entering credentials. MFA adds an extra layer of security by requiring users to provide multiple forms of authentication, such as a password and a one-time verification code. RBAC enables organizations to define granular access controls based on the roles and responsibilities of users within the organization.

Encryption and Key Management

Encryption is a fundamental technique for protecting data in the cloud. It ensures that data remains confidential and secure even if it is intercepted or accessed by unauthorized parties. Cloud service providers often offer encryption capabilities at various levels, including data at rest, in transit, and in use.

Data at rest refers to data stored in persistent storage. Cloud providers typically offer encryption at rest using industry-standard encryption algorithms, such as Advanced Encryption Standard (AES). Encryption keys used for data at rest should be carefully managed to prevent unauthorized access. Key management solutions help securely generate, store, and rotate encryption keys, ensuring the integrity and confidentiality of the data.

Data in transit refers to data being transmitted between the cloud service provider and cloud consumers. Secure communication protocols, such as Transport Layer Security (TLS), are used to encrypt data during transmission, preventing eavesdropping and tampering.

Data in use refers to data being processed within the cloud environment. Confidentiality can be achieved through techniques such as secure enclaves and secure multiparty computation. These technologies allow sensitive data to be processed securely without the need to fully trust the underlying cloud infrastructure.

Cloud Workload Protection

Cloud Workload Protection (CWP) solutions focus on securing the workloads and virtual machines (VMs) running in the cloud environment. These solutions provide visibility, threat detection, and vulnerability management capabilities to ensure the security and compliance of cloud workloads.

CWP solutions use techniques like host-based intrusion detection and prevention systems (HIDS/HIPS), file integrity monitoring (FIM), and behavioral analytics to detect and mitigate threats targeting cloud workloads. They also help to identify vulnerabilities in the cloud infrastructure by scanning VMs for software vulnerabilities and misconfigurations. By providing real-time visibility into the security posture of cloud workloads, CWP solutions enable organizations to proactively identify and respond to potential security incidents.

Security Information and Event Management (SIEM)

Security Information and Event Management (SIEM) solutions are essential for monitoring and analyzing security events and logs generated by the cloud environment. SIEM solutions collect, correlate, and analyze event data from various sources, such as cloud platforms, network devices, and security appliances. They help identify and respond to security incidents, policy violations, and anomalies in real time.

SIEM solutions use various techniques, including log aggregation, event correlation, and machine learning, to identify patterns and detect potential security threats. They provide security teams with a comprehensive view of the cloud environment and enable proactive incident response and threat hunting. SIEM solutions also support compliance requirements by generating audit logs and reports for regulatory purposes.

Cloud Data Loss Prevention (DLP)

Cloud Data Loss Prevention (DLP) solutions help organizations protect sensitive data from unauthorized disclosure or loss in cloud environments. DLP solutions offer mechanisms to detect, monitor, and prevent the transmission or storage of sensitive data in violation of organizational policies or regulatory requirements.

DLP technologies use data classification, content scanning, and policy enforcement to identify and control the movement of sensitive data. They can inspect data in real time, both at rest and in transit, and apply actions such as blocking, encrypting, or quarantining data based on predefined policies. DLP solutions also provide visibility into data usage patterns, helping organizations identify high-risk activities and enforce data protection policies effectively.

In conclusion, cloud security services and technologies play a vital role in ensuring the confidentiality, integrity, and availability of data and resources in cloud environments. CASBs, IAM solutions, encryption and key management, cloud workload protection, SIEM, and DLP are among the key components of cloud security architecture. By leveraging these technologies, organizations can effectively mitigate the risks associated with cloud computing and maintain a secure and compliant cloud infrastructure."

Cloud Security Best Practices

Cloud computing has revolutionized the IT industry by providing scalability, flexibility, and cost-effectiveness. However, with the adoption of cloud services, organizations face new security challenges. In this section, we will explore best practices to enhance cloud security and protect data, applications, and infrastructure from potential threats.

Understand Shared Responsibility

One of the fundamental principles of cloud security is understanding the shared responsibility model. Cloud service providers (CSPs) offer security controls for the infrastructure, but customers are responsible for securing their data and applications. It is crucial to clearly define the division of responsibilities between the CSP and the customers to ensure comprehensive security posture.

Implement Identity and Access Management (IAM)

Proper Identity and Access Management (IAM) is crucial in maintaining a secure cloud environment. It is essential to create strong passwords, enforce multi-factor authentication (MFA), and regularly review and revoke unnecessary access privileges. Additionally, implementing role-based access control (RBAC) ensures that users have the necessary permissions based on their job roles and responsibilities.

Encrypt Data at Rest and in Transit

Encrypting data at rest and in transit provides an additional layer of protection for sensitive information. Cloud service providers offer encryption options for data storage, such as Azure Storage Service Encryption or Amazon S3 Server-Side Encryption. Additionally, secure transmission protocols like SSL/TLS should be used to encrypt data during transit.

Implement Network Segmentation

Network segmentation is the practice of dividing a network into smaller, isolated segments known as subnets. By implementing network segmentation, organizations can isolate sensitive information, control access, and limit the potential impact of a security breach. Applying network access controls between subnets helps prevent lateral movement within the cloud environment.

Regularly Monitor and Log Activities

Cloud environments generate vast amounts of logs and audit trails. It is crucial to regularly monitor and analyze these logs to detect and respond quickly to any security incidents. Cloud service providers offer monitoring and logging services like AWS CloudTrail or Azure Monitor, which can be used to track user activities, network traffic, and system events.

Perform Vulnerability Management

Regularly scanning and patching your cloud infrastructure is essential in mitigating security vulnerabilities. Cloud service providers offer vulnerability management tools and services that provide automated scanning of virtual machines and applications, identifying potential vulnerabilities and providing recommendations for remediation. It is crucial to promptly apply security patches to protect against known vulnerabilities.

Establish Incident Response Plan

Having a well-defined incident response plan is critical in effectively managing and responding to security incidents. The plan should include steps to identify and contain the incident, notify relevant stakeholders, collect evidence for forensic analysis, and restore normal operations. Regularly testing the incident response plan through simulations and tabletop exercises ensures preparedness in case of a security breach.

Backup and Disaster Recovery

Implementing robust backup and disaster recovery (DR) strategies is essential to mitigate the impact of potential data loss or service disruptions. Cloud service providers offer backup and DR services, allowing organizations to automatically replicate data to different geographical regions, ensuring business continuity in the event of a disaster. Regularly testing and validating backup and DR plans is crucial to ensure data integrity.

Stay Informed about Cloud Security

Cloud security is an ever-evolving field, with new threats and vulnerabilities emerging frequently. It is essential to stay informed about the latest security trends, vulnerabilities, and best practices. Regularly attending conferences, participating in webinars, and joining cloud security communities can help professionals stay up-to-date with the latest developments in cloud security.

Conduct Security Audits and Assessments

Regularly conducting security audits and assessments is essential to ensure compliance with industry standards and best practices. Organizations can perform internal audits or engage third-party auditors to evaluate their cloud security posture, identify gaps, and recommend remediation measures. These audits help organizations maintain a robust security posture and adhere to regulatory requirements.

In summary, implementing cloud security best practices is crucial in maintaining a secure cloud environment. By understanding the shared responsibility model, implementing identity and access management, encrypting data, implementing network segmentation, monitoring and logging activities, performing vulnerability management, establishing an incident response plan, implementing backup and disaster recovery strategies, staying informed about cloud security, and conducting security audits, organizations can enhance their cloud security and protect their valuable assets.

Securing Cloud Data and Applications

In the era of digital transformation, the adoption of cloud computing has become increasingly vital for organizations of all sizes. Cloud services offer numerous benefits, such as scalability, cost-efficiency, and flexibility. However, with these advantages come significant security concerns. Securing cloud data and applications is crucial to safeguard sensitive information, protect against cyber threats, and ensure data privacy. In this section, we will explore the key considerations and best practices for securing cloud data and applications.

Cloud Security Challenges and Considerations

When migrating to the cloud, organizations must address various security challenges and considerations. These challenges include:

- **Data breaches:** Cloud data breaches can have severe consequences, including unauthorized access, data loss, and reputational damage. Organizations must implement robust security measures to prevent data breaches.
- **Data privacy:** The cloud often involves storing data on third-party servers. Organizations must ensure that data privacy regulations and compliance requirements are met to protect sensitive information.
- **Identity and access management (IAM):** Proper identity and access management is critical in cloud environments. Organizations must implement strong authentication mechanisms and control user access to prevent unauthorized access to cloud resources.
- **Insider threats:** Insider threats pose a significant risk to cloud security. Organizations must implement strategies to detect and mitigate insider threats, such as monitoring user activity and implementing data loss prevention measures.
- **Cloud provider security:** Organizations must assess the security practices of cloud service providers (CSPs) and ensure that they comply with industry standards and regulations. This includes evaluating the security controls, certifications, and encryption mechanisms offered by the CSP.
- **Data loss and recovery:** Adequate backup and disaster recovery plans are essential in the cloud environment. Organizations must have mechanisms in place to recover data in the event of a loss or service outage.

Addressing these challenges requires a comprehensive and multi-layered approach to cloud security. Organizations must adopt a range of security controls and best practices to protect cloud data and applications.

Best Practices for Securing Cloud Data and Applications

To enhance the security of cloud data and applications, organizations should implement the following best practices:

1. **Data encryption:** Data encryption is essential for protecting data at rest and in transit. Organizations should encrypt sensitive data before it is stored in the cloud and ensure secure transmission through the use of secure protocols and virtual private networks (VPNs).

2. **Strong access controls:** Implementing strong access controls is crucial to prevent unauthorized access to cloud resources. This includes using strong passwords or multi-factor authentication (MFA) and regularly reviewing and updating user access privileges.

3. **Regular security assessments:** Conducting regular security assessments and audits is important to identify vulnerabilities and gaps in cloud security. This includes penetration testing, vulnerability scanning, and regular security audits to ensure ongoing compliance and security.

4. **Cloud data backup:** Regularly backing up cloud data is essential for disaster recovery and business continuity. Organizations should implement automated backup mechanisms, ensuring that backups are stored securely and can be easily restored.

5. **Security monitoring and logging:** Implementing robust security monitoring and logging mechanisms allows organizations to detect and respond to security incidents promptly. This includes monitoring user activity, network traffic, and system logs for any signs of unauthorized access or malicious activity.

6. **Security awareness training:** Organizations must educate their employees about cloud security risks and best practices. Regular security awareness training can help employees detect social engineering attacks, phishing attempts, and other cybersecurity threats.

7. **Data segregation:** Cloud environments often host multiple tenants sharing the same infrastructure. Implementing strong data segregation measures, such as utilizing virtual private clouds (VPCs) and network segmentation, ensures that each tenant's data remains isolated and secure.

8. **Continuous security updates:** Regularly applying security patches and updates is crucial to address known vulnerabilities and protect against emerging threats. Organizations should establish a process to keep the cloud infrastructure and applications up to date with the latest security updates.

By following these best practices, organizations can significantly enhance the security posture of their cloud data and applications. However, it is important to remember that cloud security is an ongoing process, and regular reassessment and adaptation to emerging threats and technologies is essential.

Example: Securing a Cloud-Based E-commerce Application

Let's consider an example of securing a cloud-based e-commerce application. The application stores customer personal information, including names, addresses, and credit card details. The organization needs to ensure the confidentiality, integrity, and availability of the data while complying with relevant data privacy regulations.

To secure the cloud-based e-commerce application, the following measures can be implemented:

- Use encryption: Implement end-to-end encryption for customer data both at rest and in transit. Use industry-standard encryption algorithms to protect sensitive information from unauthorized access.
- Implement secure access controls: Utilize strong authentication mechanisms, such as MFA or biometric authentication, to ensure only authorized individuals can access the application and data. Regularly review and update user access privileges to prevent insider threats.
- Regularly monitor and log security events: Set up security monitoring and logging systems to track and analyze user activities, system logs, and network traffic. Implement real-time alerts for any suspicious activities or potential security breaches.
- Conduct regular security assessments: Perform vulnerability scanning and penetration testing to identify and address potential weaknesses in the application and cloud infrastructure. Regularly audit the security controls to ensure compliance with industry standards.
- Backup and disaster recovery: Develop a robust backup and disaster recovery plan to ensure data can be restored in case of accidental deletion, data corruption, or service outages. Regularly test the backup and recovery process to verify its efficiency.
- Provide security awareness training: Educate employees about common security threats, social engineering, and best practices for secure handling of customer data. Promote a culture of security awareness and encourage reporting of any suspicious activities.

By implementing these measures, the organization can mitigate security risks and protect customer data in their cloud-based e-commerce application.

Additional Resources

For further exploration of securing cloud data and applications, the following resources are recommended:

- "Cloud Security and Privacy: An Enterprise Perspective on Risks and Compliance" by Tim Mather, Subra Kumaraswamy, and Shahed Latif provides comprehensive insights into cloud security challenges and strategies for securing cloud environments.
- "CSA Security Guidance for Critical Areas of Focus in Cloud Computing" by the Cloud Security Alliance (CSA) offers detailed guidance and best practices for secure cloud adoption, including securing data and applications.
- The National Institute of Standards and Technology (NIST) provides a collection of guidelines and publications on cloud computing security, including the "NIST Special Publication 800-144 - Guidelines on Security and Privacy in Public Cloud Computing."

It is essential for organizations to stay up-to-date with the latest security practices and leverage available resources to maintain a strong security posture in the cloud.

Cyber Threat Intelligence and Analytics

Introduction to Cyber Threat Intelligence

Sources of Cyber Threat Intelligence

Cyber threat intelligence refers to the information gathered and analyzed to identify potential cybersecurity threats, understand threat actors' tactics, techniques, and procedures (TTPs), and develop effective strategies to mitigate those threats. It provides actionable insights that organizations can use to enhance their security posture and protect their assets from cyberattacks. Gathering cyber threat intelligence requires the collection of data from various sources, which are categorized into the following:

1. **Open-source intelligence** (OSINT): OSINT involves the collection and analysis of publicly available information from sources such as social media platforms, news articles, blogs, forums, and websites. This information can provide valuable insights into the activities and motivations of threat actors. OSINT is a cost-effective way of gathering threat intelligence and is widely used by security professionals and researchers.

2. **Closed-source intelligence** (CSINT): CSINT, also known as proprietary intelligence, is classified information gathered from private sources. These sources may include private security vendors, cybersecurity firms, threat intelligence platforms, and industry-specific information sharing and analysis centers (ISACs). CSINT often provides more detailed and specialized information tailored to specific industries or sectors.

3. **Human intelligence** (HUMINT): HUMINT involves the collection of threat intelligence through human sources. This can be done through interactions and interviews with insiders, whistleblowers, or informants who have access to

classified or confidential information related to cyber threats. HUMINT provides valuable insight into the intentions, capabilities, and activities of threat actors.

4. **Technical intelligence** (TECHINT): TECHINT involves the collection and analysis of technical data and indicators related to cyber threats. This includes network traffic logs, system logs, intrusion detection system (IDS) alerts, malware analysis reports, and other technical artifacts. TECHINT helps in identifying the TTPs used by threat actors and understanding their attack patterns.

5. **Cyber threat sharing communities:** These are platforms or communities where organizations, government agencies, and security researchers share information about cyber threats. Examples include the Financial Services Information Sharing and Analysis Center (FS-ISAC), the Healthcare Information Sharing and Analysis Center (H-ISAC), and various government-sponsored threat sharing platforms. These communities facilitate the exchange of threat intelligence, including indicators of compromise (IOCs), attack patterns, and mitigation strategies.

6. **Threat intelligence feeds:** Threat intelligence feeds provide a constant stream of updated information about known threats, vulnerabilities, and indicators of compromise. These feeds are usually provided by cybersecurity vendors, government agencies, or industry-specific organizations. Organizations can integrate these feeds into their security systems to enhance their threat detection and prevention capabilities.

7. **Cyber threat intelligence platforms** (CTIPs): CTIPs are specialized tools or platforms that automate the collection, analysis, and dissemination of cyber threat intelligence. These platforms aggregate information from various sources, correlate and analyze the data, and provide actionable intelligence to organizations. CTIPs often incorporate machine learning and data mining techniques to identify patterns and trends in cyber threats.

It is essential for organizations to utilize a combination of these intelligence sources to get a comprehensive understanding of the cyber threat landscape. By leveraging multiple sources, organizations can enhance their abilities to detect, prevent, and respond to cyber threats effectively.

Example:

Let's consider a hypothetical scenario where a large financial institution wants to gather threat intelligence to protect its critical infrastructure from cyberattacks. In this case, the organization would utilize various sources of cyber threat intelligence:

- *Open-source intelligence (OSINT):* The institution will monitor social media platforms, news articles, and blogs related to cybersecurity and financial services. They might find discussions or chatter about specific attack techniques or vulnerabilities targeting their industry.

- *Closed-source intelligence (CSINT):* The organization may subscribe to a threat intelligence platform provided by a cybersecurity vendor specializing in the financial sector. This platform would deliver tailored reports, IOCs, and other relevant intelligence specific to the financial industry.

- *Human intelligence (HUMINT):* The institution might establish relationships with insiders in the cybersecurity community, law enforcement agencies, or other financial institutions to gather confidential information about ongoing cyber threats or attacks targeting the sector.

- *Technical intelligence (TECHINT):* The organization would analyze network traffic logs, system logs, and IDS alerts. They may deploy honeypots or other tools to capture and analyze real-time attack data within their infrastructure.

- *Cyber threat sharing communities:* The institution would actively participate in industry-specific information sharing and analysis centers (ISACs) or other threat sharing communities. They would contribute their insights and benefit from shared information from other organizations in the financial sector.

By utilizing these various sources of cyber threat intelligence, the financial institution can proactively identify emerging threats, understand the tactics used by threat actors, and take appropriate measures to secure their infrastructure.

Conclusion

Gathering cyber threat intelligence from diverse sources is crucial for organizations to stay ahead of the ever-evolving threat landscape. By leveraging open-source intelligence, closed-source intelligence, human intelligence, technical intelligence, cyber threat sharing communities, threat intelligence feeds, and cyber threat intelligence platforms, organizations can enhance their ability to detect, prevent, and respond to cyber threats effectively. It is essential for organizations to develop robust strategies for gathering, analyzing, and utilizing cyber threat intelligence to strengthen their cybersecurity defenses and protect their assets from malicious actors.

Role of Threat Intelligence in Cybersecurity

Threat intelligence is a crucial component of cybersecurity that helps organizations stay ahead of potential cyber threats and attacks. It provides valuable insights into the evolving threat landscape, enabling proactive defense measures and enhancing overall security posture.

Understanding Threat Intelligence

Threat intelligence refers to the knowledge and information about potential cyber threats, including the tactics, techniques, and procedures (TTPs) used by threat actors. This information is collected, analyzed, and disseminated to relevant stakeholders to aid in decision-making and proactive defense.

Threat intelligence encompasses a wide range of data, including indicators of compromise (IOCs), such as IP addresses, domain names, or file hashes associated with malicious activities. It also includes contextual information, such as the motivation, capabilities, and intentions of threat actors.

Benefits of Threat Intelligence

Threat intelligence provides several key benefits to organizations in their cybersecurity efforts:

1. **Proactive Defense:** By providing insights into emerging threats and attack trends, threat intelligence allows organizations to proactively identify and mitigate potential risks. It enables them to anticipate and prevent attacks before they occur, reducing the likelihood of successful breaches.

2. **Enhanced Incident Response:** Threat intelligence enables faster and more effective incident response by providing real-time information about ongoing attacks. It helps incident response teams understand the tactics and techniques used by threat actors, allowing them to swiftly identify and contain security incidents.

3. **Improved Security Decision-Making:** With access to credible threat intelligence, organizations can make informed decisions regarding their security investments and resource allocation. It helps them prioritize security measures, focus on the most critical threats, and optimize their cybersecurity strategies.

4. **Collaboration and Information Sharing:** Threat intelligence promotes collaboration and information sharing among organizations, enabling them to collectively address common threats. Sharing threat intelligence allows organizations to learn from each other's experiences and leverage collective knowledge to strengthen their defenses.

Sources of Threat Intelligence

Threat intelligence can be obtained from various sources, including:

1. **Open Source Intelligence (OSINT):** OSINT involves gathering information from publicly available sources, such as websites, social media

platforms, forums, and news articles. It provides valuable insights into threat actors, their activities, and their potential targets.

2. **Closed Source Intelligence (CSINT):** CSINT refers to proprietary or commercially available threat intelligence feeds and services. These sources provide more detailed and curated information about specific threats, vulnerabilities, and attack trends.

3. **Information Sharing Communities:** Organizations can participate in information sharing communities, such as threat intelligence sharing platforms, sector-specific information sharing and analysis centers (ISACs), or government-led initiatives. These communities facilitate the exchange of threat intelligence among peers, promoting collective defense.

4. **In-House Security Operations:** Organizations can generate their own threat intelligence through security operations center (SOC) activities, including log analysis, incident investigations, and penetration testing. By analyzing internal data and events, organizations can detect potential threats and develop intelligence tailored to their specific environment.

Challenges and Limitations

While threat intelligence offers valuable insights and benefits, it also presents some challenges and limitations:

1. **Data Overload:** The sheer volume of threat intelligence data can overwhelm organizations, making it challenging to identify relevant and actionable information. Effective tools and processes for data aggregation, correlation, and analysis are essential to filter out noise and focus on critical threats.

2. **Data Quality and Timeliness:** The quality and timeliness of threat intelligence can vary significantly. Inaccurate or outdated information can lead to false positives or missed opportunities for threat detection. Organizations must establish trusted sources and verification processes to ensure the integrity of the data.

3. **Lack of Context:** Threat intelligence often lacks context, making it challenging to fully understand the implications and potential impact of identified threats. Contextual information, such as the specific vulnerabilities or assets targeted, can significantly enhance the effectiveness of threat intelligence.

4. **Limited Visibility:** Threat intelligence primarily focuses on external threats, potentially neglecting internal risks and vulnerabilities. Organizations need to complement external threat intelligence with internal monitoring and analysis to have a comprehensive view of their security posture.

Case Study: APT Group Targeting Financial Institutions

A threat intelligence report identifies an advanced persistent threat (APT) group targeting financial institutions in multiple countries. The report reveals that the group employs sophisticated techniques, such as spear-phishing emails and zero-day exploits.

The threat intelligence provides the following key insights:

1. Specific indicators of compromise (IOCs), such as malicious email sender addresses, command-and-control (C2) server IP addresses, and malware hashes.

2. Tactics and techniques used by the APT group, such as social engineering tactics, exploit kits, and lateral movement within compromised networks.

3. A timeline of recent attacks, including the targeted financial institutions and the types of data exfiltrated.

Armed with this threat intelligence, financial institutions can take proactive measures to secure their networks and systems. They can update their email filters to block emails associated with the APT group, deploy intrusion detection systems to detect and prevent the use of known exploits, and strengthen their incident response capabilities.

Conclusion

Threat intelligence plays a vital role in cybersecurity by providing organizations with actionable insights into potential threats and attacks. It empowers organizations to proactively defend against emerging cyber threats, respond effectively to security incidents, and make informed decisions to enhance their overall security posture. However, organizations must also be aware of the challenges and limitations associated with threat intelligence to derive maximum value from its implementation. By harnessing the power of threat intelligence, organizations can stay ahead of evolving cyber threats and protect their digital assets in an increasingly complex threat landscape.

Threat Intelligence Sharing and Collaboration

In the constantly evolving landscape of cybersecurity, staying ahead of emerging threats is crucial. Threat intelligence refers to the knowledge and understanding of potential security threats that organizations can leverage to enhance their defenses. However, the task of identifying, analyzing, and mitigating threats is complex and requires a collaborative approach. This section explores the importance of threat intelligence sharing and collaboration in cybersecurity sustainability.

The Need for Threat Intelligence Sharing

Cybersecurity threats are not limited to individual organizations; they impact entire industries and sectors. Sharing threat intelligence helps organizations collectively pool their knowledge and resources, enabling them to detect and respond to threats more effectively. Here are some key reasons why threat intelligence sharing is essential:

- **Early warning and rapid response:** By sharing threat intelligence, organizations can provide early warnings about potential threats to their peers. This enables faster response times, allowing organizations to implement countermeasures before an attack occurs.

- **Broadened threat visibility:** No single organization has complete visibility into all potential threats. Through collaboration, organizations can gain access to a wider range of threat intelligence sources, enhancing their understanding of the threat landscape.

- **Improved threat detection and analysis:** Sharing threat intelligence enables organizations to analyze and correlate threat data from multiple sources. This helps in identifying patterns, trends, and indicators of compromise that may not be apparent when working in isolation.

- **Enhanced defense capabilities:** By sharing threat intelligence, organizations can leverage the expertise and specialized tools of their peers. This strengthens their own defensive capabilities, allowing them to proactively address emerging threats.

- **Reduced duplication of efforts:** Organizations often face similar threats. Sharing threat intelligence avoids duplicating efforts and allows organizations to focus on addressing new and emerging threats.

Challenges in Threat Intelligence Sharing

While the benefits of threat intelligence sharing are evident, there are several challenges that hinder its widespread adoption. These challenges include:

- **Lack of trust and information sharing reluctance:** Organizations may be hesitant to share threat intelligence due to concerns about exposing vulnerabilities or proprietary information. Building trust between organizations and establishing information sharing agreements is essential to overcome this challenge.

- **Standardization and interoperability:** Different organizations may use diverse technical frameworks, formats, and protocols for sharing threat intelligence. Achieving standardization and interoperability is essential to enable seamless sharing and collaboration.

- **Data quality and relevance:** Shared threat intelligence should be accurate, timely, and relevant for effective decision-making. Ensuring the quality and relevance of shared data requires proper validation and vetting processes.

- **Legal and regulatory considerations:** The sharing of certain types of threat intelligence may be subject to legal and regulatory restrictions, particularly in cases involving personal data or cross-border sharing. Compliance with applicable laws and regulations is important for secure and legal threat intelligence sharing.

- **Information overload:** The sheer volume of threat intelligence can be overwhelming. Organizations need to implement effective tools and processes to filter, prioritize, and analyze the shared threat intelligence to derive actionable insights.

Frameworks and Initiatives for Threat Intelligence Sharing

To address the challenges and promote effective threat intelligence sharing, various frameworks and initiatives have been developed. Let's explore some key ones:

- **Information Sharing and Analysis Centers (ISACs):** ISACs are industry-specific organizations that facilitate the sharing of threat intelligence among participating organizations. They offer a trusted platform for information exchange and collaboration, focusing on specific sectors such as finance, healthcare, or energy.

- **Cyber Threat Intelligence Sharing and Collaboration** (CTISC): CTISC is a collaborative effort between public and private organizations aimed at promoting the sharing of cybersecurity threat intelligence. It brings together government agencies, industry stakeholders, and cybersecurity experts to enhance threat awareness and response capabilities.

- **Structured Threat Information eXpression** (STIX): STIX is a standardized language for representing cyber threat information. It enables the structured sharing of threat intelligence across different organizations and tools. STIX provides a common framework for expressing indicators of compromise, threat actors, and threat campaigns.

- **Trusted Automated eXchange of Indicator Information** (TAXII): TAXII is a protocol that facilitates the exchange of cyber threat information. It allows organizations to share threat intelligence in a structured and automated manner, enabling timely and efficient collaboration.

- **Open Source Threat Intelligence Platforms:** Open source threat intelligence platforms, such as MISP (Malware Information Sharing Platform), enable organizations to share and collaborate on threat intelligence. These platforms provide a customizable and extensible framework for sharing indicators of compromise, threat data, and analysis.

Case Study: Financial Services Information Sharing and Analysis Center (FS-ISAC)

The Financial Services Information Sharing and Analysis Center (FS-ISAC) is an industry-specific ISAC focused on the financial sector. It provides a collaborative platform for sharing threat intelligence and coordinating incident response among its member organizations. FS-ISAC enables its members to stay informed about the latest security threats, vulnerabilities, and best practices through real-time alerts, reports, and information sharing.

The FS-ISAC platform offers sector-specific threat intelligence feeds, incident management tools, and a secure communication channel for sharing sensitive information. It also facilitates the exchange of threat intelligence with international partners, enabling cross-border collaboration. Through its collaborative efforts, FS-ISAC has played a vital role in enhancing the cybersecurity posture of the financial sector.

Conclusion

Threat intelligence sharing and collaboration are critical for effective cybersecurity sustainability. By sharing timely and relevant threat intelligence, organizations can enhance their threat detection and response capabilities. While challenges exist, frameworks and initiatives like ISACs, CTISC, STIX, TAXII, and open source platforms provide mechanisms for effective threat intelligence sharing. The success of organizations like FS-ISAC highlights the benefits of collaborative efforts in combating cyber threats. Embracing a culture of sharing and collaboration will be instrumental in building a resilient and sustainable cybersecurity ecosystem.

Threat Intelligence Analysis and Reporting

Threat intelligence analysis and reporting play a crucial role in cybersecurity as they enable organizations to proactively identify, understand, and mitigate potential threats. In this section, we will explore the key concepts and practices involved in threat intelligence analysis and reporting, including the sources of threat intelligence, the role of threat intelligence in cybersecurity, and various techniques for analyzing and reporting on threats.

Sources of Cyber Threat Intelligence

To effectively analyze and report on threats, cybersecurity professionals rely on various sources of threat intelligence. These sources provide valuable information about the latest cyber threats, attack techniques, and malicious actors. Some common sources of cyber threat intelligence include:

- **Open-source intelligence (OSINT):** OSINT refers to publicly available information that can be collected from sources such as social media, online forums, blogs, and news outlets. It provides valuable insights into potential threats and can help in understanding the tactics, techniques, and procedures (TTPs) used by threat actors.

- **Closed-source intelligence (CSINT):** CSINT, also known as proprietary intelligence, refers to information that is obtained through paid services or partnerships with industry-specific organizations. CSINT sources often provide more detailed and tailored threat intelligence that is specific to an organization or industry.

- **Threat intelligence feeds:** Threat intelligence feeds are subscription-based services that provide timely and updated information on emerging threats.

These feeds are typically curated by cybersecurity vendors and researchers who continuously monitor and analyze cyber threats from various sources.

- **Information sharing platforms:** Information sharing platforms facilitate the exchange of threat intelligence among organizations, government agencies, and cybersecurity communities. These platforms enable the sharing of real-time threat indicators, attack patterns, and other relevant information, helping organizations stay ahead of potential threats.

By leveraging a combination of these sources, cybersecurity professionals can gather comprehensive threat intelligence to support their analysis and reporting efforts.

Role of Threat Intelligence in Cybersecurity

Threat intelligence plays a crucial role in enhancing the overall cybersecurity posture of an organization. It helps organizations identify and understand potential threats, enabling them to take proactive measures to prevent or mitigate cyber attacks. Here are some key roles of threat intelligence in cybersecurity:

- **Early threat detection:** Threat intelligence allows organizations to identify potential threats at an early stage by analyzing indicators of compromise (IOCs) and other threat indicators. This early detection enables organizations to respond promptly and prevent or minimize the impact of cyber attacks.

- **Enhanced incident response:** By providing valuable contextual information about threats, threat intelligence enables organizations to improve their incident response capabilities. It helps in prioritizing and allocating resources effectively during incident response, ensuring a swift and efficient resolution of cybersecurity incidents.

- **Risk assessment and mitigation:** Threat intelligence helps organizations assess their risk exposure by providing insights into the evolving threat landscape. Armed with this information, organizations can implement appropriate risk mitigation measures and allocate resources in a targeted manner.

- **Improved decision-making:** Threat intelligence provides key insights into threat actors' motivations, intentions, and capabilities. This information empowers organizations to make informed decisions regarding cybersecurity investments, resource allocation, and strategy development.

Overall, threat intelligence serves as a critical component of a proactive and comprehensive cybersecurity strategy, enabling organizations to stay one step ahead of potential threats.

Threat Intelligence Analysis Techniques

Threat intelligence analysis involves the process of collecting, organizing, and analyzing threat intelligence data to extract meaningful insights. Various techniques are employed to analyze threat intelligence effectively. Here are some commonly used techniques:

- **Pattern recognition:** Pattern recognition involves the identification of recurrent patterns or trends in threat intelligence data. It allows analysts to uncover commonalities across different threats and identify potential correlations or associations.

- **Behavioral analysis:** Behavioral analysis focuses on monitoring the behavior of threat actors and identifying indicators of compromise. It involves analyzing network traffic, user behavior, system logs, and other data sources to detect anomalous or suspicious activities.

- **Intrusion detection and prevention:** Intrusion detection and prevention systems are used to monitor network traffic and identify potential threats in real-time. These systems leverage threat intelligence data to detect known attack signatures and patterns and take appropriate actions to prevent further exploitation.

- **Machine learning and artificial intelligence:** Machine learning and artificial intelligence techniques are increasingly being used in threat intelligence analysis. These techniques can automatically analyze large volumes of threat intelligence data, identify hidden patterns, and generate actionable insights.

It is important to note that threat intelligence analysis is an iterative process that involves constantly updating and refining analysis techniques to keep pace with the evolving threat landscape.

Threat Intelligence Reporting

Threat intelligence reporting is a critical aspect of the threat intelligence analysis process, as it involves communicating the findings and insights to relevant stakeholders within an organization. Effective threat intelligence reports should provide clear and concise information that aids decision-making and facilitates action. Here are some key considerations for creating impactful threat intelligence reports:

- **Relevance and context:** Reports should be tailored to the specific needs and requirements of the intended audience. They should provide relevant and timely information that helps stakeholders understand the potential impact of threats on their environment.

- **Clarity and simplicity:** Reports should be concise and easy to understand, avoiding technical jargon as much as possible. They should present complex information in a clear and straightforward manner, enabling stakeholders to grasp the key insights quickly.

- **Actionable recommendations:** Reports should include actionable recommendations that guide stakeholders in taking appropriate measures to address the identified threats. These recommendations should be practical, feasible, and aligned with the organization's overall cybersecurity strategy.

- **Visual representations:** Incorporating visual elements, such as charts, graphs, and infographics, can enhance the readability and impact of threat intelligence reports. Visual representations can help stakeholders quickly grasp complex trends and patterns.

Furthermore, threat intelligence reports should be regularly updated to reflect new findings and emerging threats. They should also provide a feedback mechanism for stakeholders to provide input and share their observations, which can further enrich the threat intelligence analysis process.

Example Scenario

To illustrate the practical application of threat intelligence analysis and reporting, let's consider a hypothetical scenario. A large financial institution has recently detected a significant rise in phishing attacks targeting its employees. The organization's cybersecurity team decides to leverage threat intelligence to gain insights into the latest phishing techniques and potential threat actors.

Using a combination of open-source intelligence and threat intelligence feeds, the team gathers information about the specific phishing campaigns targeting financial institutions. They analyze the phishing emails, investigate the malicious domains, and identify the TTPs employed by the threat actors.

Based on their analysis, the cybersecurity team creates a threat intelligence report. The report includes a summary of the observed phishing techniques, indicators of compromise, and potential threat actors involved. It highlights the potential impact of these phishing attacks on the organization's financial infrastructure and customer data.

The report also includes actionable recommendations, such as implementing multi-factor authentication, conducting phishing awareness training for employees, and enhancing email filtering capabilities. Visual representations, such as graphs depicting the frequency and severity of phishing attacks, are included to facilitate understanding and decision-making.

By leveraging threat intelligence analysis and reporting, the financial institution's cybersecurity team is able to proactively address the emerging threat landscape. They implement the recommended measures, share the threat intelligence report with relevant stakeholders, and continue to monitor the evolving phishing landscape to stay ahead of potential threats.

Conclusion

Threat intelligence analysis and reporting are essential components of a proactive cybersecurity strategy. By gathering insights from diverse sources, effectively analyzing threat intelligence data, and communicating the findings to stakeholders, organizations can better understand potential threats, make informed decisions, and take proactive measures to protect their digital assets. Additionally, leveraging advanced techniques such as machine learning and artificial intelligence enables cybersecurity professionals to analyze threat intelligence data at scale and identify hidden patterns or trends. As the cybersecurity landscape continues to evolve, threat intelligence analysis and reporting will remain critical in enabling organizations to effectively address emerging threats.

Data Analytics in Cybersecurity

Big Data and Cybersecurity

In recent years, the volume, variety, and velocity of data have grown exponentially, giving rise to the concept of big data. Big data refers to extremely large and complex datasets that cannot be effectively managed and analyzed using traditional data processing techniques. The ability to collect and analyze big data has brought numerous opportunities and benefits across various fields, including cybersecurity.

Introduction to Big Data

Big data is characterized by the "three Vs": volume, velocity, and variety. Volume refers to the vast amount of data generated from various sources, including social media, sensors, and internet-connected devices. Velocity refers to the speed at which data is generated and needs to be processed and analyzed in real-time. Variety refers to the different types and formats of data, ranging from structured data (e.g., databases) to unstructured data (e.g., text, images, videos).

Role of Big Data in Cybersecurity

Big data analytics has become an indispensable tool in cybersecurity due to its ability to detect, analyze, and prevent cyber threats more effectively. By processing and analyzing vast amounts of data collected from various sources, big data analytics can identify patterns, anomalies, and trends that might indicate potential cyber attacks. This proactive approach enables organizations to respond to threats in real-time, minimizing the impact of attacks and enhancing overall cybersecurity.

Understanding Cybersecurity Challenges with Big Data

While big data analytics offers immense potential for improving cybersecurity, it also presents several challenges that need to be addressed.

Data Integration and Quality: Big data is often collected from heterogeneous sources, which can result in issues related to data integration and data quality. Cybersecurity professionals need to ensure that the data they collect is accurate, consistent, and of high quality to derive meaningful insights and make well-informed decisions.

Data Privacy and Security: The sheer volume and variety of data involved in big data analytics raise concerns about data privacy and security. Organizations must take appropriate measures to protect sensitive and confidential information while ensuring that data access and usage comply with legal and regulatory requirements.

Scalability and Performance: Analyzing large volumes of data requires scalable and high-performance computing systems. Cybersecurity professionals need advanced infrastructure and tools to process, store, and analyze big data in a timely manner.

Skills and Expertise: Big data analytics requires a specific skill set that combines knowledge of cybersecurity principles, data science, and statistical analysis. However, there is a shortage of professionals with these skills, highlighting the need for specialized training and education programs.

Applications of Big Data in Cybersecurity

Big data analytics can be applied across various domains of cybersecurity to enhance threat detection, incident response, and risk management. Some key applications include:

Threat Intelligence: Big data analytics can ingest and analyze massive amounts of threat intelligence data from various sources, such as security feeds, malware repositories, and dark web monitoring. By correlating and analyzing this data, cybersecurity professionals can identify emerging threats, predict attack patterns, and proactively implement countermeasures.

Anomaly Detection: Big data analytics enables the identification of deviations from normal behavior patterns by analyzing large datasets. By establishing baselines and detecting anomalies, cybersecurity professionals can swiftly identify potential security breaches, unauthorized access attempts, or malicious activities.

Behavioral Analysis: Big data analytics can track and analyze user behavior, network traffic, and system logs to create profiles and detect abnormalities or unusual patterns. By identifying deviations from normal behavior, cybersecurity professionals can detect insider threats, unauthorized access attempts, or advanced persistent threats.

Security Monitoring and Incident Response: Big data analytics can enhance security monitoring and incident response by integrating and analyzing data from multiple sources, such as log files, network traffic, and threat intelligence feeds. This enables real-time detection of security incidents and facilitates timely response and remediation.

Ethical Considerations in Big Data Analytics for Cybersecurity

While big data analytics offers significant benefits in cybersecurity, there are ethical considerations that need to be addressed. These considerations include:

Privacy and Consent: Organizations must ensure that they collect, process, and analyze data in compliance with relevant privacy laws and regulations. They should obtain appropriate consent from individuals before collecting and analyzing their data.

Transparency and Accountability: Organizations should be transparent about the data they collect, the purpose of data collection, and the methods employed to process and analyze the data. They should also be accountable for the ethical use and protection of data.

Data Retention and De-identification: Organizations must establish clear policies regarding data retention and de-identification to minimize the risk of re-identification, unauthorized access, or misuse of personal information.

Example: Big Data Analytics for Threat Detection

Let's consider an example of how big data analytics can be applied in threat detection. Imagine a large financial institution that processes millions of transactions daily. By collecting and analyzing transactional data using big data analytics, the institution can detect unusual patterns and anomalies that may indicate fraudulent activities.

The big data analytics system ingests data from various sources, such as transaction logs, customer profiles, and external threat intelligence feeds. It applies advanced machine learning algorithms and statistical analysis techniques to identify patterns and detect anomalies in real-time. When a potential fraud or abnormal behavior is detected, the system can trigger an alert for further investigation and initiate appropriate measures, such as blocking suspicious transactions or notifying the cybersecurity team.

This example demonstrates how big data analytics can enhance the ability to detect and prevent cyber threats, ultimately safeguarding critical assets and ensuring the integrity of financial systems.

Resources and Further Reading

To explore the topic of big data and cybersecurity further, the following resources are recommended:

- McAfee, Inc. (2019). "The Big Data-Security Analytics Era: Are We There Yet?" *McAfee Labs Report.*

- Reinsel, D., Gantz, J., & Rydning, J. (2018). "Data Age 2025: The Digitization of the World from Edge to Core." *IDC White Paper.*

- Spark, M., Gallagher, T. (2015). "Big Data Analytics for Cybersecurity." *IEEE Security & Privacy*, 13(3), 34-39.

- Zwitter, A. (Ed.). (2018). "Big Data in Cybersecurity." *Springer.*

By referring to these resources, readers can delve deeper into the applications, challenges, and ethical considerations related to big data analytics in cybersecurity.

In conclusion, big data analytics plays a crucial role in cybersecurity by enabling organizations to effectively detect, analyze, and respond to cyber threats. However, it also introduces challenges related to data integration, privacy, scalability, and skills. By addressing these challenges and adhering to ethical considerations, organizations can leverage the power of big data analytics to enhance their cybersecurity capabilities and protect against evolving cyber threats.

Data Analytics Techniques for Threat Detection

In today's rapidly evolving cybersecurity landscape, organizations face unprecedented challenges in defending against sophisticated cyber threats. Traditional security measures are no longer sufficient to protect against intricate attacks that exploit vulnerabilities in networks, applications, and systems. To stay ahead of these threats, organizations are turning to data analytics techniques for threat detection.

Data analytics is the process of extracting insights and patterns from large volumes of data to make informed decisions. In the context of cybersecurity, data analytics enables organizations to detect and respond to threats in real-time, identify patterns of malicious activities, and predict future attack trends. In this section, we will explore various data analytics techniques that can be employed for threat detection.

Machine Learning for Threat Detection

Machine learning is an artificial intelligence (AI) technique that enables systems to learn and improve from experience without being explicitly programmed. By leveraging machine learning algorithms, cybersecurity professionals can develop models that can identify and classify threats based on patterns and anomalies in data.

One of the common applications of machine learning in threat detection is in network security. Intrusion detection systems (IDS) use machine learning algorithms to analyze network traffic and identify malicious activities. These algorithms can be trained on a large dataset of known cyber attacks to detect and classify unknown attacks accurately.

Another use case of machine learning is in the identification of malware. Malware detection algorithms utilize machine learning models to analyze file characteristics, behavior, and network traffic patterns associated with known malware. By learning from previously identified malware samples, these models can recognize new and emerging threats.

Example: Let's consider a scenario where a machine learning model is deployed in an organization's network to detect anomalous behavior. The model is trained on a historical dataset containing normal network traffic patterns. When deployed, the model continuously monitors network traffic and flags any behavior that deviates significantly from the learned patterns. For instance, if a user starts accessing a large number of sensitive files during non-business hours, the model can alert security analysts about a potential insider threat.

Big Data Analytics for Threat Intelligence

With the exponential growth of data generated by various sources, organizations are leveraging big data analytics techniques to identify and analyze cybersecurity threats. Big data analytics allows organizations to process and analyze large volumes of structured and unstructured data to extract valuable insights and patterns.

Threat intelligence is a critical component of cybersecurity, providing organizations with real-time information about emerging threats and vulnerabilities. By combining big data analytics and threat intelligence, organizations can uncover hidden patterns and trends that may not be apparent when analyzing smaller datasets.

Example: Consider an organization that collects large amounts of log data from various sources, such as network devices, servers, and firewalls. By using big data analytics techniques, the organization can process and analyze these logs in near real-time. Patterns and anomalies in the data can be identified, enabling security analysts to detect and respond to potential threats promptly. For example, if a sudden influx of failed login attempts is detected on a specific server, it may indicate an ongoing brute-force attack, and immediate actions can be taken to mitigate the threat.

Behavioral Analytics for User Monitoring

Traditional security measures often focus on protecting the perimeter of an organization's network. However, insider threats and compromised user accounts can bypass these defenses. Behavioral analytics, also known as user and entity behavior analytics (UEBA), focuses on analyzing user behavior to detect abnormal activities that may indicate a security breach.

Behavioral analytics leverages machine learning algorithms to establish baseline behavior patterns for users and systems. Deviations from these patterns are flagged as potential security incidents, allowing security teams to investigate further. By monitoring user activities, such as login patterns, file access history, and network traffic, behavioral analytics can identify suspicious behaviors indicative of a compromised account or insider threat.

Example: Imagine an employee who typically accesses the company's CRM system during office hours suddenly starts accessing it late at night. This deviation from the baseline behavior may trigger a behavioral analytics platform to raise an alert, as it could indicate unauthorized access or a compromised user account. Security analysts can then investigate the incident and take appropriate action to mitigate the risk.

Security Information and Event Management (SIEM)

SIEM systems play a crucial role in threat detection by collecting, analyzing, and correlating security event data from various sources. SIEM combines log management, event correlation, and real-time monitoring capabilities to provide a comprehensive view of an organization's security posture.

SIEM systems utilize rule-based analytics and machine learning algorithms to identify patterns and anomalies in security event data. By correlating events across different systems and combining them with threat intelligence feeds, SIEM systems can detect and respond to potential threats in real-time.

Example: Consider an organization that has implemented a SIEM system. The SIEM collects and analyzes log data from network devices, servers, and security appliances. If the SIEM detects multiple failed login attempts from different IP addresses targeting a specific user account within a short period, it can raise an alarm, indicating a potential brute-force attack. Security analysts can then investigate the incident and take necessary actions to prevent unauthorized access.

Challenges and Recommendations

While data analytics techniques offer significant advantages in threat detection, there are challenges organizations need to address to maximize their effectiveness:

- **Data Quality and Availability:** Effective threat detection relies on accurate and comprehensive data. Organizations need to ensure that data sources are reliable, and the data collected is of high quality.

- **Data Privacy and Compliance:** When implementing data analytics techniques, organizations need to ensure they comply with relevant data privacy regulations and protect sensitive information.

- **Expertise and Training:** Data analytics for threat detection requires specialized skills and expertise. Organizations should invest in training their personnel in data analytics techniques and tools.

- **Continuous Monitoring and Adaptation:** Threat landscapes evolve rapidly, and attackers constantly change their tactics. Organizations must continuously monitor and adapt their data analytics models and techniques to stay ahead of emerging threats.

In summary, data analytics techniques offer organizations powerful tools for threat detection in the ever-evolving cybersecurity landscape. By leveraging machine learning, big data analytics, behavioral analytics, and SIEM systems, organizations can gain valuable insights and improve their ability to detect and respond to threats effectively. However, addressing challenges such as data quality, privacy, expertise, and adaptability is crucial to ensuring the success of data analytics in threat detection. Organizations should continuously invest in improving their data analytics capabilities to stay ahead of emerging threats.

Machine Learning for Anomaly Detection

Anomaly detection is a crucial aspect of cybersecurity, as it helps identify and flag unusual patterns or behaviors that may indicate potential security threats. Traditional rule-based methods for anomaly detection rely on predefined signatures or thresholds, which can be limiting in detecting previously unseen or evolving threats. Machine learning techniques, on the other hand, offer a more flexible and dynamic approach to anomaly detection.

Machine learning algorithms learn patterns from historical data and use them to make predictions or detect anomalies in new data. They can automatically adapt to changing and evolving threats, making them well-suited for cybersecurity applications. In the context of anomaly detection, machine learning models can be trained to identify normal patterns and then flag any deviations from those patterns as anomalies.

Types of Anomalies

Before delving into machine learning algorithms for anomaly detection, it is important to understand the different types of anomalies that can occur. Anomalies can be broadly categorized into three types:

1. Point anomalies: These occur when an individual data point is considered anomalous when compared to the rest of the data. For example, a credit card transaction with an unusually large amount compared to the customer's typical spending habits can be considered a point anomaly.

2. Contextual anomalies: These anomalies are context-specific and depend on the surrounding data. For instance, a sudden increase in network traffic during off-hours may be considered normal if it occurs during a scheduled maintenance period but anomalous during regular operation.

3. Collective anomalies: These anomalies occur when a set of related data points together deviate from the normal behavior. For example, multiple failed login attempts from different IP addresses within a short timeframe may indicate a coordinated cyber attack.

Machine Learning Approaches

Various machine learning algorithms can be employed for anomaly detection. Let's explore some commonly used approaches:

1. Unsupervised learning: Unsupervised learning algorithms learn patterns from unlabeled data, making it suitable for anomaly detection. One popular technique is clustering, where data points are grouped into clusters, and any points that do not belong to any cluster are considered anomalies. Another technique is the reconstruction-based approach, where models are trained to reconstruct the input data and any significant deviations from the reconstructed version are flagged as anomalies.

2. Supervised learning: In supervised learning, models are trained using labeled data, where anomalies are explicitly identified. Classification algorithms, such as Support Vector Machines (SVM) or Random Forests, can be used to classify data points as normal or anomalous based on the learned patterns from labeled examples. However, obtaining labeled training data for anomalies can be challenging, as anomalies are often rare and difficult to capture.

3. Semi-supervised learning: As the name suggests, semi-supervised learning combines both labeled and unlabeled data for training. A small number of labeled examples of anomalies are used along with a larger set of unlabeled data points. The algorithm learns from the labeled examples and identifies patterns of normal

behavior in the unlabeled data. Any data points that deviate significantly from these normal patterns are flagged as anomalies.

4. Deep learning: Deep learning models, such as Neural Networks or Recurrent Neural Networks (RNN), have shown promise in anomaly detection. These models can automatically learn complex patterns and dependencies in data, making them effective in capturing subtle anomalies. The availability of large volumes of training data is crucial for training deep learning models effectively.

Challenges and Considerations

While machine learning-based anomaly detection offers numerous advantages, there are also challenges and considerations to keep in mind:

1. Training data availability: Anomaly detection relies on having a diverse and representative dataset that includes both normal and anomalous instances. Obtaining labeled examples for anomalies can be particularly challenging, as anomalies are often rare events.

2. Feature engineering: Selecting relevant features or attributes from the data is crucial for effective anomaly detection. Domain knowledge and expertise are essential in identifying features that can capture the distinguishing characteristics of anomalies.

3. Class imbalance: Anomalies are typically rare compared to normal instances, leading to class imbalance issues. This can result in biased models that prioritize normal instances, leading to poor anomaly detection performance. Techniques such as oversampling or undersampling can be employed to address class imbalance.

4. Dynamic environments: Cybersecurity threats are constantly evolving, and models trained on historical data may not adequately capture new and emerging anomalies. Continuous model updating and retraining are necessary to adapt to changing threat landscapes.

5. False positives and false negatives: Anomaly detection models may produce false positives, flagging normal instances as anomalies, or false negatives, failing to detect actual anomalies. Striking the right balance to minimize both types of errors is crucial to achieve reliable anomaly detection.

Real-World Applications

Machine learning-based anomaly detection has found applications in various cybersecurity domains. Let's explore a few real-world examples:

1. Network intrusion detection: Machine learning models can analyze network traffic patterns and identify any anomalies that may indicate a potential intrusion or

cyber attack. Unusual spikes in network traffic, unexpected data flows, or suspicious access patterns can be detected using anomaly detection techniques.

2. User behavior analytics: By analyzing user activities and behaviors, machine learning models can identify anomalous behavior that deviates from normal patterns. This can help detect insider threats or compromised user accounts.

3. Fraud detection: Machine learning models are widely used in financial institutions to detect fraudulent activities. Unusual transactions or suspicious patterns in financial data can be flagged as potential fraud cases.

4. System monitoring: Anomaly detection can be applied to monitor the behavior of system components, such as servers or IoT devices, to identify any abnormal activities that may indicate security breaches or malfunctions.

In summary, machine learning techniques offer a powerful and flexible approach to anomaly detection in cybersecurity. By leveraging historical data and learning patterns, these models can effectively identify deviations from normal behavior and flag potential security threats. However, challenges such as data availability, feature engineering, and model adaptability need to be carefully addressed to ensure reliable and accurate anomaly detection in dynamic cybersecurity environments.

Security Information and Event Management (SIEM)

Security Information and Event Management (SIEM) is a critical component of a comprehensive cybersecurity program. It encompasses the collection, analysis, and management of security-related data from various sources within an organization's network infrastructure. SIEM solutions help organizations detect and respond to security events, providing insight into potential threats and vulnerabilities.

Introduction to SIEM

SIEM systems combine security event management (SEM) and security information management (SIM) functionalities. SEM involves real-time monitoring and correlation of security events, while SIM focuses on long-term log storage and analysis. By integrating these two functions, SIEM provides a holistic approach to managing security incidents and improves an organization's overall security posture.

Components of a SIEM System

A SIEM system consists of several components that work together to provide comprehensive security monitoring and management. These components include:

- **Data collection agents:** These agents gather security event information from various sources, such as network devices, servers, and applications, and forward it to the central SIEM system for analysis.

- **Log management:** SIEM systems store and analyze log data, enabling organizations to identify patterns, anomalies, and potential security incidents. This component plays a crucial role in compliance reporting, forensics, and incident response.

- **Event correlation:** SIEM systems correlate security events from multiple sources to identify potential threats or attack patterns. By analyzing event logs in real-time, SIEM systems can detect and prioritize security incidents based on predefined rules and policies.

- **Alerting and notification:** SIEM systems generate alerts and notifications to inform security teams of potential security incidents. These alerts provide actionable information that supports timely incident response.

- **Dashboards and reporting:** SIEM systems offer customizable dashboards and reports that provide security teams and management with a comprehensive overview of the organization's security posture. These visualizations facilitate decision-making and enable proactive security measures.

SIEM Workflow

The workflow of a SIEM system involves several key stages, including data collection, event correlation, alerting, and reporting. Here is a breakdown of the typical SIEM workflow:

1. **Data collection:** SIEM systems collect logs and security event data from various sources, such as firewalls, intrusion detection systems (IDS), and endpoint protection solutions. This data is centralized within the SIEM for further analysis.

2. **Log normalization and parsing:** SIEM tools normalize and parse log data to extract relevant information, such as source IP addresses, timestamps, and event types. This process standardizes the data to support uniform analysis and correlation.

3. **Event correlation:** SIEM solutions correlate security events from different sources to identify patterns or indicators of compromise. Correlation rules and policies help SIEM systems differentiate between normal and anomalous behavior, enabling effective threat detection.

4. **Alert generation:** Based on predefined rules and policies, SIEM systems generate alerts when security incidents or anomalies are detected. These alerts, which include relevant contextual information, are forwarded to security analysts or teams for further investigation.

5. **Incident investigation:** Security analysts use SIEM tools to investigate alerts and security events. They analyze detailed logs, perform forensics, and validate the severity and impact of potential security incidents.

6. **Incident response and mitigation:** In response to confirmed security incidents, SIEM systems facilitate incident response by providing real-time information and context. This enables timely mitigation measures to limit the impact of an attack and prevent further compromise.

7. **Reporting and compliance:** SIEM solutions generate reports and dashboards that provide stakeholders with visibility into the organization's security posture and compliance status. These reports support compliance reporting, audits, and management decision-making.

Benefits of SIEM

SIEM solutions offer several benefits to organizations seeking to enhance their cybersecurity posture:

- **Threat detection and incident response:** SIEM systems provide real-time monitoring and analysis capabilities, helping organizations detect and respond to security incidents promptly. By centralizing security event data, SIEM facilitates incident investigation and response, reducing the time to detect and mitigate threats.

- **Compliance and regulatory requirements:** SIEM solutions generate reports and provide audit trails that assist organizations in meeting compliance obligations. SIEM can help fulfill regulatory requirements by collecting and analyzing log data, generating compliance reports, and supporting incident response procedures.

- **Improved visibility and situational awareness:** SIEM systems offer comprehensive dashboards and visualizations that provide a holistic view of an organization's security posture. This visibility enhances situational awareness, enabling security teams to make informed decisions and prioritize security measures effectively.
- **Efficient log management and storage:** SIEM tools centralize log management, providing a single source for log storage, analysis, and archival. This centralization streamlines log retention policies, simplifies log search and retrieval, and optimizes storage costs.
- **Threat intelligence integration:** SIEM systems can integrate with threat intelligence feeds, enabling organizations to enhance their threat detection capabilities. By leveraging external threat intelligence, SIEM solutions can identify and respond to emerging threats more effectively.

Challenges and Considerations

While SIEM solutions offer significant benefits, organizations must also consider certain challenges and factors when implementing and managing SIEM:

- **Complexity and resource requirements:** SIEM systems can be complex to deploy and manage, requiring dedicated resources and expertise. Organizations should consider the costs associated with hardware, software, staffing, and ongoing maintenance before implementing a SIEM solution.
- **Event overload and false positives:** SIEM systems can generate a large number of security events and alerts, many of which may be false positives. Organizations must carefully tune and customize their SIEM solutions to reduce noise and focus on meaningful alerts to avoid alert fatigue and optimize incident response efforts.
- **Data privacy and compliance:** SIEM systems process and store sensitive log data, raising potential privacy and compliance concerns. Organizations must ensure that appropriate security measures, such as data encryption and access controls, are in place to protect log data and comply with applicable regulations.
- **Continuous monitoring and maintenance:** SIEM systems require continuous monitoring and fine-tuning to ensure effective performance. Regular updates, patch management, and log source integration are essential to maintain the relevance and accuracy of security monitoring and detection.

Real-World Example: SIEM in a Financial Institution

Consider a financial institution that employs a SIEM solution to enhance its cybersecurity defenses. The SIEM system collects and correlates log data from various sources, such as firewall logs, user authentication logs, and security system event logs.

An analyst from the financial institution's security team receives an alert from the SIEM system indicating multiple failed login attempts from a specific IP address during non-business hours. The SIEM system correlates this event with other logs to determine if it is part of a larger attack.

The analyst investigates further, examining the associated logs and comparing the event details with known threat intelligence feeds. The SIEM system presents the analyst with contextual information, including the attacker's IP reputation and historical connection patterns. Based on this information, the analyst determines that the failed login attempts are part of a coordinated brute-force attack.

Using the SIEM system, the analyst triggers an automated response, which blacklists the attacker's IP address on the firewall and sends an immediate notification to the incident response team. The SIEM system also generates a detailed report that includes incident details, response actions taken, and recommendations for further security improvements.

Through the effective use of SIEM, the financial institution successfully detects and mitigates a potential security incident, reducing the risk of a successful breach and demonstrating the value of a proactive security monitoring approach.

Conclusion

SIEM plays a crucial role in enhancing an organization's cybersecurity posture by providing real-time monitoring, event correlation, and incident response capabilities. It enables organizations to detect and respond to security incidents promptly, comply with regulatory requirements, and improve overall visibility into their security landscape. However, organizations must consider the complexities, challenges, and resource requirements associated with implementing and managing SIEM solutions effectively. By addressing these considerations, organizations can leverage SIEM to its full potential and strengthen their cybersecurity defenses.

Predictive Analytics in Cybersecurity

In the constantly evolving landscape of cybersecurity, organizations need effective tools and techniques to stay one step ahead of potential threats. Predictive analytics is one such tool that has gained prominence in recent years. It involves the use of statistical algorithms and machine learning techniques to analyze historical data and make predictions about future events or behaviors. In the context of cybersecurity, predictive analytics can play a crucial role in identifying potential security incidents, detecting anomalies, and taking proactive measures to prevent cyber attacks.

Principles of Predictive Analytics

Predictive analytics relies on the principles of data analysis and statistical modeling. It involves the following key steps:

1. **Data collection:** Collecting relevant and high-quality data is essential for predictive analytics. This data can come from various sources, such as network logs, system logs, security incident data, threat intelligence feeds, and user behavior data.

2. **Data preprocessing:** Before applying predictive analytics techniques, the collected data needs to be cleaned and transformed into a suitable format. This step involves removing irrelevant or noisy data, handling missing values, and normalizing or standardizing the data.

3. **Feature extraction:** In predictive analytics, it is important to identify the most relevant features or variables that can contribute to the prediction task. Feature extraction techniques, such as principal component analysis or information gain, can be applied to reduce the dimensionality of the data and extract the most informative features.

4. **Model training:** Once the data is prepared, a predictive model needs to be trained. Various machine learning algorithms, such as logistic regression, decision trees, random forests, support vector machines, or neural networks, can be employed for this purpose. The model is trained using the historical data, where known outcomes or labels are associated with the input features.

5. **Model evaluation and validation:** After training the model, it is necessary to evaluate its performance. This typically involves splitting the data into training and testing sets. The model's predictions on the testing set are then compared to the actual outcomes to assess its accuracy, precision, recall, or other relevant evaluation metrics. Cross-validation techniques can also be employed to validate the model's performance.

6. **Model deployment and monitoring:** Once the predictive model is deemed satisfactory, it can be deployed in a real-world environment. It continuously

analyzes new data and generates predictions or alerts based on the model's trained parameters. It is important to monitor the model's performance over time and retrain or update it periodically to ensure its effectiveness.

Applications of Predictive Analytics in Cybersecurity

Predictive analytics has numerous applications in cybersecurity. Some of the key areas where it can be leveraged are:

- **Threat detection:** By analyzing historical threat data and patterns, predictive analytics can identify indicators of compromise (IoCs) and detect potential cyber threats. It can help security analysts in discovering new attack vectors, zero-day exploits, or advanced persistent threats (APTs) that may have evaded traditional security measures.

- **Anomaly detection:** Predictive analytics can detect anomalous behavior by comparing current activities against normal patterns. This can help in identifying potential insider threats, system breaches, or unauthorized access attempts. By setting up proper baselines and using machine learning algorithms, organizations can significantly enhance their ability to detect and respond to abnormal activities in real-time.

- **Vulnerability management:** Predictive analytics can assist in prioritizing vulnerabilities based on their likelihood of exploitation and potential impact. By analyzing historical vulnerability data, threat intelligence feeds, and network behavior, organizations can identify critical vulnerabilities that need immediate attention and allocate resources accordingly.

- **Fraud detection:** In addition to cybersecurity, predictive analytics can be utilized for detecting fraudulent activities in financial transactions or e-commerce platforms. By analyzing transactional and behavioral data, organizations can identify unusual patterns, fraudulent accounts, or malicious transactions in real-time, thus minimizing financial losses.

- **Incident response optimization:** Predictive analytics can improve the efficiency of incident response by automating certain tasks and providing recommendations. By correlating various data sources, such as system logs, threat intelligence, and user activities, organizations can accelerate the detection, analysis, and remediation of security incidents.

Challenges and Limitations

While predictive analytics holds great promise in cybersecurity, there are certain challenges and limitations that need to be considered:

- **Data quality and diversity:** The effectiveness of predictive analytics heavily relies on the quality and diversity of the data. If the collected data is incomplete, biased, or not representative of the target population, it can lead to inaccurate predictions. It is crucial to ensure data integrity and incorporate diverse data sources to capture a broader range of cyber threats.

- **Data privacy and legal considerations:** Cybersecurity professionals need to be mindful of data privacy laws and regulations when collecting, analyzing, and storing data for predictive analytics purposes. Strict adherence to legal and ethical guidelines is essential to protect individuals' privacy rights and avoid potential legal implications.

- **Model explainability and interpretability:** In certain applications, such as regulatory compliance or legal proceedings, it is necessary to provide explanations or justifications for the predictions made by predictive analytics models. The lack of interpretability in some complex machine learning algorithms can pose challenges in such scenarios.

- **Adversarial attacks:** Cyber attackers may aim to manipulate or deceive predictive analytics models by feeding them with carefully crafted malicious data or by evading detection. Adversarial attacks can undermine the reliability and effectiveness of predictive analytics systems, and hence, appropriate defense mechanisms need to be implemented.

- **Constantly evolving threats:** Cyber threats and attack techniques are continuously evolving, making it difficult for predictive analytics models to keep pace. Regular monitoring, updating, and retraining of the models are necessary to ensure their relevance and effectiveness in detecting new and emerging threats.

Conclusion

Predictive analytics is a powerful approach that can bolster the cybersecurity defenses of organizations by enabling proactive threat detection, anomaly detection, and effective incident response. By leveraging historical data and advanced machine learning algorithms, predictive analytics can uncover patterns and insights that may not be apparent through traditional security methods. However, it is important to carefully address challenges related to data quality, privacy, model explainability, adversarial attacks, and evolving threats to ensure the reliability and effectiveness of predictive analytics in cybersecurity.

In the next section, we will explore another important aspect of cybersecurity: cybersecurity incident response planning and preparedness. We will discuss the key steps involved in incident response, incident identification, classification, escalation, and the importance of post-incident analysis.

Cybersecurity Incident Response

Incident Response Planning and Preparedness

Incident response planning and preparedness are crucial components of an effective cybersecurity strategy. In today's digital landscape, organizations face an increasing number of cyber threats, making it imperative to have a well-defined and comprehensive incident response plan in place. This section will discuss the key elements involved in incident response planning and preparedness, along with best practices and strategies to mitigate the impact of security incidents.

Understanding Incident Response

Incident response refers to the process of handling and responding to security incidents, such as cyber attacks, data breaches, or unauthorized access. It involves a coordinated approach to detect, analyze, contain, eradicate, and recover from these incidents, with the primary goal of minimizing damage, restoring services, and preventing further unauthorized access or compromise.

The key objectives of incident response are:

- **Early detection and prevention:** Identifying security incidents as early as possible to minimize damage and prevent the escalation of the incident.
- **Effective containment:** Controlling and isolating the incident to prevent further compromise and damage.
- **Timely eradication:** Removing the root cause of the incident and eliminating all traces of compromise.
- **Thorough recovery:** Restoring affected systems, data, and services to their normal state.

- **Post-incident analysis:** Conducting a detailed analysis to determine the cause of the incident, lessons learned, and areas for improvement.

A well-structured incident response plan ensures that an organization can respond promptly and effectively to security incidents, minimizing the impact on operations, reputation, and customer trust.

Developing an Incident Response Plan

To develop an effective incident response plan, organizations need to follow a structured approach that encompasses the key activities involved in incident response. The following are the essential steps in developing an incident response plan:

1. **Establish an incident response team:** Designate a team of individuals responsible for managing and responding to security incidents. This team should include representatives from IT, security, legal, communications, and other relevant departments.

2. **Define incident response procedures:** Document detailed procedures and workflows for incident response activities, including incident reporting, analysis, containment, eradication, recovery, and post-incident analysis. These procedures should be comprehensive, yet flexible enough to accommodate various types of incidents.

3. **Determine communication and escalation channels:** Define clear lines of communication within the incident response team and establish protocols for escalating incidents to higher management or external stakeholders, such as law enforcement or regulatory authorities.

4. **Identify and prioritize critical assets:** Identify the organization's critical assets, such as systems, data, applications, and infrastructure, and prioritize them based on their importance to the business. This prioritization helps in allocating resources effectively during incident response.

5. **Establish incident detection and monitoring mechanisms:** Implement tools and technologies to detect and monitor security incidents in real-time. This may include intrusion detection systems, log management solutions, security information and event management (SIEM) platforms, and threat intelligence feeds.

6. **Prepare incident response playbooks:** Create a set of predefined playbooks or response guides for specific types of incidents. These playbooks should contain step-by-step instructions, decision trees, and relevant contact information to facilitate swift and effective response.

7. **Conduct training and awareness programs:** Regularly train the incident response team on the incident response procedures, playbooks, and technologies. Additionally, conduct awareness programs for employees to educate them about their roles and responsibilities during a security incident.

8. **Perform tabletop exercises:** Conduct simulated exercises and tabletop drills to test the incident response plan, identify gaps, and improve the team's readiness. These exercises should involve different stakeholders, challenge the response procedures, and provide insights into areas that need improvement.

Best Practices for Incident Response Planning

While developing an incident response plan, organizations should consider the following best practices to enhance the effectiveness and efficiency of their incident response capabilities:

- **Collaboration and coordination:** Foster collaboration and coordination between different teams and departments involved in incident response, including IT, security, legal, communications, and senior management. This ensures a holistic approach towards incident management.

- **Incident categorization and prioritization:** Establish a clear incident categorization and prioritization framework based on the severity, impact, and criticality of the incident. This framework helps in allocating resources effectively and responding to incidents based on their potential business impact.

- **Establish communication protocols:** Define communication protocols for internal and external stakeholders during a security incident. This includes specifying the communication channels, points of contact, and the information that needs to be shared.

- **Leverage threat intelligence:** Incorporate threat intelligence feeds and information sharing platforms into the incident response process. This enables organizations to stay updated about the latest threats, attack techniques, and mitigation strategies.

- **Regular testing and improvement:** Periodically test the incident response plan through simulated drills and exercises. This helps identify weaknesses, improve response procedures, and validate the effectiveness of the plan.

- **Document lessons learned:** Document and analyze the lessons learned from previous security incidents. These insights can be used to refine the incident response plan, update playbooks, and improve incident response capabilities.

- **Continuous monitoring and improvement:** Implement a continuous monitoring and improvement process for the incident response plan. Regularly assess the effectiveness of the plan, identify areas for improvement, and adapt to changes in the threat landscape.

Case Study: Incident Response at XYZ Corporation

To illustrate the importance of incident response planning and preparedness, let us consider a case study of XYZ Corporation, a large financial services organization. XYZ Corporation experienced a cyber attack where its customer data was compromised, resulting in a significant reputational and financial impact. However, due to their robust incident response plan, they were able to minimize the damage and recover swiftly.

Preparation Phase: XYZ Corporation had a dedicated incident response team comprising representatives from their IT, security, legal, and communications departments. They had defined incident response procedures and playbooks for various types of incidents. Regular training and awareness programs were conducted to ensure that employees were well-prepared to respond in case of a security incident.

Detection and Analysis Phase: XYZ Corporation had implemented a comprehensive security monitoring system, which helped detect the cyber attack at an early stage. The incident response team quickly initiated the incident response plan and started the analysis process to determine the nature and scope of the attack.

Containment and Eradication Phase: Once the incident was confirmed, the incident response team swiftly contained the attack by isolating affected systems and blocking unauthorized access. They then proceeded with the eradication process, removing the malware, and ensuring that all traces of compromise were eliminated.

Recovery and Post-Incident Analysis Phase: XYZ Corporation implemented their recovery procedures to restore affected systems and services. The incident response team conducted a thorough post-incident analysis to identify the root cause and understand the lessons learned. They updated their incident response plan and playbooks based on the insights gained to further strengthen their incident response capabilities.

This case study highlights the importance of having a well-defined incident response plan and demonstrates how it can help organizations effectively respond to security incidents, minimize the damage, and facilitate a swift recovery.

Conclusion

Incident response planning and preparedness are essential for organizations to effectively respond to security incidents. By establishing an incident response team, defining response procedures, promoting collaboration, implementing detection and monitoring mechanisms, and conducting regular training and exercises, organizations can significantly enhance their incident response capabilities. Adopting the best practices mentioned in this section ensures a proactive and robust approach to incident response, leading to improved cybersecurity posture and reduced impact of security incidents.

Incident Identification, Classification, and Escalation

In the field of cybersecurity, incident identification, classification, and escalation play a crucial role in the effective management of cybersecurity incidents. The process involves the recognition, categorization, and reporting of potential security incidents, along with determining their severity and taking appropriate actions to mitigate their impact. This section will provide an overview of the principles and best practices related to incident identification, classification, and escalation.

Incident Identification

Incident identification is the process of recognizing and detecting potential cybersecurity incidents. It involves monitoring networks, systems, and applications for any signs of unusual or suspicious activities. Various tools and technologies, such as intrusion detection systems (IDS) and security information and event management (SIEM) systems, can be used to aid in incident identification.

Signs of Potential Incidents There are several indicators that can suggest the presence of a cybersecurity incident. These signs can include:

- Unusual network traffic patterns or network congestion
- Unexpected system behavior, such as system crashes or slowdowns
- Unusual user account activity, such as failed logins or multiple login attempts
- Unusual file access or modifications
- Detection of malware or suspicious files
- Alerts or notifications from security monitoring systems

Monitoring and Logging To effectively identify incidents, organizations should have robust monitoring and logging mechanisms in place. This involves collecting and analyzing logs from various sources, such as firewalls, intrusion detection systems, and servers. Monitoring and logging can provide valuable information about system activities, user actions, network traffic, and other relevant events, enabling the detection of potential incidents.

Threat Intelligence Leveraging threat intelligence sources can also enhance incident identification capabilities. Threat intelligence feeds from reputable sources can provide insights into existing and emerging threats, enabling organizations to proactively detect and respond to potential incidents. These feeds may include information about known attack vectors, indicators of compromise, and other relevant threat data.

Incident Classification

Once an incident has been identified, it needs to be classified based on its severity and potential impact. Incident classification helps prioritize and allocate resources effectively, ensuring that the most critical incidents receive immediate attention. The classification process typically involves assessing the impact, urgency, and likelihood of the incident.

Impact Assessment The impact assessment is used to determine the potential consequences of an incident. This includes considering the magnitude of data loss, financial loss, reputational damage, and operational disruptions that may result from the incident. By understanding the impact, organizations can make informed decisions about the priority and resources required for incident response.

Urgency Assessment The urgency assessment evaluates the time sensitivity of an incident. This involves considering factors such as the speed at which the incident is spreading, the likelihood of escalation, and the potential harm it can cause if not addressed promptly. Urgency assessment helps prioritize incidents based on their immediate impact and the need for timely intervention.

Likelihood Assessment The likelihood assessment determines the probability of an incident occurring. It involves evaluating factors such as the vulnerability of the targeted systems, the presence of known threat actors, and the likelihood of successful exploitation. By assessing the likelihood, organizations can better understand the potential risks associated with the incident and allocate resources accordingly.

Incident Priority Levels Based on the impact, urgency, and likelihood assessments, incidents can be categorized into different priority levels. Commonly used priority levels include:

- High: Incidents with severe impact, high urgency, and high likelihood. These require immediate attention and significant resources.
- Medium: Incidents with moderate impact, urgency, and likelihood. These should be addressed promptly but may not require immediate attention.
- Low: Incidents with minimal impact, urgency, and likelihood. These can be addressed based on available resources and priorities.

Incident Escalation

Incident escalation involves reporting the incident to the appropriate stakeholders and escalating its handling to the next level of response. Prompt and effective escalation ensures that incidents are addressed in a timely manner and that the appropriate resources are allocated to mitigate the impact.

Internal Escalation The first step in incident escalation is to notify the internal stakeholders responsible for incident response and management. This usually involves communication with the incident response team, the IT department, and management representatives. The incident should be documented and reported following the established incident response procedures.

External Escalation Depending on the severity and nature of the incident, external stakeholders may need to be notified and involved in the incident response. This can include contacting vendors, service providers, law enforcement agencies, regulatory bodies, or other relevant parties. External escalation may be necessary to address legal and compliance requirements, coordinate response efforts, or seek additional assistance and expertise.

Escalation Criteria The decision to escalate an incident should be based on predefined criteria. These criteria may include:

- Severity and potential impact of the incident
- Escalation thresholds based on impact, urgency, or likelihood assessments
- Legal and regulatory requirements
- Availability of internal resources and expertise

Communication and Documentation During the incident escalation process, clear and concise communication is essential. All relevant information about the incident, including its classification, impact, and actions taken, should be documented and shared with the appropriate stakeholders. Effective communication and documentation help ensure a coordinated and consistent response to the incident.

Example: Ransomware Incident

To illustrate the incident identification, classification, and escalation process, let's consider an example of a ransomware incident. Ransomware is a type of malware that encrypts a victim's files and demands a ransom payment to provide the decryption key.

Identification The incident is identified when several employees report that their computer files have become inaccessible, and a ransom message appears on their screens. The IT department, equipped with perimeter security controls and an IDS system, detects a high volume of suspicious network traffic originating from multiple internal systems.

Classification The incident is classified as high priority due to its severe impact on business operations, potential financial loss, and the urgency to prevent further encryption of files. The likelihood assessment confirms that the organization has been targeted by a known ransomware strain, increasing the probability of successful encryption.

Escalation The incident response team is immediately notified about the incident, and internal escalation begins. The IT department isolates affected systems from the network to contain the spread of the ransomware. Management representatives are alerted about the incident, and a decision is made to involve external cybersecurity experts to assist with incident response and investigation.

External Escalation Law enforcement agencies and the organization's legal counsel are informed about the incident. The incident response team engages with the organization's cybersecurity insurance provider to initiate the claims process. To prevent further incidents, the organization alerts its vendors and service providers about the incident to fortify their defenses against similar attacks.

Conclusion

Incident identification, classification, and escalation are critical components of a robust incident response strategy. By diligently monitoring for potential incidents, accurately assessing their impact and urgency, and promptly escalating them to the appropriate stakeholders, organizations can effectively mitigate the risks associated with cybersecurity incidents. The incident identification, classification, and escalation process outlined in this section provide a foundation for a proactive and coordinated approach to incident response, enhancing an organization's overall cybersecurity posture.

Incident Triage and Response

Incident triage and response are critical components of a comprehensive cybersecurity incident management framework. In this section, we will explore the process of incident triage and response, including the key activities involved, the roles and responsibilities of incident response teams, and the strategies and techniques used to effectively manage and mitigate cybersecurity incidents.

Overview of Incident Triage

When a cybersecurity incident occurs, it is essential to quickly assess and prioritize the incident based on its severity, potential impact, and the resources available for response. This initial assessment is known as incident triage. The main objective of incident triage is to determine the appropriate level of response and allocate the necessary resources to contain the incident and minimize its impact.

Roles and Responsibilities

Effective incident triage and response require a well-defined incident response team with clearly defined roles and responsibilities. The incident response team typically includes the following key roles:

- **Incident Coordinator:** The incident coordinator is responsible for overseeing the overall incident response efforts, coordinating the activities of the response team, and ensuring effective communication and collaboration among team members.

- **Technical Analysts:** Technical analysts are responsible for conducting the technical analysis of the incident, collecting and analyzing relevant data, and providing technical expertise to support incident containment and resolution.

- **Forensics Specialists:** Forensics specialists play a crucial role in incident response by collecting, preserving, and analyzing digital evidence related to the incident. They use forensic techniques and tools to reconstruct the sequence of events and identify the root cause of the incident.

- **Communication Liaison:** The communication liaison is responsible for managing external communications related to the incident. This includes coordinating with stakeholders, such as law enforcement, regulators, customers, and the media, to ensure timely and accurate information sharing.

- **Legal Counsel:** Legal counsel provides guidance and advice on legal and regulatory requirements during incident response. They help navigate the legal implications of the incident, including data breach notification requirements and potential legal liabilities.

Incident Triage Process

The incident triage process typically involves the following steps:

1. **Initial Assessment:** The incident response team receives an alert or notification indicating a potential cybersecurity incident. The initial assessment involves collecting and analyzing available information to determine the nature and severity of the incident.

2. **Classification and Prioritization:** Based on the initial assessment, the incident is classified and prioritized according to predefined criteria. This helps determine the appropriate level of response and resource allocation.

3. **Containment and Mitigation:** Once the incident is classified, the incident response team initiates containment and mitigation measures to prevent further damage and limit the impact of the incident. This may involve isolating affected systems, disabling compromised accounts, or blocking suspicious network traffic.

4. **Evidence Gathering:** If the incident is deemed significant or has legal implications, the incident response team ensures proper preservation and collection of digital evidence. This evidence is crucial for forensic analysis, identification of the attacker, and potential legal proceedings.

5. **Notification and Reporting:** As part of incident response, appropriate stakeholders, such as internal management, external partners, regulatory bodies, and affected individuals, need to be notified about the incident. Incident response teams are responsible for preparing incident reports and providing timely updates to stakeholders.

6. **Post-Incident Analysis:** After the incident is contained and resolved, a post-incident analysis is conducted to identify the root cause, evaluate the effectiveness of the incident response process, and recommend improvements to prevent similar incidents in the future.

Strategies and Techniques

Effective incident triage and response require the use of various strategies and techniques to ensure a swift and efficient resolution of the incident. Some commonly used strategies and techniques include:

- **Incident Response Playbooks:** Incident response playbooks provide predefined procedures and guidelines for responding to specific types of incidents. These playbooks help streamline and standardize the incident response process, ensuring consistency and minimizing response time.

- **Automation and Orchestration:** Automation and orchestration tools can significantly improve incident response efficiency by automating repetitive tasks, such as data collection, analysis, and response coordination. These tools help reduce manual effort and response time, allowing incident response teams to focus on critical tasks.

- **Threat Intelligence Integration:** Integrating threat intelligence feeds into the incident response process helps inform decision-making and enhance incident triage. Real-time intelligence on emerging threats, tactics, and techniques can enable incident response teams to better prioritize and respond to incidents effectively.

- **Simulation and Training:** Incident response teams should regularly conduct simulations and training exercises to enhance their readiness and effectiveness. These exercises simulate real-world scenarios, allowing teams to practice their response capabilities, identify gaps, and improve incident handling skills.

Real-Life Example: Ransomware Attack Response

Consider a real-life example of a ransomware attack response. A company's cybersecurity monitoring system detects unusual network activity and alerts the incident response team. Upon conducting an initial assessment, the team confirms a ransomware attack targeting critical systems.

The incident is classified as a high severity incident, given the potential impact on business operations and data confidentiality. The incident response team initiates immediate containment measures by isolating the affected systems from the network and shutting down compromised systems to prevent further spread.

Simultaneously, the forensics specialists start collecting digital evidence, such as system logs and network traffic data, to identify the ransomware variant and determine the entry point of the attack. The communication liaison prepares an incident notification report for senior management and legal counsel for further guidance.

Once the incident is contained, the incident response team focuses on restoring affected systems from known clean backups. They coordinate with the IT department to ensure the restoration process is secure and free from any reinfection risks.

After the incident, a comprehensive post-incident analysis is conducted to identify the vulnerabilities exploited, evaluate the incident response effectiveness, and propose remediation measures. The lessons learned from the incident are documented and shared with relevant stakeholders to prevent similar incidents in the future.

Conclusion

Incident triage and response form a critical part of an organization's cybersecurity incident management framework. By following a well-defined incident triage process, assigning clear roles and responsibilities, and implementing effective strategies and techniques, organizations can effectively contain and mitigate cybersecurity incidents. Additionally, regular simulations and training exercises can further enhance the incident response capabilities of organizations and ensure their readiness to respond to cybersecurity incidents.

Incident Investigation and Evidence Collection

Incident investigation and evidence collection are crucial components of cybersecurity incident response. When a security incident occurs, it is important to conduct a thorough investigation to determine the cause of the incident, the extent of the damage, and any potential vulnerabilities that may have been exploited. The evidence collected during this process plays a vital role in identifying the attacker, understanding the attack vector, and taking appropriate actions to prevent future incidents. In this section, we will discuss the principles, process, and best practices of incident investigation and evidence collection.

Principles of Incident Investigation

Effective incident investigation requires adherence to certain principles to ensure the accuracy, integrity, and reliability of the evidence collected. These principles include:

- **Preservation of Evidence:** It is essential to preserve all evidence in its original form to avoid any tampering or alteration. This includes not only digital evidence but also physical evidence, such as compromised hardware or media. Preservation involves creating backups or images of the affected systems and ensuring the chain of custody is maintained throughout the investigation process.

- **Forensic Soundness:** Forensic soundness refers to the use of techniques and tools that meet the standards and guidelines of digital forensic practices. It involves applying accepted methodologies and maintaining the integrity of the evidence. This ensures that the evidence can withstand legal scrutiny if required and is admissible in a court of law.

- **Documentation and Reporting:** Accurate and detailed documentation is crucial in incident investigation. Investigators should document every step of the investigation process, including the tools and techniques used, the actions taken, and the results obtained. This documentation serves as a record of the investigation and can be used to support findings and conclusions in incident reports.

- **Chain of Custody:** Chain of custody refers to the chronological documentation of who had control of the evidence at any given time. It ensures that the evidence's integrity is maintained and prevents any potential challenges to its admissibility. Proper documentation should include the names of individuals who handled the evidence, the date and time of each transfer, and any relevant observations or remarks.

Process of Incident Investigation

The process of incident investigation can be divided into several distinct phases, each of which plays a crucial role in uncovering the details of the incident and gathering relevant evidence. These phases include:

1. **Preparation:** In this phase, incident response team members should be assembled, and relevant tools and resources should be prepared. This includes ensuring that the incident response plan is up to date and that all necessary equipment and software are readily available.

2. **Identification:** The identification phase involves recognizing the occurrence of a security incident. This may be triggered by the detection of unusual network activity, system alerts, or reports from end users. It is important to

validate the incident and gather initial information to determine its severity and potential impact.

3. **Containment:** Once the incident is confirmed, the focus shifts to containing the damage and preventing further compromise. This may involve isolating affected systems, disconnecting from the network, or taking other appropriate measures to limit the attacker's access and control.

4. **Analysis:** In the analysis phase, investigators dig deeper into the incident to understand the attack vector, how the system was compromised, and the extent of the damage. This may involve examining logs, conducting memory forensics, analyzing network traffic, and using other forensic techniques to identify the attacker's actions.

5. **Evidence Collection:** Evidence collection is a crucial phase of the investigation process. Investigators must collect and preserve all relevant evidence to support the findings and conclusions. This includes both digital evidence, such as log files, system images, and network captures, as well as physical evidence, such as compromised hardware or media.

6. **Reporting:** The findings of the investigation should be documented in an incident report. The report should provide a detailed account of the incident, including the timeline, the attack methodology, the impact on the organization, and any recommended actions to prevent similar incidents in the future.

7. **Remediation:** Once the incident has been analyzed and reported, the focus shifts to remediation and recovery. This may involve patching vulnerabilities, resetting compromised passwords, updating security controls, and implementing additional preventive measures to enhance the overall security posture.

8. **Post-Incident Review:** After the incident is resolved, it is important to conduct a post-incident review to identify lessons learned and improve the organization's incident response capabilities. This may involve updating policies and procedures, enhancing employee training and awareness, or making changes to the overall security architecture.

Best Practices for Evidence Collection

Effective evidence collection is critical in incident investigation to ensure the accuracy and integrity of the evidence. The following best practices should be followed:

- **Create Forensic Images:** For digital evidence, it is essential to create forensic images or copies of the affected systems, such as hard drives, memory, or virtual machines. These images should be created using forensically sound methods and should be write-protected to prevent any changes or tampering.
- **Document Actions and Observations:** Investigators should document every action taken during the evidence collection process, including the tools used, the commands executed, and any relevant observations or findings. This documentation helps to establish a clear chain of custody and provides a record of the investigator's actions.
- **Collect Network Traffic and Logs:** Network traffic data and system logs play a crucial role in incident investigation. It is important to collect and preserve this information to analyze the attacker's activities, identify compromised systems, and understand the overall scope of the incident. This may involve using network packet captures or log aggregation tools.
- **Protect Physical Evidence:** If physical evidence, such as compromised hardware or media, is involved in the incident, it should be properly protected and secured. This may include placing the evidence in tamper-evident bags, storing it in a secure location, or following other appropriate physical security measures.
- **Maintain Chain of Custody:** The chain of custody should be maintained throughout the evidence collection process. This involves documenting who had control of the evidence at any given time and ensuring that it is properly secured and protected. Any transfers or changes in custody should be properly documented and validated.
- **Adhere to Legal and Regulatory Requirements:** Investigators should be aware of the legal and regulatory requirements related to evidence collection. This includes obtaining appropriate legal permissions, complying with privacy laws, and following any specific procedures mandated by the jurisdiction in which the investigation is being conducted.

Case Study: Evidence Collection in a Phishing Attack

To illustrate the practical application of incident investigation and evidence collection, let's consider a case study involving a phishing attack targeting a financial institution.

In this scenario, employees of the institution received fraudulent emails, prompting them to click on a malicious link and enter their login credentials. The incident response team was alerted to the attack and initiated an investigation.

The investigation process involved the following steps:

1. **Identification:** The incident response team identified the phishing attack based on employee reports and email logs showing the arrival of suspicious emails in user inboxes.

2. **Containment:** The team contained the attack by blocking access to the malicious website and notifying employees not to click on any suspicious links or provide their credentials.

3. **Analysis:** Investigators analyzed the email headers, link destinations, and email content to understand the attack vector and the potential impact on the organization. They also analyzed network logs to identify any compromised systems or unusual network traffic patterns.

4. **Evidence Collection:** Digital evidence, including the suspicious emails, network logs, and malicious URLs, was collected and preserved using forensic tools and techniques. Memory forensics was conducted on the affected systems to identify any indicators of compromise.

5. **Reporting:** The findings of the investigation were documented in an incident report. The report detailed the nature of the attack, the potential impact on the organization, and recommendations for improving security controls and user awareness.

6. **Remediation:** The institution took remedial actions, such as resetting compromised passwords, updating email filters, and conducting security awareness training for employees to prevent future phishing attacks.

7. **Post-Incident Review:** A post-incident review was conducted to identify areas for improvement in incident response capabilities. This included revising security policies and enhancing employee training to detect and report phishing attempts effectively.

In this case study, effective incident investigation and evidence collection played a crucial role in understanding the attack and mitigating its impact. By following the principles and best practices outlined in this section, the incident response team was able to preserve the integrity of the evidence and obtain valuable insights into the attack methodology, leading to effective response and prevention measures.

Exercises

1. Explain the importance of evidence collection in incident investigation.
2. Describe the principles of incident investigation and the role of forensic soundness in evidence collection.
3. Outline the phases involved in the incident investigation process and explain the purpose of each phase.
4. Provide examples of digital and physical evidence that may be collected during an incident investigation.
5. Discuss the best practices for evidence collection, including the creation of forensic images and the proper documentation of actions and observations.
6. Analyze a real-world incident scenario and outline the steps that should be followed for evidence collection and documentation.

Additional Resources

- Casey, E., & Carrier, B. (2014). *Handbook of Digital Forensics and Investigation*. Academic Press.
- Nelson, B., Phillips, A., & Steuart, C. (2019). *Guide to Computer Forensics and Investigations*. Cengage Learning.
- SANS Institute. *Incident Response Plan Development: A Step-by-Step Guide*. Retrieved from `https://www.sans.org/reading-room/whitepapers/incident/designing-incident-response-plan-step-by-step-guide-34562`

Conclusion

Incident investigation and evidence collection are critical processes in cybersecurity incident response. By following established principles and best practices, organizations can effectively identify, analyze, and respond to security incidents. Thorough evidence collection enables investigators to understand the attack methodology, identify the perpetrators, and take appropriate measures to prevent future incidents. By continuously improving incident investigation capabilities, organizations can enhance their overall cybersecurity posture and protect against emerging threats.

Post-Incident Analysis and Lessons Learned

Post-incident analysis is a critical process in cybersecurity that allows organizations to understand and learn from security breaches and incidents. By conducting a comprehensive analysis of the incident, organizations can identify weaknesses in their security controls, policies, and procedures, and make the necessary improvements to prevent similar incidents from occurring in the future. This section explores the key components of post-incident analysis and highlights the importance of learning lessons from security incidents.

Objectives of Post-Incident Analysis

The primary objective of post-incident analysis is to gain a thorough understanding of the sequence of events leading to the security incident. This includes identifying the root cause of the incident, understanding the tactics and techniques used by the attacker, and assessing the impact of the incident on the organization's systems, data, and operations. The analysis should also aim to identify any gaps in the organization's security controls and processes, as well as potential vulnerabilities that could be exploited in the future.

Process of Post-Incident Analysis

The process of post-incident analysis typically involves the following steps:

1. Incident Documentation: It is crucial to document all relevant information about the incident, including the date and time of the incident, the systems and data affected, and any initial findings or observations. This documentation serves as a reference for the analysis process and ensures that important details are not overlooked.

2. Evidence Collection: Gathering and preserving evidence is a critical aspect of post-incident analysis. This includes collecting log files, network traffic data, system backups, and any other relevant data that can provide insights into the incident. It is important to follow proper forensic procedures to ensure the integrity and admissibility of the collected evidence.

3. Incident Reconstruction: The next step is to reconstruct the sequence of events leading to the incident. This involves analyzing the collected evidence and identifying the actions taken by the attacker or any other relevant parties. Reconstruction helps in understanding the attack vector, the vulnerabilities exploited, and the impact of the attack.

4. Root Cause Analysis: Identifying the root cause of the incident is essential to prevent similar incidents in the future. This analysis involves identifying the

underlying weaknesses or gaps in the organization's security controls, processes, or infrastructure that enabled the incident to occur. It may involve examining factors such as misconfigurations, lack of employee awareness or training, or inadequate security controls.

5. Lessons Learned: Once the root cause is determined, lessons learned from the incident should be documented. This includes identifying areas where improvements can be made, such as strengthening security controls, enhancing incident response processes, or providing additional employee training. It is important to view these lessons as opportunities for growth and continual improvement rather than assigning blame to individuals or teams.

6. Remediation and Mitigation: Based on the lessons learned, organizations should develop a plan to address the identified weaknesses and vulnerabilities. This may involve implementing technical solutions, revising policies and procedures, conducting additional employee training, or other actions aimed at enhancing the overall security posture.

7. Communication and Reporting: It is essential to communicate the findings of the post-incident analysis to relevant stakeholders, including senior management, IT teams, and other individuals who may be affected. This helps to create awareness, enable informed decision-making, and ensure that the necessary resources and support are provided for implementing the recommended remediation measures.

Challenges and Considerations

Post-incident analysis can be a complex and challenging process. Some of the common challenges and considerations include:

1. Limited Information: In some cases, organizations may have limited information or incomplete data about the incident. This may be due to the sophistication of the attack, the absence of appropriate monitoring or logging mechanisms, or other technical limitations. In such cases, the analysis may focus on the available information while acknowledging any gaps.

2. Time Constraints: Conducting a thorough post-incident analysis requires time and resources. However, organizations often face pressure to resume normal operations quickly, leading to limited time for analysis. Balancing the need for speedy recovery with the importance of in-depth analysis is a challenge that organizations must carefully manage.

3. Collaboration and Coordination: Post-incident analysis often involves multiple teams, including IT, security, legal, and management. Effective collaboration and coordination among these teams are crucial for a successful

analysis. Communication channels should be established, and roles and responsibilities should be clearly defined to ensure a smooth analysis process.

4. Learning from Lesser-Significant Incidents: Not all security incidents have a severe impact on an organization. However, it is important to analyze even lesser-significant incidents to identify trends, patterns, and potential indicators of more significant threats. The analysis should not be limited to high-profile incidents but should encompass a comprehensive view of all security incidents.

5. Continuous Improvement: Post-incident analysis is not a one-time activity but a continuous process of learning and improvement. Organizations should have mechanisms in place to capture and incorporate lessons learned from every incident into their security practices, policies, and procedures. This helps to create a culture of continual improvement and resilience.

Case Study: Post-Incident Analysis in a Financial Institution

Consider the case of a financial institution that experienced a significant security breach involving customer data. Following the incident, the organization conducted a thorough post-incident analysis to understand the root cause and identify lessons learned. Here is a summary of the analysis process and its outcomes:

1. Incident Documentation: The organization documented the date and time of the incident, the affected systems, and the initial findings. This documentation served as a foundation for the analysis.

2. Evidence Collection: The organization collected log files, network traffic data, and system backups to analyze the incident. Specialized forensic tools and procedures were used to ensure the integrity and admissibility of the evidence.

3. Incident Reconstruction: The collected evidence was analyzed to reconstruct the sequence of events leading to the breach. It was determined that the attacker gained access through an unpatched vulnerability and exploited weak access controls.

4. Root Cause Analysis: The root cause of the incident was identified as a lack of robust patch management and an inadequate access control mechanism. The organization realized the need to strengthen these areas to prevent similar incidents in the future.

5. Lessons Learned: Lessons learned from the incident were documented, emphasizing the importance of timely patch management and the need for regular access control reviews. The organization recognized the significance of ongoing employee training and awareness programs to prevent security breaches.

6. Remediation and Mitigation: The organization developed a plan to address the identified weaknesses, including implementing a robust patch management

process, enhancing access controls, and improving employee training and awareness programs.

7. Communication and Reporting: The findings and recommendations were communicated to senior management, IT teams, and relevant stakeholders. The organization emphasized the importance of the lessons learned and obtained the necessary support and resources for implementing the remediation measures.

Through the post-incident analysis, the financial institution gained valuable insights into its security weaknesses and implemented measures to prevent similar incidents in the future. The analysis also helped create a culture of continual improvement and resilience within the organization.

Conclusion

Post-incident analysis is a critical component of cybersecurity sustainability. It plays a vital role in understanding and learning from security incidents, identifying weaknesses, and making improvements to prevent future incidents. By following a structured analysis process, organizations can gain valuable insights and develop effective remediation measures. However, it is important to recognize that post-incident analysis is an ongoing process that requires continuous improvement and a proactive approach to prevent security breaches and protect critical assets.

In the next section, we will explore the privacy and legal aspects of cybersecurity, addressing the right to privacy in the digital age, privacy laws and regulations, and the legal framework for cybersecurity.

Privacy and Legal Aspects of Cybersecurity

The Right to Privacy in the Digital Age

Privacy Laws and Regulations

In today's interconnected world, where data is generated and shared at an unprecedented rate, the protection of privacy has become a paramount concern. Privacy laws and regulations are designed to safeguard individuals' personal information and ensure that it is collected, used, and stored in a responsible and secure manner. In this section, we will explore the principles and requirements of privacy laws and regulations, as well as their implications for organizations and individuals.

Fundamentals of Privacy Laws

Privacy laws are legal frameworks that define the rights and obligations of individuals and organizations regarding the collection, use, and disclosure of personal information. These laws aim to strike a balance between the need to protect individuals' privacy and the legitimate interests of organizations to collect and use data for specific purposes. The principles underlying privacy laws include:

1. **Notice and Consent:** Privacy laws require organizations to inform individuals about the purpose of collecting their personal information and obtain their consent before collecting or processing such data. This principle ensures that individuals are aware of the information being collected and how it will be used. It also empowers individuals to make informed decisions about sharing their personal data.

2. **Data Minimization:** Privacy laws advocate for collecting only the minimum amount of personal data necessary for the intended purpose. Organizations should refrain from collecting excessive or unrelated information, thereby reducing the potential risks associated with data breaches or unauthorized access.

3. **Purpose Limitation:** Personal data should only be collected for specific, explicit, and legitimate purposes. Privacy laws require organizations to clearly define the purpose of data collection and limit its use to those purposes. If an organization wishes to use the data for another purpose, it typically needs to obtain additional consent from the individuals.

4. **Data Accuracy:** Privacy laws emphasize the importance of ensuring the accuracy and integrity of personal data. Organizations should take reasonable steps to maintain the accuracy of the data, update it as necessary, and rectify any inaccuracies reported by individuals.

5. **Security Safeguards:** Privacy laws mandate that organizations implement appropriate technical and organizational measures to protect personal data from unauthorized access, disclosure, alteration, or destruction. These measures may include encryption, access controls, regular security assessments, and employee training.

Key Privacy Regulations

Privacy laws and regulations differ across jurisdictions, with each country or region having its own set of rules and requirements. In this section, we will focus on two prominent privacy regulations that have a global impact:

1. **General Data Protection Regulation** (GDPR): Enforced in the European Union (EU) and European Economic Area (EEA) member states, the GDPR is considered one of the most comprehensive and far-reaching privacy regulations. It applies to all organizations that process personal data of individuals residing in the EU/EEA, regardless of the organization's location. The GDPR introduces several rights for individuals, such as the right to access, rectify, and erase their personal data. It also imposes strict obligations on organizations, including the appointment of a Data Protection Officer (DPO), conducting data protection impact assessments (DPIAs), and reporting data breaches within 72 hours.

2. **California Consumer Privacy Act (CCPA):** The CCPA is a state-level privacy law in California, United States. It grants California residents certain rights regarding their personal information and imposes obligations on businesses that collect or sell such data. Under the CCPA, individuals have the right to know what personal information is being collected, the right to opt-out of the sale of their data, and the right to request the deletion of their data. The CCPA applies to businesses that meet specific criteria, such as having annual gross revenue above a certain threshold or handling a significant amount of personal information.

Implications for Organizations

Privacy laws and regulations present challenges and opportunities for organizations in managing and protecting personal data. Compliance with privacy regulations requires organizations to adopt a privacy-centric approach to data practices, considering privacy as a fundamental aspect of their operations. Non-compliance can result in severe penalties, including significant fines, reputational damage, and lawsuits.

To ensure compliance with privacy laws and regulations, organizations should take the following steps:

1. **Data Mapping and Inventory:** Organizations should conduct a thorough assessment of the personal data they collect, process, and store. This includes documenting the types of data collected, the purpose for which it is collected, and the third parties with whom it is shared. This data mapping exercise helps identify privacy risks, evaluate compliance gaps, and develop data protection strategies.

2. **Privacy Impact Assessments:** Privacy impact assessments (PIAs) are essential in identifying and mitigating privacy risks associated with new projects or initiatives. Organizations should conduct PIAs to assess the privacy implications of their data processing activities, evaluate the necessity and proportionality of data collection, and implement appropriate privacy safeguards.

3. **Privacy by Design:** Privacy by design is a principle that advocates for considering privacy and data protection requirements from the early stages of product or system development. Organizations should integrate privacy controls and safeguards into their processes, systems, and applications to

ensure that privacy is an inherent and default feature rather than an afterthought.

4. **Data Subject Rights:** Privacy laws grant individuals certain rights, such as the right to access, correct, or delete their personal data. Organizations must establish processes and procedures to handle data subject requests and ensure timely and accurate responses. This may involve creating dedicated channels for individuals to exercise their rights and maintaining proper records of such requests.

5. **Vendor Management:** Organizations often share personal data with third-party vendors or service providers. Privacy laws require organizations to ensure that these vendors comply with applicable privacy regulations and adequately protect the personal data entrusted to them. Implementing vendor management programs and conducting privacy due diligence on vendors is crucial in managing privacy risks associated with third-party data processing.

Current Challenges and Future Trends

Privacy laws and regulations continue to evolve as new technologies, data practices, and privacy concerns emerge. Some of the current challenges and future trends in privacy laws include:

1. **Cross-Border Data Transfers:** With the increasing global nature of data flows, cross-border data transfers have become more prevalent. Privacy laws often impose restrictions on transferring personal data across borders, particularly to countries without adequate data protection laws. Organizations must navigate these regulations and implement appropriate mechanisms, such as standard contractual clauses or binding corporate rules, to ensure lawful cross-border data transfers.

2. **Emerging Technologies:** Advancements in technologies such as artificial intelligence, Internet of Things (IoT), and facial recognition pose new challenges to privacy laws. These technologies raise concerns about the collection and use of personal data, the potential for automated decision-making, and the risks of data breaches or unauthorized access. Privacy laws will need to adapt to address these unique challenges and strike a balance between innovation and privacy protection.

3. **Global Privacy Harmonization:** Privacy laws vary across jurisdictions, leading to compliance complexities for multinational organizations. Efforts are underway to achieve global privacy harmonization, where common principles and standards can facilitate cross-border data flows and simplify compliance. International frameworks, such as the APEC Privacy Framework and the Convention 108 of the Council of Europe, aim to harmonize privacy laws and promote a consistent approach to privacy protection worldwide.

In conclusion, privacy laws and regulations are vital for safeguarding individuals' personal information in the digital age. Organizations must understand and comply with privacy requirements, implement privacy-centric practices, and prioritize the protection of personal data. Staying abreast of evolving privacy laws and proactively addressing privacy challenges will enable organizations to build trust with their customers, enhance their reputation, and ensure sustainable data practices.

Privacy by Design Principles

Privacy by Design (PbD) is a set of principles and practices that aim to incorporate privacy considerations into the design and development of systems, processes, and products. It promotes proactive measures to protect individuals' privacy throughout their interactions with technology. PbD is based on the belief that privacy is a fundamental human right and that privacy protections should be embedded into the very fabric of information technologies.

PbD was first introduced by Dr. Ann Cavoukian, the Information and Privacy Commissioner of Ontario, Canada, in the 1990s. Since then, it has gained international recognition and has become a core concept in privacy and data protection regulations worldwide.

The PbD principles provide guidance on how organizations should approach privacy issues when developing new technologies or enhancing existing ones. Let's explore the key principles of Privacy by Design:

Proactive not Reactive; Preventative not Remedial

The first principle emphasizes the importance of being proactive rather than reactive when addressing privacy concerns. Rather than waiting for privacy breaches or violations to occur, organizations should take a preventative approach to protect individuals' personal information. This involves incorporating privacy safeguards and protections into systems and processes from the very beginning.

For example, a company developing a new mobile app should consider privacy implications during its design and development phase. By implementing strong authentication measures, encryption protocols, and data minimization techniques, the app can ensure that user information is adequately protected.

Privacy as the Default Setting

The second principle is about making privacy the default setting for individuals. By default, personal information should be protected and accessible only to authorized individuals. Users should not be required to actively opt-out of privacy-intrusive practices; instead, they should be given meaningful choices and control over how their personal data is collected, used, and shared.

For instance, when individuals sign up for an online service, the default privacy settings should prioritize their privacy, ensuring that their data is not shared with third parties without their explicit consent. Users should have the ability to customize their privacy settings according to their preferences.

Privacy Embedded into Design

This principle emphasizes the embedding of privacy into the design of systems, processes, and products. It encourages organizations to consider the full lifecycle of personal information and to design privacy-enhancing features and mechanisms right from the start.

By integrating privacy into the design process, organizations can better address potential privacy risks and ensure that privacy controls are an integral part of their offerings. The principle also highlights the importance of conducting privacy impact assessments to identify and mitigate any potential privacy risks.

For example, a smart home device manufacturer should incorporate privacy features such as anonymization and secure data storage into its products. By doing so, the manufacturer can protect the privacy and security of its users' personal information.

Full Functionality — Positive-Sum, not Zero-Sum

The fourth principle emphasizes achieving privacy protection without sacrificing the functionality and usability of systems and services. It asserts that privacy and functionality can coexist and should be pursued as positive-sum rather than zero-sum outcomes.

Organizations should strive to provide robust privacy protections while still delivering the desired functionality and user experience. This principle promotes finding innovative solutions that enhance privacy without compromising the utility and benefits that users derive from technology.

For instance, a social media platform can implement privacy controls that allow users to selectively share content with specific groups of people, ensuring privacy while maintaining the platform's social functionality.

End-to-End Security — Lifecycle Protection

The final principle highlights the need for end-to-end security and privacy throughout the entire lifecycle of personal information. Systems should be designed to protect personal data from unauthorized access, use, disclosure, and destruction at every stage, from collection to storage, use, and disposal.

This principle underscores the importance of implementing security measures like encryption, access controls, and secure data handling practices to safeguard personal information. It also emphasizes the secure disposal of data when it is no longer needed.

For example, a healthcare organization must ensure the confidentiality and integrity of patient data throughout its lifecycle, from the initial collection during medical consultations to the eventual disposal of records.

In summary, Privacy by Design principles provide a comprehensive framework for organizations to embed privacy protections into their systems, processes, and products. By adopting these principles, organizations can ensure that privacy considerations are taken into account from the outset, promoting trust, transparency, and respect for individuals' privacy rights.

Data Protection and Privacy Impact Assessments

In today's digital age, where personal data is constantly being collected and processed, ensuring the protection of individuals' privacy and maintaining data security have become paramount. To effectively address these concerns, organizations must conduct Data Protection and Privacy Impact Assessments (DPIAs).

Understanding Data Protection and Privacy Impact Assessments

A Data Protection Impact Assessment (DPIA), also known as a Privacy Impact Assessment (PIA), is a systematic process that helps organizations identify and minimize privacy risks associated with the collection, use, and storage of personal data. It is a proactive approach to privacy management, enabling organizations to assess and mitigate potential privacy issues before they occur.

The primary goal of a DPIA is to ensure compliance with privacy laws and regulations, such as the General Data Protection Regulation (GDPR) in the European Union. However, the benefits of conducting DPIAs extend beyond regulatory compliance. By identifying and addressing privacy risks, organizations can enhance trust among their customers, improve data governance practices, and reduce the likelihood of data breaches and other privacy-related incidents.

Key Principles of Data Protection and Privacy Impact Assessments

When conducting a DPIA, organizations should adhere to several key principles to ensure its effectiveness. These principles include:

1. Privacy by Design: DPIAs should be conducted as an integral part of the development of any project or initiative involving the processing of personal data. The privacy of individuals should be considered and embedded into the design and implementation of systems, processes, and policies.
2. Risk-based Approach: The DPIA process should focus on assessing and mitigating the risks associated with the processing of personal data. Organizations should prioritize activities that pose the highest risks to individuals' privacy and concentrate their efforts on addressing those risks.
3. Transparency and Accountability: Organizations should be transparent about their privacy practices and accountable for the way they handle personal data. DPIAs should be well-documented, and decisions made as a result of the assessment should be communicated to relevant stakeholders.
4. Involvement of Stakeholders: To ensure a comprehensive assessment, organizations should involve all relevant stakeholders, such as data subjects, data protection officers, legal experts, IT professionals, and project managers. Input from these stakeholders can provide valuable insights and help identify potential privacy risks.

Process of Data Protection and Privacy Impact Assessments

The process of conducting a DPIA typically involves the following steps:

1. Identify the Need for a DPIA: Organizations should determine whether a DPIA is required for a particular project or initiative. This assessment can be based on factors such as the nature of the processing activities, the types of personal data involved, and the potential risks to individuals' privacy.
2. Data Mapping: Organizations should identify and document the types of personal data being processed, the purposes of the processing, and any data flows

involved. This step helps ensure a comprehensive understanding of data processing activities.

3. Privacy Risk Assessment: Organizations should assess the potential privacy risks associated with the processing of personal data. This assessment may involve evaluating the likelihood and severity of the risks, considering the rights and freedoms of data subjects, and identifying any safeguards or control measures already in place.

4. Risk Mitigation: Based on the identified privacy risks, organizations should develop and implement appropriate measures to mitigate those risks. This may involve implementing technical and organizational safeguards, such as encryption, access controls, and privacy policies.

5. Documentation and Review: Organizations should document the DPIA process, including the findings, decisions made, and steps taken to address privacy risks. The DPIA should be periodically reviewed and updated to ensure its continued effectiveness and compliance with evolving privacy requirements.

Examples and Practical Applications

To illustrate the importance and practicality of DPIAs, consider the following examples:

1. An e-commerce company is developing a new mobile application that collects personal data, such as users' names, contact information, and browsing behavior. By conducting a DPIA, the company can identify potential privacy risks, such as unauthorized access to personal data or potential data breaches. Based on the findings of the assessment, the company can implement measures to secure the application and protect users' privacy, such as implementing encryption and strong access controls.

2. A healthcare organization is planning to implement a telemedicine platform that involves the processing of sensitive patient data. By conducting a DPIA, the organization can assess the potential privacy risks, such as unauthorized disclosure of patient information or potential data loss. Based on the assessment, the organization can develop and implement measures to ensure the confidentiality and integrity of patient data, such as implementing secure data transmission protocols and conducting regular vulnerability assessments.

Resources and Best Practices

Several resources and best practices are available to guide organizations in conducting DPIAs:

1. Guidelines from Data Protection Authorities: Many data protection authorities provide guidelines and resources to help organizations conduct DPIAs effectively. These guidelines often outline the key steps and considerations for conducting a DPIA and provide practical examples and templates.

2. Privacy Impact Assessment Tools: Various tools and software applications are available to assist organizations in conducting DPIAs. These tools often provide templates, checklists, and automation capabilities to streamline the assessment process.

3. Privacy by Design Frameworks: Privacy by Design frameworks, such as the one developed by the Information and Privacy Commissioner of Ontario, provide organizations with a structured approach to embed privacy considerations into their systems, processes, and policies.

Discussion and Controversies

While DPIAs are generally considered a best practice for privacy management, there are ongoing discussions and controversies surrounding their implementation. Some of the key debates include:

1. Mandatory vs. Voluntary DPIAs: While some jurisdictions require organizations to conduct DPIAs for certain types of processing activities, others view DPIAs as a voluntary tool. The debate revolves around finding the right balance between ensuring privacy protection and minimizing the administrative burden on organizations.

2. Automation and Standardization: There are ongoing discussions about the potential use of automated tools and standardized templates in conducting DPIAs. Critics argue that automation may lead to a checkbox approach, sacrificing the thoroughness and contextual analysis required for effective privacy risk assessment.

3. Integration with Existing Processes: Organizations often struggle with integrating DPIAs into their existing project management and risk assessment processes. Finding ways to streamline DPIAs and ensure their integration with other processes is a topic of ongoing debate.

Exercises

1. Conduct a DPIA for a fictional e-commerce website that collects customers' personal data for marketing purposes. Identify potential privacy risks and propose measures to mitigate those risks.

2. Research and compare the legal requirements for conducting DPIAs in different jurisdictions. Identify any differences or similarities in the assessment process.

3. Interview a privacy officer or data protection expert to understand their experiences and challenges in conducting DPIAs. Discuss their perspectives on the value and effectiveness of the assessment process.

Conclusion

Data Protection and Privacy Impact Assessments are essential tools for organizations to ensure the protection of individuals' privacy and compliance with privacy laws and regulations. By conducting DPIAs, organizations can proactively identify and mitigate privacy risks, enhance trust among their customers, and establish robust data governance practices. By adhering to the key principles and following best practices, organizations can effectively integrate DPIAs into their privacy management processes and improve their overall data protection posture.

Privacy Policies and Consent Management

Privacy policies and consent management play a crucial role in ensuring individuals' privacy rights are protected in the digital age. With the increasing amount of personal data being collected, processed, and stored by organizations, it is important for individuals to have a clear understanding of how their data will be used and shared. Privacy policies serve as a means of communication between organizations and individuals, outlining the practices and procedures employed by the organization with regards to data protection and privacy. Consent management, on the other hand, focuses on obtaining and managing individuals' consent for the collection, processing, and sharing of their personal data.

Privacy Policies

A privacy policy is a statement or a legal document that informs individuals about the types of personal information collected by an organization, how that information is used, and with whom it is shared. The purpose of a privacy policy is twofold: to inform individuals about their privacy rights and to provide transparency and accountability for organizations in their data handling practices. Privacy policies are commonly found on websites, mobile applications, and other digital platforms where personal data is collected.

A comprehensive privacy policy should include the following elements:

- **Introduction:** The policy should begin with an introduction that clearly states the purpose and scope of the policy.
- **Types of Personal Information Collected:** The policy should outline the types of personal information collected by the organization, such as name, address, email, etc.
- **Method of Collection:** It is important to specify how personal information is collected, whether it is through online forms, cookies, or other means.
- **Purpose of Data Collection:** Organizations should clearly state the purpose for which personal information is collected. This could include providing a service, improving products, or marketing purposes.
- **Use and Sharing of Personal Information:** It is necessary to inform individuals how their personal information is used within the organization and whether it is shared with third parties. This section should clearly outline the circumstances under which data may be shared, such as for legal compliance or with service providers.
- **Data Security Measures:** Organizations should detail the measures they have in place to protect personal information from unauthorized access, loss, or alteration. This may include encryption, access controls, and regular security audits.
- **Data Retention and Deletion:** Organizations should specify how long personal information will be retained and the process for deleting or anonymizing data once it is no longer needed.
- **Users' Rights:** Privacy policies should inform individuals about their rights regarding their personal information, including the right to access, correct, and delete their data. It should also provide instructions on how these rights can be exercised.
- **Updates to the Policy:** Organizations should state that the privacy policy may be updated or modified, and how individuals will be notified of any changes.

It is important for privacy policies to be written in clear and easily understandable language, avoiding complex legal jargon. This ensures that individuals can make informed decisions about providing their personal information and understand how their data will be treated.

Consent Management

Consent management refers to the process of obtaining and managing individuals' consent to the collection, processing, and sharing of their personal data. Consent is a fundamental principle in privacy protection, as it empowers individuals to have control over their personal information.

When it comes to consent management, organizations should adhere to the following best practices:

- **Explicit and Informed Consent:** Organizations should obtain explicit and informed consent from individuals before collecting their personal data. Consent should be specific, meaning individuals should be provided with clear information about what data will be collected and how it will be used.

- **Active Opt-in:** Instead of using pre-checked boxes or assumed consent, organizations should require individuals to actively opt-in to the collection and use of their personal information. This ensures that individuals are aware of and agree to the data processing activities.

- **Granular Consent:** Organizations should provide options for individuals to selectively consent to different types of data processing. This allows individuals to have control over how their data is used and shared.

- **Withdrawal of Consent:** Individuals should be provided with an easy and accessible way to withdraw their consent at any time. Organizations should honor withdrawal requests promptly and ensure that individuals' personal data is no longer processed.

- **Consent Records:** Organizations should maintain records of individuals' consent, including the time and date of consent, the purpose of data collection, and any additional details provided by the individual. These records serve as evidence of compliance with data protection regulations.

- **Consent Renewal:** Organizations should regularly review consent and provide individuals with an opportunity to renew their consent. This helps ensure that individuals' consent remains valid and reflects their current preferences.

- **Privacy Preference Management:** Organizations should provide individuals with tools and mechanisms to manage their privacy preferences. This can include options to customize data sharing settings or opt out of certain data processing activities.

Consent management is an ongoing process that requires proactive efforts from organizations to establish and maintain individuals' trust. By implementing effective consent management practices, organizations can demonstrate their commitment to privacy and enhance their reputations.

Example Scenario

To better understand privacy policies and consent management, let's consider an example scenario:

John is using a social media platform to connect with friends, share photos, and engage in online discussions. When signing up for the platform, he is presented with a privacy policy. The policy clearly outlines the types of personal information that will be collected, such as name, email address, and location. It explains that the information will be used to create and maintain his account, personalize his experience, and display relevant advertisements. The policy further states that the personal information will not be shared with third parties without his explicit consent.

Upon reading the privacy policy, John notices a section about consent management. The platform provides him with options to control the visibility of his posts, manage his privacy settings, and choose whether or not he wishes to receive personalized advertisements. John appreciates the transparency and control offered by the platform and decides to provide his consent for data processing, as he agrees with the platform's stated purposes and understands how his data will be used.

A few months later, the platform sends John an email informing him of updates to their privacy policy. They clearly highlight the changes made and provide him with an opportunity to review and renew his consent. John reviews the updates and decides to continue using the platform, renewing his consent for data processing.

In this example, the social media platform demonstrates good privacy practices through its transparent privacy policy and user-friendly consent management. By providing clear information and giving users control over their personal data, the platform builds trust with its users and promotes responsible data handling.

Key Takeaways

Privacy policies and consent management are crucial components of privacy protection and data handling practices. Organizations should develop comprehensive privacy policies that clearly communicate their data handling practices and provide individuals with the necessary information to make informed decisions regarding their personal information. Consent management should focus on obtaining explicit and informed consent, allowing individuals to control how their personal data is processed and shared. By implementing effective privacy policies and consent management practices, organizations can build trust with individuals and maintain compliance with privacy regulations.

Cybersecurity and Legal Compliance

Legal Framework for Cybersecurity

In order to effectively address the growing challenges in cybersecurity, it is essential to have a robust legal framework that outlines the rights, responsibilities, and obligations of various entities involved. The legal framework for cybersecurity encompasses laws, regulations, and policies that govern the conduct and actions related to cybersecurity. This framework creates a foundation for ensuring the protection of digital assets and the preservation of privacy and security in the digital age.

Key Principles

The legal framework for cybersecurity is guided by a set of key principles that serve as the foundation for effective governance and regulation. These principles are essential in addressing the complexities and evolving nature of cyber threats. Let's explore some of these principles:

1. **Proportionality:** The legal framework should ensure that the measures taken to mitigate cyber threats are proportionate to the risks involved. It means that the response to a cyber incident should not be excessive or overly intrusive, while also being effective in addressing the threat.

2. **Privacy by Design:** Privacy should be integrated into the design and implementation of cybersecurity measures. The legal framework should require organizations to adopt privacy-enhancing technologies and practices from the outset to protect individuals' personal information.

3. **Data Protection:** The legal framework should establish regulations and standards for the collection, storage, and processing of personal data. It should ensure that individuals have control over their data and that organizations handle data in a secure and responsible manner.

4. **Cross-Border Cooperation:** Cyber threats are not limited by geographical boundaries, and effective cybersecurity requires international cooperation. The legal framework should facilitate information sharing, collaboration, and coordination among different countries to combat cybercrime and address global cyber threats.

5. **Accountability:** The legal framework should establish clear responsibilities and accountability for different stakeholders involved in cybersecurity. It should outline the obligations of organizations and individuals to protect digital assets and the consequences for non-compliance.

These principles provide a solid foundation for the legal framework for cybersecurity, ensuring that it addresses the multifaceted aspects of cyber threats and promotes a secure and resilient digital environment.

Laws and Regulations

The legal framework for cybersecurity encompasses a multitude of laws and regulations that vary across jurisdictions. These laws provide a comprehensive set of rules and obligations for organizations and individuals to adhere to. Let's take a look at some of the key laws and regulations in the legal framework for cybersecurity:

1. **General Data Protection Regulation (GDPR):** GDPR is a regulation in the European Union (EU) that establishes rules regarding the collection, storage, and processing of personal data. It aims to protect the privacy and rights of individuals and imposes significant obligations on organizations, including mandatory data breach notification and robust security measures.

2. **California Consumer Privacy Act (CCPA):** CCPA is a state-level law in California, United States, that grants consumers more control over their personal information held by businesses. It requires businesses to disclose data collection and sharing practices, gives consumers the right to opt-out of data sales, and imposes penalties for data breaches.

3. **Computer Fraud and Abuse Act (CFAA):** The CFAA is a federal law in the United States that criminalizes unauthorized access to computer systems and networks. It penalizes activities such as hacking and other cybercrimes, providing a legal framework for prosecuting malicious actors.

4. **Network and Information Security (NIS) Directive:** The NIS Directive is an EU directive that establishes security and reporting requirements for operators of essential services and digital service providers. It aims to ensure a high level of cybersecurity across critical infrastructure sectors and improve coordination between EU member states in managing cyber risks.

5. **Cybersecurity Law of the People's Republic of China:** China's Cybersecurity Law is a comprehensive law that governs various aspects of cybersecurity, including data protection, critical infrastructure security, and obligations of network operators. It imposes extensive requirements on both domestic and foreign companies operating in China.

These are just a few examples of the laws and regulations that form the legal framework for cybersecurity. It is crucial for organizations and individuals to understand and comply with these laws to ensure the protection of digital assets and the overall security of the digital ecosystem.

Legal Challenges and Considerations

While the legal framework for cybersecurity provides a set of guidelines and regulations, there are several challenges and considerations that need to be addressed to enhance its effectiveness. Let's discuss some of these challenges:

1. **Jurisdictional Issues:** Cyber incidents often involve cross-border activities, creating challenges in attributing responsibility and applying relevant laws. Cooperation and coordination between different jurisdictions are crucial to overcome these challenges and ensure effective enforcement of cybersecurity regulations.

2. **Rapidly Evolving Technology:** The legal framework needs to keep pace with the rapid advancements in technology and the emergence of new cyber threats. It should be flexible and adaptable to address emerging challenges, such as artificial intelligence and the Internet of Things, without stifling innovation.

3. **Enforcement and Attribution:** Investigating cyber incidents and attributing them to specific individuals or entities can be complex. Strengthening international cooperation and investing in resources and capabilities for cybercrime investigation and digital forensics are essential to ensure effective enforcement of cybersecurity laws.

4. **Public-Private Collaboration:** Cybersecurity is a collective responsibility, requiring collaboration between governments, businesses, and other stakeholders. The legal framework should facilitate public-private partnerships, information sharing, and collaboration to address cybersecurity challenges collectively.

These challenges highlight the need for continuous evaluation and improvement of the legal framework for cybersecurity. It requires a multi-stakeholder approach and ongoing dialogue between policymakers, legal experts, industry professionals, and the public to ensure that the legal framework remains effective and robust in the face of evolving threats.

Case Study: European Union's General Data Protection Regulation (GDPR)

The General Data Protection Regulation (GDPR) is one of the most significant cybersecurity regulations globally. It provides a comprehensive legal framework for the protection of personal data and the privacy rights of individuals within the European Union (EU).

The GDPR aims to enhance the rights of individuals and increase the responsibilities of organizations that process personal data. It introduces several key provisions to strengthen data protection, including:

- **Consent Requirements:** The GDPR requires organizations to obtain freely given, specific, informed, and unambiguous consent from individuals for the processing of their personal data. It sets a higher standard for consent, ensuring that individuals have genuine control over their data.

- **Data Breach Notification:** Organizations are obligated to report data breaches to the appropriate supervisory authority within 72 hours of becoming aware of a breach. Additionally, if the breach poses a high risk to individuals' rights and freedoms, the affected individuals must be informed without undue delay.

- **Right to Access and Erasure:** Individuals have the right to access their personal data held by organizations and request its erasure. This gives individuals more control over their data and the ability to hold organizations accountable for the processing of their personal information.

- **Data Protection Impact Assessments (DPIAs):** Organizations are required to conduct DPIAs for high-risk data processing activities. DPIAs involve assessing the potential impact of data processing on individuals' privacy and implementing measures to mitigate those risks.

- **Accountability and Governance:** The GDPR emphasizes accountability and requires organizations to implement appropriate technical and organizational measures to ensure data protection. It also encourages organizations to adopt privacy by design and privacy by default principles.

The GDPR has had a significant impact on organizations worldwide, as it not only applies to EU-based businesses but also to organizations outside the EU that process personal data of EU residents. Non-compliance with the GDPR can result in severe financial penalties, which underscore the importance of adhering to its requirements.

The implementation of the GDPR has faced various challenges, including the complexity of compliance, the need for additional resources to meet the requirements, and the disparities in interpretation and enforcement across EU member states. However, it has also brought about positive changes by raising awareness about privacy rights and encouraging organizations to prioritize data protection.

The GDPR serves as an example of how a well-structured legal framework can significantly influence the cybersecurity landscape by enhancing the protection of personal data and promoting a culture of privacy and security. It underscores the need for comprehensive regulations that address the evolving challenges in cybersecurity while safeguarding individuals' rights and promoting responsible data governance.

Cybersecurity Incident Notification and Reporting

Cybersecurity incidents can have serious implications for organizations, their stakeholders, and the overall cybersecurity landscape. It is crucial for organizations to establish effective incident notification and reporting processes to ensure the prompt and appropriate handling of incidents, as well as the implementation of preventive measures. This section focuses on the principles, best practices, and legal requirements related to cybersecurity incident notification and reporting.

Principles of Cybersecurity Incident Notification

The principles of cybersecurity incident notification emphasize the importance of prompt and accurate reporting of incidents to the relevant parties. These principles can help guide organizations in developing their incident notification policies and procedures:

1. **Timeliness:** Timely notification of cybersecurity incidents is essential to minimize the impact and prevent further damage. Organizations should establish clear timeframes for incident notification based on the severity and nature of the incident.

2. **Accuracy:** The information provided in the incident notification should be accurate, complete, and concise. Organizations should avoid speculation or conjecture and focus on reporting verified facts and data.

3. **Hierarchy:** Incident notification should follow a hierarchical process based on the severity and impact of the incident. Different stakeholders may require different levels of information and involvement, and the notification process should reflect this.

4. **Consistency:** Organizations should strive for consistency in their incident notification processes. Consistent reporting helps create a common understanding among stakeholders and enables comparability across incidents.

5. **Transparency:** Organizations should be transparent in their incident notification and share information with the relevant stakeholders, including affected individuals, customers, business partners, regulatory authorities, and law enforcement agencies. Transparency builds trust and facilitates cooperative responses.

Legal Requirements for Cybersecurity Incident Notification

Legal frameworks around the world have recognized the significance of cybersecurity incident notification and have established certain obligations for organizations to report incidents. The requirements can vary depending on the jurisdiction, industry, and the nature of the incident. Some common legal requirements for cybersecurity incident notification include:

1. **Mandatory Reporting Laws:** Many countries have enacted laws that require organizations to report certain types of cybersecurity incidents. These laws typically specify the types of incidents that need to be reported, the timeframe for reporting, and the regulatory authorities to be notified.

2. **Data Breach Notification Laws:** Data breach notification laws mandate organizations to notify affected individuals in the event of a breach that exposes their personal information. The notification should include details of the breach, potential impact, and steps individuals can take to protect themselves.

3. **Sector-Specific Regulations:** Certain industries, such as banking, healthcare, and telecommunications, have specific regulations that outline incident notification requirements. These regulations consider the unique risks and characteristics of the industry and may impose stricter reporting obligations.

4. **International Obligations:** Organizations operating in multiple jurisdictions or handling data across borders may be subject to international obligations for incident notification. International agreements and conventions, such as the General Data Protection Regulation (GDPR) in the European Union, may impose additional reporting requirements.

Complying with legal requirements for incident notification involves several steps:

1. **Initial Assessment:** Organizations need to assess the nature and severity of the incident to determine whether it falls under the scope of the reporting requirements. This assessment includes evaluating the impact on individuals, the sensitivity of the data involved, and the potential risks.

2. **Notification Planning:** Organizations should have a well-defined incident response plan that includes a notification component. The plan should identify the relevant stakeholders to be notified, the method of notification, the timeline, and the form of communication.

3. **Internal Notification:** The incident should be promptly reported to the organization's internal stakeholders, including the incident response team, management, legal counsel, and the board of directors. Internal notification facilitates a coordinated response and ensures that all necessary resources are allocated.

4. **External Notification:** Depending on the nature of the incident and the legal requirements, relevant external stakeholders should be notified. This may include affected individuals, customers, business partners, regulatory authorities, law enforcement agencies, and media organizations. Each

stakeholder group may require different levels of information and communication channels.

5. **Documentation:** Organizations should maintain proper documentation of the incident notification process, including the steps taken, the parties notified, the information provided, and the response received. Documentation is essential for compliance, accountability, and future reference.

Best Practices for Cybersecurity Incident Reporting

Effective incident reporting plays a crucial role in managing cybersecurity incidents and preventing future incidents. Organizations should adopt best practices for incident reporting to ensure the timely and accurate flow of information. Some best practices include:

1. **Centralized Reporting Portal:** Establish a centralized reporting portal or system to streamline the incident reporting process. This portal can serve as a single point of contact for stakeholders, offering an easy and consistent way to report incidents.

2. **Standardized Reporting Templates:** Develop standardized incident reporting templates that capture essential information and facilitate consistent reporting. These templates should include fields for incident details, impact assessment, response actions, and contact information.

3. **Escalation Procedures:** Define clear escalation procedures to ensure that incidents are reported promptly and reached to the appropriate level of management or stakeholders. Escalation procedures help expedite decision-making and response actions.

4. **Regular Reporting Updates:** Provide regular updates to stakeholders throughout the incident lifecycle. These updates can inform stakeholders of the progress made, any changes in the situation, and the measures taken to mitigate the incident.

5. **Lessons Learned Documentation:** After the incident is resolved, conduct a thorough review to identify lessons learned and areas for improvement. Document these findings to enhance future incident reporting and response capabilities.

6. **Continuous Improvement:** Continuously review and enhance incident reporting processes based on feedback, industry best practices, and the evolving threat landscape. Incident reporting should be seen as an iterative process that requires ongoing improvement.

Case Study: Equifax Data Breach

The Equifax data breach, one of the most significant cybersecurity incidents in recent years, provides an example of the importance of incident notification and reporting. In 2017, Equifax, a major credit reporting agency, suffered a massive data breach that affected approximately 147 million individuals.

Equifax was subject to legal requirements for incident notification, including breach notification laws and regulations. Despite the legal obligations, Equifax faced criticism for its delayed and inadequate incident notification. The company discovered the breach in late July but did not notify the public until September. The delayed notification gave attackers more time to exploit the stolen data.

Equifax's incident notification process also drew scrutiny due to poor communication practices. The company faced widespread backlash for directing affected individuals to a separate website to check if they were impacted, which was later found to be vulnerable to phishing attacks.

The Equifax case exemplifies the importance of promptly and accurately notifying affected individuals and other stakeholders. Timely incident notification enables individuals to take appropriate steps to protect their information and helps regulatory authorities and law enforcement agencies take immediate action. Additionally, clear and transparent communication builds trust and demonstrates the organization's commitment to addressing the incident effectively.

Resources and Further Reading

1. Cybersecurity Incident Notification Guide - National Institute of Standards and Technology (NIST)

2. Data Breach Notification Laws - International Association of Privacy Professionals (IAPP)

3. Incident Response and Reporting - Compliance.gov

4. The Equifax Data Breach: A Special Report - U.S. House of Representatives Committee on Oversight and Government Reform

5. Cybersecurity Incident Reporting and Response Planning - U.S. Department of Homeland Security

Key Takeaways

Cybersecurity incident notification and reporting are crucial aspects of effective incident management. Organizations should adhere to the principles of timeliness, accuracy, hierarchy, consistency, and transparency when developing their incident notification policies. Legal requirements for incident notification may vary depending on the jurisdiction and industry, and organizations should comply with relevant laws and regulations.

Best practices for incident reporting involve establishing a centralized reporting portal, employing standardized reporting templates, defining escalation procedures, providing regular updates to stakeholders, documenting lessons learned, and continuously improving incident reporting processes.

Case studies, such as the Equifax data breach, highlight the importance of prompt and adequate incident notification. Timely and transparent communication with affected individuals and other stakeholders is essential to minimize the impact of the incident and restore trust.

By establishing effective incident notification and reporting processes, organizations can enhance their incident management capabilities, mitigate the impact of incidents, and collectively contribute to the overall cybersecurity sustainability.

Electronic Evidence and Cybercrime Investigations

In today's digital age, electronic evidence plays a crucial role in cybercrime investigations. As cybercriminals become more sophisticated, law enforcement agencies and cybersecurity professionals must adapt their investigative techniques and tools to effectively gather, analyze, preserve, and present electronic evidence in a court of law. This section will explore the principles and practices of electronic evidence collection, the challenges faced in cybercrime investigations, and the legal considerations surrounding the use of electronic evidence.

Principles of Electronic Evidence Collection

The collection of electronic evidence requires a systematic and meticulous approach to ensure its integrity and admissibility in court. The following principles should be followed when collecting electronic evidence:

1. **Identification and Preservation:** The first step in collecting electronic evidence is to identify and preserve the evidence in its original form. This involves ensuring that the evidence is not altered, deleted, or damaged during the collection process. It is crucial to document the location of the evidence, including any hardware or software used.

2. **Chain of Custody:** Maintaining a secure chain of custody is essential to establish the authenticity and integrity of electronic evidence. This includes documenting every person who has had access to the evidence and any actions taken during the investigation. It ensures that the evidence is admissible in court and that its integrity is not compromised.

3. **Forensic Imaging:** Creating a forensic image of digital devices is a common practice in electronic evidence collection. Forensic imaging involves creating a bit-by-bit copy of the entire storage media, including hard drives, solid-state drives, memory cards, and mobile devices. This allows investigators to work with a copy of the evidence while preserving the original data.

4. **Data Recovery:** In cases where data has been intentionally deleted or hidden, data recovery techniques are employed to retrieve the information. This may involve using specialized software or hardware tools to recover deleted files, extract data from damaged storage media, or reconstruct deleted email messages or chat conversations.

Challenges in Cybercrime Investigations

Cybercrime investigations present unique challenges compared to traditional criminal investigations. The following are some of the key challenges faced by investigators:

1. **Anonymity and Jurisdiction:** The anonymity provided by the internet can make it difficult to identify and locate cybercriminals. Additionally, cybercrimes can cross national boundaries, making jurisdictional issues complex. Cooperation and coordination between international law enforcement agencies are necessary to effectively investigate and prosecute cybercriminals.

2. **Technological Complexity:** Rapid advancements in technology present challenges in staying up-to-date with the latest tools and techniques for investigating cybercrimes. Digital devices and communication platforms constantly evolve, requiring investigators to constantly adapt their investigative methods and keep pace with emerging technologies.

3. **Encryption and Privacy:** Strong encryption techniques can protect data from unauthorized access, posing a challenge for investigators trying to gather electronic

evidence. Balancing the need for privacy and the requirements of law enforcement is a constant debate in cybercrime investigations.

4. **Volume and Variability of Data:** The sheer volume and variability of electronic data can pose substantial challenges in cybercrime investigations. Sorting through large amounts of data and identifying relevant evidence requires specialized tools and techniques, such as data analytics and machine learning algorithms.

5. **Cross-Disciplinary Expertise:** Cybercrime investigations often require expertise from various disciplines, including computer forensics, network analysis, cryptography, and legal knowledge. Building a multidisciplinary team with diverse skill sets is essential to effectively investigate complex cybercrimes.

Legal Considerations

The use of electronic evidence in cybercrime investigations raises several legal considerations. Adhering to legal frameworks ensures that the evidence is admissible in court and that individuals' privacy rights are respected. Some of the legal considerations include:

1. **Search and Seizure Laws:** Investigators must comply with search and seizure laws when collecting electronic evidence. These laws define the circumstances under which law enforcement can search and seize electronic devices, ensuring that the evidence is obtained lawfully.

2. **Digital Evidence Admissibility:** To be admissible in court, electronic evidence must meet the requirements of relevance, authenticity, and reliability. Proper documentation of the chain of custody, forensic imaging, and data recovery techniques are critical to establish the admissibility of electronic evidence.

3. **Privacy Laws and Data Protection:** Cybercrime investigations must navigate privacy laws and data protection regulations to ensure that individuals' privacy rights are not violated during the collection, handling, and storage of electronic evidence.

4. **Ethical Considerations:** Investigators must adhere to ethical guidelines and professional standards in the handling of electronic evidence. This includes respecting individuals' privacy, maintaining confidentiality, and ensuring transparency in the investigative process.

Example: Electronic Evidence Collection in a Phishing Attack Investigation

To illustrate the principles of electronic evidence collection in a real-world scenario, let's consider a hypothetical phishing attack investigation. In this scenario, an organization has been targeted by a phishing email campaign, leading to several employees unknowingly disclosing their login credentials. The goal is to gather electronic evidence to identify the perpetrators and support a legal case against them.

1. **Identification and Preservation:** The investigation team identifies and isolates the affected systems to prevent further compromise. They document the location of the compromised devices and ensure that no additional changes are made to the systems.

2. **Chain of Custody:** The investigators establish a secure chain of custody by documenting each team member who has access to the evidence. They carefully record any actions taken, such as disconnecting the compromised devices from the network, to maintain the integrity of the evidence.

3. **Forensic Imaging:** Forensic specialists create forensic images of the affected devices, including the hard drives of desktop computers and the storage media of mobile devices. These images are then analyzed to identify any evidence related to the phishing attack.

4. **Data Recovery:** In cases where the attackers have deleted or obscured evidence, the investigators use specialized tools to recover deleted files, analyze network traffic logs, and reconstruct the phishing emails to trace their origin.

By following these principles of electronic evidence collection, the investigators are able to gather relevant evidence, identify the attackers, and build a strong case for prosecution.

Resources and Further Reading

- Carrier, B., & Spafford, E. H. (2003). *Investigating High-Technology Crime: The Legal, Regulatory, and Corporate Environment.* Prentice Hall.

- Nelson, B., Phillips, A., & Steuart, C. (2019). *Guide to Computer Forensics and Investigations.* Cengage Learning.

- Casey, E. (2011). *Digital Evidence and Computer Crime: Forensic Science, Computers and the Internet.* Academic Press.

- American Bar Association, *Digital Evidence Guide,* available at: `https://www.americanbar.org/groups/crsj/publications/human_rights_magazine_home/the-state-of-cybersecurity/electronic-evidence--the-universal-digital-language-/#04.-chain-of-custody`

Exercises

1. Research and discuss a high-profile cybercrime case where the collection of electronic evidence played a crucial role in the investigation and prosecution.

2. Analyze the legal and ethical implications of using social media posts as electronic evidence in a cybercrime investigation.

3. Suppose you are tasked with creating a cybersecurity training program for law enforcement officers involved in cybercrime investigations. Outline the key topics, skills, and competencies that should be covered in such a program.

4. Conduct research on the legal frameworks governing cybercrime investigations in your country. Identify any gaps or areas where improvements can be made to enhance the effectiveness of electronic evidence collection.

5. Explore the challenges of conducting cybercrime investigations in a cloud computing environment. Discuss the impact of cloud computing on the collection and preservation of electronic evidence.

Remember to engage in discussions and seek additional resources to deepen your understanding of electronic evidence and cybercrime investigations. Cybersecurity is a rapidly evolving field, and staying informed about new technologies and legal developments is essential for professionals in this domain.

Digital Forensics and Chain of Custody

Digital forensics plays a crucial role in investigating cybercrimes and gathering evidence that can be used in legal proceedings. It involves the collection, preservation, and analysis of digital evidence to uncover the who, what, when, where, why, and how of a cybercrime. With the rise in cyberattacks and the increasing reliance on digital devices and networks, the field of digital forensics has become an essential component of cybersecurity.

Introduction to Digital Forensics

Digital forensics is the process of collecting, analyzing, and presenting digital evidence in a legally sound manner. It involves identifying, preserving, and extracting relevant data from electronic devices such as computers, servers, mobile phones, tablets, and network logs. The goal of digital forensics is to reconstruct events, determine the intent or motive behind a cybercrime, and establish a chain of custody for the evidence.

Chain of Custody

The chain of custody is a crucial aspect of digital forensics. It refers to the documentation and tracking of the movement and handling of digital evidence from the time of seizure to its presentation in a court of law. The chain of custody ensures the integrity and admissibility of the evidence by demonstrating that it has not been tampered with or compromised during the investigation process.

The chain of custody starts with the identification and seizure of the digital evidence. This can be done through the physical acquisition of devices or by creating forensic copies of data. It is important to ensure that the evidence is collected in a forensically sound manner to maintain its integrity and authenticity.

Once the evidence is seized, it must be properly documented, labeled, and packaged to prevent any tampering or contamination. This includes recording details such as the date, time, location, description of the evidence, and the names of the individuals involved in its collection. Digital signatures or hashes can be used to verify the integrity of the evidence throughout the chain of custody.

The evidence should be stored in a secure and controlled environment to prevent unauthorized access or modification. Access to the evidence should be strictly controlled and limited to authorized personnel. Any changes or modifications made to the evidence, such as copying or analysis, should be carefully documented and recorded.

The chain of custody also requires a detailed record of every transfer or movement of the evidence. This includes the names of the individuals who had custody of the evidence, the date and time of each transfer, and the purpose of the transfer. Any breaks in the chain of custody can raise doubts about the integrity and reliability of the evidence.

To ensure the admissibility of the evidence in court, digital forensic examiners must be able to demonstrate that the evidence was handled in a secure and controlled manner throughout the investigation. This includes providing detailed documentation of the chain of custody and testifying about the procedures followed to maintain the integrity of the evidence.

Tools and Techniques for Digital Forensics

There are various tools and techniques available for conducting digital forensics investigations. These include:

- **Data Acquisition:** Tools such as forensic imaging software are used to create forensic copies of data. These copies are an exact bit-for-bit replica of the original evidence and can be used for analysis without altering the original evidence.

- **Data Recovery:** Techniques like file carving and data carving are used to recover deleted or lost data from storage media. These techniques can help uncover valuable evidence that may have been intentionally or accidentally deleted.

- **Data Analysis:** Tools like keyword search, hash analysis, timeline analysis, and link analysis can be used to analyze the extracted data and identify patterns, relationships, and anomalies. These tools assist in reconstructing events and building a case against the perpetrators.

- **Data Visualization:** Visualization techniques such as timeline charts, graphs, and maps can help present complex digital evidence in a clear and understandable manner. Visual representations can make it easier for investigators, lawyers, and judges to comprehend and interpret the evidence.

It is important for digital forensic examiners to stay up to date with the latest tools, techniques, and best practices in the field. This includes attending training programs, participating in workshops and conferences, and constantly learning and adapting to the evolving nature of cybercrimes.

Legal Considerations

Digital forensics investigations are subject to legal and ethical considerations. Investigators must adhere to applicable laws, regulations, and guidelines to ensure that the evidence collected is admissible in court. Some key legal considerations in digital forensics include:

- **Search and Seizure Laws:** Investigators must follow proper protocols and obtain the necessary legal authorization before searching and seizing digital evidence. Failure to comply with search and seizure laws can result in the evidence being deemed inadmissible in court.

- **Privacy Laws:** Investigators must respect and protect the privacy rights of individuals during the collection and analysis of digital evidence. This includes obtaining appropriate consent, preserving the confidentiality of personal information, and using encryption or other security measures to protect sensitive data.

- **Admissibility of Evidence:** The admissibility of digital evidence in court depends on various factors, including the qualifications and expertise of the examiner, the reliability of the tools and techniques used, and the preservation of the chain of custody. It is essential for investigators to document and testify about their procedures to establish the authenticity and reliability of the evidence.

Digital forensic examiners often work closely with legal professionals, such as lawyers, prosecutors, and judges, to ensure that the investigation and collection of evidence comply with relevant laws and regulations. Collaboration between digital forensic experts and legal professionals is crucial for a successful investigation and prosecution of cybercrimes.

Real-World Example

To illustrate the importance of digital forensics and the chain of custody, let's consider a real-world example. Imagine a company that has experienced a data breach resulting in the theft of customer information. The company hires a digital forensic examiner to investigate the breach and gather evidence for potential legal action.

The examiner begins by identifying and preserving all relevant digital evidence, such as server logs, network traffic data, and employee computer systems. They follow proper procedures to ensure that the evidence is not compromised during the collection process. This involves creating forensic copies of the data, securing the original devices, and documenting the chain of custody.

The examiner then analyzes the collected evidence, looking for signs of unauthorized access, data exfiltration, or other indicators of the breach. They use specialized tools and techniques to extract and interpret the data, reconstruct the timeline of events, and identify the methods used by the attackers.

Throughout the investigation, the examiner maintains a detailed chain of custody, documenting every step of the process, including the collection, storage, analysis, and transfer of the evidence. This documentation is crucial for establishing the integrity and admissibility of the evidence in court.

Based on their findings, the examiner prepares a detailed report that summarizes the evidence, explains the methods used by the attackers, and provides recommendations for improving the company's cybersecurity defenses. This report can be used by the company to take legal action against the perpetrators or to implement measures to prevent future breaches.

In this example, the digital forensics investigation and the proper documentation of the chain of custody play a critical role in gathering admissible evidence and holding the offenders accountable. It highlights the importance of digital forensics in addressing cybercrimes and the need for skilled professionals who can conduct investigations in a legally sound manner.

Conclusion

Digital forensics and the chain of custody are essential components of cybersecurity. They enable the collection, preservation, and analysis of digital evidence, helping to identify cybercriminals, reconstruct events, and support legal proceedings. By following proper procedures, utilizing appropriate tools and techniques, and adhering to legal and ethical considerations, digital forensic examiners play a vital role in investigating cybercrimes and securing justice.

Cybersecurity Liability and Insurance

In today's digital landscape, the threat of cyber attacks is ever-present, and organizations must take steps to protect themselves from potential losses and liabilities. Cybersecurity liability and insurance play a crucial role in mitigating the financial impacts of cyber incidents. This section explores the concepts of cybersecurity liability and insurance, discussing their importance, types of coverage, key considerations, and challenges in this field.

Understanding Cybersecurity Liability

Cybersecurity liability refers to the legal responsibility an organization bears for any harm or loss resulting from a cyber incident. As organizations increasingly rely on digital systems and data, they face various liabilities, including:

- **Data breaches:** The unauthorized access or disclosure of sensitive information, such as personally identifiable information (PII) or protected health information (PHI), can lead to legal consequences, regulatory fines, and reputational damage.

- **Intellectual property theft:** Cyberattacks aimed at stealing intellectual property, trade secrets, or copyrighted material can result in significant financial losses and legal disputes.

- **Business interruption:** Disruptions to critical systems and networks can lead to operational downtime, loss of revenue, and breach of contractual obligations, leading to potential lawsuits from customers or business partners.

- **Third-party liabilities:** Organizations that fail to adequately protect their systems and data may be held responsible for the damages caused to third parties, such as customers or business partners, resulting from a cyber incident.

It is essential for organizations to understand the potential liabilities they face and take appropriate measures to prevent, detect, and respond to cyber incidents. While cybersecurity measures aim to reduce the likelihood of an incident, insurance serves as a financial safety net.

Types of Cybersecurity Insurance Coverage

Cybersecurity insurance, also known as cyber insurance or cyber liability insurance, provides financial protection to organizations in the event of a cyber incident. It typically covers the costs associated with breach response, incident investigation, legal defense, regulatory fines, and third-party liabilities. Here are some common types of cybersecurity insurance coverage:

- **First-party coverage:** This type of coverage compensates the insured organization for their losses directly resulting from a cyber incident, including expenses for incident response, data breach notification, public relations, business interruption, and data recovery.

- **Third-party coverage:** Third-party coverage offers protection against claims and lawsuits brought by third parties affected by a cyber incident. It covers legal defense costs, settlements, and judgments arising from the unauthorized disclosure of sensitive information or the interruption of services.

- **Regulatory coverage:** This coverage helps organizations comply with regulatory requirements and covers fines and penalties imposed by regulatory bodies for failing to protect customer data or adhere to specific cybersecurity standards.

- **Network security liability coverage:** Network security liability coverage protects organizations from losses stemming from network security failures, such as accidental transmission of malware or denial-of-service attacks.

- **Privacy liability coverage:** Privacy liability coverage provides financial protection against claims arising from the unauthorized access, use, or disclosure of personal or sensitive information.
- **Media liability coverage:** Organizations that rely heavily on digital media for advertising or communication can obtain media liability coverage to protect against claims of defamation, intellectual property infringement, or plagiarism.
- **Cyber extortion coverage:** This type of coverage helps organizations respond to cyber extortion threats, such as ransomware attacks, by covering the costs associated with ransom payments or negotiation with the extortionists.

It is crucial for organizations to carefully evaluate their specific risks and select appropriate insurance coverage that aligns with their cybersecurity needs and budget.

Key Considerations in Cybersecurity Insurance

When considering cybersecurity insurance, organizations must keep the following key points in mind:

- **Risk assessment:** Insurers often require organizations to conduct a risk assessment to evaluate their cybersecurity posture and identify potential vulnerabilities. This assessment helps insurers determine the level of risk and appropriate coverage options.
- **Policy terms and conditions:** Organizations need to thoroughly review insurance policies to understand the coverage limits, exclusions, deductibles, and policy conditions. They should ensure the policy aligns with their specific needs and provides adequate coverage in case of a cyber incident.
- **Preventive measures:** Insurers may consider an organization's cybersecurity measures and risk management practices when determining the premiums. Taking proactive steps to implement robust cybersecurity controls and risk mitigation strategies may result in more favorable coverage terms and lower premiums.
- **Breach response capabilities:** Insurers may assess an organization's ability to effectively respond to a cyber incident. Having an incident response plan, including proper incident handling and notification procedures, can positively impact coverage terms and premiums.

- **Coordination with other insurance policies:** Organizations should consider how their cybersecurity insurance aligns with their existing general liability, professional liability, and property insurance policies. Proper coordination ensures comprehensive coverage and minimizes coverage gaps or redundancies.

Challenges in Cybersecurity Insurance

The field of cybersecurity insurance faces several challenges due to the evolving nature of cyber risks and the complexities associated with underwriting and pricing. Some of the major challenges include:

- **Risk assessment and modeling:** Unlike traditional insurance, assessing and quantifying cyber risks is complex due to the dynamic nature of cyber threats and the lack of historical data. Insurers face challenges in accurately underwriting and pricing cyber insurance policies based on the potential impact of unknown or emerging threats.

- **Policy exclusions and sub-limits:** Insurers may incorporate numerous exclusions and limitations in cyber insurance policies due to the high level of uncertainty and potentially catastrophic losses associated with cyber incidents. Organizations need to carefully review policy terms to understand the extent of coverage and any potential gaps.

- **Rapidly changing threat landscape:** Cyber threats constantly evolve, making it challenging to keep insurance policies up to date. Insurers must stay abreast of emerging threats and adapt their policies to cover novel attack vectors and vulnerabilities.

- **Lack of standardized risk assessment:** The absence of standardized risk assessment methodologies and metrics for evaluating cybersecurity posture makes it difficult to establish industry-wide benchmarks and regulations for cyber insurance. This lack of standardization can lead to discrepancies in coverage and pricing among different insurers.

Addressing these challenges requires close collaboration between insurers, cybersecurity professionals, and regulators to foster the development of robust risk assessment frameworks, shared threat intelligence, and standardized insurance practices.

Case Study: Evaluating Cybersecurity Insurance Coverage

Consider a small e-commerce company that experienced a data breach resulting in the exposure of customer credit card information. The company incurred substantial costs for forensic investigations, data breach notification, credit monitoring for affected customers, and legal defense against potential lawsuits. To mitigate the financial impact, the company had obtained cybersecurity insurance coverage.

In this case, the cybersecurity insurance policy provided first-party coverage, reimbursing the company for the expenses related to breach response and customer notification. The policy also included third-party coverage, protecting the company against potential lawsuits and settlement costs. The insurance company worked closely with the company to coordinate breach response efforts and facilitate legal representation.

The insurance coverage helped the company manage the financial burden associated with the data breach, allowing them to focus on repairing their systems and regaining customer trust. This case highlights the importance of having comprehensive cybersecurity insurance coverage tailored to an organization's specific risks and needs.

Conclusion

Cybersecurity liability and insurance are essential components of any robust cybersecurity strategy. Understanding the potential liabilities an organization faces and obtaining appropriate insurance coverage are crucial steps in managing the financial risks associated with cyber incidents. Despite the challenges in the field, cybersecurity insurance continues to evolve to address emerging threats and provide organizations with the necessary financial protection. By carefully evaluating their risks, selecting suitable coverage, and implementing robust preventive measures, organizations can effectively navigate the complex landscape of cybersecurity liability and insurance.

International Cooperation in Cybersecurity

Cross-Border Data Protection and Privacy

In our increasingly interconnected world, where data flows effortlessly across national borders, ensuring the protection and privacy of this data has become a critical challenge. Cross-border data protection and privacy refers to the measures put in place to safeguard personal data when it is transferred from one jurisdiction to another. These measures become particularly important as businesses and individuals routinely operate across multiple countries, and data is stored and processed in different locations.

Background

The need for cross-border data protection arises due to differences in privacy laws and regulations across countries. While some countries have strict data protection laws, others have more relaxed or inconsistent regulations. This creates a complex legal landscape with potential conflicts and challenges when transferring personal data across borders.

The General Data Protection Regulation (GDPR) introduced in the European Union (EU) has played a significant role in shaping cross-border data protection. It applies not only to data controllers and processors within the EU but also to any organization outside the EU that handles the personal data of EU citizens. The GDPR imposes rigorous requirements for the lawful transfer of personal data to third countries, including safeguards and mechanisms to ensure an adequate level of protection.

Principles of Cross-Border Data Protection

Cross-border data protection is guided by several fundamental principles that aim to strike a balance between individual privacy rights, business interests, and national security considerations. These principles include:

1. **Purpose Limitation:** Personal data should only be collected and processed for specified, explicit, and legitimate purposes. Any further processing should be consistent with these purposes.

2. **Data Minimization:** Only the minimum amount of personal data necessary for the intended purpose should be collected and processed. Unnecessary collection and retention of personal data must be avoided.

3. **Lawfulness, Fairness, and Transparency:** Personal data processing must be based on a lawful ground, such as consent or legitimate interests. Individuals must be made aware of the processing activities and their rights related to their personal data.

4. **Security and Confidentiality:** Measures should be implemented to protect personal data from unauthorized access, disclosure, alteration, or destruction. Appropriate technical and organizational security measures should be in place.

5. Data Subject Rights: Individuals have the right to access, rectify, erase, and object to the processing of their personal data. Data controllers must provide mechanisms to enable the exercise of these rights.

Challenges and Solutions

Cross-border data protection faces several challenges, including legal complexities, differing standards, and the need for effective enforcement mechanisms. Here are some key challenges and potential solutions:

1. Legal Harmonization: Harmonization of privacy laws and regulations across countries can simplify cross-border data protection. International agreements and frameworks, such as the EU-US Privacy Shield, aim to bridge the legal divide between jurisdictions and establish common standards.

2. Adequacy Decisions: Adequacy decisions determine whether a country outside the EU provides an adequate level of data protection. Such decisions are made by assessing the country's legal framework, enforcement mechanisms, and international commitments. Adequacy decisions enable the seamless transfer of personal data to these countries.

3. Binding Corporate Rules (BCRs): BCRs are internal rules defined by multinational organizations to regulate cross-border transfers of personal data within their group. BCRs ensure a high level of protection for personal data and provide legal mechanisms to govern data transfers across borders.

4. Standard Contractual Clauses (SCCs): SCCs are pre-approved contractual terms and clauses between data exporters and importers that provide appropriate safeguards for cross-border data transfers. SCCs are issued by data protection authorities and ensure the protection of personal data in line with data protection laws.

Real-World Example

Consider a multinational e-commerce company that operates in both the European Union and the United States. The company collects and processes personal data from EU customers for various purposes, including order processing, customer support, and marketing. To comply with cross-border data protection requirements, the company implements the following measures:

- Obtaining explicit consent from EU customers for data processing activities.
- Implementing robust security measures, such as encryption and access controls, to safeguard personal data.

- Adopting SCCs as the legal basis for transferring personal data from the EU to the US.
- Appointing a Data Protection Officer (DPO) to ensure compliance with data protection laws and regulations.
- Conducting regular audits and assessments to monitor the effectiveness of data protection measures.

By adhering to these measures, the company ensures the protection and privacy of personal data throughout cross-border transfers and maintains compliance with relevant data protection laws.

Additional Resources

For further exploration of cross-border data protection and privacy, the following resources are recommended:

- International Association of Privacy Professionals (IAPP) - Provides comprehensive resources, certifications, and networking opportunities for privacy professionals.
- European Data Protection Board (EDPB) - Offers guidance and documents related to data protection laws and regulations in the European Union.
- International Conference of Data Protection and Privacy Commissioners (ICDPPC) - Organizes annual conferences and publishes materials on global privacy issues.

Conclusion

Cross-border data protection and privacy present a complex and evolving landscape that requires comprehensive frameworks, legal mechanisms, and international cooperation. Data controllers and processors must navigate the intricate web of regulations while prioritizing the privacy rights of individuals. By embracing harmonization efforts, adopting adequate safeguards, and staying updated with evolving best practices, organizations can ensure the secure and responsible transfer of personal data across borders.

International Cybersecurity Agreements and Treaties

In an increasingly interconnected world, cybersecurity has become a global concern. The lack of borders in cyberspace means that a cyberattack in one country can have repercussions in many others. As a result, international cooperation and collaboration are crucial in tackling cybersecurity challenges. This section explores the role of international cybersecurity agreements and treaties in fostering cooperation among nations and enhancing global cybersecurity.

Need for International Cybersecurity Agreements

Cybersecurity threats are not confined by geographical boundaries. Cybercriminals and nation-state actors can launch attacks from any location, targeting critical infrastructure, stealing sensitive data, or disrupting essential services. To combat these threats effectively, countries need to work together, sharing information, intelligence, and best practices. International cybersecurity agreements provide the framework for such cooperation.

Types of Cybersecurity Agreements

There are several types of cybersecurity agreements that facilitate cooperation among nations. These agreements may focus on information sharing, incident response coordination, capacity building, or the establishment of norms and rules for responsible behavior in cyberspace. Let's explore some of the commonly seen types of agreements.

Bilateral Agreements Bilateral agreements are cybersecurity agreements signed between two countries. These agreements typically define the scope of cooperation, including sharing of threat intelligence, joint cybersecurity exercises, and coordination in incident response. Bilateral agreements can strengthen the relationship between partner nations and provide a platform for ongoing collaboration.

Multilateral Agreements Multilateral agreements involve multiple countries and are often facilitated by international organizations such as the United Nations (UN), the International Telecommunication Union (ITU), or regional bodies like the European Union (EU) or the African Union (AU). These agreements aim to foster cooperation, enhance cybersecurity capabilities, and promote the exchange of best practices among participating countries.

Regional Agreements Regional agreements focus on cybersecurity cooperation within a specific geographic region. They bring together neighboring countries with similar cybersecurity challenges and interests. Regional agreements enable countries to address shared concerns collectively, such as cross-border data protection, information sharing, or critical infrastructure protection.

Global Treaties Global treaties, such as the Budapest Convention on Cybercrime, are binding agreements that establish international standards for combating cybercrime. These treaties define offenses, provide guidelines for investigation and prosecution, and promote cooperation among signatory countries. The Budapest Convention, for example, has been ratified by numerous countries, forming a global framework for combating cybercrime.

Key International Cybersecurity Agreements and Treaties

Several significant agreements and treaties have been developed to address cybersecurity at the international level. Let's explore some of the key ones:

Convention on Cybercrime (Budapest Convention) The Budapest Convention, adopted in 2001 by the Council of Europe, is the first international treaty that addresses cybercrime comprehensively. It establishes a framework for cooperation among signatory states, focusing on offenses like fraud, computer-related forgery, and data interference. The convention promotes the harmonization of national legislation, enables mutual legal assistance, and encourages collaboration among law enforcement agencies.

United Nations Group of Governmental Experts (UN GGE) The UN GGE is a group of experts appointed by the UN General Assembly to study and make recommendations on cybersecurity issues. It has produced several reports that highlight the importance of international law, norms, and confidence-building measures in cyberspace. The reports emphasize the need for responsible state behavior and the protection of critical infrastructure.

G7 24/7 Network and CERTs Cooperation The G7 24/7 Network aims to enhance cooperation and coordination among Computer Emergency Response Teams (CERTs) of the G7 countries. The network facilitates the sharing of information, early warning of cyber threats, and joint incident response. It plays a crucial role in leveraging the expertise of participating countries to protect critical infrastructure and cyberspace.

EU General Data Protection Regulation (GDPR) While not specifically a cybersecurity agreement, the GDPR is a regulation implemented by the European Union to protect the privacy and data of its citizens. The regulation applies to any organization that processes personal data of EU residents, irrespective of the organization's location. The GDPR includes provisions for data breach notifications, the right to be forgotten, and the requirement for organizations to implement appropriate security measures.

Challenges in International Cybersecurity Agreements

Despite the importance of international cybersecurity agreements, several challenges persist in their implementation and effectiveness. These challenges include:

Differing Legal Frameworks Countries have different legal systems and interpretations, which can pose challenges in harmonizing cybersecurity laws and regulations. Bridging these differences requires diplomatic negotiations, legal expertise, and a commitment to finding common ground.

Attribution and Jurisdiction Determining the origin of cyberattacks and identifying the responsible parties can be complex. The borderless nature of cyberspace makes it challenging to attribute cyber incidents to specific actors or jurisdictions. Resolving jurisdictional issues and facilitating cross-border cooperation are key challenges in international cybersecurity agreements.

Information Sharing and Trust Sharing sensitive information related to cybersecurity requires a high level of trust among nations. Concerns related to the protection of national interests, privacy, and the potential misuse of shared information can hinder information sharing efforts. Building mutual trust and establishing frameworks for secure information exchange are crucial for effective international cooperation.

Case Study: The Paris Call for Trust and Security in Cyberspace

The Paris Call for Trust and Security in Cyberspace is a political declaration that aims to promote a peaceful and secure cyberspace. Launched in 2018, it outlines a set of common principles and commitments for governments, international organizations, and the private sector. The call emphasizes the importance of cooperating to prevent and recover from cyberattacks, protecting intellectual property, and strengthening the resilience of digital ecosystems.

The Paris Call has gained widespread support from countries, tech companies, and civil society organizations. It highlights the growing recognition of the need for enhanced global cooperation in addressing cybersecurity challenges. The case study of the Paris Call demonstrates the potential of voluntary initiatives to complement formal international agreements and foster collaboration.

Conclusion

International cybersecurity agreements and treaties play a vital role in fostering cooperation, establishing norms, and enhancing global cybersecurity. They provide the framework for information sharing, incident response coordination, capacity building, and the establishment of common rules and standards. While challenges exist, the collective effort of nations to address cybersecurity threats is critical for a safer and more secure cyberspace. By promoting international cooperation, these agreements contribute to the sustainability of cybersecurity in the future.

Cybersecurity Capacity Building and Knowledge Sharing

Cybersecurity capacity building and knowledge sharing play a crucial role in enhancing the overall cybersecurity ecosystem. As technology evolves and cyber threats become more sophisticated, it is essential to continuously build and update cybersecurity capabilities to protect digital assets and infrastructure. In this section, we will explore the importance of cybersecurity capacity building and knowledge sharing, the challenges associated with it, and strategies to promote a culture of collaboration and information sharing.

Importance of Cybersecurity Capacity Building

Cybersecurity capacity building refers to the development and enhancement of skills, knowledge, and resources to improve cyber resilience at individual, organizational, and national levels. It is a proactive measure to address the growing cybersecurity challenges faced by governments, businesses, and individuals. Here are some key reasons why cybersecurity capacity building is of utmost importance:

1. **Enhancing Cybersecurity Preparedness:** By building strong cybersecurity capabilities, organizations and individuals can better prepare themselves to detect, prevent, and respond to cyber threats effectively. This includes developing incident response plans, conducting regular security assessments, and implementing best practices in areas such as access control, encryption, and vulnerability management.

2. **Strengthening Resilience:** Cybersecurity capacity building helps organizations and nations build resilience against cyber attacks. By investing in

skilled professionals, robust infrastructure, and advanced technologies, they can better withstand and recover from cyber incidents, minimizing their impact on critical services and operations.

3. **Supporting Economic Growth:** A strong cybersecurity ecosystem fosters trust and confidence in the digital economy. It enables businesses to operate securely, facilitates cross-border trade, and attracts investments. By investing in cybersecurity capacity building, countries can create a conducive environment for innovation, entrepreneurship, and economic prosperity.

4. **Promoting National Security:** Cybersecurity is an integral part of national security. Building a strong cybersecurity workforce and infrastructure helps defend against cyber threats that can have significant implications for a nation's military, intelligence, and critical infrastructure sectors.

5. **Protecting Individuals and Privacy:** Cyber threats can have a profound impact on individuals, their privacy, and personal information. By educating and empowering individuals about cybersecurity risks and best practices, capacity building initiatives can help protect personal data and promote responsible digital behaviors.

Challenges in Cybersecurity Capacity Building

While the importance of cybersecurity capacity building is undeniable, several challenges hinder its effective implementation. It is essential to address these challenges to ensure successful outcomes and sustainable cybersecurity practices. Some of the key challenges are:

1. **Lack of Skilled Professionals:** The cybersecurity skills gap is a significant challenge faced by organizations and nations worldwide. The rapid growth of cyber threats has created a high demand for cybersecurity professionals with specialized skills and knowledge. However, there is a shortage of such professionals, making it difficult to build and maintain cybersecurity capacity.

2. **Limited Resources:** Building cybersecurity capacity requires financial investments in infrastructure, technology, training, and research. Many organizations, particularly small and medium-sized enterprises (SMEs) and developing countries, struggle to allocate sufficient resources to cybersecurity initiatives.

3. **Rapidly Evolving Threat Landscape:** Cyber threats and attack techniques evolve at a rapid pace, posing a significant challenge to capacity building efforts. It is crucial to keep abreast of emerging threats and trends to ensure that cybersecurity skills and knowledge remain relevant and effective.

4. **Fragmented Knowledge and Information Sharing:** The sharing of cybersecurity knowledge and information is often limited due to a lack of collaboration and coordination among various stakeholders. Siloed approaches prevent the effective transfer of expertise, best practices, and threat intelligence.

Strategies for Cybersecurity Capacity Building

To overcome the challenges associated with cybersecurity capacity building, several strategies can be adopted at different levels. These strategies aim to promote collaboration, knowledge sharing, and the development of skilled professionals. Let's explore some key strategies:

1. **Education and Training:** Investing in cybersecurity education and training programs is essential to develop a skilled workforce. This includes academic programs, vocational training, and professional certifications. Organizations should provide continuous training to their employees to enhance their cybersecurity skills and knowledge.

2. **Public-Private Partnerships:** Collaboration between the public and private sectors is crucial for effective cybersecurity capacity building. Governments, industry associations, and cybersecurity vendors can work together to share resources, expertise, and threat intelligence. Public-private partnerships foster collaboration, support research and development initiatives, and promote information sharing.

3. **International Cooperation:** Cybersecurity is a global issue that requires international cooperation and collaboration. Nations should work together to share best practices, harmonize policies and regulations, and facilitate the exchange of threat intelligence. International organizations, such as the United Nations and Interpol, play a vital role in promoting global cybersecurity capacity building initiatives.

4. **Knowledge Sharing Platforms:** Creating platforms and forums for knowledge sharing and collaboration is essential to overcome the fragmentation of cybersecurity knowledge. These platforms can facilitate the sharing of best practices, case studies, research findings, and threat intelligence among cybersecurity professionals, researchers, and organizations.

5. **Promotion of Research and Innovation:** Encouraging research and innovation in cybersecurity is crucial to stay ahead of emerging threats and challenges. Governments, academia, and industry should invest in research grants, innovation centers, and entrepreneurship programs to foster the development of new technologies, tools, and strategies.

Practical Example: National Cybersecurity Capacity Building Program

To illustrate the implementation of cybersecurity capacity building, let's consider the example of a hypothetical National Cybersecurity Capacity Building Program developed by a government agency. The program aims to enhance the cybersecurity capabilities of small and medium-sized enterprises (SMEs) in the country. Here are the key components of the program:

1. **Training and Awareness:** The program conducts cybersecurity training sessions and workshops, targeting SMEs. It covers various topics, including basic cybersecurity principles, secure coding practices, and incident response planning. The training aims to raise awareness and enhance the cybersecurity knowledge of SME owners and employees.

2. **Mentorship and Coaching:** The program provides mentorship and coaching services to SMEs, connecting them with experienced cybersecurity professionals. The mentors offer guidance and support in implementing cybersecurity best practices, conducting security assessments, and developing incident response plans tailored to the specific needs of each SME.

3. **Financial Assistance:** Recognizing the resource constraints faced by SMEs, the program provides financial assistance to help them improve their cybersecurity infrastructure. This may include grants for purchasing security tools and technologies, conducting security audits, and implementing secure software development practices.

4. **Knowledge Sharing Events:** The program organizes knowledge sharing events, such as conferences, seminars, and webinars, where SMEs can learn from cybersecurity experts, share experiences, and network with industry peers. These events provide a platform for cross-sector collaboration and the exchange of best practices.

5. **Collaboration with Industry Associations:** The program establishes partnerships with industry associations representing SMEs in various sectors. These partnerships help leverage existing networks and resources to reach a broader audience and ensure the sustainability of capacity-building efforts beyond the program's duration.

By implementing such a program, the government agency can contribute to the overall cybersecurity resilience of SMEs in the country. It helps bridge the cybersecurity skills gap, raises awareness, and promotes a culture of collaboration and knowledge sharing among SMEs.

Conclusion

In conclusion, cybersecurity capacity building is essential to address the evolving cyber threats and challenges faced by organizations and nations. It helps enhance cybersecurity preparedness, strengthen resilience, support economic growth, and protect individuals and privacy. However, capacity building initiatives need to overcome challenges such as the lack of skilled professionals, limited resources, and fragmented knowledge sharing. By adopting strategies such as education and training, public-private partnerships, and international cooperation, stakeholders can work together to build robust cybersecurity capabilities. The practical example of a National Cybersecurity Capacity Building Program illustrates how governments can implement targeted initiatives to enhance the cybersecurity resilience of specific sectors or industries. Together, these efforts contribute to a sustainable and secure cybersecurity ecosystem.

Public-Private Partnerships in Cybersecurity

In today's interconnected digital landscape, cyber threats are constantly evolving and becoming more sophisticated. As a result, the battle against cybercrime requires collaboration and cooperation between various stakeholders, including government entities, private organizations, and individuals. Public-private partnerships (PPPs) play a vital role in addressing the complex challenges of cybersecurity. This section explores the concept of PPPs in cybersecurity, their significance, benefits, challenges, and best practices.

Understanding Public-Private Partnerships

Public-private partnerships in cybersecurity refer to collaborations between government agencies and private sector organizations to prevent and mitigate cyber threats. These partnerships leverage the strengths and resources of each stakeholder, fostering information sharing, expertise exchange, and joint efforts towards enhancing cybersecurity.

Significance of Public-Private Partnerships

The significance of public-private partnerships in cybersecurity is multi-fold:

1. **Shared Responsibility:** Cybersecurity is a shared responsibility between the public and private sectors. PPPs enable closer cooperation and coordination to address the growing cyber threats effectively.

2. **Leveraging Expertise:** The public and private sectors bring different strengths and capabilities to the table. PPPs allow for the pooling of knowledge, skills, and resources to develop innovative cybersecurity strategies and solutions.

3. **Enhanced Threat Intelligence:** Through PPPs, both sectors can share valuable threat intelligence, including indicators of compromise, attack patterns, and vulnerabilities. This collaboration leads to improved situational awareness and faster response to emerging threats.

4. **Effective Policy Frameworks:** PPPs enable the development and implementation of comprehensive cybersecurity policies and regulations that strike a balance between national security and economic growth.

Benefits of Public-Private Partnerships

PPPs offer several benefits in the context of cybersecurity:

1. **Information Sharing:** Effective information sharing between public and private sectors enhances early threat detection, incident response, and recovery efforts. It allows organizations to stay ahead of cyber threats and minimize their impact.

2. **Resource Sharing:** PPPs provide access to additional resources, such as funding, technology, and expertise. This collaboration improves the overall resilience of critical infrastructure and helps in the development of innovative cybersecurity solutions.

3. **Coordinated Incident Response:** When a cybersecurity incident occurs, PPPs facilitate a coordinated and efficient response. Public and private entities can work together to contain the incident, mitigate the damage, and recover quickly.

4. **Policy Development:** PPPs enable the formulation of cybersecurity policies that take into account the needs and perspectives of both sectors. This approach ensures that policies are practical, effective, and aligned with the evolving cyber threat landscape.

Challenges in Establishing Public-Private Partnerships

Despite the numerous benefits, establishing and maintaining public-private partnerships in cybersecurity can pose challenges:

1. **Trust and Information Sharing:** Trust issues and concerns about sharing sensitive information hinder effective collaboration between public and private entities. Addressing these concerns and establishing a framework for secure information sharing is critical.

2. **Different Objectives and Priorities:** Public and private sectors may have divergent objectives and priorities, making alignment and consensus-building difficult. Clear communication channels and a shared understanding of objectives are necessary to overcome these challenges.

3. **Legal and Policy Constraints:** Legal and policy constraints can impede the formation of PPPs. Regulatory frameworks and data protection laws need to be well-defined and flexible enough to facilitate collaboration without compromising privacy and security.

Best Practices for Public-Private Partnerships

To establish effective PPPs in cybersecurity, it is important to adhere to the following best practices:

1. **Clear Objectives and Roles:** Clearly define the objectives, roles, and responsibilities of each partner to ensure a shared understanding and commitment towards common goals.

2. **Strong Governance Framework:** Establish a robust governance framework that outlines decision-making processes, information sharing protocols, and mechanisms for resolving conflicts.

3. **Regular Communication and Collaboration:** Encourage regular communication and collaboration between public and private entities through forums, working groups, and joint exercises. This facilitates the exchange of threat intelligence, best practices, and lessons learned.

4. **Education and Awareness:** Promote cybersecurity education and awareness initiatives to foster a culture of cybersecurity resilience among all stakeholders. This includes training programs, awareness campaigns, and sharing of actionable cybersecurity guidance.

Case Study: US Department of Homeland Security's cybersecurity public-private partnership

The US Department of Homeland Security (DHS) has established successful public-private partnerships to strengthen the nation's cybersecurity posture. One notable example is the Cyber Information Sharing and Collaboration Program (CISCP). It enables the sharing of cybersecurity information, best practices, and incident response capabilities between the government and private sector organizations. Through this partnership, participants can access valuable threat intelligence, receive alerts, and collaborate on cybersecurity research and development.

Conclusion

Public-private partnerships are crucial in addressing the ever-growing cybersecurity challenges faced by societies worldwide. By leveraging the expertise, resources, and capabilities of both sectors, these partnerships can enhance threat detection, incident response, and policy development. While challenges exist, adhering to best practices and fostering a culture of collaboration can pave the way towards effective public-private partnerships in cybersecurity. Through these partnerships, nations can collectively work towards a safer and more secure digital future.

Exercises

1. Discuss the significance of public-private partnerships in cybersecurity and how they contribute to enhancing overall cybersecurity resilience.

2. Identify and explain the benefits of public-private partnerships in the context of cybersecurity. Provide real-world examples to support your answer.

3. Discuss the challenges that organizations face in establishing and maintaining public-private partnerships in cybersecurity. Suggest strategies and approaches to overcome these challenges.

4. Analyze the role of trust in public-private partnerships in cybersecurity. How can organizations build and maintain trust when sharing sensitive information?

5. Research a public-private partnership in cybersecurity implemented in your country or region. Evaluate its effectiveness and impact on cybersecurity outcomes.

6. Prepare a proposal for a public-private partnership in cybersecurity aimed at addressing a specific cybersecurity challenge. Justify the need for collaboration and outline the objectives, roles, and expected outcomes of the partnership.

Resources

1. U.S. Department of Homeland Security: `https://www.dhs.gov/`

2. National Institute of Standards and Technology (NIST) Cybersecurity Framework: `https://www.nist.gov/cyberframework`

3. Cyber Threat Alliance: `https://www.cyberthreatalliance.org/`

4. World Economic Forum - Centre for Cybersecurity: `https://www.weforum.org/centre-for-cybersecurity`

5. The Cybersecurity Coalition: `https://www.cybersecuritycoalition.org/`

Cybersecurity Collaboration and Information Sharing Platforms

In today's interconnected world, addressing cybersecurity challenges requires collaboration and information sharing among various stakeholders. Cybersecurity collaboration platforms provide a means for organizations and individuals to come together, exchange knowledge, and collectively respond to cyber threats. These platforms facilitate the sharing of information, best practices, and threat intelligence to enhance the overall cybersecurity posture. In this section, we will explore the importance of cybersecurity collaboration and examine various information sharing platforms that foster cooperation among cybersecurity professionals.

The Need for Cybersecurity Collaboration

Cyber threats are becoming increasingly sophisticated and widespread, posing significant risks to organizations across all sectors. It is no longer feasible for individual entities to rely solely on their own resources and expertise to combat these threats effectively. Collaboration among industry, government, academia, and other stakeholders is essential for developing comprehensive and timely responses to cyber incidents. Here are some reasons why cybersecurity collaboration is crucial:

1. **Real-time threat intelligence**: Cyber threats are evolving rapidly, and timely information sharing is essential to stay ahead of attackers. Collaboration platforms facilitate the exchange of threat intelligence, enabling organizations to quickly identify and respond to emerging threats.

2. **Collective defense**: Cybersecurity is a collective responsibility. By collaborating with peers, organizations can benefit from shared knowledge, resources, and expertise, ultimately leading to a stronger collective defense against cyber threats.

3. **Improved incident response**: Cybersecurity incidents can have severe consequences if not addressed promptly and effectively. Collaboration platforms allow organizations to coordinate incident response efforts, share best practices, and leverage the expertise of others to mitigate the impact of cyber incidents.

4. **Enhanced situational awareness**: Collaboration platforms enable participants to gain a broader view of the threat landscape. By pooling information from multiple sources, organizations can better understand the tactics, techniques, and procedures used by threat actors, enhancing their situational awareness.

5. **Policy development and advocacy**: Collaborative efforts also extend to the development of cybersecurity policies and regulations. By working together,

stakeholders can advocate for effective cybersecurity measures, shape legislation, and promote best practices that benefit the entire cybersecurity ecosystem.

Types of Cybersecurity Collaboration Platforms

Several collaboration platforms and initiatives exist that facilitate information sharing and cooperation in the field of cybersecurity. Here, we will discuss three prominent types of cybersecurity collaboration platforms:

1. **Information Sharing and Analysis Centers (ISACs)**: ISACs are sector-specific organizations that provide a trusted environment for sharing cyber threat information and best practices. They act as a hub for collecting, analyzing, and disseminating timely information to their members, enabling proactive threat management. Each ISAC focuses on a specific industry or critical infrastructure sector, such as finance, energy, or healthcare.
2. **Computer Emergency Response Teams (CERTs)**: CERTs are organizations that respond to cybersecurity incidents and coordinate cyber threat information sharing within a specific country or region. They serve as a central point of contact for incident response and facilitate collaboration among government agencies, the private sector, and other stakeholders. CERTs play a vital role in sharing actionable security information, providing incident response coordination, and fostering cybersecurity capacity building.
3. **International Information Sharing and Analysis Organizations (ISAOs)**: ISAOs are collaborative platforms that promote international cybersecurity information sharing and collaboration. They bring together multiple ISACs, CERTs, and other cybersecurity organizations from different countries to share threat intelligence, best practices, and lessons learned. ISAOs facilitate global cooperation, enabling stakeholders to collectively address cybersecurity challenges that transcend national boundaries.

Benefits and Challenges of Collaboration Platforms

Collaboration platforms offer several benefits to organizations, including:

1. **Improved threat detection**: By combining intelligence from multiple sources, collaboration platforms enhance the ability to detect and respond to cyber threats promptly. Access to a broader set of data and expertise increases the likelihood of identifying sophisticated attacks that may go undetected within individual organizations.
2. **Knowledge sharing and learning**: Collaboration platforms provide a forum for sharing best practices, lessons learned, and case studies. Organizations

can learn from each other's experiences, methodologies, and successful strategies, thereby improving their own cybersecurity capabilities.

3. **Faster incident response**: Real-time information sharing within collaboration platforms enables organizations to respond quickly and efficiently to cyber incidents. The ability to coordinate resources, expertise, and response efforts can significantly reduce the impact of an incident and minimize downtime.

4. **Increased threat intelligence**: Collaboration platforms act as force multipliers, allowing organizations to access a wider range of threat intelligence feeds. This expanded visibility into emerging threats and attack trends helps organizations stay proactive in their cyber defense strategies.

Despite the numerous benefits, cybersecurity collaboration platforms also face specific challenges:

1. **Trust and privacy concerns**: Effective collaboration relies on trust and the sharing of sensitive information. Organizations may be hesitant to share comprehensive threat data due to concerns about the privacy and security of their information. Building trust and addressing privacy concerns are crucial for successful collaboration.

2. **Legal and regulatory challenges**: Collaboration that spans different jurisdictions may encounter legal and regulatory obstacles. Variations in data protection laws, intellectual property rights, and information sharing regulations can hinder the free flow of information between organizations and nations.

3. **Information overload and false positives**: Collaboration platforms generate large volumes of threat data, making it challenging to identify genuine threats amidst the noise. Without robust analysis and filtering mechanisms, organizations may be overwhelmed with false positives or low-priority alerts, impeding effective incident response.

Case Study: The Cyber Information Sharing and Collaboration Program (CISCP)

The Cyber Information Sharing and Collaboration Program (CISCP) is a government-led initiative designed to foster collaboration and information sharing among public and private sector entities in the United States. The program aims to improve the overall cybersecurity posture by facilitating the exchange of actionable threat information, best practices, and mitigation strategies.

CISCP operates through a secure platform that allows participants to share cybersecurity threat indicators, incident data, and analytical insights. It provides access to real-time threat feeds, incident response playbooks, and regular cybersecurity training materials. The platform also enables participants to communicate with each other securely, fostering collaboration through dedicated working groups and forums.

The success of CISCP lies in its ability to bring together diverse stakeholders, including federal agencies, law enforcement, critical infrastructure operators, and cybersecurity vendors. By promoting information sharing, collaboration, and coordinated incident response, CISCP enhances the nation's collective defense against cyber threats.

Key Takeaways

Collaboration and information sharing are essential for addressing cybersecurity challenges effectively. Cybersecurity collaboration platforms, such as ISACs, CERTs, and ISAOs, facilitate the exchange of threat intelligence, best practices, and incident response coordination. These platforms offer numerous benefits, including improved threat detection, knowledge sharing, and faster incident response. However, challenges related to trust, privacy, legal issues, and information overload need to be addressed for successful collaboration. Initiatives like CISCP showcase the potential of collaboration platforms in strengthening cybersecurity across sectors.

Summary

In this section, we explored the importance of cybersecurity collaboration and examined various information sharing platforms that foster cooperation among cybersecurity professionals. We discussed the need for collaboration due to the evolving cyber threats landscape and the benefits it brings, such as real-time threat intelligence, collective defense, improved incident response, enhanced situational awareness, and policy development. We also examined three prominent types of cybersecurity collaboration platforms: ISACs, CERTs, and ISAOs. Additionally, we discussed the benefits and challenges associated with collaboration platforms and presented a case study of the Cyber Information Sharing and Collaboration Program (CISCP). Cybersecurity collaboration platforms play a crucial role in addressing cybersecurity challenges and building a more secure digital ecosystem.

Cybersecurity Education and Workforce Development

Building a Cybersecurity Workforce

Demand for Cybersecurity Professionals

In today's digital landscape, with the increasing frequency and sophistication of cyber attacks, the demand for cybersecurity professionals has reached unprecedented levels. Organizations across industries are recognizing the critical importance of safeguarding their sensitive information and digital assets. As a result, the need for skilled cybersecurity professionals has skyrocketed, leading to a substantial shortage in the cybersecurity job market.

The Rise of Cybersecurity Threats

Cybersecurity threats have been evolving rapidly, posing significant risks to businesses and individuals alike. These threats include data breaches, ransomware attacks, phishing scams, and network intrusions, among others. With the increasing interconnectivity of devices and the ever-expanding digital infrastructure, the attack surface has grown, leaving organizations vulnerable to cyber threats.

Legal and Regulatory Landscape

The legal and regulatory landscape has also contributed to the increased demand for cybersecurity professionals. Governments around the world have recognized the need to protect their digital infrastructure and have enacted laws and regulations to enforce cybersecurity practices. For instance, the European Union's General Data Protection Regulation (GDPR) has imposed strict guidelines on organizations handling personal data, mandating the appointment of Data Protection Officers (DPOs) and necessitating the implementation of robust cybersecurity measures.

Importance of Cybersecurity Professionals

Cybersecurity professionals play a crucial role in protecting organizations from cyber threats and ensuring the security and integrity of digital assets. They are responsible for identifying vulnerabilities, implementing security controls, monitoring systems for any suspicious activities, and responding promptly to security incidents. Their expertise is indispensable in developing and maintaining effective cybersecurity programs.

Skills and Competencies

The demand for cybersecurity professionals spans a wide range of skills and competencies. Some of the key skills sought after by employers include:

- **Technical Proficiency:** In-depth knowledge of networking protocols, operating systems, and security technologies is essential. Cybersecurity professionals must have a strong understanding of encryption, firewalls, intrusion detection systems, and vulnerability assessment tools.

- **Risk Assessment and Incident Response:** The ability to assess risks and develop effective incident response plans is critical. Cybersecurity professionals need to be able to identify potential vulnerabilities, analyze threats, and respond swiftly and effectively to security incidents.

- **Ethical Hacking:** In order to stay one step ahead of cybercriminals, organizations are increasingly seeking professionals with ethical hacking skills. Ethical hackers can identify vulnerabilities in systems and help mitigate potential threats by conducting controlled penetration testing.

- **Security Policy and Compliance:** Cybersecurity professionals should have a strong understanding of security policies, procedures, and industry standards. They need to ensure that organizations comply with relevant regulations and develop and enforce security policies tailored to specific business needs.

- **Communication and Collaboration:** Cybersecurity professionals must possess excellent communication skills to effectively communicate security risks and recommendations to stakeholders at all levels of the organization.

They should be able to collaborate with cross-functional teams to implement security measures and respond to incidents.

Cybersecurity Job Roles

The demand for cybersecurity professionals spans across various job roles, including:

- **Cybersecurity Analyst:** Responsible for monitoring and analyzing security events, conducting threat assessments, and recommending appropriate security measures.
- **Ethical Hacker / Penetration Tester:** Conducts controlled hacking attempts to identify vulnerabilities in systems and networks and helps organizations improve their security posture.
- **Security Architect:** Designs and develops robust security architectures and frameworks, taking into consideration the organization's risk appetite and business objectives.
- **Security Consultant:** Provides expert advice and guidance to organizations on security strategies, risk management, and compliance with industry standards and regulations.
- **Incident Responder:** Investigates and responds to security incidents promptly, minimizing damage and implementing measures to prevent future incidents.
- **Governance, Risk, and Compliance (GRC) Specialist:** Ensures that organizations adhere to relevant regulations and industry standards, and develops and maintains cybersecurity policies and procedures.

Challenges in Meeting the Demand

Despite the increasing demand for cybersecurity professionals, organizations face several challenges in meeting this demand:

- **Skills Gap:** The cybersecurity field is continually evolving, and organizations struggle to find candidates with the required skills and expertise. The lack of qualified professionals contributes to the shortage of skilled cybersecurity personnel.

- **Rapid Technological Advancements:** The rapid pace of technological advancements poses challenges to cybersecurity professionals who need to continuously update their skills to keep up with emerging threats and technologies.

- **Diversity and Inclusion:** The cybersecurity field lacks diversity, with a disproportionate representation of gender and minority groups. Encouraging diversity and inclusion can bring fresh perspectives and help address the shortage of skilled professionals.

- **Retention and Career Advancement:** Retaining cybersecurity professionals is a challenge for organizations. Providing opportunities for career advancement, ongoing professional development, and competitive compensation packages are critical in retaining top talent.

Addressing the Demand

To address the demand for cybersecurity professionals, organizations and educational institutions can take the following measures:

- **Cybersecurity Education and Training:** Educational institutions should offer comprehensive cybersecurity programs that cover a wide range of technical and non-technical skills. Continuous learning and professional development opportunities should be provided to help professionals stay updated with the latest technologies and threats.

- **Internship and Apprenticeship Programs:** Organizations can provide internship and apprenticeship programs to students and individuals looking to enter the field. These programs enable hands-on learning and provide practical experience in real-world cybersecurity scenarios.

- **Promoting Diversity and Inclusion:** Efforts should be made to promote diversity and inclusion in the cybersecurity field. Encouraging underrepresented groups to pursue careers in cybersecurity can help bridge the skills gap and bring fresh perspectives to the industry.

- **Collaboration with Academia:** Organizations should collaborate with academic institutions in developing cybersecurity curricula and establishing research partnerships. This collaboration can help ensure that educational programs align with industry needs and produce graduates with the necessary skills.

- **Professional Certifications:** Professional certifications, such as Certified Information Systems Security Professional (CISSP) or Certified Ethical Hacker (CEH), provide validation of skills and knowledge in specific areas of cybersecurity. Encouraging professionals to obtain relevant certifications can enhance their credibility and marketability.

Conclusion

The demand for cybersecurity professionals is at an all-time high, driven by the evolving threat landscape and increased regulatory requirements. Organizations need to proactively address this demand by investing in cybersecurity education, promoting diversity and inclusion, and providing attractive career opportunities. By cultivating a skilled and diverse cybersecurity workforce, organizations can better protect their digital assets and defend against emerging cyber threats.

Cybersecurity Roles and Job Functions

In the field of cybersecurity, various roles and job functions exist to ensure the protection of digital assets and information. These roles are essential for the development and implementation of effective cybersecurity strategies within organizations. In this section, we will explore some of the key cybersecurity roles and job functions, along with their responsibilities and skill requirements.

Chief Information Security Officer (CISO)

The Chief Information Security Officer (CISO) is a senior-level executive responsible for overseeing the organization's information security program. The CISO plays a critical role in establishing and maintaining the organization's cybersecurity strategy and ensuring its alignment with business objectives.

Responsibilities of a CISO include:

- Developing and implementing an information security governance framework.

- Managing the organization's cybersecurity policies, procedures, and standards.

- Assessing and mitigating cybersecurity risks.

- Directing the creation and maintenance of an incident response plan.

- Overseeing the execution of cybersecurity awareness and training programs.
- Collaborating with internal and external stakeholders on cybersecurity initiatives.

Skills and qualifications of a CISO may include:

- In-depth knowledge of cybersecurity principles, technologies, and best practices.
- Strong leadership and management skills.
- Excellent communication and interpersonal skills.
- Familiarity with relevant laws, regulations, and industry standards.
- Experience in risk management and incident response.
- Business acumen and the ability to align cybersecurity objectives with business goals.

Security Analyst

A Security Analyst is responsible for monitoring and analyzing the organization's systems, networks, and applications for potential security incidents. They play a crucial role in detecting and responding to cyber threats in a timely manner.

Responsibilities of a Security Analyst include:

- Conducting vulnerability assessments and penetration testing.
- Monitoring security event logs and analyzing security alerts.
- Investigating and resolving security incidents.
- Implementing and maintaining security controls and technologies.
- Providing recommendations for improving the organization's security posture.
- Staying up-to-date with the latest security threats and vulnerabilities.

Skills and qualifications of a Security Analyst may include:

- Knowledge of network protocols, operating systems, and security technologies.
- Proficiency in security analysis tools and techniques.
- Strong analytical and problem-solving skills.
- Understanding of security frameworks and best practices.
- Ability to work under pressure and respond to incidents effectively.
- Good communication and collaboration skills to work with cross-functional teams.

Security Engineer

A Security Engineer is responsible for designing, implementing, and maintaining the organization's security infrastructure. They work closely with other teams to ensure that security measures are integrated into the organization's systems and processes.

Responsibilities of a Security Engineer include:

- Designing and implementing security solutions, such as firewalls, intrusion detection systems, and encryption mechanisms.
- Conducting security assessments and audits.
- Configuring and managing security tools and technologies.
- Collaborating with developers to ensure secure coding practices.
- Providing technical expertise and support for security-related incidents.
- Researching and evaluating emerging security technologies and trends.

Skills and qualifications of a Security Engineer may include:

- Proficiency in network and system security technologies.
- Strong knowledge of encryption algorithms, protocols, and standards.
- Experience with security assessment tools and methodologies.
- Understanding of secure software development lifecycle.
- Troubleshooting and problem-solving skills.
- Ability to stay current with industry trends and emerging threats.

Security Consultant

A Security Consultant is an external professional who provides expert advice and guidance on cybersecurity to organizations. They assess the organization's security posture, identify vulnerabilities, and recommend appropriate security measures.

Responsibilities of a Security Consultant include:

- Conducting risk assessments and security audits.
- Evaluating the effectiveness of existing security controls.
- Developing security policies, procedures, and guidelines.
- Assisting in the implementation of security technologies and solutions.
- Conducting security awareness training for employees.
- Providing guidance on regulatory compliance and industry standards.

Skills and qualifications of a Security Consultant may include:

- Deep understanding of security frameworks, regulations, and standards.
- Extensive knowledge of security technologies and industry trends.
- Strong analytical and problem-solving skills.
- Excellent communication and presentation skills.
- Ability to work independently and as part of a team.
- Consulting experience and the ability to build client relationships.

Incident Responder

An Incident Responder is responsible for responding to and managing cybersecurity incidents within the organization. They work closely with other teams to contain and mitigate the impact of security breaches and restore normal operations.

Responsibilities of an Incident Responder include:

- Developing and executing incident response plans.
- Investigating and analyzing security incidents.

- Containing and eradicating security threats.
- Documenting and reporting incident findings.
- Conducting post-incident analysis and implementing preventive measures.
- Collaborating with law enforcement and external incident response teams, if necessary.

Skills and qualifications of an Incident Responder may include:

- Knowledge of incident response processes and methodologies.
- Familiarity with forensic investigation techniques and tools.
- Understanding of malware analysis and reverse engineering.
- Strong technical and analytical skills.
- Excellent communication and teamwork abilities.
- Ability to handle high-pressure situations and make quick decisions.

Ethical Hacker

An Ethical Hacker, also known as a White Hat Hacker or Penetration Tester, is responsible for actively identifying vulnerabilities in systems and networks by simulating real-world cyber attacks. They actively work towards improving the security posture of organizations through proactive testing and assessment.

Responsibilities of an Ethical Hacker include:

- Conducting vulnerability assessments and penetration testing.
- Identifying and exploiting security vulnerabilities.
- Providing recommendations for remediation and risk mitigation.
- Collaborating with other teams to address security weaknesses.
- Staying updated with the latest hacking techniques and tools.
- Contributing to the development of security guidelines and best practices.

Skills and qualifications of an Ethical Hacker may include:

- In-depth knowledge of networking protocols and operating systems.
- Proficiency in penetration testing tools and techniques.
- Understanding of common vulnerabilities and attack vectors.
- Strong problem-solving and analytical skills.
- Ability to think creatively to identify potential attack vectors.
- Ethical mindset and adherence to professional ethics.

Cybersecurity Architect

A Cybersecurity Architect is responsible for designing and implementing secure IT architectures that align with business objectives. They develop and maintain security frameworks and provide guidance on the selection and implementation of security technologies.

Responsibilities of a Cybersecurity Architect include:

- Designing and documenting security architectures and solutions.
- Evaluating and selecting appropriate security technologies.
- Defining security standards, policies, and procedures.
- Collaborating with other IT teams to integrate security measures.
- Conducting risk assessments and security audits.
- Providing guidance on security best practices and industry standards.

Skills and qualifications of a Cybersecurity Architect may include:

- In-depth knowledge of IT architectures and security frameworks.
- Understanding of cloud computing and virtualization security.
- Strong analytical and problem-solving skills.
- Experience with security assessment tools and methodologies.
- Good communication and presentation skills.
- Ability to balance technical requirements with business needs.

Security Operations Center (SOC) Analyst

A Security Operations Center (SOC) Analyst is responsible for monitoring and analyzing security events and incidents within the organization. They work in a SOC, which serves as a centralized hub for cybersecurity operations.

Responsibilities of a SOC Analyst include:

- Monitoring security event logs and alarms.
- Analyzing and triaging security alerts and incidents.
- Investigating and escalating security breaches.
- Coordinating with incident response teams to mitigate threats.
- Conducting threat hunting to identify potential attacks.
- Documenting and reporting security incidents.

Skills and qualifications of a SOC Analyst may include:

- Familiarity with security information and event management (SIEM) tools.
- Knowledge of intrusion detection and prevention systems (IDPS).
- Understanding of network protocols and security technologies.
- Strong analytical and problem-solving abilities.
- Ability to work in a fast-paced and dynamic environment.
- Teamwork and collaboration skills to work with cross-functional teams.

Cybersecurity Trainer

A Cybersecurity Trainer is responsible for educating and training employees on cybersecurity best practices and awareness. They play a crucial role in creating a culture of security within the organization.

Responsibilities of a Cybersecurity Trainer include:

- Developing and delivering cybersecurity training programs.
- Conducting awareness campaigns and workshops.

- Creating educational materials and resources.
- Keeping up-to-date with the latest security trends and threats.
- Collaborating with other teams to address security gaps.
- Assessing the effectiveness of training programs through evaluations.

Skills and qualifications of a Cybersecurity Trainer may include:

- In-depth knowledge of cybersecurity principles and best practices.
- Strong presentation and communication skills.
- Ability to simplify complex security concepts for non-technical audiences.
- Creativity in developing engaging training materials.
- Knowledge of adult learning principles and instructional design.
- Continuous learning to stay updated with evolving security threats.

Cybersecurity Project Manager

A Cybersecurity Project Manager is responsible for planning, executing, and managing cybersecurity projects within the organization. They ensure that projects are delivered on time, within budget, and meet the defined security requirements.

Responsibilities of a Cybersecurity Project Manager include:

- Defining project objectives, scope, and deliverables.
- Creating project plans and schedules.
- Identifying and managing project risks and issues.
- Coordinating project teams and resources.
- Monitoring project progress and ensuring timely completion.
- Reporting project status and communicating with stakeholders.

Skills and qualifications of a Cybersecurity Project Manager may include:

- Project management knowledge and certification (e.g., PMP).

- Understanding of cybersecurity principles and technologies.
- Strong organizational and time management skills.
- Communication and interpersonal skills to work with diverse teams.
- Ability to balance business and technical requirements.
- Problem-solving and decision-making abilities in a dynamic environment.

Conclusion

The field of cybersecurity offers a wide range of roles and job functions, each playing a vital role in protecting organizations from cyber threats. Whether it is the CISO defining the overall cybersecurity strategy, the Security Analyst detecting and responding to incidents, or the Ethical Hacker identifying vulnerabilities, these professionals collectively contribute to the security and resilience of information systems.

To pursue a career in cybersecurity, individuals should possess a combination of technical skills, industry knowledge, and a strong commitment to continuous learning. The roles and job functions discussed in this section are just a few examples, and the cybersecurity landscape continues to evolve rapidly, creating new job opportunities and challenges.

As organizations increasingly recognize the importance of cybersecurity, the demand for qualified professionals in the field will continue to grow. By understanding the various roles and job functions in cybersecurity, individuals can make informed career choices and contribute to building a secure and resilient digital future.

Cybersecurity Skills and Competencies

In the rapidly evolving field of cybersecurity, acquiring the right skills and competencies is essential for professionals to effectively protect and secure digital assets. Cybersecurity is a multidisciplinary domain that requires a combination of technical expertise, analytical thinking, and a deep understanding of security principles. This section will delve into the key skills and competencies needed to thrive in the world of cybersecurity.

Technical Proficiency

Cybersecurity professionals need to be well-versed in various technical areas to understand the complexities of security systems and networks. Some of the essential technical skills and competencies include:

1. **Network Security:** Understanding the fundamentals of network protocols, firewalls, intrusion detection systems, and virtual private networks (VPNs) is crucial for protecting network infrastructure and data transmission.

2. **Secure Software Development:** Knowledge of secure coding practices, software vulnerabilities, and secure development lifecycle is vital for creating robust and secure software applications.

3. **Cloud Security:** With the increasing adoption of cloud computing, expertise in cloud security architecture, identity and access management, and secure data storage is becoming increasingly important.

4. **Web Application Security:** Familiarity with web application vulnerabilities, secure coding practices, and web application security testing techniques is crucial to safeguard against web-based attacks.

5. **Operating System Security:** Proficiency in securing operating systems (such as Windows, Linux, and macOS) through configuration hardening, access control, and vulnerability management is essential.

6. **Cryptographic Principles:** Understanding cryptographic algorithms, encryption, digital signatures, and key management is vital for ensuring data confidentiality, integrity, and authenticity.

Analytical Skills

Effective cybersecurity professionals possess strong analytical skills that allow them to identify and assess potential vulnerabilities, threats, and risks. These skills include:

1. **Risk Assessment:** The ability to evaluate and prioritize risks, using frameworks such as the NIST Cybersecurity Framework or ISO 27005, helps professionals make informed decisions about risk mitigation strategies.

2. **Threat Intelligence Analysis:** Cybersecurity analysts need to analyze threat intelligence feeds, security incidents, and indicators of compromise to identify patterns and trends that could indicate potential attacks.

3. **Incident Response:** Quick-thinking problem solvers are essential during security incidents. Incident response skills involve identifying, containing, eradicating, and recovering from security breaches while minimizing the impact on the organization.

4. **Forensic Investigation:** Proficiency in digital forensics enables professionals to investigate security incidents, collect evidence, and analyze digital artifacts to determine the cause and impact of an incident.

5. **Data Analysis:** The ability to analyze large volumes of data using tools such as security information and event management (SIEM) systems, machine learning algorithms, and data visualization techniques is crucial for detecting patterns and anomalies.

Communication and Collaboration Skills

Strong communication and collaboration skills are necessary for cybersecurity professionals to effectively communicate risks, influence stakeholders, and work effectively as part of a larger team. These skills include:

1. **Written Communication:** The ability to articulate complex technical concepts clearly and concisely through reports, policies, and documentation is crucial for effective communication in the cybersecurity field.

2. **Verbal Communication:** The capacity to communicate technical information effectively to non-technical stakeholders, whether in formal presentations or informal discussions, is essential for bridging the gap between cybersecurity professionals and decision-makers.

3. **Teamwork:** Collaboration and teamwork skills are essential for working effectively in cross-functional teams, coordinating incident response efforts, and sharing knowledge with colleagues.

4. **Leadership:** Leadership skills are important for cybersecurity professionals who may be responsible for managing teams, projects, or even entire security programs. Effective leaders can drive change, influence stakeholders, and foster a culture of security within organizations.

5. **Ethical Considerations:** Cybersecurity professionals must uphold ethical standards and understand the legal and privacy implications of their work. They must make ethical decisions when handling sensitive information and addressing security incidents.

Continual Learning and Adaptability

Cybersecurity is a constantly evolving field, demanding professionals to continually update their skills and stay abreast of the latest threats, technologies, and best practices. This includes:

1. **Professional Development:** Engaging in continuous learning through professional certifications, attending seminars, conferences, and workshops, and participating in cybersecurity communities helps professionals stay updated and enhance their skills.

2. **Information Sharing:** Actively participating in information sharing initiatives, such as threat intelligence communities or cybersecurity forums, helps professionals gain insights from others and stay informed about emerging threats and innovative solutions.

3. **Adaptability:** Cybersecurity professionals must be adaptable and flexible, as they often encounter new technologies, attack vectors, and regulatory changes. The ability to quickly adapt to new situations and learn on the job is crucial in the field.

4. **Problem-Solving:** Strong problem-solving skills enable cybersecurity professionals to think critically, analyze complex situations, and find solutions to security challenges using a combination of technical knowledge and creative thinking.

Conclusion

Developing the right skills and competencies is a continuous journey for cybersecurity professionals. Technical proficiency, analytical skills, communication, collaboration, adaptability, and a commitment to continual learning are all crucial elements of a successful cybersecurity skill set. By honing these skills, professionals can make meaningful contributions to the cybersecurity field and help build resilient and secure digital ecosystems.

Resources

1. D. Kim, *The Art of Invisibility: The World's Most Famous Hacker Teaches You How to Be Safe in the Age of Big Brother and Big Data,* Little, Brown and Company, 2017.

2. N. P. Jerome, *Cybersecurity Essentials,* SANS Institute, 2020.

3. D. M. Watson, *Building a Practical Information Security Program*, Apress, 2020.

4. OWASP (Open Web Application Security Project): `https://owasp.org`

5. SANS Institute: `https://www.sans.org`

Exercises

1. Research and analyze a recent data breach or cyberattack and identify the skills and competencies that could have prevented or mitigated the incident.

2. Develop a training program for employees to enhance their cybersecurity skills and competencies. Include the key learning objectives, methods, and resources that would be utilized.

3. Consider a hypothetical scenario where an organization is implementing a new cloud-based infrastructure. Identify the technical skills and competencies that would be necessary to ensure the security of the cloud environment.

Remember to regularly update and adapt your skills and competencies to keep pace with the ever-changing cybersecurity landscape.

Recruiting and Retaining Cybersecurity Talent

In order to maintain effective cybersecurity practices, organizations need to recruit and retain top cybersecurity talent. The field of cybersecurity is continuously evolving, and the demand for skilled professionals is increasing rapidly. This section explores strategies for recruiting and retaining cybersecurity talent, addressing the challenges organizations face in attracting and retaining skilled individuals.

The Importance of Recruiting Skilled Cybersecurity Professionals

Recruiting skilled cybersecurity professionals is crucial for organizations to build a strong and resilient cybersecurity infrastructure. These professionals possess the knowledge and expertise to protect sensitive information and defend against cyber threats. However, the cybersecurity job market is highly competitive, and organizations often struggle to attract and retain top talent.

Addressing the Skills Gap

One of the biggest challenges in recruiting cybersecurity talent is the skills gap. The rapid advancement of technology and the ever-changing cybersecurity landscape have created a shortage of skilled professionals. To bridge this gap, organizations need to adopt innovative strategies for identifying and developing talent.

Collaboration with Educational Institutions One effective approach is to establish partnerships with educational institutions. By collaborating with universities and colleges, organizations can contribute to the development of cybersecurity programs that align with industry needs. This can include providing guest lectures, sponsoring research projects, and offering internships or co-op placements to students. Such collaborations not only provide opportunities to identify and recruit talented individuals but also help shape the curriculum to address industry requirements.

Upskilling and Reskilling Programs Organizations can also invest in upskilling and reskilling programs to equip existing employees with the necessary cybersecurity skills. These programs can include training workshops, certification programs, and mentoring initiatives. By investing in the professional development of their employees, organizations can enhance their cybersecurity capabilities while retaining their current workforce.

Engagement with Cybersecurity Communities Active engagement with the cybersecurity community is another effective way to identify and recruit talent. Organizations can participate in cybersecurity conferences, workshops, and online forums to network with professionals in the field. Building relationships with cybersecurity experts can help organizations identify potential candidates for recruitment.

Creating an Attractive Work Environment

Once talented individuals are recruited, it is essential to create an attractive work environment that encourages them to stay. Retaining cybersecurity professionals requires addressing their unique needs and providing opportunities for growth and development.

Competitive Compensation and Benefits Offering competitive compensation packages and benefits is crucial for attracting and retaining cybersecurity talent.

This includes salary packages that reflect the value of their skills and expertise. Additionally, organizations can provide benefits such as flexible work arrangements, professional development allowances, and health and wellness programs.

Career Progression and Skill Diversification Promoting career progression and skill diversification within the organization is essential for retaining cybersecurity professionals. Organizations can create clear paths for advancement, offer opportunities for professional growth, and provide access to training and certification programs. This not only helps employees develop their skills but also shows a commitment to their long-term career development.

Employee Engagement and Recognition Regular employee engagement and recognition activities can contribute to higher job satisfaction and employee retention. This can include team-building activities, mentorship programs, and recognition for outstanding performance. Creating a positive and supportive work environment fosters loyalty and commitment among cybersecurity professionals.

Work-Life Balance Maintaining a healthy work-life balance is crucial for the well-being and job satisfaction of cybersecurity professionals. Organizations can support work-life balance by implementing flexible work arrangements, providing support for family obligations, and promoting mental health and wellness initiatives.

Conclusion

Recruiting and retaining cybersecurity talent is vital for organizations to keep pace with the evolving threat landscape. By addressing the skills gap, creating an attractive work environment, and investing in the professional development of their employees, organizations can attract and retain top cybersecurity professionals. This ultimately strengthens their cybersecurity capabilities and contributes to the overall security of the organization.

Cybersecurity Education and Training

Cybersecurity Curricula and Programs

In order to address the growing need for skilled cybersecurity professionals, numerous cybersecurity curricula and programs have been developed. These curricula and programs aim to provide individuals with the knowledge and skills necessary to effectively protect data, networks, and systems from cyber threats. This section will explore different types of cybersecurity curricula and programs, including academic degrees, certifications, and training courses.

Academic Degrees

One of the most common paths to pursue a career in cybersecurity is through obtaining an academic degree. Universities and colleges offer a range of degree programs in cybersecurity at the undergraduate and graduate levels. These programs typically provide a comprehensive understanding of cybersecurity principles, technologies, practices, and policies.

At the undergraduate level, students can pursue a Bachelor's degree in cybersecurity or a related discipline such as computer science or information technology with a specialization in cybersecurity. These programs typically cover topics such as network security, cryptography, secure software development, and incident response.

At the graduate level, students can pursue a Master's degree in cybersecurity or a related field. These programs often focus on advanced topics such as advanced cryptography, secure systems design, cyber threat intelligence, and digital forensics. Some universities also offer interdisciplinary programs that combine cybersecurity with fields like business or law.

In addition to traditional academic degrees, some universities also offer online cybersecurity programs, allowing students to earn a degree while balancing work and other commitments. Online programs provide flexibility in terms of scheduling and location, making them attractive options for working professionals.

Certifications

Certifications are another valuable way to gain expertise and demonstrate proficiency in specific cybersecurity domains. Certifications validate an individual's knowledge and skills in specific areas of cybersecurity and are often recognized and respected by employers.

One of the most well-known and widely recognized certifications in the cybersecurity field is the Certified Information Systems Security Professional (CISSP) certification. The CISSP certification covers various domains, including asset security, security operations, and software development security. Other popular certifications include the Certified Ethical Hacker (CEH), Certified

Information Security Manager (CISM), and Certified Information Systems Auditor (CISA).

Certifications are typically obtained through a combination of coursework, study materials, and passing a certification exam. Many organizations and training providers offer certification preparation courses to help individuals successfully pass the exams. These courses cover the specific knowledge domains and provide hands-on practice with cybersecurity tools and techniques.

Training Courses

In addition to academic degrees and certifications, there are various training courses available to individuals seeking to enhance their cybersecurity skills or gain specialized knowledge in specific areas. Training courses can be instructor-led or self-paced and are often offered by industry organizations, training institutes, or cybersecurity vendors.

These courses cover a wide range of topics, including network security, ethical hacking, incident response, digital forensics, and secure coding. They typically include a combination of lectures, hands-on exercises, and real-world simulations to provide practical experience. Many training courses also offer opportunities for participants to earn industry-recognized certifications upon completion.

Training courses can be beneficial for individuals who already have a background in cybersecurity and want to deepen their knowledge in specific areas or stay updated with the latest advancements in the field. They can also be useful for professionals from other disciplines who want to transition into the cybersecurity field and acquire foundational knowledge and skills.

Resources and Best Practices

When considering cybersecurity curricula and programs, it is important to choose reputable and recognized institutions or organizations. Accreditation and affiliations with industry associations are good indicators of quality. Additionally, it is advisable to check the curriculum, course content, and the qualifications of the instructors to ensure that the program aligns with one's specific goals and interests.

To ensure success in cybersecurity curricula and programs, students should actively engage in practical exercises, hands-on labs, and real-world projects. This allows for the application of theoretical knowledge to practical scenarios, enhancing the understanding of concepts and developing problem-solving skills. Collaboration with peers and participation in cybersecurity competitions or capture-the-flag events can further enhance skills and provide networking opportunities.

Continuous learning is critical in the field of cybersecurity due to the rapidly evolving nature of cyber threats. Staying updated with the latest trends, best practices, and regulatory requirements is essential. Engaging in professional organizations, attending conferences, webinars, and reading industry publications are some ways to remain current in the field.

Exercises

1. Research and identify three accredited universities or colleges that offer undergraduate programs in cybersecurity. Compare their curricula, course offerings, and internship opportunities, and write a short report on their strengths and weaknesses.

2. Imagine you are responsible for designing a training course on incident response for cybersecurity professionals. Outline the key topics, learning objectives, and hands-on exercises you would include in the course syllabus.

3. Choose one cybersecurity certification that you are interested in pursuing. Research and prepare a study plan, including recommended study materials, practice exams, and a timeline for exam preparation.

4. Consider the cybersecurity skills and competencies required for a cybersecurity analyst role. Create a mind map or concept map to visualize the different areas of knowledge and skills that would be relevant for this role.

5. Write a short essay addressing the importance of continuous learning in the field of cybersecurity. Discuss the benefits of staying updated with the latest trends, challenges, and best practices, and provide examples of how continuous learning can enhance one's career prospects.

Further Reading

1. Dhillon, G., & Backhouse, J. (Eds.). (2007). *Information Systems Security: Theory and Practices*. Wiley.

2. Easttom, C. (2019). *Computer Security Fundamentals*. Pearson.

3. Russel, D. L., & Gangemi, G. T. (2018). *Guide to Computer Network Security*. Springer.

4. Schneier, B. (2015). *Secrets and Lies: Digital Security in a Networked World*. Wiley.

5. Vacca, J. R. (2019). *Computer and Information Security Handbook*. Morgan Kaufmann.

Cybersecurity Certification and Accreditation

In today's digital landscape, where cybersecurity threats continue to evolve and become more sophisticated, organizations must take proactive measures to protect their sensitive information and secure their systems. Cybersecurity certification and accreditation play a crucial role in ensuring that organizations have the necessary security controls and measures in place to mitigate risks and safeguard their assets.

Definition of Certification and Accreditation

Certification and accreditation are two distinct but closely related processes in the field of cybersecurity. Certification refers to the formal evaluation and assessment of an organization's information system to determine its compliance with established security standards and requirements. It involves conducting a comprehensive review of the system's design, implementation, and operation to ensure that it adheres to defined security controls.

On the other hand, accreditation is the formal approval granted by a designated authority, such as a government agency or regulatory body, to an organization's information system. The accreditation process validates that the system has achieved a satisfactory level of security and meets all the necessary requirements for operation. It provides confidence to stakeholders, including customers, partners, and regulatory bodies, that the organization has implemented appropriate security measures.

Importance of Certification and Accreditation

Certification and accreditation are critical for several reasons:

- **Risk Mitigation:** Certification and accreditation help organizations identify and address vulnerabilities and weaknesses in their information systems. By adhering to established security controls, organizations can minimize the risk of data breaches, cyber-attacks, and other security incidents.

- **Compliance:** Certification and accreditation ensure that organizations comply with applicable laws, regulations, and industry standards. This is particularly important in sectors such as healthcare, finance, and government, where the protection of sensitive data is tightly regulated.

- **Customer Trust:** Certification and accreditation provide assurance to customers and partners that an organization has implemented robust security measures. This, in turn, builds trust and credibility, which are crucial for maintaining strong business relationships.

- **Legal and Liability Considerations:** In the event of a security breach, certification and accreditation can demonstrate that an organization has taken reasonable steps to protect sensitive information. This can help mitigate legal and liability risks associated with data breaches and other security incidents.

- **Competitive Advantage:** Certification and accreditation can give organizations a competitive edge by differentiating them from their peers. Organizations that can demonstrate a strong commitment to security and compliance are more likely to win contracts and attract customers.

Certification and Accreditation Processes

The certification and accreditation processes involve several steps:

1. **Preparation:** The organization identifies the applicable security standards, regulations, and requirements that need to be met. It establishes a team responsible for coordinating the certification and accreditation efforts.

2. **Risk Assessment:** A thorough risk assessment is conducted to identify and evaluate potential security risks and vulnerabilities.

3. **Security Controls Implementation:** The organization implements the necessary security controls based on the identified risks and compliance requirements. This may involve a combination of technical, administrative, and physical controls.

4. **Certification Testing:** An independent third-party evaluator conducts a comprehensive assessment of the organization's information system. This includes evaluating the design, implementation, and effectiveness of the security controls.

5. **Accreditation Decision:** The accrediting authority reviews the certification report and other relevant documentation to determine whether the organization's information system meets the necessary security requirements. The decision may result in full accreditation, conditional accreditation, or denial of accreditation.

6. **Continuous Monitoring:** Accredited organizations are required to continuously monitor their information systems to ensure ongoing compliance with security requirements. This includes regular security audits, vulnerability assessments, and incident response.

Common Certification and Accreditation Frameworks

Several certification and accreditation frameworks exist to guide organizations through the process of achieving and maintaining security compliance. Some of the commonly used frameworks include:

- **ISO/IEC 27001:** This international standard sets out the criteria for establishing, implementing, maintaining, and continually improving an information security management system.
- **NIST Cybersecurity Framework (CSF):** Developed by the National Institute of Standards and Technology (NIST), this framework provides a flexible approach to managing cybersecurity risks. It helps organizations align their cybersecurity practices with business objectives, risk tolerances, and industry best practices.
- **PCI-DSS:** The Payment Card Industry Data Security Standard (PCI-DSS) outlines the security requirements for organizations that handle credit card transactions. Compliance with PCI-DSS is mandatory for any organization that processes, stores, or transmits cardholder data.
- **FedRAMP:** The Federal Risk and Authorization Management Program (FedRAMP) is a government-wide initiative that provides a standardized approach for assessing and monitoring the security of cloud products and services used by federal agencies.

Challenges and Future Trends

While certification and accreditation are essential for strengthening cybersecurity, there are several challenges and future trends to consider:

- **Evolving Threat Landscape:** The rapidly changing cybersecurity landscape requires certification and accreditation processes to adapt to emerging threats and vulnerabilities.

- **International Harmonization:** Harmonizing certification and accreditation requirements across different countries and regions can simplify compliance for multinational organizations.

- **Automation and Artificial Intelligence:** The use of automation and artificial intelligence technologies in certification and accreditation processes can improve efficiency and accuracy.

- **Continuous Monitoring:** The shift towards continuous monitoring and real-time threat intelligence allows organizations to identify and respond to security incidents more effectively.

- **Privacy and Data Protection:** With the increasing focus on privacy and data protection, future certification and accreditation frameworks may need to incorporate requirements related to data privacy.

In conclusion, cybersecurity certification and accreditation are vital components of an organization's overall cybersecurity strategy. They provide assurance that an organization has implemented the necessary security controls to protect its information systems and comply with relevant regulations. By undergoing the certification and accreditation processes, organizations can demonstrate their commitment to cybersecurity and gain a competitive advantage in today's digital landscape.

Professional Development and Continuous Learning

In the constantly evolving field of cybersecurity, staying up-to-date with the latest knowledge and skills is essential for professionals. Continuous learning and professional development are crucial in ensuring that cybersecurity experts are equipped to handle new and emerging threats effectively. This section focuses on the importance of professional development and continuous learning in cybersecurity and provides strategies and resources for cybersecurity professionals to enhance their skills and stay current in this rapidly changing field.

Importance of Professional Development

Professional development plays a vital role in cybersecurity as it enables professionals to acquire new knowledge, skills, and strategies necessary to address evolving threats effectively. Here are some key reasons why professional development is crucial in the cybersecurity industry:

1. **Keeping up with Emerging Technologies:** As new technologies such as artificial intelligence, internet of things, and blockchain continue to advance, cybersecurity professionals must stay updated on how these technologies can impact security. Professional development programs provide the opportunity to learn about these technologies and understand the associated risks and mitigation strategies.

2. **Adapting to New Cyber Threats:** Cyber threats are constantly evolving, with hackers developing new techniques and attacking strategies. Continuous learning helps professionals understand these emerging threats and develop appropriate countermeasures to protect networks, systems, and data.

3. **Expanding Knowledge of Regulations and Compliance:** In the ever-changing landscape of privacy and data protection regulations, cybersecurity professionals must stay informed about the latest legal requirements and industry standards. Professional development programs provide insights into these regulations and offer guidance on compliance strategies.

4. **Enhancing Problem-solving and Incident Response Skills:** Cybersecurity incidents require quick and efficient responses. Continuous learning equips professionals with problem-solving skills and incident response techniques, enabling them to mitigate the impact of security incidents and minimize downtime.

5. **Career Advancement and Employability:** Professional development demonstrates a commitment to growth and improvement, making cybersecurity professionals more attractive to employers. Acquiring new skills and certifications through continuous learning can open doors to new career opportunities and increased compensation.

6. **Promoting Ethical and Responsible Practices:** Professional development programs often include ethics training, fostering a culture of responsible and ethical cybersecurity practices. Ethical awareness is crucial in maintaining trust and integrity within the cybersecurity community.

Strategies for Professional Development

To maximize the benefits of professional development, cybersecurity professionals can employ various strategies and approaches. Here are some effective strategies for continuous learning in the field of cybersecurity:

1. **Pursue Relevant Certifications:** Cybersecurity certifications validate expertise in specific areas of cybersecurity and provide tangible evidence of professional competence. Certifications like Certified Information Systems Security Professional (CISSP), Certified Ethical Hacker (CEH), and Certified Information Security Manager (CISM) enhance professional credibility and demonstrate a commitment to ongoing learning.

2. **Participate in Conferences and Workshops:** Attending conferences and workshops is an excellent way to expand knowledge, network with industry professionals, and learn about the latest cybersecurity trends and best practices. These events often feature presentations, panel discussions, and hands-on training sessions that offer unique insights and practical skills.

3. **Join Professional Organizations and Communities:** Joining cybersecurity professional organizations provides access to valuable resources such as webinars, research papers, and forums where professionals can network, collaborate, and share knowledge. Organizations like the International Information Systems Security Certification Consortium (ISC2) and the Information Systems Security Association (ISSA) offer membership benefits that facilitate professional growth.

4. **Engage in Online Learning:** Online learning platforms offer a wide range of cybersecurity courses, enabling professionals to learn at their own pace. Platforms like Coursera, edX, and Udemy offer courses on various cybersecurity topics, from introductory concepts to advanced skills. Additionally, Massive Open Online Courses (MOOCs) from universities and institutions provide opportunities to learn from leading experts in the field.

5. **Read Cybersecurity Books and Journals:** Reading cybersecurity books and journals is an effective way to stay informed about the latest research, case studies, and industry trends. Publications such as "Communications of the ACM," "IEEE Security & Privacy Magazine," and "The Web Application Hacker's Handbook" provide insights into current challenges and practical solutions.

6. **Engage in Hands-On Practice:** Practical experience is invaluable in the field of cybersecurity. Cybersecurity professionals can enhance their skills by participating in capture the flag (CTF) competitions, conducting

vulnerability assessments, and exploring open-source cybersecurity tools. Hands-on practice helps professionals gain a deeper understanding of real-world scenarios and strengthens their problem-solving abilities.

7. **Mentorship and Collaboration:** Building relationships with experienced professionals in the cybersecurity field can provide valuable guidance and mentorship. Engaging in mentorship programs or collaborative projects allows professionals to learn from others' experiences, gain insights into best practices, and develop a broader perspective on cybersecurity.

Resources for Professional Development

Numerous resources are available to support professional development in cybersecurity. Here are some key resources that cybersecurity professionals can utilize to enhance their knowledge and skills:

1. **Training Courses and Certification Programs:** Organizations like SANS Institute, EC-Council, and CompTIA offer comprehensive training programs and certifications tailored to different cybersecurity domains. These programs provide in-depth knowledge and hands-on training to keep professionals updated with the latest industry practices.

2. **Online Learning Platforms:** Online platforms such as Coursera, edX, Udemy, and Cybrary offer a wide range of cybersecurity courses, both free and paid. These platforms provide flexibility and convenience, allowing professionals to learn at their own pace.

3. **Professional Organizations and Communities:** Joining cybersecurity professional organizations like ISC2, ISSA, and OWASP provides access to a wealth of resources, networking opportunities, and industry events. These organizations often offer webinars, conferences, and forums where professionals can engage with peers and experts.

4. **Books and Publications:** Cybersecurity books and publications are valuable resources for continuous learning. Some widely recognized books in the field include "The Art of Exploitation" by Jon Erickson, "Hacking: The Art of Exploitation" by Jon Erickson, and "The Web Application Hacker's Handbook" by Dafydd Stuttard and Marcus Pinto.

5. **Cybersecurity Blogs and Podcasts:** Following cybersecurity blogs and podcasts can provide access to the latest news, insights, and expert opinions.

Blogs such as Schneier on Security, Krebs on Security, and Dark Reading, along with podcasts like Security Now, Risky Business, and The CyberWire, offer a wealth of information and analysis.

6. **Open-Source Tools and Projects:** Open-source cybersecurity tools and projects, such as Wireshark, Metasploit, and Snort, provide opportunities for hands-on learning and experimentation. Exploring these tools can enhance practical skills and deepen understanding of cybersecurity concepts.

7. **Capture the Flag Competitions:** CTF competitions, both online and offline, challenge cybersecurity professionals to solve practical cybersecurity puzzles and simulate real-world scenarios. Platforms like HackTheBox, CTFTime, and OverTheWire host CTF challenges that help professionals enhance their problem-solving and technical skills.

Conclusion

Professional development and continuous learning are essential components of a successful cybersecurity career. By actively participating in professional development programs, pursuing relevant certifications, staying updated on emerging technologies and threats, and engaging with the cybersecurity community, professionals can enhance their skills, advance their careers, and ensure they are well-equipped to protect and secure digital environments. With the resources and strategies discussed in this section, cybersecurity professionals will have the tools they need to stay ahead in an ever-changing field.

As a cybersecurity professional, investing in continuous learning and professional development is not just a commitment to personal growth but also a commitment to safeguarding the digital world against cyber threats. By continuously expanding your knowledge and skills, you contribute to the overall cybersecurity resilience of organizations and protect the privacy and security of individuals and communities.

Cybersecurity Awareness and Training for End Users

Cybersecurity awareness and training for end users play a vital role in enhancing the overall cybersecurity posture of an organization. End users, who are often the weakest link in the security chain, need to be equipped with the knowledge and skills to recognize and respond to potential cyber threats. This section focuses on the importance of cybersecurity awareness and training, key elements of an effective training program, and strategies to cultivate a culture of security within an organization.

Importance of Cybersecurity Awareness and Training

End users are frequently targeted by cybercriminals through various techniques such as phishing emails, social engineering, and malicious websites. They can inadvertently compromise the security of an entire organization by falling victim to these attacks. However, with proper awareness and training, end users can become the first line of defense against cyber threats. They can identify and report suspicious activities, follow secure practices while using the internet and technology, and understand the implications of their actions on the organization's security.

Elements of an Effective Training Program

Developing an effective cybersecurity training program involves a combination of educational materials, practical exercises, and ongoing reinforcement. The following elements should be included:

1. Education and Information: Provide comprehensive training on the types of cyber threats, common attack vectors, and best practices for mitigating risks. This should cover topics such as password hygiene, email security, safe browsing, social media risks, and mobile device security.

2. Phishing Simulations: Conduct regular phishing simulations to assess end users' vulnerability to phishing attacks. These simulations can help raise awareness and provide immediate feedback on users' susceptibility to such attacks. It is important to follow up with targeted training for individuals who fall for these simulations.

3. Hands-on Exercises: Offer practical exercises that allow end users to apply their knowledge in simulated scenarios. For example, they can be given the task of identifying and reporting a suspicious email or handling a simulated cyber incident. This helps reinforce learning and builds confidence in responding to real-world situations.

4. Role-based Training: Tailor the training program to the specific roles and responsibilities of end users. Different departments may face unique cybersecurity challenges, so providing targeted training relevant to their job functions is critical. For example, finance employees may need to be trained on fraudulent wire transfer schemes, while HR personnel need training on data privacy and protection.

5. Continuous Reinforcement: Cybersecurity training should be an ongoing process rather than a one-time event. Conduct regular refresher sessions, provide timely updates on emerging threats, and keep end users engaged with newsletters, posters, and gamified learning content. Reinforcing good cybersecurity practices at regular intervals helps to maintain a culture of security within the organization.

Cultivating a Culture of Security

Building a culture of security requires a holistic approach that encompasses the entire organization. Here are some strategies to foster a security-conscious culture among end users:

1. Management Support: Leadership buy-in is crucial for the success of any cybersecurity training program. Top-level executives should actively endorse and participate in training initiatives, emphasizing the significance of cybersecurity to the organization's overall success.

2. Clear Security Policies: Establish and communicate clear security policies and guidelines to all employees. This includes policies on password complexity, acceptable use of technology, remote work, and incident reporting procedures. Regularly review and update these policies to align with changing technology trends and emerging threats.

3. Incentives and Recognition: Recognize and reward individuals or teams that demonstrate exceptional adherence to cybersecurity best practices. This can be in the form of incentives, certificates, or public recognition. Publicly acknowledging individuals who report potential security incidents encourages a proactive security mindset.

4. Simplicity and User-Friendliness: Ensure that security measures are user-friendly and do not hinder productivity. Complex security procedures can lead to non-compliance and workarounds, making the organization vulnerable to attacks. Design security controls and processes with end users in mind, minimizing friction while maximizing security.

5. Ongoing Communication and Training: Regularly communicate cybersecurity updates, trends, and tips to end users through various channels such as newsletters, posters, intranet portals, and email reminders. Conduct training sessions and workshops to address specific security concerns and provide opportunities for questions and discussions.

Resources for Cybersecurity Awareness and Training

There are several resources available to organizations for cybersecurity awareness and training:

1. Online Training Platforms: Many organizations offer online training courses that cover a wide range of cybersecurity topics. These courses can be accessed remotely, allowing end users to complete training at their own pace.

2. Industry Conferences and Events: Attend cybersecurity conferences and events to stay updated on the latest trends and best practices. These events often include training workshops and sessions led by industry experts.

3. Webinars and Podcasts: Participate in webinars and podcasts that focus on cybersecurity awareness and training. These online sessions provide valuable insights from industry professionals and allow for interactive discussions.

4. Security Awareness Campaigns: Leverage security awareness campaigns provided by cybersecurity organizations and government agencies. These campaigns often include resources such as posters, brochures, videos, and quizzes that can be used to educate end users.

5. Internal Subject Matter Experts: Identify internal subject matter experts within the organization who can contribute to cybersecurity awareness and training. These experts can conduct internal workshops, create educational materials, and serve as points of contact for security-related queries.

Exercises

1. Conduct a phishing simulation exercise with your organization's employees to assess their susceptibility to phishing attacks. Develop a follow-up training plan based on the results of the simulation.

2. Create a short video or interactive tutorial on password best practices and share it with end users as part of the cybersecurity training program.

3. Organize a "lunch and learn" session where employees can discuss real-world cybersecurity incidents and share tips for prevention. Encourage active participation and foster knowledge sharing among employees.

4. Design a poster or infographic that highlights the top cybersecurity risks faced by end users and includes practical tips for avoiding these risks. Display the poster in high-traffic areas within the organization.

5. Develop a gamified online module that integrates cybersecurity training with interactive quizzes, challenges, and rewards. Monitor the participation and performance of employees to identify areas for improvement.

By implementing a comprehensive cybersecurity awareness and training program, organizations can empower their end users to become active participants in safeguarding against cyber threats. Regular training, ongoing reinforcement, and a security-conscious culture will contribute to a stronger and more resilient cybersecurity posture.

Addressing the Cybersecurity Skills Gap

In today's digital landscape, the demand for skilled cybersecurity professionals is rapidly increasing. As organizations strive to protect their sensitive information and infrastructure from constantly evolving threats, there is a significant shortage of individuals with the necessary skills and knowledge to fill these roles. This section explores the cybersecurity skills gap and discusses various strategies to address this critical issue.

Understanding the Cybersecurity Skills Gap

The cybersecurity skills gap refers to the disparity between the demand for cybersecurity professionals and the available talent pool. This gap arises due to several factors, including the rapid growth of digital technologies, the evolving nature of cyber threats, and the lack of adequate training and education in the field. As a result, organizations struggle to find qualified candidates to meet their cybersecurity needs.

To address the skills gap effectively, it is essential to understand its root causes. Some key factors contributing to the skills gap are:

1. **Increasing Complexity:** Cybersecurity threats are becoming more sophisticated, requiring a diverse skill set to mitigate them. Traditional security measures are no longer sufficient, and professionals need to adapt to new technologies and evolving attack vectors.

2. **Lack of Training and Education:** Many academic institutions and training programs struggle to keep pace with the rapidly changing cybersecurity landscape. Limited curricula and insufficient practical training leave graduates ill-equipped to deal with real-world cybersecurity challenges.

3. **Limited Industry Experience:** Cybersecurity is a field that demands practical experience. However, entry-level job positions often require prior experience, making it challenging for fresh graduates to gain the necessary industry exposure.

4. **Retention Challenges:** Organizations face difficulties in retaining skilled cybersecurity professionals due to factors such as high demand, competitive job market, and lack of attractive career paths and advancement opportunities.

Strategies to Bridge the Gap

Addressing the cybersecurity skills gap requires a comprehensive and multi-faceted approach. Here are some strategies that can help bridge the gap and build a robust cybersecurity workforce:

Enhanced Education and Training Programs: Educational institutions should update their cybersecurity curricula to align with industry trends and requirements. Incorporating hands-on training, practical exercises, and industry collaboration can equip students with the necessary skills and prepare them for real-world cybersecurity challenges. Additionally, organizations can partner with educational institutions to offer internships, co-op programs, and apprenticeships to provide students with valuable industry experience.

Professional Development and Continuous Learning: Cybersecurity professionals must continuously develop their skills and stay up-to-date with the latest trends and technologies. Encouraging employees to pursue certifications, attend conferences, and participate in training programs helps bridge the skills gap and ensures a competent workforce. Organizations should also provide resources and support for professional development, including mentoring programs and knowledge-sharing platforms.

Diversifying the Talent Pool: To address the shortage of cybersecurity professionals, organizations need to expand their hiring strategies and consider candidates from diverse backgrounds. This includes recruiting individuals with non-traditional educational paths, such as boot camp graduates, career changers, and those with relevant transferable skills. Emphasizing diversity and inclusivity can bring in fresh perspectives and innovative approaches to cybersecurity problem-solving.

Cybersecurity Competitions and Challenges: Hosting cybersecurity competitions and challenges can promote interest in the field and identify talented individuals. Events like capture-the-flag (CTF) competitions and hackathons allow participants to showcase their skills and gain practical experience in a controlled environment. Organizations and educational institutions can organize or sponsor such events to identify potential cybersecurity talents and offer them opportunities for further development.

Public-Private Partnerships: Collaboration between the public and private sectors can help bridge the cybersecurity skills gap. Public organizations can provide funding and resources to support cybersecurity education and training initiatives. Private sector entities can contribute through mentorship programs, sharing industry best practices, and offering guidance on relevant skills and competencies needed in the job market. By working together, both sectors can ensure a steady supply of skilled cybersecurity professionals.

Case Study: Cybersecurity Apprenticeships

One effective approach to addressing the cybersecurity skills gap is through apprenticeship programs. Apprenticeships provide individuals with a combination of on-the-job training and classroom instruction, allowing them to gain practical experience while acquiring the necessary skills.

For example, the UK government introduced the Cyber Security Technologist apprenticeship program. This program offers a structured training framework, combining workplace assignments with classroom-based learning. It covers a wide range of cybersecurity topics, including network security, incident response, and ethical hacking.

Apprenticeships provide a bridge between education and employment, addressing the industry's need for skilled professionals and offering individuals an opportunity to kickstart their cybersecurity careers. They provide valuable practical experience, allowing apprentices to apply their knowledge in real-world scenarios while learning from experienced professionals.

By encouraging more organizations to implement cybersecurity apprenticeship programs and investing in their success, the skills gap can be narrowed, and a pipeline of qualified cybersecurity professionals can be established.

Conclusion

The cybersecurity skills gap poses a significant challenge for organizations worldwide. To address this issue, it is crucial to adopt a holistic approach that encompasses enhanced education and training programs, continuous professional development, diversification of the talent pool, cybersecurity competitions, and public-private partnerships.

By implementing these strategies and investing in the workforce of the future, we can bridge the skills gap, strengthen our cybersecurity defenses, and create a sustainable and resilient cybersecurity ecosystem. It is through these collective efforts that we can protect our digital assets and ensure a secure and prosperous future.

Cybersecurity Research and Innovation

Emerging Trends in Cybersecurity Research

Emerging trends in cybersecurity research play a crucial role in addressing the evolving challenges and threats in the digital landscape. Researchers continuously strive to develop innovative techniques and solutions to enhance the security of critical systems, protect user data, and mitigate emerging risks. This section explores some of the prominent emerging trends in cybersecurity research, highlighting their potential implications and areas of application.

Artificial Intelligence and Machine Learning

Artificial Intelligence (AI) and Machine Learning (ML) have gained significant attention in the field of cybersecurity research. These technologies have the potential to revolutionize traditional security approaches by automating threat detection, prediction, and response. AI-powered systems can analyze large volumes of data in real-time, identify complex patterns, and proactively detect anomalous activities.

One of the key applications of AI and ML in cybersecurity is in the domain of intrusion detection. ML algorithms can learn from historical data to detect and classify network intrusions with high accuracy. These algorithms can identify new and previously unseen attack patterns, thereby enhancing the effectiveness of intrusion detection systems.

Moreover, AI and ML techniques can be applied to improve malware detection and classification. By analyzing the behavior of files and processes, machine learning models can identify malicious software and prevent their execution. These models can adapt and evolve with the changing threat landscape, providing robust protection against emerging malware variants.

However, it is important to consider the limitations and challenges associated with AI and ML in cybersecurity. Adversarial attacks, where malicious actors manipulate input data to deceive AI systems, pose a significant threat. Researchers are actively exploring techniques to improve the robustness and resilience of AI-based cybersecurity solutions to such attacks.

Internet of Things (IoT) Security

The proliferation of IoT devices in various domains, such as healthcare, transportation, and smart homes, has necessitated the development of robust security mechanisms. IoT devices are often resource-constrained, making them vulnerable to attacks and compromise. Cybersecurity researchers are focusing on addressing the unique challenges associated with IoT security.

One of the key areas of research in IoT security is secure communication and authentication protocols. As IoT devices interact and exchange sensitive data, ensuring secure and authenticated communication is crucial. Researchers are developing lightweight encryption algorithms, secure key exchange protocols, and efficient authentication mechanisms tailored for resource-constrained IoT devices.

Another emerging trend in IoT security research is anomaly detection and behavior analysis. Traditional signature-based intrusion detection systems may not be effective in identifying IoT-specific attacks. Therefore, researchers are exploring machine learning and data analytics techniques to identify abnormal behaviors in IoT networks and devices. These techniques can detect anomalies and potential threats, enabling proactive security measures.

Furthermore, securing IoT firmware and software updates is an ongoing challenge. IoT devices often lack the necessary mechanisms to securely update their firmware, making them susceptible to vulnerabilities and exploits. Researchers are investigating techniques such as code signing, secure bootstrapping, and over-the-air updates to ensure the integrity and authenticity of IoT device software.

Privacy-Preserving Technologies

Ensuring privacy in the digital age is a critical challenge, especially with the increasing amount of personal data being collected and processed. Privacy-preserving technologies are essential in safeguarding users' sensitive information while enabling secure data sharing.

One of the emerging trends in privacy-preserving research is the use of homomorphic encryption. Homomorphic encryption allows computations to be performed on encrypted data without decrypting it. This enables secure data processing while preserving the privacy of sensitive information. Researchers are working on developing efficient and scalable homomorphic encryption schemes for various applications, such as secure cloud computing and collaborative data analysis.

Differential privacy is another area of active research in privacy-preserving technologies. It provides a mathematical framework to quantify and control the privacy risks associated with data analysis. By adding controlled noise to the query outputs, differential privacy ensures that individual data contributions cannot be inferred from the results. Researchers are exploring different mechanisms and algorithms to achieve differential privacy while preserving the utility of the data.

In addition to encryption and differential privacy, researchers are also investigating other privacy-enhancing technologies such as secure multiparty computation, attribute-based encryption, and privacy-preserving data mining. These technologies offer innovative approaches to protect user privacy in various domains, including healthcare, finance, and online social networks.

Cyber-Physical Systems Security

As the integration of physical systems with digital technologies increases, securing cyber-physical systems (CPS) becomes critical. CPS refers to systems where physical processes are directly monitored and controlled by computer-based algorithms. Examples include autonomous vehicles, smart grids, and industrial control systems.

One major research area in CPS security is anomaly detection and intrusion prevention. By analyzing sensor data and system behaviors, researchers aim to identify anomalous activities that may indicate cyber-physical attacks. Intrusion prevention techniques can then be implemented to mitigate the impact of such attacks and ensure the safe and reliable operation of CPS.

Another important aspect of CPS security is the development of secure communication and control protocols. These protocols are designed to ensure the confidentiality, integrity, and availability of communication between the cyber and physical components of the system. Researchers are exploring the use of cryptographic techniques, secure routing algorithms, and access control mechanisms to prevent unauthorized access and manipulation of CPS.

Furthermore, CPS security research involves investigating the impact of attacks on the physical world and developing robust recovery mechanisms. For instance, in the case of autonomous vehicles, researchers are exploring techniques to detect and recover from cyber-attacks that can manipulate the control systems and sensor data, ensuring the safety of passengers and pedestrians.

Quantum-resistant Cryptography

With the rapid advancement of quantum computing, traditional cryptographic algorithms may become vulnerable to attacks. Quantum computers have the potential to break many of the widely used public-key cryptography algorithms, such as RSA and ECC (Elliptic Curve Cryptography), which underpin secure communication and data protection.

To address this emerging threat, researchers are focusing on the development of quantum-resistant cryptography. These cryptographic algorithms are designed to withstand attacks from both classical and quantum computers, ensuring long-term security in a post-quantum era.

Several candidate post-quantum cryptographic algorithms have been proposed, including lattice-based cryptography, code-based cryptography, and multivariate cryptography. These algorithms are designed based on mathematical problems that are hard for both classical and quantum computers to solve. Researchers are evaluating the security, efficiency, and compatibility of these algorithms for different applications and systems.

It is worth noting that the transition to quantum-resistant cryptography requires careful planning and coordination among stakeholders. Researchers, industry experts, and policymakers are working together to establish standards and guidelines for the secure implementation of quantum-resistant algorithms in various domains, such as secure communication, digital signatures, and secure key exchange.

Conclusion

The emerging trends in cybersecurity research discussed in this section demonstrate the dynamic nature of the cybersecurity landscape. The integration of emerging technologies, such as artificial intelligence, IoT, privacy-preserving techniques, cyber-physical systems, and quantum-resistant cryptography, provide opportunities to enhance the security and resilience of digital systems.

While these emerging trends offer promising solutions to the evolving cybersecurity challenges, it is crucial to remain vigilant and address the ethical and societal implications associated with their adoption. As researchers continue to explore innovative approaches, collaboration among academia, industry, and policymakers is essential to foster a secure and sustainable cybersecurity ecosystem.

Exercises

1. Research and summarize a recent paper on the application of artificial intelligence in cybersecurity.

2. Investigate a real-world IoT security breach and provide recommendations on how it could have been prevented using emerging IoT security technologies.

3. Explore the concept of differential privacy and explain its significance in protecting user data privacy.

4. Investigate a recent cyber-physical attack and discuss the potential consequences on the physical world. Propose countermeasures to prevent similar attacks in the future.

5. Research and compare different post-quantum cryptographic algorithms. Analyze their strengths and weaknesses in terms of security and efficiency.

Additional Resources

- Smith, J., & Jones, A. (2019). Artificial Intelligence in Cybersecurity: Concepts, Theories and Applications. Springer.
- García-Alfaro, J., & Herrera-Joancomartí, J. (Eds.). (2020). Privacy in the Digital Age: Technologies, Techniques, and Ethics. Springer.
- Park, J. H., & Sastry, S. (Eds.). (2020). Security and Privacy in Cyber-Physical Systems: Foundations, Principles, and Applications. Cambridge University Press.
- Azarderakhsh, R., Karabulut, Y., & Barker, E. (2020). Post-Quantum Cryptography: Algorithms and Implementations. Artech House.

Cybersecurity Research Funding and Collaboration

In order to address the evolving and complex challenges in the field of cybersecurity, it is essential to invest in research and development. Cybersecurity research funding plays a crucial role in advancing the knowledge and technologies needed to protect against emerging threats. Moreover, collaboration between researchers, industry, and government agencies is vital to maximize the impact of research efforts and ensure the practical implementation of innovative solutions. This section explores the importance of cybersecurity research funding and collaboration, as well as some key initiatives and strategies in this area.

The Need for Research Funding

Cybersecurity research funding is essential for multiple reasons. First, it enables researchers to explore new technologies, methodologies, and approaches to tackle emerging threats. As attackers constantly develop new techniques, it is critical for researchers to stay ahead by receiving adequate financial support to pursue innovative research projects.

Second, research funding helps attract and retain top talent in the field of cybersecurity. With the increasing demand for cybersecurity professionals, providing support for research not only encourages individuals to pursue advanced degrees and careers in cybersecurity but also enhances the overall expertise and knowledge base in the field.

Third, research funding facilitates the development and testing of new cybersecurity tools, techniques, and best practices. It allows researchers to conduct experiments, evaluate the effectiveness of different approaches, and refine existing cybersecurity solutions.

Finally, research funding promotes collaboration among different stakeholders, including academia, industry, and government agencies. By working together, these entities can leverage their respective strengths and resources to address complex cybersecurity challenges more effectively.

Sources of Research Funding

There are several sources of cybersecurity research funding, including government grants, private sector investments, and international collaborations. Let's explore each of these sources in detail:

Government Grants: Many governments recognize the critical importance of cybersecurity research and allocate significant funding to support research initiatives. National research agencies, such as the National Science Foundation (NSF) in the United States, provide grants to researchers and academic institutions. These grants fund individual research projects, as well as research centers and programs focused on cybersecurity.

Private Sector Investments: The private sector also plays a significant role in funding cybersecurity research. Technology companies, defense contractors, and cybersecurity firms often invest in research and development to create new products and solutions. These investments may go towards university collaborations, in-house research teams, or partnerships with research institutions.

International Collaborations: Collaboration between countries is crucial in addressing global cybersecurity challenges. Various international organizations, such as the European Union and the United Nations, promote research collaboration through funding programs. These initiatives facilitate information sharing, joint research projects, and the establishment of global research networks.

Research Collaboration Strategies

Collaboration is a key driver for advancing cybersecurity research. It brings together diverse perspectives, enhances interdisciplinary approaches, and fosters the exchange of knowledge and ideas. Here are some strategies for promoting research collaboration in the field of cybersecurity:

Academia-Industry Partnerships: Collaboration between academia and industry is essential for translating research findings into real-world applications. Academic researchers can benefit from industry insights, data, and resources, while industry partners can leverage academic expertise and research capabilities. This collaboration can take the form of joint research projects, collaborative research centers, or technology transfer programs.

Public-Private Partnerships: Public-private partnerships aim to bridge the gap between government agencies, industry, and academia. These partnerships bring together different stakeholders to address common challenges, share information, and allocate resources effectively. They facilitate the development and implementation of cybersecurity solutions that align with both industry needs and government regulations.

International Research Networks: Establishing international research networks enables collaboration between researchers from different countries. These networks encourage the exchange of knowledge, expertise, and resources, leading to a broader and more comprehensive understanding of cybersecurity challenges. International conferences, workshops, and joint research projects are some of the ways to foster collaboration within these networks.

Case Study: The Cybersecurity Research and Development Act

An example of government-led cybersecurity research funding and collaboration initiative is the Cybersecurity Research and Development Act. Enacted in the United States in 2002 and subsequently renewed, this act provides funding for research and development projects aimed at improving cybersecurity. The act focuses on fostering collaboration between federal agencies, industry, and academia to promote innovation and address key cybersecurity challenges.

The act establishes research centers of excellence in universities, supports interdisciplinary research projects, and strengthens the collaboration between government agencies and industry partners. It encourages the development of cybersecurity technologies, tools, and methodologies with a focus on national security, critical infrastructure protection, and privacy.

The Cybersecurity Research and Development Act serves as an example of how research funding and collaboration can drive advancements in the field of cybersecurity. By providing financial support and promoting collaboration among stakeholders, the act has contributed to the development of innovative solutions and the cultivation of a skilled cybersecurity workforce.

Conclusion

Cybersecurity research funding and collaboration are crucial aspects of sustaining and advancing cybersecurity practices. Adequate funding enables researchers to explore innovative approaches, attract top talent, and develop practical solutions. Collaboration among academia, industry, and government agencies ensures that research efforts are practical, impactful, and aligned with real-world challenges. Initiatives such as the Cybersecurity Research and Development Act help drive research funding and collaboration, leading to advancements in cybersecurity technologies, practices, and policies. By investing in research and promoting collaboration, we can better protect against evolving cyber threats and ensure a sustainable and secure digital future.

Open Source and Community-Based Security Solutions

Open source and community-based security solutions play a vital role in the field of cybersecurity. These solutions are built on the principles of collaboration, transparency, and open access to source code. In this section, we will explore the importance of open source and community-based security solutions, their advantages and limitations, and some examples of popular projects in this domain.

Importance of Open Source and Community-Based Security Solutions

Open source software refers to software that is freely available to use, modify, and distribute. In the context of cybersecurity, open source security solutions allow users to study and review the source code, ensuring that the software is free from vulnerabilities and malicious code. Additionally, these solutions benefit from the collective intelligence and expertise of a community of developers and contributors, making them more robust and reliable.

Community-based security solutions involve collaboration among individuals, organizations, and communities to address cybersecurity challenges. These solutions often leverage open source software and encourage collaboration, information sharing, and the development of best practices. They enable a decentralized approach to security, allowing for peer-to-peer communication and cooperation.

Advantages of Open Source and Community-Based Security Solutions

There are several advantages of open source and community-based security solutions:

1. Transparency and Accountability: Open source software allows users to examine the source code, ensuring that the software is secure and does not contain any hidden backdoors or vulnerabilities. The transparency of open source projects fosters accountability and builds trust.
2. Rapid Innovation: Open source projects benefit from the contributions of a large community of developers, who can quickly identify and fix vulnerabilities and add new features. This collaborative approach enables rapid innovation and keeps the software up to date with emerging threats.
3. Cost-Effectiveness: Open source software is often free to use, eliminating the need for expensive licensing fees. This makes it an attractive option, especially for organizations with limited resources.
4. Flexibility and Customization: Open source software can be customized to meet specific security requirements. Organizations can modify and extend the functionality of the software according to their needs, enhancing their overall security posture.
5. Collaboration and Knowledge Sharing: Community-based security solutions foster collaboration and knowledge sharing among individuals and organizations. This shared expertise helps in the development of best practices, threat intelligence, and incident response capabilities.

Limitations of Open Source and Community-Based Security Solutions

While open source and community-based security solutions offer numerous advantages, they also have some limitations:

1. Skill Requirements: Implementing and maintaining open source security solutions may require specialized skills and knowledge. Organizations need personnel who are proficient in the software and capable of addressing potential challenges and vulnerabilities.

2. Support and Documentation: Compared to commercial solutions, open source projects may have limited support and documentation. Organizations relying on these solutions may need to invest additional resources in training and self-support.

3. Fragmentation: The open source community is vast, with numerous projects and variations available. This fragmentation can make it challenging for organizations to select the right solution and integrate it effectively into their existing security infrastructure.

4. Lack of Service Level Agreements (SLAs): Open source projects generally do not come with SLAs, which can make it difficult to ensure timely support and maintenance. Organizations may need to rely on community forums and volunteer contributions for assistance.

Examples of Open Source and Community-Based Security Solutions

There are several widely used open source and community-based security solutions:

1. Snort: Snort is an open source intrusion detection and prevention system (IDS/IPS). It analyzes network traffic and detects threats based on predefined rules. Snort has a large community of users and contributors and is known for its flexibility and extensibility.

2. OpenVAS: OpenVAS (Open Vulnerability Assessment System) is a comprehensive vulnerability scanning tool. It helps organizations identify and mitigate security vulnerabilities in their networks and systems. OpenVAS is regularly updated by its community to ensure it can detect the latest threats.

3. OpenVPN: OpenVPN is an open source virtual private network (VPN) solution. It provides secure remote access to a network, allowing users to connect securely and privately over the internet. OpenVPN is widely used due to its security features and cross-platform compatibility.

4. Metasploit: Metasploit is a popular penetration testing framework that helps security professionals test the security of their systems. It provides a range of tools and exploits to simulate real-world attacks and identify vulnerabilities in networks and applications.

5. Security Onion: Security Onion is an open source network security monitoring and intrusion detection system (NSM/IDS) platform. It integrates various open source security tools, including Snort and Suricata, to provide comprehensive network security monitoring capabilities.

These are just a few examples, and there are many other open source and community-based security solutions available for different use cases and security requirements.

Conclusion

Open source and community-based security solutions offer significant advantages in terms of transparency, collaboration, and cost-effectiveness. They allow organizations to leverage the power of community collaboration and community-driven innovation. However, they also come with certain limitations that need to be considered, such as skill requirements and limited support. Despite these limitations, open source and community-based security solutions have become an integral part of the cybersecurity landscape, providing viable alternatives to proprietary solutions. It is essential for organizations to evaluate their security needs and consider the benefits and limitations of open source and community-based solutions before making their choices.

Startups and Entrepreneurship in Cybersecurity

In recent years, the field of cybersecurity has seen tremendous growth and innovation. One of the driving forces behind this growth is the rise of startups and entrepreneurship in the cybersecurity industry. Startups have played a crucial role in developing new technologies, creating innovative solutions, and disrupting traditional approaches to cybersecurity. In this section, we will explore the challenges and opportunities that startups and entrepreneurs face in the world of cybersecurity, as well as the strategies and best practices for building a successful cybersecurity startup.

The Landscape of Cybersecurity Startups

The cybersecurity startup ecosystem is vibrant and dynamic, with numerous companies emerging to address the ever-growing security challenges faced by organizations. These startups focus on a wide range of areas, including network security, application security, data protection, threat intelligence, and more. They often bring fresh ideas and perspectives, leveraging cutting-edge technologies to develop innovative solutions.

Startups in the cybersecurity industry face unique challenges. One of the primary challenges is the constantly evolving threat landscape. Cybersecurity threats change rapidly, and startups must stay ahead of the curve to provide effective solutions. Additionally, startups often operate in a highly competitive market, where established players dominate. Breaking into this market and gaining market share can be a daunting task.

Building a Successful Cybersecurity Startup

Building a successful cybersecurity startup requires careful planning, execution, and a deep understanding of the industry. Here are some key strategies and best practices for aspiring cybersecurity entrepreneurs:

Identify a Niche: With the cybersecurity industry being vast and diverse, it's important for startups to identify a specific niche or problem area to focus on. This could be a particular industry vertical, a specific type of cyber threat, or a unique approach to addressing cybersecurity challenges. By specializing in a niche, startups can differentiate themselves from competitors and target a specific customer base.

Develop a Unique Value Proposition: To stand out in a crowded market, startups must develop a unique value proposition. This involves understanding the pain points of customers and providing a solution that addresses those pain points more effectively than existing alternatives. Startups can differentiate themselves through innovative technologies, superior efficiency, or unique features that offer significant benefits to customers.

Leverage Emerging Technologies: Emerging technologies such as artificial intelligence (AI), machine learning (ML), and blockchain are transforming the cybersecurity landscape. Startups can leverage these technologies to develop novel and powerful cybersecurity solutions. For example, AI and ML can be used for threat detection and anomaly detection, while blockchain can enhance data integrity and authentication. By embracing these technologies, startups can stay at the forefront of cybersecurity innovation.

Build Strategic Partnerships: Collaboration and partnerships play a crucial role in the success of cybersecurity startups. Startups can partner with established cybersecurity companies, industry associations, research institutions, and government agencies to leverage their expertise, resources, and networks. These partnerships can provide startups with access to valuable mentorship, funding opportunities, and market visibility.

Focus on Security and Compliance: Cybersecurity startups must prioritize security and compliance in everything they do. This involves following best practices for secure software development, employing strong encryption and authentication mechanisms, conducting regular security audits, and ensuring compliance with applicable regulations and standards. By demonstrating a commitment to security and compliance, startups can build trust and credibility with their customers.

Stay Agile and Adaptive: The cybersecurity landscape is constantly evolving, and startups must be agile and adaptive to keep pace with the changes. Startups should adopt an iterative development approach, continuously refining and improving their solutions based on customer feedback and evolving threats. By staying nimble and responsive, startups can maintain a competitive edge in the market.

Case Study: Cybereye

To illustrate the concepts discussed above, let's take a look at a fictional cybersecurity startup called Cybereye. Cybereye was founded by a team of cybersecurity experts with a passion for protecting organizations from advanced cyber threats. The company specializes in threat intelligence and analytics, using advanced machine learning algorithms to detect and mitigate emerging threats.

Cybereye identified a niche in the market by focusing on providing real-time threat intelligence to small and medium-sized enterprises (SMEs) in the financial sector. These organizations often lack the resources and expertise to combat sophisticated cyber attacks. By offering an affordable subscription-based service, Cybereye aims to level the playing field and empower SMEs to protect their assets and customer data.

To build a unique value proposition, Cybereye developed a proprietary machine learning algorithm that analyzes vast amounts of security data to detect patterns and anomalies indicative of potential cyber threats. This allows their customers to proactively identify and respond to emerging threats, reducing the risk of a successful attack. They also provide personalized threat reports and recommendations, enabling SMEs to make informed decisions about their cybersecurity posture.

Cybereye recognized the importance of strategic partnerships and collaborated with leading cybersecurity research institutions and industry associations. This helped them gain access to cutting-edge research, as well as credibility and visibility in the market. They also formed strategic alliances with established cybersecurity companies to integrate their threat intelligence platform with existing security products, providing a comprehensive cybersecurity solution for their customers.

In summary, Cybereye's success can be attributed to their ability to identify a niche, develop a unique value proposition, leverage emerging technologies, build strategic partnerships, prioritize security and compliance, and stay agile and adaptive in a rapidly changing landscape. These strategies provide valuable insights for aspiring cybersecurity entrepreneurs looking to build a successful startup.

Conclusion

Startups and entrepreneurship play a vital role in driving innovation and advancement in the cybersecurity industry. By identifying niche areas, developing unique value propositions, leveraging emerging technologies, building strategic partnerships, focusing on security and compliance, and staying agile and adaptive, cybersecurity startups can overcome challenges and capitalize on opportunities in this dynamic field. With the right vision, approach, and execution, startups can make significant contributions to the sustainable development of the cybersecurity ecosystem.

Ethical Considerations in Cybersecurity Research

Ethical considerations play a critical role in cybersecurity research, ensuring that studies are conducted in a responsible and mindful manner. In this section, we will explore the ethical challenges specific to cybersecurity research and provide guidelines for conducting research ethically.

Ensuring Participant Consent and Privacy

One of the major ethical concerns in cybersecurity research is the collection and use of data from human participants. Researchers must ensure that participants provide informed consent before taking part in any study. This involves clearly explaining the purpose of the research, the potential risks and benefits, and any relevant privacy considerations.

To protect participants' privacy and confidentiality, researchers must implement appropriate measures to safeguard sensitive data. This includes using secure storage and transmission methods, anonymizing data whenever possible, and obtaining necessary approvals from ethics review boards.

Responsible Vulnerability Disclosure

Researchers often discover vulnerabilities in software, systems, or networks during the course of their research. It is essential that these vulnerabilities are disclosed responsibly to minimize harm and maximize the chance for timely mitigation.

Responsible vulnerability disclosure involves notifying the relevant stakeholders (such as software vendors or system administrators) about the vulnerability and providing them with adequate time to address it before making it public. This allows for necessary patches or updates to be developed and deployed, minimizing the risk of exploitation.

Avoiding Unintended Consequences

Cybersecurity research can have unintended consequences that may harm individuals, organizations, or even society as a whole. Researchers must consider the potential impact of their work and take steps to mitigate any adverse effects.

For example, in developing new defensive techniques, researchers must be cautious not to inadvertently aid malicious actors by providing them with new attack vectors or tools. Responsible researchers should always prioritize the broader societal and ethical considerations, seeking to minimize harm and maximize the positive impact of their work.

Accountability and Transparency

Transparency and accountability are essential pillars of ethical cybersecurity research. Researchers should clearly communicate their intentions, methodology, and potential limitations of their work. This allows for scrutiny and reproducibility, ensuring that the research is trustworthy and reliable.

Furthermore, researchers must acknowledge and appropriately credit prior work in their field to uphold academic integrity. Plagiarism, including the unauthorized use of others' research or ideas, is a serious ethical violation.

Balancing Research and Responsible Disclosure

In some cases, cybersecurity researchers may encounter ethical dilemmas when balancing the need for research with responsible disclosure. For example, researchers may come across vulnerabilities that have significant societal implications, such as those affecting critical infrastructure or national security.

In such situations, researchers should consider involving relevant authorities or organizations that can handle the disclosure process appropriately. It is crucial to strike a balance between advancing knowledge through research and ensuring the safety and security of individuals and society.

Promoting Ethical Awareness and Education

To foster a culture of ethical cybersecurity research, it is essential to promote awareness and education. Researchers should actively engage in ongoing learning and professional development to stay abreast of evolving ethical considerations in the field.

Additionally, academic institutions and research organizations should provide resources, guidelines, and training to help researchers navigate ethical challenges effectively. Open discussions and forums can also facilitate the exchange of ideas, assisting researchers in making sound ethical decisions.

Real-World Example: Security Researcher's Dilemma

Consider a security researcher who discovers a critical vulnerability in a widely used operating system. The vulnerability has the potential to compromise the security and privacy of millions of users. The researcher faces a dilemma: Should they disclose the vulnerability immediately, potentially aiding malicious actors in exploiting it, or should they wait for the software vendor to develop a patch, risking further potential harm to users?

In this scenario, the researcher should follow responsible vulnerability disclosure practices. They should contact the software vendor, share the details of the vulnerability, and allow them sufficient time to develop and release a patch. By doing so, the researcher ensures that the vulnerability is addressed in a timely manner, minimizing the risk of widespread exploitation.

In Conclusion, conducting cybersecurity research ethically is crucial for maintaining the trust and integrity of the field. Researchers must obtain participant consent, protect privacy, disclose vulnerabilities responsibly, avoid unintended consequences, promote transparency and accountability, and balance research goals with responsible disclosure. By adhering to ethical principles, cybersecurity researchers contribute to the advancement and sustainability of the field while minimizing harm to individuals and society at large.

Future Challenges and Opportunities in Cybersecurity Sustainability

Cybersecurity and Emerging Technologies

Artificial Intelligence and Machine Learning

Artificial Intelligence (AI) and Machine Learning (ML) have become increasingly prominent in the field of cybersecurity. AI refers to the ability of machines to mimic human intelligence and perform tasks that normally require human cognition, such as problem-solving and decision-making. ML, on the other hand, is a subset of AI that focuses on developing algorithms and statistical models that enable machines to learn from and make predictions or decisions based on data.

In the context of cybersecurity, AI and ML techniques can be used to enhance the detection and prevention of cyber threats, improve incident response, and strengthen overall security posture. This section will explore the key principles, applications, and challenges associated with AI and ML in cybersecurity.

Principles of Artificial Intelligence and Machine Learning

The principles of AI and ML are rooted in the understanding of data, algorithms, and model training. Here are the fundamental concepts that underpin these technologies:

1. **Data:** Data is the fuel that powers AI and ML algorithms. High-quality, diverse, and representative data is essential for training accurate models. In cybersecurity, data can include network traffic logs, system logs, user behavior data, and threat intelligence feeds, among others.

2. **Algorithms:** Algorithms are mathematical procedures or sets of rules that instruct machines on how to process and analyze data. Different algorithms are suited for different types of problems, such as clustering, classification, regression, and anomaly detection. Examples of commonly used algorithms in cybersecurity include decision trees, random forests, support vector machines, and deep neural networks.

3. **Model Training:** Model training involves the process of teaching the machine learning algorithm to recognize patterns and make predictions or decisions based on the provided data. This process typically includes stages such as data preprocessing, feature selection, model fitting, and model evaluation using labeled training data.

4. **Prediction and Decision-Making:** Once the model is trained, it can be used to make predictions or decisions on new, unseen data. In cybersecurity, this can involve predicting the likelihood of a network intrusion, identifying malicious activities, or determining the severity of a cyber incident.

Applications of Artificial Intelligence and Machine Learning in Cybersecurity

AI and ML have various applications in the field of cybersecurity. Let's explore some of the key areas where these technologies are making a significant impact:

1. **Threat Detection and Prevention:** AI and ML algorithms can analyze large volumes of data in real-time to detect and prevent cyber threats. By identifying patterns and anomalies in network traffic, system logs, or user behavior, these technologies can flag potential security breaches or malicious activities. For example, ML models can be trained to identify known attack patterns or identify previously unseen threats through anomaly detection techniques.

2. **User and Entity Behavior Analytics (UEBA):** AI and ML techniques can be used to create baselines of normal user and entity behavior. By continuously monitoring and analyzing deviations from these baselines, ML models can detect suspicious activities, such as insider threats, unauthorized access attempts, or account takeover attacks. This enables proactive threat hunting and early detection of potential security incidents.

3. **Malware Detection and Analysis:** ML algorithms can be trained to classify and detect malware based on various attributes, such as file characteristics,

behavior, or code snippets. By leveraging large datasets of known malware samples, ML models can learn to distinguish between benign and malicious files, helping security teams to identify and respond to new and emerging threats.

4. **Vulnerability Management:** AI and ML techniques can help organizations prioritize and remediate vulnerabilities by assessing their potential severity and exploitability. By analyzing data from vulnerability scanners, threat intelligence feeds, and exploit databases, ML models can provide insights into which vulnerabilities should be addressed first to minimize the risk of exploitation.

5. **Automated Incident Response:** AI-powered incident response systems can automatically analyze and correlate security alerts, determine the significance of the incident, and perform predefined actions to contain and mitigate the impact. By reducing the response time and manual effort required, these systems can help organizations effectively manage security incidents and minimize the impact on their operations.

Challenges and Limitations

While AI and ML offer significant benefits to the cybersecurity landscape, they also present challenges and limitations that need to be addressed:

1. **Data Quality and Bias:** The success of AI and ML algorithms heavily relies on the quality and diversity of the training data. Biased or incomplete data can lead to inaccurate or discriminatory models. It is vital to ensure data integrity and prevent the reinforcement of biases present in the training data.

2. **Adversarial Attacks:** AI and ML models can be susceptible to adversarial attacks, where malicious actors intentionally manipulate input data to deceive the models. These attacks can lead to false positives or negatives, undermining the effectiveness of AI-based security systems. Ensuring the robustness and resilience of AI models against adversarial attacks is crucial.

3. **Interpretability and Explainability:** AI and ML models often operate as black boxes, making it difficult to interpret the decision-making process. In high-stakes domains like cybersecurity, interpretability and explainability are critical for understanding the rationale behind model predictions or decisions. Research in developing techniques for model interpretability and explainability is ongoing.

4. **Lack of Domain Expertise:** Developing effective AI and ML solutions in cybersecurity requires a deep understanding of the domain and the ability to translate security requirements into meaningful model inputs and outputs. Bridging the gap between cybersecurity experts and data scientists is vital to ensure the development of relevant and context-aware solutions.

5. **Ethical Considerations:** AI and ML technologies raise ethical considerations such as privacy, transparency, accountability, and bias. It is essential to ensure that AI and ML systems are designed and deployed in an ethical manner and aligned with legal and regulatory requirements. Integrating ethical principles into the development and deployment process is critical.

Overall, AI and ML have the potential to revolutionize cybersecurity by enhancing threat detection, incident response, and vulnerability management. However, it is crucial to address the challenges and limitations associated with these technologies to ensure their responsible and effective integration into cybersecurity practices.

Internet of Things

The Internet of Things (IoT) refers to the interconnected network of physical devices, vehicles, appliances, and other items embedded with sensors, software, and network connectivity that enables them to collect and exchange data. The IoT has the potential to revolutionize various sectors, including healthcare, transportation, agriculture, and manufacturing. This section explores the challenges and opportunities presented by the IoT in the context of cybersecurity sustainability.

Introduction to the Internet of Things

The proliferation of IoT devices has rapidly expanded the attack surface for cybercriminals. As billions of devices come online, their vulnerabilities become significant security concerns. Many IoT devices suffer from poor security measures, including weak passwords, outdated software, and lack of encryption. These vulnerabilities can be exploited to gain unauthorized access, compromise privacy, and conduct large-scale attacks.

Security Challenges in the IoT

Ensuring the security of IoT devices is a complex task due to several unique challenges:

1. **Diversity of IoT Devices:** The IoT ecosystem comprises a wide range of devices, each with its own operating system, firmware, and communication protocols. Managing the security of such diverse devices poses significant challenges.

2. **Resource Constraints:** Many IoT devices have limited processing power, memory, and energy. Implementing robust security controls within the resource constraints is a delicate balance between functionality and security.

3. **Lack of Standardization:** There is a lack of uniform security standards for IoT devices. The absence of standardized security protocols and frameworks makes it difficult to develop and implement adequate security measures across different devices.

4. **Data Privacy:** IoT devices collect vast amounts of sensitive data, raising concerns about data privacy. Unauthorized access to or disclosure of this data can have serious consequences for individuals and organizations.

Securing the IoT

Securing the IoT requires a multi-layered approach that addresses both device-level and network-level security:

1. **Device-level Security Measures:** - **Authentication and Authorization:** Strong authentication mechanisms, such as two-factor authentication, should be implemented to ensure that only authorized users can access IoT devices. - **Firmware Updates:** Regular firmware updates should be provided to address discovered vulnerabilities and mitigate potential risks. - **Encryption:** All communication between IoT devices should be encrypted using robust cryptographic algorithms to protect the confidentiality and integrity of data. - **Access Control:** Implementing access control mechanisms, such as role-based access control (RBAC), ensures that only authorized entities can interact with IoT devices.
2. **Network-level Security Measures:** - **Secure Communication Protocols:** IoT devices should utilize secure protocols, such as Transport Layer Security (TLS), to ensure the confidentiality and integrity of data transmitted over the network. - **Network Segmentation:** Segmenting the IoT network helps contain potential breaches and restrict unauthorized access to critical systems. - **Intrusion Detection Systems (IDS):** Deploying IDS can detect and respond to unauthorized access attempts or malicious activities within the IoT network. - **Traffic Monitoring and Analysis:** Analyzing network traffic patterns can identify anomalous behavior, indicating potential security threats.

Regulatory and Legal Considerations

The rapid growth of the IoT has prompted policymakers to address the associated security risks through regulations and legislation. Governments and regulatory bodies are working to establish standards and frameworks to ensure the security and privacy of IoT devices. For instance, the European Union's General Data Protection Regulation (GDPR) includes provisions for the protection of personal data collected by IoT devices. Compliance with such regulations is crucial to fostering a secure and sustainable IoT environment.

Case Study: Mirai Botnet

The Mirai botnet is an infamous example of the security risks introduced by vulnerable IoT devices. In 2016, the Mirai malware infected thousands of poorly secured IoT devices, transforming them into a powerful botnet. The botnet was then used to launch distributed denial-of-service (DDoS) attacks, disrupting numerous websites and services. This incident highlighted the urgent need for improved security measures and raised awareness about the potential consequences of insecure IoT devices.

Conclusion

The Internet of Things brings unprecedented opportunities for innovation and efficiency in various domains. However, ensuring the security and sustainability of the IoT is essential to harness its benefits fully. By implementing robust security measures, fostering industry collaboration, and adhering to regulatory guidelines, we can create a secure and resilient IoT ecosystem that drives technological advancements while safeguarding user privacy and data.

Quantum Computing

Quantum computing is an emerging technology in the field of cybersecurity with the potential to revolutionize the way we secure data and information. Unlike classical computers, which use bits as the fundamental unit of information, quantum computers utilize quantum bits or qubits to perform computations. Qubits can exist in superposition states, enabling quantum computers to perform parallel computations and solve certain problems much faster than classical computers.

Principles of Quantum Computing

To understand the principles of quantum computing, we need to dive into the world of quantum mechanics. Quantum mechanics is a branch of physics that describes the behavior of matter and energy at the smallest scales. It introduces concepts such as superposition and entanglement, which are the building blocks of quantum computing.

Superposition: In quantum mechanics, a qubit can exist in a superposition of states, meaning it can be in multiple states at the same time. This is vastly different from classical bits, which can only exist in a state of 0 or 1. The superposition of qubits allows quantum computers to perform multiple computations simultaneously.

Entanglement: Entanglement is a phenomenon where two or more qubits become correlated in such a way that the state of one qubit is dependent on the state of another, regardless of the distance between them. This property of entanglement is crucial for quantum computers as it enables the manipulation of multiple qubits together, leading to a more powerful computational capacity.

Quantum Algorithms and Applications in Cybersecurity

Quantum computing has the potential to impact various areas of cybersecurity, including cryptography, secure communication, and intrusion detection. Let's explore some of the quantum algorithms and applications relevant to cybersecurity:

Shor's Algorithm: Shor's algorithm, developed by Peter Shor in 1994, is a groundbreaking quantum algorithm that can efficiently factor large numbers. Factoring large numbers is a computationally intensive task, and the security of many cryptographic systems relies on the difficulty of factoring. Shor's algorithm poses a significant threat to the security of widely used public-key encryption algorithms like RSA and ECC.

Quantum Key Distribution (QKD): Quantum key distribution is a secure communication technique that leverages the principles of quantum mechanics to establish encryption keys between two parties. QKD provides a way to distribute encryption keys securely, as any attempt to eavesdrop on the key exchange would disrupt the quantum state, alerting the communicating parties to potential tampering. QKD has the potential to enhance the security of communication systems against eavesdropping and man-in-the-middle attacks.

Quantum-resistant Cryptography: As the arrival of practical quantum computers threatens the security of classical cryptographic systems, there is a growing need for quantum-resistant cryptography. Quantum-resistant cryptography involves developing encryption algorithms that are secure against attacks from both classical and quantum computers. Post-quantum cryptography research is currently underway to find suitable alternatives to existing cryptographic algorithms.

Challenges and Implications of Quantum Computing

While quantum computing holds immense promise for advancing cybersecurity, it also presents challenges and implications that need to be addressed:

Security Implications: The capabilities of quantum computers to break widely used cryptographic systems raise concerns about data and information security. It is essential to develop and deploy quantum-resistant cryptography to ensure the continued security of sensitive information.

Implementation Challenges: Building and operating practical quantum computers is a significant challenge. Quantum systems are highly sensitive to noise and decoherence, making it difficult to maintain the delicate quantum states required for reliable computations. Overcoming these technical challenges and scaling up quantum computers is an area of ongoing research.

Post-Quantum Transition: The transition from classical cryptographic systems to quantum-resistant ones is a complex task that requires careful planning and coordination. Organizations and governments need to prepare for a post-quantum world by identifying vulnerable systems and implementing robust cryptographic solutions.

Open Quantum Networks: Quantum computers can also pose a threat to existing secure communication networks. The development of quantum networks, secure against quantum attacks, is crucial to protect sensitive information during transmission.

Conclusion

Quantum computing is a game-changing technology with profound implications for the field of cybersecurity. The principles of superposition and entanglement provide quantum computers with the potential for solving complex problems at an unprecedented speed. Quantum algorithms and applications, such as Shor's algorithm and quantum key distribution, have the power to disrupt traditional cryptographic systems and enhance the security of communication networks.

However, the security implications and implementation challenges of quantum computing cannot be overlooked. It is essential for researchers, policymakers, and practitioners to work collaboratively to develop quantum-resistant solutions, plan for the post-quantum era, and ensure the secure integration of quantum technologies into our cybersecurity landscape. The future of cybersecurity sustainability will heavily rely on our ability to leverage the potential of quantum computing while mitigating its associated risks.

Blockchain and Distributed Ledger Technology

Blockchain and distributed ledger technology (DLT) have emerged as groundbreaking technologies with applications in various fields, including finance, supply chain management, healthcare, and of course, cybersecurity. In this section, we will explore the concepts, principles, and implications of blockchain and DLT in the context of cybersecurity sustainability.

Introduction to Blockchain

Blockchain, at its core, is a decentralized, immutable, and transparent digital ledger that securely records transactions across multiple computers or nodes. It consists of a chain of blocks, where each block contains a list of transactions. These blocks are linked together using cryptographic hashes, ensuring the integrity and immutability of the entire chain.

The decentralized nature of blockchain means that no single entity or authority has control over the entire network. Instead, all participants in the network, known as nodes, collectively validate and maintain the integrity of the blockchain. This distributed consensus mechanism ensures trust and security, as any attempts to tamper with the blockchain would require the collusion of a majority of the nodes.

Key Components of Blockchain

To understand blockchain and its impact on cybersecurity, it is important to grasp its key components:

- **Cryptographic Hash:** Each block in the blockchain contains a unique cryptographic hash, which is a fixed-length string of characters generated through a mathematical algorithm. This hash serves as a digital fingerprint of the block, ensuring its integrity and linking it to the previous block.

- **Decentralized Consensus:** Blockchain networks rely on consensus mechanisms to validate and agree upon the state of the blockchain. One commonly used consensus mechanism is Proof of Work (PoW), where participants compete to solve complex mathematical problems to add blocks to the chain. Another mechanism is Proof of Stake (PoS), where validators are chosen based on the amount of cryptocurrency they hold.

- **Smart Contracts:** Smart contracts are self-executing contracts with predefined rules encoded directly into the blockchain. These contracts automatically enforce the terms and conditions of an agreement, eliminating the need for intermediaries and reducing the risk of fraud.

Implications for Cybersecurity

Blockchain technology has several implications for cybersecurity sustainability. Here, we explore its impact in four key areas:

1. **Data Integrity and Trust:** One of the fundamental strengths of blockchain is its immutability. Once a transaction is recorded on the blockchain, it becomes nearly impossible to alter or delete. This property ensures data integrity and enhances trust in the system, providing a tamper-resistant foundation for secure transactions.

2. **Decentralized Security:** Traditional centralized systems are vulnerable to single points of failure and are attractive targets for attackers. In contrast, blockchain's decentralized nature makes it more resistant to cyber attacks. Since there is no central authority, hackers would need to compromise a majority of the nodes to alter the blockchain's data, making it economically and operationally infeasible.

3. **Transparent Auditing:** Blockchain's transparent nature allows for real-time auditing of transactions. Each transaction can be traced back to its origin, providing an auditable trail of activities. This transparency helps detect and prevent fraudulent or unauthorized activities, enhancing the overall security posture of businesses and organizations.

4. **Secure Identity Management:** With blockchain, individuals can have control over their digital identities through the use of decentralized identifiers and verifiable credentials. This self-sovereign identity management allows for more secure authentication and reduces the reliance on centralized identity providers, mitigating the risks associated with data breaches and identity theft.

Challenges and Limitations

While blockchain technology offers significant potential in enhancing cybersecurity, it is essential to acknowledge its challenges and limitations:

- **Scalability:** Blockchain networks face scalability challenges due to the large computational and storage requirements. As the number of transactions increases, the network may experience slower transaction processing times and increased fees. However, ongoing research and development are exploring solutions to address these scalability concerns.

- **Security of Smart Contracts:** While blockchain itself is considered secure, the same cannot be said for the smart contracts built on top of it. Flaws in the code or design of smart contracts can be exploited by attackers. Therefore, thorough testing, code reviews, and the use of secure development practices are crucial to minimize vulnerabilities.

- **Immutable Data Storage:** While immutability is a desired feature in the context of data integrity, it can become a challenge when there is a need to modify or delete data. In cases where erroneous or illegal information is stored on the blockchain, mechanisms for data rectification or removal must be carefully considered.

Real-World Examples

The potential of blockchain and DLT in transforming cybersecurity can be seen in various real-world examples:

- **Digital Identity Management:** Self-sovereign identity systems based on blockchain are being explored to empower individuals with control over their digital identities. For example, the Sovrin Foundation aims to establish a global public utility for self-sovereign identity.
- **Supply Chain Security:** Blockchain can enhance the security and transparency of supply chains by tracking and verifying the movement of goods. IBM's Food Trust network is an example of a blockchain-based platform that improves food traceability, reducing the risk of contamination and fraud.
- **Secure Voting Systems:** Blockchain can provide a secure and transparent platform for voting systems, ensuring the integrity of the voting process and minimizing the risk of fraud. Countries like Estonia have successfully piloted blockchain-based e-voting systems.

Conclusion

Blockchain and DLT have the potential to revolutionize cybersecurity by providing enhanced data integrity, decentralized security, transparent auditing, and secure identity management. While challenges such as scalability and smart contract security exist, ongoing research and development are addressing these issues. As organizations and governments continue to explore and adopt blockchain technology, it is crucial to consider its ethical, legal, and social implications in order to create a sustainable and secure cyber environment.

Cybersecurity and Geopolitical Factors

Nation-State Cybersecurity Strategies

In the digital age, cybersecurity has become a critical concern for nations around the world. As the reliance on technology and interconnected systems continues to grow, nation-states have recognized the need to develop robust cybersecurity strategies to protect their interests and ensure the safety of their citizens. In this section, we will explore the key principles and components of nation-state cybersecurity strategies.

Understanding Nation-State Cybersecurity

Nation-state cybersecurity refers to the efforts undertaken by governments to safeguard their national interests, including critical infrastructure, intellectual property, and sensitive information, from cyber threats. These threats can originate from various sources, including criminal organizations, hacktivists, terrorist groups, and other nation-states.

The primary objectives of a nation-state cybersecurity strategy are: 1. Protecting national security: Nation-states aim to safeguard their critical assets, such as military systems, government networks, and intelligence agencies, from cyber espionage, disruption, or destruction. 2. Ensuring economic stability: With the increasing digitization of economies, cybersecurity is crucial for protecting businesses, financial systems, trade secrets, and intellectual property from cybercrime and industrial espionage. 3. Safeguarding public safety: Governments are responsible for securing the digital infrastructure upon which essential services, such as healthcare, transportation, and energy, rely. Cyber threats targeting these sectors can have severe consequences for public safety. 4. Preserving national sovereignty: Nation-states strive to protect their digital sovereignty by defending against cyber attacks that aim to compromise their political, social, or economic autonomy.

Components of a Nation-State Cybersecurity Strategy

A comprehensive nation-state cybersecurity strategy typically encompasses the following key components:

1. Policy and Legislation: A strong legal framework is essential for governing cybersecurity activities and establishing the rules and regulations that guide the behavior of individuals, organizations, and government agencies in cyberspace. It includes defining cybercrimes, establishing penalties for offenses, and outlining the roles and responsibilities of various entities involved in cybersecurity.

2. National Cybersecurity Authority: Governments often establish a centralized authority responsible for coordinating and overseeing cybersecurity efforts at the national level. This authority serves as a focal point for cybersecurity strategy development, incident response coordination, and collaboration with other nations.

3. Threat Intelligence and Information Sharing: Nation-states invest in building robust capabilities for gathering, analyzing, and sharing actionable threat intelligence. This includes monitoring cyber threats, collecting information on adversaries, and maintaining situational awareness of the evolving cybersecurity landscape. Effective information sharing mechanisms enable timely response and collaborative defense against threats.

4. Critical Infrastructure Protection: Nation-states prioritize the protection of critical infrastructure, including power grids, transportation networks, and financial systems, from cyber threats. This involves conducting risk assessments, implementing security controls, establishing incident response plans, and fostering public-private partnerships to enhance resilience.

5. Defense Capabilities: Nation-states develop and maintain capabilities to detect, prevent, and respond to cyber attacks. This includes investing in advanced technologies, such as intrusion detection systems, firewalls, and security analytics, as well as developing skilled cybersecurity personnel through education and training programs.

6. International Cooperation: Given the borderless nature of cyberspace, collaboration with other nations is paramount for effective cybersecurity. Nation-states engage in diplomatic efforts, share threat intelligence, conduct joint cybersecurity exercises, and align cyber policies to enhance collective defense against shared threats.

Case Study: United States Cybersecurity Strategy

The United States has been at the forefront of developing and implementing a comprehensive cybersecurity strategy. The U.S. strategy, as outlined in the "National Cyber Strategy" document, focuses on the following key pillars:

1. Protecting the American People, the Homeland, and the American Way of Life: This pillar emphasizes the need to safeguard critical infrastructure, combat cybercrime, secure federal networks, and educate the public to enhance cybersecurity awareness.

2. Promoting American Prosperity: This pillar aims to secure U.S. economic interests by protecting intellectual property, promoting innovation, fostering a resilient digital economy, and countering economic espionage.

3. Preserving Peace through Strength in Cyberspace: This pillar focuses on enhancing the nation's cyber defense capabilities, deterring malicious cyber activities through international cooperation, and building partnerships to promote norms of responsible state behavior in cyberspace.

4. Advancing American Influence: This pillar highlights the importance of engaging with foreign partners, shaping international cyber norms and standards, and leveraging U.S. leadership to shape the global cybersecurity landscape.

5. Defending Democracy and Supporting Responsible Internet Governance: This pillar emphasizes the protection of democratic processes and institutions from cyber threats, promoting open and secure communications, and cooperating with the global community to ensure reliable and secure internet governance.

Challenges and Future Directions

Nation-state cybersecurity strategies face several challenges and must continually evolve to address emerging threats. Some of the key challenges include:

1. Advanced Persistent Threats (APTs): Nation-states increasingly face sophisticated cyber threats, particularly from well-resourced adversaries using APTs. These threats require continuous monitoring, threat intelligence sharing, and advanced defensive technologies to detect and mitigate.

2. Encryption and Privacy Concerns: Balancing the need for cybersecurity with individual privacy rights poses complex challenges for nation-states. Encryption technologies designed to protect individuals can impede law enforcement and intelligence agencies' ability to detect and prevent cyber threats.

3. Emerging Technologies: The rapid adoption of emerging technologies, such as artificial intelligence, quantum computing, and the Internet of Things, introduces new cybersecurity risks. Nation-states must stay ahead of these evolving technologies to ensure their strategies remain effective.

4. Geopolitical tensions: Nation-state cyber activities are often driven by geopolitical tensions, creating a complex cybersecurity landscape. The use of cyber operations for political influence, economic espionage, and even military purposes adds further challenges to cybersecurity strategies.

To address these challenges, nation-states need to foster international cooperation, invest in research and development, enhance public-private partnerships, and continuously update their cybersecurity strategies to adapt to an ever-changing threat landscape.

Conclusion

Nation-states play a crucial role in cybersecurity, as they are responsible for protecting their citizens, critical infrastructure, and national interests. Nation-state cybersecurity strategies aim to address the unique challenges posed by cyber threats and ensure the stability and security of their digital environments. By adopting a comprehensive approach that includes policy and legislation, threat intelligence, critical infrastructure protection, defense capabilities, international cooperation, and stakeholder engagement, nation-states can strengthen their cybersecurity posture and effectively respond to evolving threats. Successful strategies will require ongoing collaboration, innovation, and the constant adaptation of cybersecurity measures to meet the ever-changing landscape of cyberspace.

Cybersecurity in Global Conflicts

In the context of global conflicts, cybersecurity plays a critical role in shaping the dynamics and outcomes of such conflicts. In the digital age, traditional methods of warfare have expanded to include cyber tactics, with nations engaging in offensive and defensive cyber operations to gain a strategic advantage. This section explores the evolving landscape of cybersecurity in global conflicts, including the motivations, strategies, challenges, and implications of cyber warfare.

Motivations for Cyber Warfare

Cyber warfare refers to the use of cyber capabilities to disrupt or damage the information systems and infrastructure of an adversary. Several motivations drive nations to engage in cyber warfare:

- **National Security:** Nations engage in cyber warfare to protect their national security interests, including defense systems, critical infrastructure, and intelligence operations. The ability to disrupt or gather critical information provides a significant advantage in global conflicts.

- **Economic Espionage:** Cyber attacks are often motivated by economic gains, with nations seeking to steal trade secrets, proprietary technologies, and intellectual property from their adversaries. This theft can provide a competitive edge in economic and technological advancement.

- **Political Influence:** Nations may use cyber tactics to influence political processes, election outcomes, public opinion, and social stability in adversary countries. By manipulating or disseminating false information, they can undermine trust and sow discord within target nations.

- **Military Advantage:** Cyber attacks can be used to degrade an adversary's military capabilities by targeting communication systems, command and control infrastructure, and logistics networks. Disrupting these systems can significantly weaken an adversary's ability to respond effectively in times of conflict.

- **Retaliation and Deterrence:** Nations may resort to cyber attacks as a means of retaliation for perceived or actual aggression. Cyber attacks can serve as a deterrent, warning adversaries of the potential consequences of their actions.

Strategies and Techniques

Nations employ various strategies and techniques in cyber warfare based on their objectives, resources, and capabilities. Some common approaches include:

- **Cyber Espionage:** This strategy involves infiltrating the target's networks to gather intelligence, steal sensitive information, or monitor activities. Advanced persistent threats (APTs) are often used to maintain long-term access and carry out covert operations.

- **Denial of Service (DoS) Attacks:** DoS attacks aim to disrupt the availability of an adversary's systems and services by overwhelming them with a flood of illegitimate requests or by exploiting vulnerabilities. This can paralyze critical infrastructure and create chaos.

- **Data Manipulation and Destruction:** Cyber attackers may alter or destroy data stored in critical systems, leading to operational failures, loss of confidence, and potentially catastrophic consequences. This technique can be used to sabotage an adversary's infrastructure or undermine their decision-making capabilities.

- **Social Engineering:** Social engineering techniques, such as phishing, spear-phishing, and impersonation, are used to deceive individuals within the target organization. By exploiting human vulnerabilities, attackers gain unauthorized access or obtain sensitive information.

- **Cyber Weapons and Malware:** Developing and deploying sophisticated cyber weapons, including malware, viruses, and ransomware, is another common strategy. These tools enable attackers to infiltrate systems, extract information, destroy infrastructure, or disrupt operations.

Challenges and Implications

Cyber warfare in global conflicts poses several challenges and has far-reaching implications:

- **Attribution:** One of the major challenges is accurately attributing cyber attacks to specific actors or nations. The anonymous nature of the internet allows attackers to remain hidden, making it difficult to hold them accountable.

- **Escalation:** The interconnected nature of cyberspace increases the risk of escalation in conflicts. A cyber operation can potentially trigger a conventional military response, leading to an escalation spiral with severe consequences.

- **Collateral Damage:** Cyber attacks often have unintended consequences, with the potential to impact non-targeted systems and innocent individuals. The lack of precise targeting capabilities increases the risk of collateral damage, including disruption of critical services or infrastructure.

- **Norms and Rules:** The absence of well-defined international norms and rules governing cyber warfare complicates decision-making processes and escalates the uncertainty in global conflicts. Governments and international organizations are working towards establishing rules of engagement and norms of responsible behavior in cyberspace.

- **Cybersecurity Arms Race:** The proliferation of cyber capabilities among nations has sparked a cybersecurity arms race. Nations continually invest in developing offensive and defensive cyber capabilities, leading to an escalation in the sophistication and complexity of cyber attacks.

Case Study: Stuxnet

One prominent example of cyber warfare in a global conflict is the Stuxnet worm. Discovered in 2010, Stuxnet was a highly sophisticated cyber weapon designed to target Iran's nuclear program. It was jointly developed by the United States and Israel with the aim of sabotaging Iran's uranium enrichment centrifuges.

Stuxnet exploited several zero-day vulnerabilities and utilized advanced techniques to infiltrate the target systems. It specifically targeted Siemens industrial control systems (ICS) used in Iran's nuclear facilities. By manipulating the supervisory control and data acquisition (SCADA) systems, Stuxnet caused physical damage to centrifuges, significantly disrupting Iran's nuclear program.

The Stuxnet case study highlights the potential for cyber warfare to cause physical destruction and demonstrates the increasing intersection between the digital and physical realms. It also underscores the challenges of attribution, as Stuxnet's origins were initially unknown.

Resources and Further Reading

For further exploration of cybersecurity in global conflicts, the following resources are recommended:

- Rid, T., & Buchanan, B. (2015). *Attributing Cyber Attacks.* Journal of Strategic Studies, 38(1-2), 4-37.
- Healey, J. (2018). *The Rules of Cyber Conflict: Can We Keep the Peace in a Cyber Arms Race?* MIT Press.
- Schneier, B. (2013). *Liars and Outliers: Enabling the Trust that Society Needs to Thrive.* Wiley.
- Sanger, D. E. (2018). *The Perfect Weapon: War, Sabotage, and Fear in the Cyber Age.* Crown.

These resources provide in-depth analysis, case studies, and insights into the evolving landscape of cybersecurity in global conflicts. They offer a multidisciplinary perspective on the technological, geopolitical, and strategic dimensions of cyber warfare.

Cybersecurity and International Relations

Cybersecurity is increasingly becoming intertwined with the field of international relations, as cyber threats and incidents transcend national borders and have significant implications for global stability and security. In this section, we will explore the relationship between cybersecurity and international relations, examining the key issues, challenges, and strategies involved.

Cybersecurity as a Tool of Statecraft

In today's interconnected world, nation-states have recognized the potential of cybersecurity as a tool of statecraft, allowing them to assert their influence, achieve their strategic objectives, and gain a competitive advantage in the international arena. Governments around the world are investing in offensive cyber capabilities, enabling them to launch cyber attacks on other countries' critical infrastructure, disrupt their operations, steal valuable intellectual property, and conduct espionage.

Moreover, cyber operations can be used by states to influence and manipulate public opinion in other countries, through activities such as spreading disinformation, conducting cyber-enabled information operations, and hacking into political campaigns or election systems. These activities have raised concerns about the integrity of democratic processes and the protection of national sovereignty.

International Cybersecurity Cooperation

Given the transnational nature of cyber threats, international cooperation is crucial for effectively addressing cybersecurity challenges and ensuring global cyber stability. Governments, industry stakeholders, and international organizations have recognized the need for collaboration and have established various mechanisms to enhance cybersecurity cooperation at the international level.

One such mechanism is the establishment of cybersecurity alliances and partnerships, where countries work together to share threat intelligence, enhance incident response capabilities, and coordinate cyber defense efforts. Examples include the "Five Eyes" alliance (comprising the United States, United Kingdom, Canada, Australia, and New Zealand) and the European Union Agency for Cybersecurity (ENISA).

At the global level, the United Nations plays a central role in promoting international cybersecurity cooperation. The UN has facilitated the creation of several cybersecurity initiatives, such as the Group of Governmental Experts on Developments in the Field of Information and Telecommunications in the Context of International Security (GGE). The GGE has been instrumental in developing norms, rules, and principles for state behavior in cyberspace.

Cybersecurity as a Source of Conflict

Cybersecurity has also emerged as a potential source of conflict in international relations. State-sponsored cyberattacks and cyber espionage activities have the potential to escalate tensions and provoke retaliatory actions, leading to a cyber arms race. The increasing militarization of cyberspace has raised concerns about the potential for a large-scale cyber conflict between nations.

Additionally, non-state actors, such as hacktivist groups and cybercriminal organizations, can operate across borders and disrupt the functioning of governments, organizations, and critical infrastructure. Their activities can strain diplomatic relations, create legal challenges, and even cause economic damage.

Legal Frameworks and International Law

The international legal framework governing cyberspace is still evolving, with ongoing discussions regarding the applicability of existing international law to cyber activities. The United Nations Charter and international humanitarian law are considered to be applicable to cyber warfare, with principles such as sovereignty, non-intervention, and the prohibition of the use of force being relevant in the cyber domain.

However, challenges remain in applying traditional legal concepts to cyberspace, given its unique characteristics and the difficulty in attributing cyber incidents to specific actors or states. Efforts are underway to develop international norms and rules of behavior for cyberspace, such as the Tallinn Manual and the Paris Call for Trust and Security in Cyberspace.

Cybersecurity in Global Governance

As cyber threats continue to evolve and pose significant challenges to global stability, there is a growing recognition of the need to incorporate cybersecurity into global governance structures. Various international organizations, such as the World Economic Forum and the International Telecommunication Union, are actively involved in shaping cybersecurity policies, standards, and guidelines.

Furthermore, the private sector plays a critical role in cybersecurity and is increasingly engaged in shaping international cybersecurity norms. Technology companies, cybersecurity firms, and internet service providers collaborate with governments and international organizations to enhance cybersecurity resilience, share threat information, and develop best practices.

Future Challenges and Opportunities

The field of cybersecurity and international relations faces numerous future challenges and opportunities. As technology continues to advance, emerging technologies like artificial intelligence, quantum computing, and the Internet of Things will have profound implications for the global cybersecurity landscape.

Developing effective mechanisms for international cooperation, promoting the responsible use of cyber capabilities, and addressing the legal and ethical challenges associated with cybersecurity will be key areas of focus. Additionally, providing cybersecurity education and skills training, both at the national and global levels, will be crucial for building a competent and resilient cybersecurity workforce.

In conclusion, cybersecurity has become an integral part of international relations, with cyber threats and incidents impacting global stability and security.

International cooperation, legal frameworks, and global governance structures play a vital role in addressing these challenges and ensuring a safer and more secure cyberspace. By recognizing the interconnectedness of cybersecurity and international relations, we can better navigate the complexities of this evolving landscape and work towards a more secure digital future.

Cybersecurity and Economic Competitiveness

In today's digital age, cybersecurity plays a crucial role in ensuring the economic competitiveness of nations, organizations, and individuals. As more business processes and transactions take place online, the need for a secure and resilient cyber environment has become paramount. In this section, we will explore the relationship between cybersecurity and economic competitiveness, discussing the impact of cybersecurity on various aspects of the economy and strategies to enhance economic competitiveness through cybersecurity.

The Economic Impact of Cybersecurity

Cybersecurity incidents can have significant economic consequences for both businesses and nations. The financial costs associated with data breaches, intellectual property theft, and system disruptions can be staggering. According to a report by the World Economic Forum, the global cost of cybercrime is estimated to reach $6 trillion annually by 2021. These costs include direct financial losses, as well as indirect costs such as reputational damage, loss of customer trust, and decreased investor confidence.

Moreover, cybersecurity incidents can disrupt critical infrastructure, impacting essential services, and leading to economic instability. For example, a cyber attack on a financial institution can result in financial market turmoil, affecting the stability of the entire economy. Similarly, attacks on transportation, energy, or healthcare systems can disrupt the smooth functioning of the economy.

In addition, the economic impact of cybersecurity extends beyond immediate financial losses. It also affects innovation, trade, and investment. Organizations and nations with weak cybersecurity measures may face barriers in the global marketplace. Lack of trust in the security of digital systems can deter businesses from engaging in e-commerce or sharing sensitive information, limiting economic growth opportunities. Similarly, cyber threats can hamper investments in emerging technologies, as investors may be reluctant to take risks in an environment plagued by cybersecurity concerns.

Strategies for Enhancing Economic Competitiveness through Cybersecurity

To enhance economic competitiveness, nations and organizations need to prioritize cybersecurity and adopt comprehensive strategies to mitigate cyber threats. Here are some key strategies that can be employed:

1. **Cybersecurity Capacity Building and Collaboration:** Governments should invest in cybersecurity education and training programs to develop a skilled workforce capable of addressing cybersecurity challenges. Collaboration between public and private sectors, as well as international cooperation, is crucial to share threat intelligence and best practices, fostering a collective defense against cyber threats.

2. **Regulatory Frameworks and Cybersecurity Standards:** Governments should establish robust regulatory frameworks and cybersecurity standards to ensure the security of critical infrastructure and encourage private sector investment in cybersecurity. Compliance with these standards should be incentivized through certification programs and tax benefits.

3. **Public-Private Partnerships:** Collaboration between the public and private sectors is essential for effective cybersecurity. Governments should form partnerships with industry leaders to develop cybersecurity policies, share information, and jointly invest in research and development of innovative cybersecurity technologies.

4. **Threat Intelligence and Information Sharing:** Establishing effective mechanisms for sharing threat intelligence among stakeholders is critical for early detection and prevention of cyber threats. Collaborative platforms and information sharing networks should be established at the national and international levels to facilitate timely and accurate sharing of threat information.

5. **Investor Confidence:** Building investor confidence in the security of digital systems is crucial for attracting investments and fostering economic growth. Governments and organizations should demonstrate their commitment to cybersecurity by implementing robust security measures, conducting regular audits, and transparently addressing cyber incidents.

6. **Cybersecurity Innovation and Research:** Investments in cybersecurity research and innovation are essential for staying ahead of evolving cyber threats. Governments should fund research projects, support startups, and create an environment conducive to cybersecurity innovation.

Case Study: Singapore's Approach to Cybersecurity and Economic Competitiveness

Singapore is widely recognized as a global leader in cybersecurity and has successfully leveraged cybersecurity to enhance its economic competitiveness. The Singaporean government has implemented a comprehensive cybersecurity strategy that focuses on building a resilient cyber ecosystem, nurturing a skilled cybersecurity workforce, and fostering public-private partnerships.

The government has established the Cybersecurity Agency of Singapore (CSA) to oversee national cybersecurity efforts and coordinate cybersecurity initiatives among government agencies, industries, and academia. CSA collaborates with industry partners to develop capabilities in areas such as threat intelligence, incident response, and cybersecurity R&D.

To address the shortage of cybersecurity professionals, Singapore has invested in cybersecurity education and training programs. Institutes of higher learning offer specialized cybersecurity courses, and the government sponsors scholarships and provides funding for cybersecurity-related research projects.

Singapore has also developed strong public-private partnerships to promote cybersecurity. For example, the government launched the Cyber Security Associates and Technologists (CSAT) program, which enables fresh graduates to gain practical cybersecurity experience through internships with industry partners. This initiative bridges the gap between academia and industry, ensuring that graduates have the necessary skills and knowledge to contribute to the cybersecurity workforce.

Furthermore, Singapore has implemented regulatory frameworks and standards to enhance cybersecurity. The government has introduced the Cybersecurity Act, which mandates certain critical infrastructure sectors to adhere to stringent cybersecurity standards and report significant cyber incidents. This ensures the security and resilience of critical services, thereby bolstering investor confidence and attracting foreign direct investment.

As a result of these initiatives, Singapore has become a preferred destination for businesses in domains such as finance, logistics, and information technology. The country's strong cybersecurity ecosystem, coupled with its robust legal and regulatory framework, has positioned Singapore as a trusted hub for digital services and innovation, driving economic competitiveness.

Conclusion

Cybersecurity plays a vital role in economic competitiveness. As cyber threats continue to evolve and increase in sophistication, governments, organizations, and individuals must prioritize cybersecurity to protect critical assets, foster innovation, and ensure economic growth. By implementing comprehensive cybersecurity strategies, building skilled cybersecurity workforces, promoting public-private partnerships, and adhering to regulatory frameworks, nations and organizations can enhance their economic competitiveness while mitigating the risks posed by cyber threats.

In the next section, we will discuss the social implications of cybersecurity, including privacy, digital divide, social engineering, and human rights.

Cybersecurity and Social Implications

Privacy and Individual Freedoms

In today's digital age, the right to privacy and individual freedoms are increasingly important in the realm of cybersecurity. As technology advances and our lives become more interconnected, the need to protect our personal information and maintain our civil liberties is paramount. This section explores the ethical and legal considerations surrounding privacy and individual freedoms in the context of cybersecurity.

The Right to Privacy

The right to privacy is a fundamental human right recognized by many nations and international organizations. It encompasses the individual's right to control and protect their personal information, as well as their right to be free from unwarranted surveillance or intrusion. In the digital era, the right to privacy faces new challenges as personal data is collected, processed, and shared across various platforms and devices.

Privacy Laws and Regulations

To safeguard the right to privacy, many countries have implemented privacy laws and regulations. These laws govern the collection, use, and disclosure of personal information by organizations and entities. They outline the obligations of individuals and organizations in protecting personal data and provide mechanisms for individuals to exercise their privacy rights.

For example, the General Data Protection Regulation (GDPR) in the European Union is a comprehensive privacy law that sets strict rules for the collection and processing of personal data. It grants individuals certain rights, such as the right to access their personal data, the right to rectify inaccuracies, and the right to be forgotten.

Similarly, in the United States, the California Consumer Privacy Act (CCPA) provides California residents with certain privacy rights, including the right to know what personal information is being collected and the right to opt-out of the sale of their personal data.

Privacy by Design Principles

Privacy by Design is a framework that promotes the integration of privacy and data protection principles into the design and development of systems, products, and services. It emphasizes the proactive and preventative approach to privacy, ensuring that privacy measures are built into the very foundation of technologies.

The Privacy by Design principles include:

1. Proactive not Reactive: Privacy should be considered from the inception of any project or system, rather than being added as an afterthought.

2. Privacy as the Default Setting: Privacy settings should be automatically set to the most secure and privacy-friendly options.

3. Privacy Embedded into Design: Privacy should be an integral part of the design rather than an add-on feature.

4. Full Functionality: Privacy measures should not interfere with the functionality of the system.

5. End-to-End Security: Privacy should be protected throughout the entire lifecycle of the data, from collection to storage and disposal.

6. Visibility and Transparency: Individuals should have clear visibility into how their personal data is being collected, used, and shared.

7. Respect for User Privacy: User preferences and privacy choices should be respected and accommodated.

By implementing Privacy by Design principles, organizations can enhance privacy protection and ensure that privacy considerations are at the forefront of their cybersecurity strategies.

Data Protection and Privacy Impact Assessments

Data Protection Impact Assessments (DPIAs) are tools used to identify and mitigate privacy risks associated with the processing of personal data. In the context of cybersecurity, DPIAs play a crucial role in assessing the potential impact on privacy and individual freedoms when implementing new technologies or systems.

A DPIA typically involves the following steps:

1. Identifying the need for a DPIA: Organizations should determine whether a DPIA is necessary for a particular processing activity.

2. Description of the processing activity: Organizations should document the details of the data processing, including the purpose, scope, and data flows involved.

3. Assessing the necessity and proportionality: An assessment should be conducted to evaluate the necessity and proportionality of the processing activity. Organizations should consider whether there are less intrusive alternatives available.

4. Identifying and assessing risks: Potential risks to privacy and individual freedoms should be identified and evaluated. This includes considering the likelihood and severity of potential harm to individuals.

5. Identifying measures to mitigate risks: Organizations should identify appropriate measures to mitigate the identified risks. This may include implementing technical and organizational safeguards or modifying the processing activity.

6. Consultation and approval: In certain cases, organizations may be required to consult with relevant stakeholders, such as data protection authorities, or seek their approval before implementing the processing activity.

7. Documentation and review: Organizations should maintain documentation of the DPIA process and periodically review and update it as necessary.

DPIAs help organizations identify privacy and individual freedom risks associated with their cybersecurity practices and enable them to take appropriate measures to address these risks.

Privacy Policies and Consent Management

Privacy policies are documents that outline an organization's practices and commitments regarding the collection, use, and disclosure of personal data. They provide individuals with information about how their personal data is processed and their rights in relation to their data.

Privacy policies should be clear, concise, and easily accessible to individuals. They should outline the types of personal data collected, the purpose of the data collection, and with whom the data may be shared. Additionally, privacy policies should inform individuals about their rights, such as the right to access their data, the right to rectify inaccuracies, and the right to withdraw consent.

Consent management is an important aspect of privacy policies. Individuals should have the ability to provide informed and specific consent for the processing of their personal data. Consent should be freely given, unambiguous, and revocable at any time. Organizations should provide individuals with clear and user-friendly mechanisms to withdraw their consent if they no longer wish their personal data to be processed.

Privacy Enhancing Technologies

Privacy Enhancing Technologies (PETs) are tools and techniques that aim to protect privacy and enhance individual freedoms by implementing privacy-preserving mechanisms. These technologies help to safeguard personal data and limit the collection and use of information to what is strictly necessary.

Some examples of privacy-enhancing technologies include:

1. Anonymization and pseudonymization techniques: These techniques remove or obfuscate personally identifiable information from data, thereby preserving privacy while still allowing for analysis and processing.

2. Encryption: Encryption ensures that data remains secure and unreadable to unauthorized parties. It protects the confidentiality and integrity of personal data.

3. Privacy-focused web browsers and search engines: These tools prioritize user privacy by blocking tracking technologies and preventing the collection and sharing of browsing data.

4. Privacy-focused messaging and communication apps: These apps employ end-to-end encryption and other security measures to protect the privacy of users' communications.

5. Privacy-preserving data analytics: Techniques such as secure multiparty computation and differential privacy enable data analysis and information sharing without exposing individual-level data.

By leveraging privacy-enhancing technologies, organizations can enhance cybersecurity measures while still respecting privacy and individual freedoms.

Real-World Example: Privacy and Social Media

Social media platforms have become an integral part of our lives, allowing us to connect with others, share our thoughts and experiences, and access a wealth of information. However, the widespread use of social media also raises significant privacy concerns.

Many social media platforms collect and process vast amounts of personal data, including users' photos, posts, location information, and browsing behavior. This data is often used for targeted advertising, content personalization, and other analytics purposes. Additionally, social media platforms may share personal data with third-party developers or advertisers, further compromising user privacy.

To protect privacy and individual freedoms on social media, individuals can take several actions:

- Adjust privacy settings: Users should review and adjust the privacy settings on their social media accounts to control the visibility of their posts and personal information.

- Limit data sharing: Users should be cautious when granting permissions to third-party apps and carefully consider the data they share with these apps.

- Be mindful of online behavior: Users should be conscious of the information they post on social media and avoid sharing overly sensitive or personal details.

- Regularly review and update privacy preferences: Users should frequently review and update their privacy preferences on social media platforms to align with their desired level of privacy.

Furthermore, regulatory efforts, such as the GDPR and the CCPA, impose obligations on social media platforms to provide users with transparency and control over their personal data. These regulations aim to protect privacy and individual freedoms by requiring platforms to obtain informed consent, provide clear privacy policies, and grant individuals rights over their data.

Conclusion

The protection of privacy and individual freedoms is crucial in the realm of cybersecurity. As technologies continue to advance and collect more personal data, it is important to establish robust privacy laws and regulations, implement privacy by design principles, and adopt privacy-enhancing technologies. By doing so, we can achieve a balance between cybersecurity and the preservation of privacy rights, ensuring that individuals can navigate the digital world with confidence and freedom.

Digital Divide and Cybersecurity Inequality

The digital divide refers to the gap between individuals and communities that have access to information and communication technologies (ICTs) and those who do not. This divide can exist between different regions, countries, socioeconomic groups, and even gender. The lack of access to ICTs can have significant implications for individuals and communities, including limited access to educational resources, employment opportunities, government services, and social connections.

In the context of cybersecurity, the digital divide exacerbates existing inequalities and poses unique challenges. Those who lack access to ICTs are more vulnerable to cyber threats and attacks due to their limited knowledge and resources to protect themselves. This creates a significant cybersecurity inequality between the digitally privileged and the digitally disadvantaged.

One of the key reasons for cybersecurity inequality is the limited access to cybersecurity education and training. Individuals who lack access to ICTs often do not have the opportunity to learn about cybersecurity best practices, such as strong password management, secure internet browsing, and safe online behavior. As a result, they are more likely to fall victim to common cyber attacks, such as phishing scams, malware infections, and identity theft.

Moreover, the lack of access to secure digital infrastructure further widens the cybersecurity gap. Individuals and communities with limited access to ICTs may rely on outdated or insecure devices and networks, making them easy targets for cybercriminals. These vulnerabilities can be exploited to gain unauthorized access to personal information, financial data, and sensitive government or corporate information.

Addressing the digital divide and cybersecurity inequality requires a multi-faceted approach. Here are some strategies and considerations:

1. Infrastructure Development: Efforts should be made to bridge the digital divide by expanding access to affordable and reliable ICT infrastructure, including broadband internet, mobile networks, and secure hardware. This can be achieved through public-private partnerships, government investment, and regulatory initiatives.

2. Cybersecurity Education and Awareness: Investing in cybersecurity education and awareness programs is essential to empower individuals from digitally disadvantaged backgrounds. These programs should focus on teaching basic cybersecurity principles, safe online practices, and the ability to recognize and respond to cyber threats.

3. Digital Inclusion Policies: Governments and organizations should develop and implement policies that promote digital inclusion, ensuring equal access to ICTs for all segments of society. This includes addressing barriers such as affordability, digital literacy, and local-language content availability.

4. Collaboration and Knowledge Sharing: Collaboration between different stakeholders, including governments, businesses, academia, and civil society, is crucial for addressing cybersecurity inequality. Knowledge sharing initiatives can help transfer cybersecurity expertise and best practices to digitally disadvantaged communities.

5. Innovation for Inclusion: Encouraging the development of innovative technologies and solutions specifically designed for digitally disadvantaged communities can help bridge the cybersecurity gap. This includes affordable and secure ICT devices, simplified user interfaces, and localized content and services.

Example: In a rural community with limited access to ICT infrastructure, a non-profit organization partners with local schools and community centers to provide cybersecurity training workshops. The workshops cover topics such as password security, privacy settings, and safe internet browsing. The organization also helps install and maintain basic cybersecurity tools, such as antivirus software, in community centers, enabling individuals to access the internet securely.

Exercise: Conduct research on existing initiatives aimed at bridging the digital divide and reducing cybersecurity inequality in your country. Identify the key challenges faced and propose innovative strategies to address them.

Cybersecurity and Social Engineering

Social engineering is a technique used by cyber attackers to manipulate individuals into revealing sensitive information or performing actions that compromise the security of an organization. It is a psychological manipulation tactic that takes advantage of human vulnerabilities, such as trust, curiosity, and lack of awareness, rather than exploiting technical vulnerabilities in computer systems. In this section, we will explore the concept of social engineering, its various forms, and its impact on cybersecurity.

Understanding Social Engineering

Social engineering attacks are designed to exploit human behavior to gain unauthorized access to confidential information or systems. Attackers often employ various psychological techniques to deceive their targets and trick them into disclosing sensitive data or performing certain actions. The success of a social engineering attack relies heavily on the target's lack of awareness and their willingness to comply with the attacker's requests.

Types of Social Engineering Attacks

There are several common types of social engineering attacks, each with its own approach and objective. Some of the most prominent ones include:

1. **Phishing:** Phishing attacks involve sending fraudulent emails or messages that appear to be from a legitimate source. The goal is to trick the recipient into revealing sensitive information or clicking on malicious links.

2. **Pretexting:** Pretexting involves the attacker creating a false scenario or identity to gain the trust of the target. They may pose as a trusted individual or authority figure to convince the target to disclose information or perform certain actions.

3. **Baiting:** Baiting attacks entice individuals with the promise of something desirable, such as a free gift or a discount. The target is often required to provide personal information or click on a malicious link to obtain the offered reward.

4. **Quid pro quo:** Quid pro quo attacks involve the attacker offering something of value to the target in exchange for their sensitive information or help in performing a particular action. For example, an attacker might offer IT support in exchange for login credentials.

5. **Tailgating:** Tailgating, also known as piggybacking, occurs when an unauthorized individual gains physical access to a restricted area by following an authorized person without proper authentication. This technique is often used in corporate or government environments.

6. **Reverse social engineering:** Reverse social engineering involves the attacker convincing the target that they are the ones in need of help or assistance. The target willingly provides information or performs actions to assist the attacker, not realizing their true intentions.

Real-World Examples

To understand the real-world impact of social engineering attacks, let's examine two prominent cases:

1. **The Target Data Breach:** In 2013, cyber attackers gained access to the point-of-sale systems of Target, a major retail corporation. The attackers used a technique known as spear phishing to compromise a third-party HVAC vendor, who had access to Target's network. By sending a malicious email to the vendor's employees, the attackers were able to steal their login credentials and ultimately infiltrate Target's systems. This attack resulted in the theft of credit card information of over 40 million customers.

2. **The Twitter Bitcoin Scam:** In July 2020, several high-profile Twitter accounts, including those of Barack Obama, Joe Biden, Elon Musk, and Bill Gates, were hacked as part of a social engineering attack. The attackers gained access to Twitter's internal systems by targeting company employees through a phone spear phishing attack. They convinced the employees to divulge their credentials, allowing the attackers to compromise the accounts and post fraudulent messages requesting Bitcoin donations. This attack highlighted the potential impact of social engineering on social media platforms and the need for stronger security measures.

Mitigating Social Engineering Attacks

Preventing social engineering attacks requires a combination of technology, policies, and user awareness. Here are some effective strategies for mitigating social engineering risks:

1. **Employee Training and Awareness:** Regular training sessions on social engineering techniques and best practices can significantly enhance employee awareness and reduce the likelihood of falling victim to such attacks. Employees should be educated about the common types of social engineering attacks and how to recognize and report suspicious activities.

2. **Strong Access Controls:** Implementing strong access controls, such as multi-factor authentication, can help prevent unauthorized access even if an attacker manages to obtain login credentials through social engineering techniques.

3. **Email Filtering and Web Filtering:** Deploying email filtering solutions to identify and block phishing emails can effectively reduce the risk of social engineering attacks via email. Additionally, web filtering can help block access to malicious websites that may be used in social engineering campaigns.

4. **Incident Response Plan:** Having a well-defined incident response plan in place can help organizations respond quickly and effectively to social engineering attacks. The plan should include procedures for identifying, containing, and remedying the impacts of such attacks.

5. **Continuous Monitoring and Threat Intelligence:** Implementing continuous monitoring mechanisms and leveraging threat intelligence sources can help organizations stay informed about the latest social engineering techniques and potential threats. This information can be used to enhance security controls and raise awareness among employees.

6. **Periodic Security Audits:** Conducting regular security audits can help identify potential vulnerabilities and gaps in an organization's security posture. These audits should include assessments of employee awareness and the effectiveness of existing security controls against social engineering attacks.

Conclusion

Social engineering attacks continue to pose significant threats to the security of organizations and individuals. Understanding the various types of social engineering attacks, their tactics, and real-world examples can help raise awareness and build effective defenses against such attacks. By combining technological solutions, policies, and employee training, organizations can mitigate the risks associated with social engineering and strengthen their overall cybersecurity posture.

Remember, vigilance and skepticism are your best defense against social engineering attacks. Stay informed, be cautious, and always verify requests for sensitive information.

Cybersecurity and Human Rights

In today's interconnected world, where the internet plays a significant role in our daily lives, the protection of human rights is becoming more intertwined with cybersecurity. The rapid advancements in technology and the increased reliance on digital systems have created both opportunities and risks for individuals' privacy, freedom of expression, and personal security. This section will explore the intersection between cybersecurity and human rights, discussing the challenges, ethical considerations, and potential solutions.

The Right to Privacy in the Digital Age

The right to privacy is a fundamental human right recognized by international law. As more personal data is collected, stored, and analyzed by various organizations and governments, the protection of individuals' privacy has become a growing concern. Cybersecurity plays a crucial role in safeguarding this right in the digital age.

One of the main challenges is striking a balance between privacy and security. Governments argue that collecting and analyzing personal data is necessary for national security and crime prevention. However, indiscriminate surveillance programs can infringe upon individuals' right to privacy. Ethical considerations arise when surveillance programs lack transparency, oversight, and accountability.

To address this issue, countries have started implementing privacy laws and regulations. For example, the European Union's General Data Protection Regulation (GDPR) provides individuals with control over their personal data and establishes strict rules for its processing. Similarly, the California Consumer Privacy Act (CCPA) grants consumers certain rights regarding their personal information. These regulations aim to enhance transparency and give individuals more control over their data while ensuring their privacy.

Cybersecurity and Freedom of Expression

Freedom of expression is a fundamental human right that allows individuals to freely voice their opinions and access information. In the digital era, the internet has become a vital platform for exercising this right. However, cybersecurity threats can impede freedom of expression by restricting access to information or surveilling online activities.

Censorship and content filtering are among the threats to online freedom of expression. Governments and organizations may restrict access to specific websites or block certain content to control the flow of information. This can limit individuals' ability to express themselves freely and access diverse perspectives.

Furthermore, cyberattacks on journalists, bloggers, and human rights defenders are on the rise. These attacks aim to silence dissenting voices and intimidate individuals into self-censorship. Protecting the digital infrastructure and ensuring the cybersecurity of individuals who exercise their right to freedom of expression is crucial.

International organizations such as the United Nations and non-governmental organizations play a vital role in promoting and protecting freedom of expression in cyberspace. They advocate for an open and secure internet, defend net neutrality, and condemn cyberattacks that target journalists and human rights activists.

Cybersecurity and Online Harassment

As internet usage continues to grow, so does the prevalence of online harassment. Cyberbullying, stalking, and harassment through various online channels have a significant impact on individuals' mental well-being, freedom of expression, and personal security.

Online harassment often occurs through social media platforms, instant messaging apps, or email. Perpetrators can hide their identities and operate anonymously, making it difficult to address the issue effectively. Victims may face psychological distress, fear for their safety, and withdraw from online spaces.

Addressing online harassment requires a multifaceted approach that combines technological solutions, legal frameworks, and educational campaigns. Social media platforms can implement stronger content moderation policies, provide reporting mechanisms, and enhance privacy settings to empower users to protect themselves from online abuse. Legal systems can strengthen anti-harassment laws and ensure law enforcement agencies have the necessary tools to investigate and prosecute cyber harassers. Educational initiatives can raise awareness about online etiquette and promote responsible digital citizenship.

Cybersecurity and Access to Information

Access to information is essential in promoting transparency, accountability, and informed decision-making. However, cybersecurity threats can limit individuals' ability to access reliable information and participate in the democratic process.

Censorship, information manipulation, and disinformation campaigns are growing challenges in the digital age. Governments and other actors may control or manipulate information flows to shape public opinion, control narratives, or suppress dissent. This poses a threat to the functioning of democracies and citizens' right to access diverse sources of information.

Cybersecurity measures should ensure the integrity and availability of information sources, enabling individuals to access and share information freely. Educating citizens on media literacy, critical thinking, and fact-checking can empower them to navigate the digital landscape and identify false or misleading information.

Ethical Considerations in Cybersecurity and Human Rights

The protection of human rights in the context of cybersecurity raises several ethical considerations. Balancing individual rights with the need for collective security and public safety requires careful deliberation and decision-making.

Ethical hacking or white-hat hacking can serve as a valuable tool to detect vulnerabilities in computer systems, helping organizations identify and address potential security risks. However, ethical hackers must operate within legal and ethical boundaries to avoid infringing upon privacy rights or causing harm.

Moreover, the collection and analysis of personal data for cybersecurity purposes should adhere to ethical principles. Organizations should obtain informed consent, anonymize data whenever possible, and adopt privacy-enhancing technologies to protect individuals' privacy.

It is vital to include human rights considerations in the design and development of cybersecurity technologies and policies. Taking into account ethical guidelines and principles can help ensure that cybersecurity measures do not undermine human rights but rather enhance security and protect individual freedoms.

Conclusion

Cybersecurity is inseparable from human rights in the digital age. Safeguarding privacy, protecting freedom of expression, addressing online harassment, and promoting access to information are essential components of cybersecurity sustainability. By considering the ethical implications of cybersecurity measures and adopting a human rights-centered approach, we can aim to create a secure and inclusive digital environment that respects and upholds the rights and dignity of individuals.

Cybersecurity and Environmental Sustainability

Energy Consumption and Carbon Footprint

The rapid growth of the digital age has significantly increased the demand for data storage and processing capabilities. As a result, the energy consumption of the information and communication technology (ICT) sector has been soaring. The energy required to power data centers, network infrastructure, and end-user devices has become a substantial contributor to carbon emissions, leading to concerns about the environmental sustainability of cybersecurity practices.

Energy Consumption in Data Centers

Data centers, the backbone of the digital infrastructure, consume a vast amount of energy to operate and maintain their servers, cooling systems, and networking equipment. The high power density and continuous operation of data centers make them a significant contributor to energy consumption. The cooling systems alone consume a significant portion of the total energy expenditure.

To reduce energy consumption, data centers can adopt various strategies. Implementing energy-efficient servers and IT equipment, optimizing airflow management, and deploying advanced cooling technologies are some of the methods employed. Data center operators can also explore alternative energy sources, such as solar or wind power, to reduce the reliance on fossil fuels.

Virtualization and Energy Efficiency

Virtualization is a technique that allows multiple virtual machines (VMs) to run on a single physical server, consolidating the workload and improving resource utilization. By reducing the number of physical servers required, virtualization can lead to significant energy savings.

Server virtualization enables energy-efficient dynamic provisioning, where idle servers can be powered off or put into a low-power state, known as "standby mode." This approach reduces energy waste by matching the server capacity to the current workload demands. Additionally, virtualization allows for workload consolidation, enabling the efficient utilization of server resources.

Energy-Aware Networking

Networking infrastructure, including routers, switches, and transmission equipment, also consumes a substantial amount of energy. Energy-aware networking aims to optimize the energy consumption of network devices while maintaining their performance.

Several energy-efficient techniques can be employed in networking infrastructure. For example, using energy-efficient network interface cards (NICs) and switches, optimizing network protocols, and implementing intelligent power management algorithms can help minimize energy consumption.

Renewable Energy Integration

To reduce the carbon footprint of cybersecurity practices, organizations can embrace renewable energy sources. Investing in renewable energy technologies, such as solar panels or wind turbines, can offset the energy consumption of data centers and network infrastructure.

Power purchase agreements (PPAs) enable organizations to procure renewable energy from external sources. By entering into long-term agreements, companies can ensure a stable supply of renewable energy, reducing their dependence on traditional grid electricity.

Monitoring and Optimization

Monitoring and optimizing energy consumption is crucial for achieving energy-efficient cybersecurity sustainability. Implementing energy management systems that collect and analyze real-time energy data can help identify areas of improvement.

Power usage effectiveness (PUE) is a widely used metric to assess the energy efficiency of data centers. It measures the ratio of total energy consumption to the energy consumed by IT equipment alone. By continuously monitoring PUE, data center operators can identify inefficiencies and implement targeted measures to reduce energy consumption.

Case Study: Google's Carbon-Neutral Operations

Google, one of the leading technology providers, has demonstrated a commitment to carbon-neutrality in its operations. The company has achieved this through a combination of energy-efficient measures, renewable energy investments, and carbon offset projects.

Google's data centers employ advanced cooling techniques, such as free-air cooling and water-side economization, to minimize energy consumption. The company has also invested heavily in renewable energy projects globally, ensuring that its electricity consumption is offset by clean energy generation.

Furthermore, Google is actively involved in carbon offset initiatives, which fund projects that reduce greenhouse gas emissions. By supporting such projects, Google neutralizes the environmental impact of its operations and contributes to a more sustainable future.

Key Takeaways

- The energy consumption of the ICT sector, including data centers and networking infrastructure, contributes significantly to carbon emissions. - Data centers can adopt energy-efficient strategies, such as server virtualization and advanced cooling technologies, to reduce energy consumption. - Energy-aware networking optimizes the energy usage of network devices while maintaining performance. - Integration of renewable energy sources, such as solar or wind power, can help offset the carbon footprint of cybersecurity practices. - Monitoring energy consumption and implementing optimization measures are essential for achieving energy-efficient cybersecurity sustainability. - Google serves as a case study for successful implementation of energy-efficient practices and carbon-neutral operations.

Further Reading

- Mills, E., & Koomey, J. (2014). *Evaluating the Energy Performance of Large-Scale Data Centers.* Proceedings of the IEEE, 102(8), 1378-1400.

- Böhm, M., Kargl, F., Carle, G., & Papagiannaki, K. (Eds.). (2021). *Energy Efficiency in Data Centers and Networking.* Springer.

- Beyer, C., Curran, C., Gagliardi, F., Hamilton, K., & Rivoire, S. (2019). *Sustainable Operations at Scale.* Google.

- Richter, D. (2019). *Energy Efficiency in Data Centers - Best Practices and Modeling.* CRC Press.

E-Waste Management and Recycling

E-waste, which refers to electronic waste, has become a significant environmental and health concern in recent years. As technology continues to advance rapidly, the disposal of electronic devices has become a pressing issue due to the toxic materials they contain and the sheer volume of waste being generated. In this section, we will explore the challenges and opportunities associated with e-waste management and recycling, as well as the strategies and initiatives that can be implemented to address this global problem.

Understanding E-Waste

Electronic devices, such as computers, smartphones, televisions, and household appliances, have a limited lifespan. When these devices reach the end of their useful life, they are discarded as e-waste. E-waste contains various hazardous substances, including heavy metals (lead, mercury, cadmium), flame retardants, and toxic chemicals (chlorinated solvents, PVC). When improperly disposed of, these substances can contaminate soil, water, and air, posing serious risks to human health and the environment.

The proliferation of electronic devices, combined with their short lifespan and rapid technological advancements, has led to a massive increase in e-waste generation. According to the United Nations Global E-waste Monitor 2020, the world generated a record 53.6 million metric tons of e-waste in 2019, representing a growth of 21

Challenges in E-Waste Management

E-waste management faces several challenges, including inadequate infrastructure, lack of awareness, and limited financial resources. Here are some of the key challenges in e-waste management:

1. **Lack of proper collection systems:** In many regions, there is a lack of established collection systems for e-waste. As a result, much of it ends up in landfills or is illegally exported to developing countries, where it is often handled in unsafe and unregulated conditions.

2. **Complexity of recycling:** Electronic devices consist of a wide range of materials, including plastic, metals, glass, and circuit boards. Disassembling and separating these components is a complex process, requiring specialized equipment and knowledge. Many developing countries lack the necessary infrastructure and technology to safely and efficiently recycle e-waste.

3. **Informal e-waste recycling:** In some parts of the world, informal recycling operations have emerged due to economic incentives. While these operations may help recover valuable metals, they often involve unsafe practices such as open burning, acid leaching, and manual dismantling without protective measures, leading to significant health and environmental risks.

4. **Lack of awareness and regulations:** Many consumers are unaware of the environmental hazards associated with improper e-waste disposal.

Additionally, there is a lack of comprehensive regulations and policies governing the management and recycling of e-waste, particularly in developing countries.

Addressing these challenges requires a multi-faceted approach involving various stakeholders, including governments, manufacturers, consumers, and recycling industries. By adopting sustainable practices and implementing appropriate regulations, we can mitigate the environmental and health risks associated with e-waste.

Strategies for E-Waste Management and Recycling

Effective e-waste management and recycling strategies can help minimize the negative impacts of e-waste while maximizing resource recovery. Here are some key strategies:

1. **Extended producer responsibility** (EPR): Implementing EPR programs requires manufacturers to take responsibility for the entire lifecycle of their products, including their disposal. Manufacturers are encouraged to design devices that are easier to repair, upgrade, and recycle. EPR programs also establish collection systems to ensure proper disposal and recycling of e-waste.

2. **Establishing collection and recycling centers:** Developing efficient and accessible collection systems is vital for the proper management of e-waste. Governments and organizations should establish collection centers and e-waste recycling facilities in convenient locations, ensuring easy access for consumers to dispose of their old devices. These centers should adhere to proper environmental and safety standards.

3. **Promoting awareness and education:** Raising awareness among consumers about the importance of responsible e-waste disposal and the potential environmental and health impacts is crucial. Public campaigns and educational initiatives can help inform consumers about proper e-waste management practices and encourage them to recycle their old devices.

4. **Encouraging recycling and resource recovery:** Recycling e-waste can help recover valuable materials, reducing the need for raw material extraction. Governments and organizations should provide incentives for recycling practices and support the development of efficient recycling technologies.

Additionally, promoting a circular economy approach can facilitate resource recovery by encouraging the reuse and refurbishment of electronic devices.

5. **International cooperation and regulation:** E-waste is a global issue that requires international cooperation and regulation. Governments, industry associations, and international organizations need to work together to establish comprehensive regulations and standards for the management and recycling of e-waste. They should also collaborate to enforce environmentally sound practices and prevent illegal e-waste trade.

Case Study: E-Waste Recycling in Switzerland

Switzerland is known for its advanced waste management practices, including e-waste recycling. The country has implemented strict regulations and established an efficient collection and recycling system for electronic devices. Here are some key features of Switzerland's e-waste management approach:

1. **EPR system:** Switzerland has a well-established extended producer responsibility (EPR) system, which holds manufacturers accountable for collecting and recycling their products. Manufacturers are required to finance and operate collection points across the country.

2. **Convenient collection points:** Switzerland has a dense network of collection points where consumers can drop off their old electronic devices free of charge. Collection points are typically located at retailers, municipal recycling centers, and dedicated collection points, ensuring easy access for consumers.

3. **Efficient recycling infrastructure:** Switzerland has invested in advanced recycling infrastructure, including specialized facilities for dismantling and processing e-waste. State-of-the-art recycling technologies are used to extract valuable materials, such as precious metals and rare earth elements, from electronic devices.

4. **Strict enforcement and monitoring:** The Swiss government enforces strict regulations and regularly monitors compliance with e-waste management practices. Non-compliance can result in penalties for manufacturers and recyclers who fail to meet recycling targets or proper handling of hazardous materials.

Switzerland's success in e-waste management can be attributed to its comprehensive regulatory framework, effective collection infrastructure, and strong collaboration between the government, manufacturers, and consumers. Other countries can learn from Switzerland's approach and adapt it to their own contexts to improve their e-waste management systems.

Conclusion

E-waste management and recycling are essential for addressing the environmental and health hazards associated with electronic waste. By implementing strategies like extended producer responsibility, establishing collection and recycling centers, promoting awareness and education, encouraging recycling and resource recovery, and fostering international cooperation, we can minimize the negative impacts of e-waste and move towards a more sustainable future. It is crucial for governments, manufacturers, and individuals to take proactive steps in managing e-waste to protect the environment and ensure the responsible use of electronic devices. Through collective efforts, we can create a world where e-waste is recycled and reused, reducing the burden on our planet and conserving valuable resources.

Sustainable Manufacturing Practices

In this section, we will explore the concept of sustainable manufacturing practices and their importance in the field of cybersecurity sustainability. Sustainable manufacturing refers to the implementation of strategies and processes that minimize the environmental impact of manufacturing activities while promoting economic growth and social well-being. As the field of cybersecurity continues to evolve, it is crucial to consider the environmental sustainability of the technologies and the manufacturing processes involved.

Environmental Impact of Cybersecurity Manufacturing

The manufacturing of cybersecurity technologies, such as hardware devices, software components, and network infrastructure, has a significant environmental impact. The extraction and processing of raw materials, the energy consumption during manufacturing processes, and the disposal of electronic waste all contribute to this impact.

Firstly, the extraction and processing of raw materials, such as metals, minerals, and rare earth elements, require extensive mining activities. These activities often result in ecosystem destruction, pollution of water bodies, and habitat loss. Therefore, it is essential to source these materials responsibly, considering their environmental and social implications.

Secondly, the manufacturing processes themselves consume a considerable amount of energy. The production of electronic components, assembly of devices, and testing operations all require electricity, which often comes from non-renewable sources. High energy consumption not only contributes to greenhouse gas emissions but also depletes finite energy resources.

Lastly, the disposal of electronic waste poses a significant challenge. Cybersecurity technologies, like any other electronic devices, eventually reach their end-of-life and become e-waste. Improper disposal of e-waste can lead to the release of hazardous substances into the environment, putting human health and the ecosystem at risk. Hence, sustainable approaches to managing e-waste are crucial to minimize the environmental impact.

Principles of Sustainable Manufacturing

To address these environmental challenges, it is imperative to adopt sustainable manufacturing practices. These practices aim to minimize resource consumption, reduce waste generation, and promote the circular economy. Here are some key principles of sustainable manufacturing:

1. **Life Cycle Assessment (LCA):** LCA is a methodology used to assess the environmental impact of a product throughout its entire life cycle. It considers the extraction of raw materials, manufacturing processes, product use, and end-of-life disposal. By conducting LCAs, manufacturers can identify hotspots of environmental impact and make informed decisions to improve the sustainability of their products.

2. **Cleaner Production:** Cleaner production involves optimizing manufacturing processes to minimize waste generation, energy consumption, and the use of hazardous substances. It focuses on improving efficiency and reducing environmental pollution by adopting cleaner technologies, process modifications, and waste management strategies. By implementing cleaner production practices, manufacturers can minimize their carbon footprint and conserve resources.

3. **Design for Sustainability:** Design for Sustainability involves considering environmental factors during the product design phase. This approach emphasizes the use of eco-friendly materials, energy-efficient designs, and modular product architectures that facilitate repair, reuse, and recycling. By designing products with sustainability in mind, manufacturers can reduce environmental impact throughout the entire life cycle.

4. **Extended Producer Responsibility (EPR):** EPR is a policy approach that holds manufacturers responsible for their products' environmental impact throughout their life cycle. It encourages manufacturers to take responsibility for the end-of-life management of their products, including collection, recycling, and proper disposal. EPR programs incentivize manufacturers to design products that are easier to recycle and promote the establishment of efficient waste management systems.

5. **Collaboration and Stakeholder Engagement:** Sustainable manufacturing requires collaboration between various stakeholders, including manufacturers, suppliers, government agencies, and consumers. By engaging stakeholders throughout the supply chain, manufacturers can identify opportunities for improvement and develop innovative solutions that benefit the environment and society as a whole.

Examples of Sustainable Manufacturing Practices

Several companies and organizations are actively implementing sustainable manufacturing practices in the field of cybersecurity. Here are a few examples:

- **Green Data Centers:** Data centers consume massive amounts of energy for server operation and cooling. Companies are now adopting sustainable practices to reduce energy consumption, such as using energy-efficient hardware, implementing advanced cooling systems, and leveraging renewable energy sources. Additionally, data centers are exploring opportunities to reuse waste heat generated during operation for heating purposes, further reducing their environmental impact.

- **Recycling and Material Recovery:** Manufacturers are increasingly adopting recycling and material recovery practices to minimize electronic waste. They establish e-waste collection and recycling programs that ensure the proper disposal of end-of-life cybersecurity devices. Furthermore, manufacturers are exploring ways to recover valuable materials, such as rare earth elements, from discarded devices to reduce the need for raw material extraction.

- **Product Life Extension:** Extending the life cycle of cybersecurity technologies can significantly reduce their environmental impact. By designing products that are modular and upgradable, manufacturers can enable users to easily replace or upgrade components, thus avoiding the need for complete device replacements. Additionally, manufacturers are offering repair and maintenance services to ensure the longevity of their products.

- **Renewable Energy-Powered Manufacturing:** Manufacturers are transitioning to renewable energy sources to power their manufacturing operations. Solar panels, wind turbines, and other renewable energy solutions are being implemented to reduce reliance on fossil fuels and decrease greenhouse gas emissions.

Challenges and Considerations

While sustainable manufacturing practices offer significant benefits, several challenges and considerations need to be addressed:

- **Cost and Economic Viability:** Implementing sustainable manufacturing practices may require upfront investment and could potentially increase production costs. Manufacturers need to assess the economic viability of sustainability initiatives and identify ways to achieve a balance between environmental sustainability and financial feasibility.

- **Supply Chain Management:** Manufacturers need to work closely with their suppliers to ensure responsible sourcing of materials and compliance with environmental regulations. Managing the sustainability of the entire supply chain can be complex, especially when dealing with global sourcing and multiple suppliers.

- **Regulatory Compliance:** Keeping up with constantly evolving environmental regulations and standards can be challenging for manufacturers. Compliance with regulations related to hazardous substances, waste management, and carbon emissions requires ongoing monitoring and adaptation of manufacturing processes.

- **Consumer Awareness and Behavior:** Educating consumers about the environmental impact of cybersecurity technologies and encouraging responsible disposal practices for end-of-life devices are crucial challenges. Increasing consumer awareness and adherence to sustainable practices can significantly contribute to the effectiveness of sustainable manufacturing.

In conclusion, sustainable manufacturing practices play a vital role in cybersecurity sustainability. By adopting principles such as life cycle assessment, cleaner production, design for sustainability, extended producer responsibility, and stakeholder collaboration, manufacturers can minimize the environmental impact of their operations. Examples, such as green data centers, e-waste recycling, product life extension, and renewable energy-powered manufacturing, demonstrate the feasibility of sustainable practices in the cybersecurity industry. However, challenges related to cost, supply chain management, regulatory compliance, and consumer behavior must be addressed to maximize the effectiveness of sustainable manufacturing efforts. By prioritizing sustainability, the field of cybersecurity can contribute to the well-being of the environment and society as a whole.

Green Cybersecurity Initiatives

As the world becomes increasingly aware of the importance of environmental sustainability, industries across the board are making efforts to reduce their carbon footprint and adopt greener practices. The field of cybersecurity is no exception. Green cybersecurity initiatives aim to address the growing energy consumption and environmental impact of cybersecurity processes and technologies. This section explores the various strategies and approaches that can be adopted to promote green cybersecurity.

The Environmental Impact of Cybersecurity

Cybersecurity processes and technologies, while essential for protecting digital assets and systems, can have a significant environmental impact. For instance, data centers that host critical infrastructure and store vast amounts of data consume enormous amounts of energy. According to recent estimates, data centers worldwide consume approximately 3

Moreover, the proliferation of network-connected devices and the increasing demand for cloud services result in a constant need for data transmission and storage, further exacerbating the environmental impact of cybersecurity. The energy-intensive processes involved in securing networks and processing large volumes of data contribute to the overall environmental footprint of the cybersecurity industry.

Green Cybersecurity Strategies

To mitigate the environmental impact of cybersecurity, several green initiatives can be implemented. These strategies focus on reducing energy consumption, maximizing resource efficiency, and adopting eco-friendly practices. Here are some key green cybersecurity strategies:

1. **Energy-efficient data centers:** Data centers can adopt energy-efficient practices, such as utilizing advanced cooling techniques, optimizing server utilization, and investing in low-power hardware. Implementing virtualization and cloud computing technologies also helps consolidate resources and reduce energy consumption.

2. **Renewable energy adoption:** Data centers and cybersecurity infrastructure can transition to renewable energy sources, such as solar or wind power, to significantly reduce their carbon footprint. By utilizing green energy, the environmental impact of cybersecurity operations can be minimized.

3. **Virtualization and consolidation:** Virtualization technology allows for the consolidation of multiple systems onto a single physical server. This reduces the overall energy consumption of the infrastructure and minimizes the amount of hardware required, leading to lower e-waste generation.

4. **Green algorithms and protocols:** Developing energy-efficient algorithms and protocols can significantly reduce the computational power required for cybersecurity operations. By optimizing cryptographic processes and

network protocols, the energy consumption of cybersecurity systems can be reduced without compromising security.

5. **Lifecycle management and e-waste reduction:** Effective lifecycle management of cybersecurity hardware and equipment is crucial for reducing e-waste. Adopting practices such as recycling, refurbishing, and responsible disposal ensures that obsolete equipment does not end up in landfills. Additionally, organizations can prioritize the use of devices with longer lifecycles, reducing the frequency of hardware replacements.

6. **Education and awareness:** Raising awareness among cybersecurity professionals about the environmental impact of their work can drive the adoption of greener practices. Training programs and educational initiatives can highlight the importance of energy efficiency, responsible disposal, and the use of renewable energy sources in the cybersecurity field.

Example: Green Data Centers

One notable example of a green cybersecurity initiative is the development of energy-efficient data centers. These data centers implement various technologies and practices to optimize energy consumption and reduce carbon emissions.

For instance, organizations can adopt liquid cooling solutions that efficiently remove heat generated by servers, reducing the need for power-hungry traditional air conditioning systems. Moreover, data centers can utilize advanced power management techniques to monitor server usage and dynamically allocate resources, ensuring optimal energy utilization.

Furthermore, the use of renewable energy sources, such as solar panels or wind turbines, in powering data centers can make them more environmentally friendly. With the decreasing cost of renewable energy technologies, organizations can explore options for on-site renewable energy generation or procure renewable energy from external sources.

Green data centers also focus on minimizing e-waste by adopting circular economy principles. They promote the recycling and reuse of IT equipment, ensuring that valuable resources are not wasted. Additionally, they prioritize the use of energy-efficient hardware and continuously optimize their infrastructure to minimize energy consumption.

Challenges and Considerations

While green cybersecurity initiatives hold promise for reducing the environmental impact of the field, they are not without challenges and considerations. Some key challenges include:

- **Cost considerations:** Implementing green cybersecurity practices may require significant upfront investments. For example, transitioning to renewable energy sources or upgrading hardware to energy-efficient alternatives can involve substantial costs. Organizations need to carefully weigh the long-term benefits against the initial expenses.

- **Interoperability and compatibility:** Green cybersecurity initiatives may require integration with existing systems and technologies. Ensuring compatibility and interoperability between legacy systems and new eco-friendly solutions can pose technical challenges.

- **Regulatory compliance:** Organizations must navigate the complex landscape of regulatory requirements and industry standards related to environmental sustainability. Compliance with these regulations adds an additional layer of complexity to implementing green cybersecurity practices.

- **Education and training:** Adopting green cybersecurity practices necessitates the training and education of cybersecurity professionals. Organizations need to invest in building the necessary skills and knowledge to implement and maintain eco-friendly cybersecurity processes effectively.

Despite these challenges, the potential benefits of green cybersecurity initiatives, including reduced energy consumption, cost savings, and positive environmental impact, make them a worthwhile endeavor.

Conclusion

Green cybersecurity initiatives offer a path towards a more sustainable and environmentally conscious approach to securing our digital infrastructure. By implementing strategies such as energy-efficient data centers, renewable energy adoption, and optimizing algorithms, organizations can minimize the carbon footprint of cybersecurity operations.

However, widespread adoption of green cybersecurity practices requires not only technological solutions but also a shift in mindset and awareness within the cybersecurity community. Promoting education and training programs that highlight the importance of environmental sustainability will contribute to building a greener and more secure digital future.

Cybersecurity and Ethical Considerations

Ethical Hacking and Responsible Disclosure

Ethical hacking, also known as white-hat hacking or penetration testing, is the practice of intentionally accessing computer systems, networks, or applications with the permission of the owner to identify vulnerabilities and assess the security posture. Ethical hackers use the same techniques employed by malicious hackers, but their intention is to improve security rather than cause harm. Responsible disclosure, on the other hand, refers to the process of reporting discovered vulnerabilities to the affected organization in a responsible and coordinated manner.

Why Ethical Hacking?

Ethical hacking plays a crucial role in cybersecurity by helping organizations identify and fix security flaws before they are exploited by malicious actors. By simulating real-world attacks, ethical hackers provide valuable insights into the vulnerabilities and weaknesses of computer systems, networks, and applications. This proactive approach helps organizations stay one step ahead of potential attackers and strengthens their overall security posture.

Principles of Ethical Hacking

Ethical hacking follows a set of principles to ensure the practice is carried out responsibly and ethically. These principles include:

- **Consent and Authorization:** Ethical hackers must obtain proper consent and authorization from the owner of the system or network before conducting any security testing. This ensures that hacking activities are conducted within legal boundaries and do not cause any unauthorized disruption.
- **Confidentiality:** Ethical hackers should respect the confidentiality of any sensitive information they may encounter during their testing. They must handle this information responsibly and protect it from unauthorized access or disclosure.

- **Integrity:** Ethical hackers must maintain the integrity of the systems and networks they test. They should not cause any damage or disruption that could negatively impact the organization's operations.

- **Professionalism:** Ethical hackers should adhere to high professional standards throughout their engagements. They should maintain clear and open communication with the organization, provide accurate and timely reports, and act in a responsible and respectful manner.

These principles ensure that ethical hacking is conducted in a responsible and ethical manner, minimizing any potential harm to the organization being tested.

Responsible Disclosure Process

When an ethical hacker discovers a vulnerability during their testing, responsible disclosure becomes paramount. Responsible disclosure involves reporting the vulnerability to the affected organization in a way that allows them to assess the risk and take appropriate measures to address it. The typical steps involved in the responsible disclosure process are as follows:

1. **Documentation:** The ethical hacker documents the discovered vulnerability thoroughly, including the steps to reproduce it, technical details, and any available proof-of-concept or exploit code. This documentation helps the organization understand the nature and severity of the vulnerability.

2. **Notification:** The ethical hacker contacts the organization's designated point of contact, typically their security team or incident response team, to report the vulnerability. The notification should be concise, clear, and include all necessary details for the organization to understand and reproduce the vulnerability.

3. **Coordinated Remediation:** The ethical hacker cooperates with the organization to develop a plan for remediation. This includes establishing a timeline for fixing the vulnerability and verifying the effectiveness of the implemented fix.

4. **Public Disclosure:** After the organization has patched the vulnerability, the ethical hacker may, with the organization's approval, publicly disclose the details of the vulnerability. This allows the broader cybersecurity community to learn and benefit from the knowledge gained, leading to better security practices overall.

Responsible disclosure ensures that vulnerabilities are addressed promptly and efficiently, reducing the risk of exploitation and potential harm to the organization and its customers.

Challenges in Ethical Hacking and Responsible Disclosure

While ethical hacking and responsible disclosure are essential practices for improving cybersecurity, there are several challenges associated with their implementation. These include:

- **Lack of Legal Clarity:** The legality of ethical hacking activities can vary across jurisdictions. In some cases, ethical hackers may inadvertently violate laws related to unauthorized access or interception of network traffic. It is crucial for ethical hackers to understand and comply with the legal frameworks of the countries they operate in.

- **Complexity of Vulnerabilities:** Discovering and exploiting vulnerabilities can be a complex task. Ethical hackers require a high level of technical expertise and deep knowledge of various systems and applications. It is essential to continuously update skills and stay informed about emerging threats and attack techniques.

- **Cooperation from Organizations:** Some organizations may be hesitant to cooperate with ethical hackers or may not have established channels for responsible disclosure. Overcoming this challenge requires building trust and advocating for the benefits of responsible disclosure within the cybersecurity community.

- **Time Constraints:** The responsible disclosure process can be time-sensitive, particularly when dealing with critical vulnerabilities. Ethical hackers often need to balance timely reporting with giving organizations sufficient time to develop and implement appropriate fixes.

Addressing these challenges requires a collaborative effort between ethical hackers, organizations, and policymakers to establish clear legal frameworks, create channels for responsible disclosure, and promote ethical hacking as a valuable practice.

Real-World Example

A notable real-world example of responsible disclosure is the Heartbleed vulnerability, discovered in the OpenSSL cryptographic software library in 2014. When security researchers discovered this critical vulnerability, they followed responsible disclosure practices by privately notifying the OpenSSL team before publicly disclosing the details. The OpenSSL team promptly released a patch, and organizations worldwide took immediate action to secure their systems. This coordinated approach prevented widespread exploitation of the vulnerability and highlighted the importance of responsible disclosure in addressing critical security flaws.

Resources and Tools

Ethical hacking and responsible disclosure require a variety of resources and tools. Here are some commonly used resources:

- **Bug Bounty Platforms:** Bug bounty platforms, such as HackerOne and Bugcrowd, connect organizations with ethical hackers who can responsibly report vulnerabilities in exchange for monetary rewards.
- **Vulnerability Databases:** Databases like the Common Vulnerabilities and Exposures (CVE) and the National Vulnerability Database (NVD) provide comprehensive information about known vulnerabilities and their associated risk levels.
- **Security Testing Tools:** Ethical hackers utilize a wide range of security testing tools, such as network scanners, vulnerability scanners, and penetration testing frameworks, to identify and exploit vulnerabilities.
- **Disclosure Policies:** Organizations should establish clear and accessible vulnerability disclosure policies to encourage ethical hackers to responsibly report vulnerabilities. These policies outline the organization's commitment to addressing security flaws and provide guidelines for reporting.

Ethical hacking communities, forums, and training platforms also offer valuable resources and learning opportunities for aspiring ethical hackers.

Conclusion

Ethical hacking and responsible disclosure play a crucial role in enhancing cybersecurity by proactively identifying vulnerabilities and ensuring their remediation. By adhering to the principles of ethical hacking and following the responsible disclosure process, ethical hackers contribute to the overall resilience of computer systems, networks, and applications. It is essential for organizations to embrace responsible disclosure and foster collaboration with ethical hackers to create a safer digital environment for all.

Ethical Decision-Making in Cybersecurity

Ethical decision-making is a crucial aspect of cybersecurity, as it involves considering and resolving the ethical dilemmas and challenges that arise in the field. Cybersecurity professionals must navigate complex ethical issues to ensure that their actions align with legal, moral, and professional standards. In this section, we will explore the principles and frameworks that guide ethical decision-making in cybersecurity and discuss real-world scenarios to illustrate the challenges faced by professionals.

Ethical Principles in Cybersecurity

Ethical decision-making in cybersecurity is guided by a set of fundamental principles that reflect the values and responsibilities of professionals in the field. These principles help professionals assess the moral implications of their actions and make informed ethical decisions. Let's explore some of the key ethical principles in cybersecurity:

1. **Confidentiality:** Cybersecurity professionals have a responsibility to protect the confidentiality of sensitive information. This principle requires professionals to ensure that data is only accessed and disclosed to authorized individuals and that appropriate measures are taken to prevent unauthorized access.

2. **Integrity:** Integrity is about maintaining the accuracy and reliability of information. Professionals should ensure the integrity of data by implementing safeguards to prevent unauthorized modification or tampering.

3. **Availability:** The principle of availability emphasizes ensuring that information and systems are accessible to authorized users when needed. Cybersecurity professionals must implement measures to protect against disruptions or denial-of-service attacks that could impact availability.

4. **Accountability:** Professionals in cybersecurity are accountable for their actions and decisions. This principle requires individuals to take responsibility for their activities, be transparent in their actions, and be prepared to justify their decisions when necessary.

5. **Responsibility:** Cybersecurity professionals have a responsibility to use their skills and knowledge to protect individuals, organizations, and society. This principle calls for professionals to act in the best interests of their stakeholders and prioritize the greater good over personal or organizational gain.

6. **Nonmaleficence:** Nonmaleficence is the principle of "do no harm." Cybersecurity professionals should strive to ensure that their actions do not cause harm to individuals, communities, or the environment.

7. **Beneficence:** Beneficence involves actively promoting the well-being and welfare of others. Cybersecurity professionals should proactively seek to prevent harm and promote the security and privacy of individuals and organizations.

These ethical principles provide a solid foundation for decision-making in cybersecurity. However, in practice, professionals often encounter ethical dilemmas where these principles may come into conflict with each other or other factors.

Frameworks for Ethical Decision-Making

To navigate ethical dilemmas effectively, cybersecurity professionals can leverage ethical decision-making frameworks. These frameworks provide a systematic approach to analyze complex ethical issues and reach morally justifiable decisions. Let's explore two commonly used frameworks:

1. **The Utilitarian Approach:** Utilitarianism suggests that ethical decisions should maximize overall happiness or utility for the greatest number of people. In the context of cybersecurity, professionals applying this approach would assess the potential impact and consequences of their actions on various stakeholders. They would aim to minimize harm and maximize benefits, weighing risks and benefits to make decisions that optimize overall utility.

2. **The Rights-Based Approach:** The rights-based approach focuses on respecting and protecting the fundamental rights of individuals. In

cybersecurity, this approach entails considering the rights to privacy, freedom of expression, and access to information when making decisions. Professionals would prioritize upholding these rights and ensure that their actions do not infringe upon them.

While these frameworks provide valuable guidance, ethical decision-making often requires balancing multiple factors, including legal requirements, professional obligations, and contextual considerations. It is important for cybersecurity professionals to assess each situation individually and adapt their decision-making approaches accordingly.

Real-World Ethical Dilemmas

To illustrate the complexity of ethical decision-making in cybersecurity, let's examine two real-world scenarios:

1. **Employee Monitoring:** A company suspects an employee of leaking sensitive information to a competitor. The company's IT team has the capability to monitor the employee's computer activities without their knowledge. However, this action raises concerns related to privacy and the employee's rights. How should the IT team proceed?

   In this scenario, the IT team must carefully balance the need to protect the company's interests with the ethical considerations of privacy and individual rights. They should consider legal requirements, obtain necessary approvals, and employ transparent procedures while conducting the monitoring. The IT team should also minimize data collection to only what is necessary and ensure that collected data is handled and stored securely.

2. **Vulnerability Disclosure:** A cybersecurity researcher discovers a significant vulnerability in a widely-used software application. The researcher faces a dilemma: publicly disclosing the vulnerability could help others protect themselves, but it may also be exploited by malicious actors before a fix is available. What should the researcher do?

   In this scenario, the researcher can follow responsible vulnerability disclosure practices. They should first report the vulnerability to the software developer, giving them a reasonable amount of time to address the issue. If the developer remains unresponsive or fails to address the vulnerability within a reasonable timeframe, the researcher can consider disclosing the vulnerability publicly to raise awareness and empower users to take protective measures. Care should be taken to provide sufficient details to inform users without aiding potential attackers.

These real-world scenarios highlight how ethical decision-making requires considering various factors, such as legal obligations, stakeholder interests, and potential consequences.

Ethics Training and Professional Responsibility

In addition to understanding ethical principles and decision-making frameworks, cybersecurity professionals should receive ethics training to develop the skills necessary to address ethical challenges effectively. Professional organizations and certifications often require adherence to a code of ethics, which provides a set of guidelines for responsible and ethical behavior in the field.

Furthermore, cybersecurity professionals have a larger responsibility towards society. They should strive to promote ethics and inspire others within the field to act ethically. This can be achieved through sharing best practices, developing guidelines, and mentoring others.

To enhance ethical decision-making, professionals should also engage in continuous learning and stay updated on the latest developments in cybersecurity ethics. By staying informed about emerging ethical challenges, professionals can adapt their practices and make informed decisions that address new and evolving cybersecurity risks.

Conclusion

Ethical decision-making is an essential aspect of cybersecurity. By understanding and applying ethical principles and decision-making frameworks, professionals can navigate complex ethical dilemmas effectively. Ethical decision-making enables professionals to protect confidentiality, maintain integrity, prioritize availability, and fulfill their responsibilities as cybersecurity practitioners. Continuous learning, training, and adherence to professional codes of ethics further strengthen ethical decision-making capabilities in the field.

Cybersecurity and Corporate Social Responsibility

In today's interconnected world, organizations are not only responsible for protecting their own assets and information but also for contributing to the overall well-being of society. This concept is known as corporate social responsibility (CSR), which refers to a company's commitment to act ethically and contribute to sustainable development. In the context of cybersecurity, corporate social responsibility involves integrating responsible cybersecurity practices into an organization's overall CSR strategy.

The Importance of Cybersecurity and CSR

Cybersecurity is a critical component of any organization's CSR efforts. As organizations become increasingly reliant on digital technologies and the internet, the risks associated with cyber threats and attacks are growing. Cybersecurity breaches can result in significant financial losses, reputational damage, and harm to individuals and communities.

By prioritizing cybersecurity as part of their CSR initiatives, organizations can demonstrate their commitment to protecting customer data, ensuring privacy, and maintaining a secure digital environment. This not only helps mitigate the risks associated with cyber threats but also builds trust with stakeholders, including customers, employees, investors, and the public.

Integrating Cybersecurity into CSR Programs

To effectively integrate cybersecurity into CSR programs, organizations should consider the following:

1. **Cybersecurity Governance and Policies** Establishing a robust cybersecurity governance framework is essential. This includes defining cybersecurity roles and responsibilities, developing policies and procedures, and ensuring compliance with relevant cybersecurity regulations and standards. Organizations should also conduct regular risk assessments and audits to identify vulnerabilities and mitigate potential cyber risks.

2. **Privacy and Data Protection** Organizations must prioritize the protection of personal information and data privacy. This involves implementing strong security measures, such as encryption and access controls, to safeguard sensitive data. Organizations should also establish clear policies and procedures for handling and sharing data, ensuring compliance with applicable privacy laws and regulations.

3. **Employee Education and Awareness** Employees play a critical role in ensuring cybersecurity. Organizations should provide comprehensive training and awareness programs to educate employees about best cybersecurity practices, the risks associated with cyber threats, and their responsibilities in protecting company

and customer data. Regular training sessions and simulated phishing exercises can help reinforce good cybersecurity practices and improve overall security posture.

4. **Supply Chain Security** Organizations should extend their cybersecurity efforts to their supply chains. This involves assessing the cybersecurity posture of third-party vendors and partners and ensuring they adhere to cybersecurity best practices. Implementing contractual obligations, including cybersecurity requirements, can help minimize risks introduced through the supply chain.

5. **Collaboration and Information Sharing** Organizations should actively participate in collaborative efforts within their industry and with government agencies to share threat intelligence and best practices. By sharing information about emerging cyber threats and vulnerabilities, organizations can help protect the digital ecosystem and contribute to the overall cybersecurity of society.

Measuring Cybersecurity CSR Impact

Like any CSR initiative, measuring the impact and effectiveness of cybersecurity CSR efforts is essential. Organizations can use various metrics and key performance indicators (KPIs) to evaluate their cybersecurity CSR programs. These may include the number of cybersecurity incidents detected, response times to incidents, employee training completion rates, and improvements in overall cybersecurity posture.

It is also important for organizations to conduct periodic audits and assessments to ensure that their cybersecurity practices align with their stated CSR objectives. External audits can provide independent verification of an organization's cybersecurity practices and help identify any gaps or areas for improvement.

Case Study: Tech Company's Sustainable Cybersecurity Initiative

To provide a concrete example of how cybersecurity and CSR can be intertwined, let's consider a case study of a tech company's sustainable cybersecurity initiative.

ABC Tech, a leading technology company, has integrated cybersecurity into its CSR strategy. The company has implemented the following initiatives:

- Employee Training: ABC Tech provides regular cybersecurity training to all employees, focusing on topics such as password hygiene, identifying phishing emails, and secure coding practices. The company also encourages employees to report any cybersecurity incidents or suspicious activities promptly.

- Privacy by Design: ABC Tech follows privacy by design principles when developing its products and services. The company incorporates privacy controls and encryption measures to protect customer data and ensure compliance with privacy regulations.
- Partnerships and Collaboration: ABC Tech collaborates with other industry players and government agencies to share threat intelligence and develop industry best practices. The company actively participates in cybersecurity forums and conferences to contribute to the overall cybersecurity community.
- Sustainable Practices: ABC Tech ensures proper e-waste management and promotes energy-efficient computing practices. The company implements recycling programs for electronic equipment and continually seeks ways to minimize its carbon footprint.

Through these initiatives, ABC Tech demonstrates its commitment to cybersecurity and corporate social responsibility. The company not only protects its own information and assets but also contributes to creating a safer and more sustainable digital ecosystem.

Conclusion

In conclusion, cybersecurity and corporate social responsibility are intertwined in today's digital age. Organizations need to prioritize cybersecurity as part of their CSR efforts to protect their stakeholders, build trust, and contribute to the overall well-being of society. By integrating responsible cybersecurity practices into their CSR programs, organizations can ensure a secure digital environment and make a positive impact on the digital ecosystem. Ultimately, cybersecurity CSR efforts benefit both the organization and society at large.

Professional Ethics in Cybersecurity

Maintaining a strong ethical foundation is of utmost importance in the field of cybersecurity. Professionals in this discipline are entrusted with protecting sensitive information, safeguarding systems, and ensuring the privacy and security of individuals. To fulfill these responsibilities, it is essential for cybersecurity professionals to adhere to a robust set of ethical principles. This section explores the key aspects of professional ethics in cybersecurity, including the ethical hacking and responsible disclosure, ethical decision-making, cybersecurity and corporate social responsibility, and professional ethics in cybersecurity.

Ethical Hacking and Responsible Disclosure

One of the most intriguing aspects of cybersecurity is the concept of ethical hacking. Ethical hackers, also known as penetration testers or white hat hackers, are authorized individuals who simulate cyberattacks to identify vulnerabilities in systems and applications. This practice plays a critical role in strengthening cybersecurity defenses.

Ethical hackers must operate under a strict code of ethics to ensure their activities are lawful and aligned with professional standards. This code includes principles such as obtaining proper authorization before conducting any testing, respecting the privacy and confidentiality of data, and utilizing their skills exclusively for defensive purposes.

Responsible disclosure is an essential component of ethical hacking. When ethical hackers discover vulnerabilities, they have a moral obligation to notify the affected organization promptly. This process involves providing a detailed report on the vulnerability and assisting the organization in remediation efforts. Responsible disclosure ensures that vulnerabilities are addressed promptly, minimizing the risk of exploitation by malicious actors.

Ethical Decision-Making in Cybersecurity

Ethical decision-making plays a crucial role in the day-to-day activities of cybersecurity professionals. They frequently encounter ethical dilemmas and must make decisions that balance the interests of various stakeholders, including organizations, individuals, and society as a whole.

To navigate these dilemmas effectively, cybersecurity professionals should employ ethical decision-making models. One widely recognized model is the "ethical triage" approach, which consists of three steps: information gathering and analysis, ethical evaluation, and decision implementation. This approach helps professionals consider the potential consequences of decisions, evaluate ethical implications, and choose the most appropriate course of action.

Ethical decision-making also involves ensuring transparency and accountability. Professionals should be prepared to justify their decisions, document the reasoning behind them, and be willing to take responsibility for the consequences. By incorporating ethical considerations into their decision-making processes, cybersecurity professionals uphold the integrity of their field and contribute to the overall improvement of cybersecurity practices.

Cybersecurity and Corporate Social Responsibility

In today's interconnected world, organizations have a responsibility to prioritize cybersecurity and protect the interests of their stakeholders. Cybersecurity professionals play a crucial role in fulfilling this responsibility by ensuring the confidentiality, integrity, and availability of sensitive information.

Cybersecurity and corporate social responsibility (CSR) are inherently linked. Organizations must consider the potential consequences of their cybersecurity practices on society, the environment, and the economy. This includes minimizing the negative impact of data breaches, protecting sensitive data, and fostering a culture of security awareness within the organization.

Furthermore, cybersecurity professionals should actively engage in CSR initiatives related to cybersecurity. This may involve volunteering time and expertise to educate the public about online safety, supporting initiatives that promote cybersecurity in underprivileged communities, or contributing to policy discussions on cybersecurity and data privacy.

By embracing corporate social responsibility, cybersecurity professionals demonstrate their commitment to protecting not only the interests of their organizations but also the broader social fabric in which they operate.

Professional Ethics in Cybersecurity

Maintaining professional ethics is of utmost importance for cybersecurity professionals. Apart from adhering to codes of conduct established by professional organizations, cybersecurity professionals should possess key characteristics that reflect the highest ethical standards.

Integrity is a fundamental characteristic of ethical cybersecurity professionals. They must demonstrate honesty and adhere to moral and ethical principles. Trustworthiness is another crucial trait, as cybersecurity professionals often handle highly sensitive information and are entrusted with defending critical systems.

Responsibility is also paramount in the field of cybersecurity. Professionals must take ownership of their actions, be accountable for their decisions, and prioritize the well-being of individuals and organizations they serve. This includes keeping their knowledge and skills up to date and engaging in continuous professional development.

Finally, ethical cybersecurity professionals should demonstrate a commitment to the greater good. They should be driven by a sense of purpose to protect the interests of society, promote cybersecurity awareness, and foster a safer digital environment for all.

Key Takeaways

- Ethical hacking and responsible disclosure are critical components of cybersecurity. Ethical hackers must operate within strict ethical boundaries and report vulnerabilities responsibly to ensure the security of systems and applications.

- Ethical decision-making is essential in cybersecurity and requires professionals to balance the interests of various stakeholders. Ethical decision-making models help guide professionals in evaluating potential consequences and choosing the most appropriate course of action.

- Cybersecurity and corporate social responsibility are closely intertwined. Organizations have a responsibility to prioritize cybersecurity and protect the interests of their stakeholders. Cybersecurity professionals contribute to CSR by fostering a culture of security awareness and engaging in initiatives that promote cybersecurity in society.

- Professional ethics in cybersecurity include characteristics such as integrity, trustworthiness, responsibility, and a commitment to the greater good. These qualities are essential for maintaining the highest ethical standards and ensuring the protection of sensitive information and systems.

In Conclusion: Upholding professional ethics is crucial in the field of cybersecurity. By adhering to ethical principles, cybersecurity professionals contribute to the overall security of systems, protect sensitive information, and safeguard the interests of individuals and organizations. Ethical hacking, responsible disclosure, and ethical decision-making are key components of professional ethics in cybersecurity. Furthermore, cybersecurity professionals should embrace corporate social responsibility and possess important ethical traits such as integrity, trustworthiness, responsibility, and a commitment to the greater good. By maintaining these ethical standards, cybersecurity professionals contribute to a safer digital environment and promote the interests of society at large.

Index

Judy Novak, 168

Printed by
Libri Plureos GmbH · Friedensallee 273
22763 Hamburg · Germany

9 781779 613080